Teaching Needy Kids
in Our Backward System

Teaching Needy Kids
in Our Backward System

42 Years of Trying

Siegfried "Zig" Engelmann

Cover Design: Kylee Colvin
Cover Photos: Zig Engelmann, Bryan Wickman, Ahren Osterbrink

For contact information
ADI Press: adihome.org
Zig's website: zigsite.com

ISBN: 978-1-880183-00-7

Printed in the United States of America.

ADI PRESS

Published by ADI Press
P.O. Box 10252
Eugene, OR 97440
(800) 995-2464

Dedicated to fallen comrades Wes Becker and Bob Mattson

Contents

Chapter 3 **Follow Through Continues**

Chapter 4 **During Follow Through**

Chapter 5 **Follow Through Evaluation**

Chapter 6 **Follow Through Aftermath**

Chapter 7 **The New Millennium**

FOREWORD

Teaching Needy Kids in Our Backward System is written by Siegfried (Zig) Engelmann, who has been a maverick in education for 42 years. His work is not highly recognized by the educational community because it has different roots. Unlike the traditional scholarly approach that is referenced to written reports and accounts, Engelmann's theories and practices derive from teaching kids, trying to accelerate their rate of learning, and using performance data to draw conclusions about how kids learn, what kinds of practices are effective, and which are hoaxes.

Zig's emphasis on acceleration stems from facts about the kids Zig has worked with the most, lower performers. He argues that if they can be taught faster than lower performers have been traditionally taught, they will be higher performers, and they'll have the broader set of life opportunities that are available only to those who do well in school.

Zig insists that we should not blame kids or their families for student failure. He wrote,

> We will take you where you are, and we'll teach you. And the extent to which you fail is our failure, not yours. We will not cop out by saying, "He can't learn." Rather, we will say, "I failed to teach him. So I better take a good look at what I did and try to figure out a better way."

The book *Theory of Instruction,* written by Zig and Doug Carnine, ends with a similar appeal:

> On the level of society: Let's stop wasting incredible human potential through unenlightened practices and theories.

> On the level of children: Let's recognize the incredible potential for being intelligent and creative possessed by even the least impressive children, and with unyielding passion, let's pursue the goal of assuming that this potential becomes reality.

More important than rhetoric are Zig's achievements. He showed that there was a cure for school failures—an educational parallel to a cure for cancer—and he showed how schools had to change to provide this cure; however, his programs and his research are often scorned by what he refers to as a backward system.

His latest book reveals his passion, philosophy, some of his major achievements, and his frustrations, through a montage of personal experiences. His rationale for the format is, "I want the reader to know that we are human, that we are not dumb, and that we tried as hard as we knew how. We showed what could be done, but our work failed to convince even one major school district to do it, even though it would be far less expensive than what they are doing now."

The most extensive demonstration that Zig and his colleagues provided was in Project Follow Through, the largest educational experiment ever conducted. Experiences in Follow Through occupy center stage in *Teaching Needy Kids in Our Backward System.*

Zig's care and concern for children is evident throughout the book. The reader will understand why many frontline educators consider Zig the most important educator of the last 100 years.

Jerry Silbert, colleague

ACKNOWLEDGMENTS

To the many people who should have been named in this book but weren't—dozens of very competent trainers and colleagues.

Also to the people who helped me put this work together by recovering things I had written (often-cryptic notes) and ancient documents, by checking the accuracy of things I thought I remembered, and by providing feedback on the various drafts of the work—Gary Davis, Jerry Silbert, Doug and Linda Carnine, my sons Owen and Kurt.

Finally, to Karen Fierman, my sometimes patient but always outspoken assistant and Tina Wells, who edited the work and helped with the design.

CHAPTER 1

1964–1968:
Before Project Follow Through

Like other years, 1964 was one of turmoil and change. The U.S. Surgeon General issued the first announcement that smoking may be "hazardous to one's health," but we kept on puffing. The first Beatles album was released in the U.S., and an effort began to keep the Leaning Tower of Pisa from toppling. Conservative Barry Goldwater became the landslide Republican presidential candidate. Jack Ruby was found guilty of killing John Kennedy's assassin, Lee Harvey Oswald. Lyndon Johnson sent 5,000 more military advisers to South Vietnam, bringing the total number of U.S. forces in Vietnam to 21,000.

More significant to my life were the fulminations occurring in the areas of civil rights and education. Three civil rights workers were murdered in Philadelphia, Mississippi. In response to de facto segregation in New York City, Blacks and Puerto Ricans boycotted public schools. Malcolm X resigned from the Nation of Islam and later delivered a disturbing address, "The Ballot or the Bullet."

Possibly the most important event for me was the Civil Rights Act of 1964, signed into law on July 2. The act outlawed prevailing discriminatory practices against women and racial minorities. It prohibited unequal voter registration criteria, outlawed discrimination in hotels, restaurants, and other public places engaged in interstate commerce, and authorized the U.S. Attorney General to file suits to force desegregation. The Civil Rights Act of 1964 was the precursor of the 1965 Elementary and Secondary Education Act, which would provide funds through Title I for children of poverty.

The social and educational issues that affected poor children would prove to be important to me because I started a new career in 1964, one that would keep me in touch with children who desperately needed effective instruction. In late spring I became a research associate at the University of Illinois Institute for Research on Exceptional Children. I considered myself very lucky, partly because I had no formal training in education and partly because I had been trying to find a position in education for over two years.

LEARNING HOW KIDS LEARN

My interest in instruction had begun when I was in advertising, doing marketing research. One of the assignments was to find out how many exposures it took for children to recognize or remember slogans presented on TV. A client who was considering a major investment in TV advertising wanted this information before setting up an advertising budget. The client was particularly interested in preschoolers.

I searched libraries for books, studies, and facts about how many trials it took for children of different ages to learn different content. I found almost nothing. Some studies from 1935 to 1960 had information about the patterns for subjects memorizing words in lists or remembering chains of unrelated digits. The pattern of learning followed a U-shaped curve, with the first and the last members of the set learned first, and those in the middle requiring more practice. Several related studies dealt with different kinds of interference that retarded the rate at which learning occurred, patterns of forgetting, and subsequent relearning.

There was also a study conducted in Russia that had data on the number of trials required to teach deaf children of different ages the letters of the manual alphabet. The trend showed that three-year-olds learned it most slowly and seven- or eight-year-olds learned it fastest.

Beyond this, I found nothing that addressed the recognition or retention of information like that conveyed through a commercial or even through normal interactions.

To get the information I needed, I assembled a group of preschoolers, presented information they would not have learned under normal conditions, and played games in which they were to use what they learn. I recorded how many trials it took for different kinds of learning to occur.

Three of the children I worked with were my preschool-aged sons, Eric, Owen, and Kurt. I taught them math, reading, and science information. The instruction continued long after the due date for my assignment. The more I worked on teaching, the less interested I became in the advertising component and the more I became intrigued with the way children learned. As they learned, I learned about teaching. I adopted the basic principle of assuming a blank slate and that any mistakes they made or confusions they developed were caused by the instruction they had received. This principle was very obvious because the only information the children received about academic topics came from my efforts to teach them.

The evidence showed that some of the examples I used generated confusion and some of the rules and explanations I presented conveyed misunderstanding. The misunderstandings were *always* consistent with the information I presented. In other words, they were not stupid kids; I was a naïve teacher. One of the many examples that led to this conclusion occurred when I was teaching Eric to tell time. He was four. The program I used had the clock divided into two halves. The left half was "before the hour;" the right, "after the hour." I presented the rule about which side shows *before* and which *after,* and I applied it to examples showing different times on the clock. Eric had consistent reversals. Finally, I said in an irritated tone, "Eric, the *right* side is *after* the hour."

On the verge of tears, he touched the left side and said, "But Dad, this is the clock's right side." He had applied what I taught him, but I hadn't seen that the rule was ambiguous. From that incident and a lot of others, I learned a simple test for the rules and specific examples I presented. If the rule or example is consistent with more than one possible interpretation (like the clock's right side), some children will learn the unintended interpretation. Learning the misrule is not guaranteed because there's another interpretation the learner might learn. Eric could have learned that the left and right referred to our left and right, rather than the clock's left and right. However, the only way to assure that there would be no mislearning was to purge the teaching presentation of any possible rules or examples that could be consistent with more than one interpretation.

From an operational standpoint this orientation translated into the immediate conclusion that if children made mistakes and confused things, it was most probably the result of learning what I had unintentionally taught. Maybe I didn't provide enough practice, or maybe what I showed and told generated the confusion, but in either case, it was probably my fault.

When I applied this approach to the time-telling program, I scrapped it and replaced it with one that did not refer to the left side or right side. The first routine children would learn involved times like 3:30 or 11:45. Children would start at the top of the clock and count by fives to the minute hand. Then they would *read* the hour hand.

I didn't realize how radical the single-interpretation principle was until I analyzed some of the other programs I was considering for teaching academic skills (reading, math) to the younger boys, Kurt and Owen. None of these programs had been shaped by this principle. Rather, they seemed to be based on the supposition that whatever the authors assumed they were teaching was what they supposed the children would learn, regardless of how obscure or misleading the directions or examples were. And if the children made mistakes, it was chalked up to their inability to learn, not the inability of the authors to design clean problems and instruction. My wife, Therese, and I constructed programs for teaching reading and math that seemed to be better at meeting the standard of not generating possible misinterpretations.

I thought I was pretty good at designing instruction that was consistent with only one interpretation until I started working with small groups of preschoolers. I could not always predict possible problems from my analysis of the instruction. For example, I taught some three-year-olds to count to three. I would say, "Count to three," and they would say "One, two, three." Everything seemed to be consistent with only one interpretation, so what problem could there be?

After they had worked on counting to three for a couple of sessions, I told them I was going to teach them how to count to five. One of the children said, "One, to, five." I asked him to count to seven. He said, "One, to, seven." I had unwittingly taught him a spurious pattern—a word game that had parallel statements:

"Count to three."
"One to three."
"Count to N."
"One to N."

Another principle I learned as I tried to design effective instruction was not to design teaching sequences so they required children to learn more than one new thing at a time. I used two questions to design a sequence: "Could the skill be taught in a way that involved fewer steps or less information?" and "How can the instruction be sequenced so that children don't have to learn more than one new thing at a time?" Implicit in these questions was the idea that the goal of instruction was to be efficient and to teach more in less time.

Early in 1964, I made a film of Owen and Kurt (four-year-old fraternal twins) working math problems—areas of rectangles, simple algebra, and other skills that were generally not mastered until children were in the fourth grade. To show that I was not "cheating," there was only one camera and no cuts in the action.

My objective was to get a job in education. I decided to present the film to various organizations and companies concerned with educating young kids. I assembled a list of eighteen prospects, including all the major educational publishers and some organizations that were doing research on how young children learn.

I found the responses of the first 17 prospects disappointing. Although they had never seen four-year-olds perform like the boys did in the film, they did not seem even slightly impressed. One of the last presentations I made was to four people from SRA (Science Research Associates), the publisher that would later publish over thirty instructional programs my colleagues and I developed. The only comments the viewers had about the film were platitudes: "Well, we certainly appreciate your sharing and I can see that we have the same interests in teaching children." Only one person in the group showed interest. He said, "That was very intriguing." I thanked him. Then he continued, "What did you use to write those problems?"

In the movie, the boys were seated on the floor. I wrote the problems with a felt pen on plate glass that was between the boys and the camera (so the viewer would be able to read the problems; however, they would appear backward).

I told the man who asked the question that I had used a felt pen. He then asked what I used to erase the problems. "A naptha rag." My answers apparently satisfied his curiosity.

The eighteenth and last entry on my list of places to contact was the prestigious Institute for Research on Exceptional Children, at the University of Illinois. After 17 unsuccessful presentations, I was strongly tempted not to try setting up a meeting. But I figured I might as well get closure before creating a plan B or calling it quits. I set up an appointment and presented to James Gallagher and Carl Bereiter. I had read about both of them. Gallagher was renowned for his work with gifted children. He was handsome and polished. Bereiter, who looked more like a tall farm boy, had recently received a very large grant, "Accelerating Intellectual Development of Preschool Children."

Unlike everybody else who had viewed the film, both men were seriously intrigued. After watching it, they asked a series of questions. The last came from Gallagher. "Could you do that again, with other children?"

"Yes."

"Well, let's find out."

They hired me as a research associate to do projects with Bereiter, Gallagher, and Stephen Quigley (a leading figure in deaf education). I was quite a few degrees beyond elation.

TEACHING FORMAL OPERATIONS TO PRESCHOOLERS

The first project I did was with Gallagher. It was a teaching demonstration designed to show that preschoolers could learn skills that developmental psychologist Jean Piaget indicated could not be "learned" by children under the age of about 12. The study began on July 23, 1964, and continued through the summer. I worked daily with two groups of five preschoolers each. Group 1 comprised African-Americans from a very poor neighborhood in Urbana; Group 2, high-performing Caucasians. The children in both groups were enrolled in summer school programs. Lessons took twenty minutes a day and occurred five days a week.

The study was timely because Piaget's theories were popular in the 1960s. He believed that cognition was somehow subsumed by development. This means the child was expected to go through various developmental stages of cognitive performance, from the sensory-motor stage through formal operations, which emerged around the age of 12. According to Piaget, it would be impossible to teach young children more advanced reasoning patterns. He based this conclusion on several poorly designed attempts by Piaget and Inhelder to teach younger children. The assumption of the study I did with Gallagher was that children's performance could be greatly accelerated if the instruction was well designed. This assumption held for the children in both groups, even though the two groups had greatly different backgrounds.

I would teach formal operations, which Piaget believed required the learner to construct propositions about propositions. Piaget assumed that the understanding of relative direction required formal operations. For the learner to know that Germany is south of Sweden but north of Italy, the learner must understand that something may be absolutely north or south. ("In which direction are you walking? ... Yes, north.") But the learner also must know that direction is relative, which means that you may go north, but you are south of something. In other words, if someone pointed to a dot on a map and asked, "Is this point north or south?" the learner who understood formal operations would demand more information: "North or south of what?"

For the central teaching I worked on different problems that had the logical structure and met Piaget's criterion of requiring propositions about propositions. For example, I used this model.

Figure 1

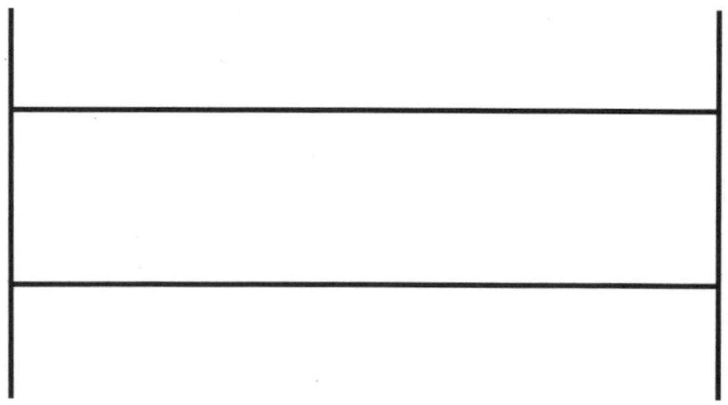

The horizontal lines in this model are the same length. Somebody could make a horizontal line shorter (by erasing part) or longer (by adding a part). If you were told simply that somebody changed the lines so the top line is longer than the bottom line, the change could have been achieved two ways: The person could have made the top line longer or erased part of the bottom line. To identify which of these options the person took, you would need more information. If you were told that the person made the top line longer than the bottom line but did not change the top line, you would know that the person made the bottom line shorter.

Another problem with the same structure involves a teeter-totter. If the teeter-totter is level and somebody changes it so the left side is down, the person who changed it could have either pushed down on the left side or pushed up on the right side. Again, you would need more information to determine which option actually occurred.

We hoped to show that if preschool children were taught how to handle different problems of this structure, they would be able to generalize to a new problem type they had never worked with or observed during the training. If they performed as we hypothesized, they would provide categorical evidence that Piaget's theory was wrong, and that with careful teaching, children's acquisition of formal-operational reasoning could be accelerated.

The learner would have to know the meanings of *same-different, longer-shorter, up-down, top-bottom, push-pull, higher-lower, if-then,* and *or.* I assumed that the children would know the meanings of these words, but I was wrong.

I kept a daily log of the activities I presented to each group and problems the children had. This log, which appears on my Website, Zigsite.com, was written formally and referred to me as "the investigator." The daily entries revealed both my ignorance and revelations.

Although the performance of the two groups seemed the same to me at the end of the first session, the Blacks (Group 1) provided me with a terrible shock at the beginning of the next lesson. I had "taught" both groups an if-then rule: "If things are not the same, they must be different." I had the kids recite and apply this rule. "If things are not the same, what do you know about those things? …" They responded in unison. The children in Group 1 found the work more reinforcing than the children in Group 2 did. On the second day, I opened the lesson for Group 1 by drawing two horizontal lines of the same length on the board. I asked the group, "Are these lines the same?"

In unison, the children responded, "If they're not the same they must be different."

I recognized that I had assumed far more than I should have. So we launched into instruction on *same* and *not same.* The children in Group 2 had no trouble with the early work. In fact they found it boring (even though one member of the group was only three years old).

As the summer progressed, the gap between the two groups increased so dramatically that the children in Group 2 learned everything I assumed they needed to solve the criterion problem weeks before most of the children in Group 1 did. So as I continued to work on the preparation program with Group 1, I taught the Group 2 children advanced map and reasoning skills, such as relative direction and identifying where a person would have to stand to be visible in the mirror to another person. In Figure 2, the oval represents a person and the thin rectangle represents a mirror. The tasks I presented required a child to touch a point on the map to show where someone could stand to see that person in the mirror. The problems I presented showed the oval in different places in the room.

Figure 2   **Figure 3**

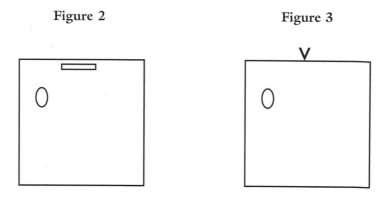

A task with the same structure (Figure 3) required children to show where they would have to stand to roll a ball so it hit a V on the wall and rolled back to the person. Note that the same problems were not repeated, so children had to learn a general scheme of how the angle of reflection changes as the angle of incidence changes.

The members of both groups were given the criterion problem (an example type they had never worked with or observed). Three of the five children in Group 1 and all but the three-year-old in Group 2 passed the test. Group 1 had required a much greater amount of instruction on skills they needed to pass the criterion problem.

For those children in Group 2 and those in Group 1 who passed the test, the program ended. For the two children in Group 1 who did not pass it, I continued to work with them every day, as much for me as for them. I needed to know how to teach them better. So I kept backing up to skills that I thought were more elementary.

By the end of the project, I was working on tasks that I should have presented at the beginning. I wished I had more time to work with them. The lowest girl in Group 1 failed the following tasks at the end of the training:

in –	Put the box in the wagon.
between –	Put it between the horse and the wagon.
behind –	Put it behind the wagon or the horse.
under –	Put it under the horse.
over –	Make the box go over the wagon.
past –	Make it go past the wagon.
pull out –	Pull the bar out.
push in –	Push the bar in.
higher –	Hold the ball up higher.
lower –	Hold the ball down lower.

Certainly there was a large range of individual differences within this group, but the group clearly knew less about the words used to give directions or describe than the higher group did. My guess was that only one of the at-risk children would have been able to keep pace with the members of Group 2 who passed the test. Although the study was not designed to show the language deficit of at-risk children, it provided information about skills, vocabulary, and operations at-risk children would have to be taught before they could learn some of the things that higher performers are ready to learn.

Even though not all the children in both groups passed the criterion test, the study showed that Piaget's notion of the relationship between development and performance was wrong. We gave the children some of the traditional Piagetian tests at the end of the study to show how they performed on other mental operations that Piaget said must be learned before they could learn formal operations. One was a test that involved water in two glasses—one narrow, one wide. The tester pours the water into the narrow glass, then pours the water into the wider glass and asks if the amount of water is the same in both glasses. All but one child in Group 2 failed the test, which meant that these children could perform some formal operations but could not pass a test that is usually passed by six-year-olds, according to Piaget's norms. The study showed clearly that there is no amorphous cognitive development or "general" operations like formal operations. There are simply specific operations that children learn as they grow up, and these specific things may be acquired through "informal," "incidental" instruction or through controlled, organized instruction.

Many academicians who read the study responded to it illogically. Several noted that the sample size was too small to determine the significance of the outcome. That analysis is illogical. If something is supposed to be universal, the performance of one child could contradict its universality. The Piagetian scheme specified a universal developmental schedule in which formal operational thinking did not emerge until children were twelve. More than one of the children acquired some formal operational skill through instruction, which means that their performance totally contradicted Piaget's universal scheme.

To me, the most important contribution of the study was knowledge. Perhaps the most important lesson for me was an extension of the idea that the instruction must convey only one interpretation. It must also start at a level that will predict success. For the lower performers, the instruction failed because it was not geared to where they needed to start and what they needed to learn before they could even begin the original program I had specified. A related issue is that with proper investigation, it is possible to discover what children don't know, why they are unable to do what some tasks require, and what a proper starting point would be.

The study also forced me to learn a number of techniques for teaching efficiently. I had to learn them because the children (and their parents) volunteered to attend the classes. If children insisted on not coming to a session, the study would have been either terminated or considerably downsized.

One of the main techniques I learned was to bill things as being difficult. "Oh, this is hard stuff and you're not going to be able to do it."

"No. We can do it," they would say. When they did it, I expressed amazement, and they laughed, pointing out that they told me they could learn it.

Another technique I used was to tell the children how smart they were. "Did you know that you're doing things that kids who are ten years old can't do? Are you smart or what?"

THE BEREITER ENGELMANN PRESCHOOL—YEAR ONE

In late August, I met with Carl Bereiter and two of his young assistants, Phil Reedford and Jean Osborn. Jean's recollection of this period was that every morning Jean and Phil would sit and comment as Carl and I discussed things—some entertaining, some boring. Jean wrote, "So when the idea of setting up a preschool was put forward our reaction was that at least we would be able to do something besides listen to talk."

This meeting started with Carl going over the discrete experiments that he had scheduled for his grant during the coming school year. Then Phil mentioned something about doing things with "culturally deprived" preschoolers.

We discussed the study that I had conducted over the summer. Then,

Carl said, "Why don't we do it all at once?" He proposed opening a preschool for disadvantaged children and using the children as subjects for some of the other experiments he'd planned. The main focus of the preschool, however, would be to accelerate the academic performance of the children. The plan was fairly well solidified during that meeting.

There would be about fifteen African-American four-year-olds from the ghetto at the north side of Champaign-Urbana. We would teach three academic subjects—reading, math, and language. I pointed out that these would be "virgin" subjects, because they would be less likely to learn the skills from other sources. We also agreed that the children should be grouped homogeneously for instruction so we wouldn't have to teach basic foundation skills to children who already had them.

Apparently our change in behavior from talking to doing was dramatic. Within less than two weeks of that meeting, the preschool opened at the McKinley Foundation in Champaign, which donated space for the half-day program. Jean Osborn was the organizing force. She recruited drivers from the League of Women Voters, contacted parents of the children who had been identified, arranged for carpools to transport the children, arranged for snacks, and attended to a myriad of other details, like first-aid kits, spare clothing, and name tags.

As part of contacting the parents, Jean, Carl, and I went to the homes of the preschoolers and explained the program to the children's mothers or grandmothers. Several houses were shacks that seemed to be on the verge of collapse. One had large cracks in the floor that revealed the ground below. The house was heated by a small wood stove. I wondered how the family survived during the winter when the temperature was in the teens.

After a couple of weeks of shakedown, the project ran smoothly. Children were placed in three small groups (high, middle, and low) and each teacher taught the same subject to each of the three groups. (Phil taught reading, Jean taught language, and I taught math.) Periods were twenty minutes with a break around 10 o'clock for recess and art, and another around 11 for music. The design for the instruction periods was something like a departmentalized school with children rotating from one instructional area to the next. At any given instructional time, three groups were being instructed: one in language, one in reading, and one in math.

The high point of their daily schedule was a music period with the entire group. Either Carl or Jean played the piano, and we sang some traditional songs (such as *London Bridge, Itsy Bitsy Spider, The Alphabet Song, The Wheels on the Bus, Ten Little Indians, Ten Little Angels,* and *Skip to My Lou*) and other songs that we made up to give children practice on things they were having difficulty learning. For example, the children had trouble saying and reversing addition statements. (Turn around 4 + 3 and you have 3 + 4.) For the song, we would have two children from the group stand in front. I would point to each child and have them switch positions as the children sang, "Sheryl and Dexter; turn it around, it says Dexter and Sheryl." Later we played a variation with three children, two holding numbers and the middle one holding a plus sign.

Another made-up song dealt with the children's difficulty in blending sounds of a word and identifying the word. To the tune of *Twinkle, Twinkle, Little Star* we sang verses like:

> The be-gin-ning says *sss,*
> D   D   D   D   D   A
> And the end-ing says *it.*
> A   A   B   B   B   A
> Put them to-geth-er,
> G   G   G   F#   F#
> And they make *sit.*
> F#   E   E   D
> The be-gin-ning says *fff,*
> D   D   D   D   D   A
> And the end-ing says *it.*
> A   A   B   B   B   A
> Put them to-geth-er,
> G   G   G   F#   F#
> And they make *fit.*
> F#   E   E   D

The children learned all the songs and seemed to enjoy the music periods nearly as much as we did. I later found it disturbing in working with at-risk schools that we had serious time and logistic problems arranging for good music periods. No school should be without music.

From the work I had done with at-risk preschoolers, we had a pretty good idea of what the "beginning" activities should be and what sorts of things we had to teach. During the first few weeks, I demonstrated some of the things I'd learned about organizing and managing the group to keep the children on task. Jean was a very fast learner, and the language looked good by the third week of instruction. The math was also impressive. I used a version of the program I had used with advantaged preschoolers. First, children learned counting objects and events (like how many times I clapped). They would learn addition, subtraction, and multiplication as different types of counting. Once they learned each operation, they would work word problems involving the operation.

During the first few weeks of the preschool, I distilled a general rule about the relationship between problems and solutions; a rule so obvious it's invisible (which is probably why I had never read or heard it), but one that has great power in the design and revision of curricula. If you know exactly the problem children have with something you're trying to teach, and if you express the problem in detail, your statement implies exactly what you need to do to solve the problem. The statement of the problem also implies exactly how to test the children on whether they no longer have the problem. For instance, if children sound out the written word *run* but can't say the word, the statement of exactly what they can't do clearly implies the remedy. "Children say the individual sounds correctly and say them in the correct order, but they cannot say the word at a normal speaking rate."

This statement of the problem does not imply a *reading* task but a *language* task that does not involve written words, simply the sounds of words. "Listen: *rrr uuu nnn.* Say it fast ... Listen: *mmm aaa t.* Say it fast ..."

Using the notion of finding the simplest possible example to start with leads to a sequence of short practice sessions that occur over many lessons, starting with easy words: "*Ham burger.* Say it fast ... *Ellu funt.* Say it fast." More difficult words would be those that were presented as sounds: "*sssiiit.* Say it fast."

Even during the first year, the preschool had a lot of visitors and received a fair amount of publicity. To people in traditional education, especially early childhood education, the program was judged singularly odious and inhumane, even though it worked well and the children liked it. Near the top of a long list of allegations about our approach was the contention that the early emphasis on academics would damage the children and stunt their development. Another was that the program wasn't consistent with the natural way children learn. The recommendations were that we shouldn't try to instruct the children but use play, manipulatives, and informal situations to pique their curiosity and provide them with opportunities to discover, rather than "forcing" instruction on them.

Near the end of the first year, a group of child developmentalists from New York City visited the project and expressed strong disagreement with our practices. After they observed the groups being taught, one of them gave a speech on how a teacher must get on the same level as the child and share the child's feelings and goals. She concluded by saying that we had no regard for children's inner feelings.

I told her that if she was so knowledgeable about children's feelings, she should have no trouble identifying which of the seven children in the math group she just observed witnessed his father being shot to death on the preceding evening. Of course she couldn't do it because all the children in the group responded with alacrity, laughed, and won all the challenges I said they couldn't possibly win.

I explained that we understood how that boy must feel, and we expressed our sorrow. But then we provided the boy with relief from his anguish by putting him in a familiar routine that took his mind off his grief and gave him an opportunity to do something energetic and consuming. Rather than thinking about the horror of the preceding night, he thought about math.

My sons Owen and Kurt were the same age as the children in our preschool. On Christmas Eve, Owen said something that made me very proud of him. We were driving through the north end ghetto en route to a friend's house in Urbana. Therese observed that not many of the houses seemed to have Christmas trees. Our boys started pointing at the houses. Owen laughed and said, "Look at the funny tree in that house."

I said, ""Owen, these people are very poor. Some of them can't afford trees. Some of the children won't even get Christmas presents."

"No Christmas presents?"

Therese told the boys that when she was young, the only Christmas present she got some years was an orange or a pair of socks.

The boys were silent for a while. Then Owen said in a tear-cracked voice, "Dad, they can have my presents."

THE BEREITER ENGELMANN PRESCHOOL—YEAR TWO

One of the reasons we learned much during the first year was that every day, after the volunteers picked up the children from the McKinley Foundation, Carl, Jean, Phil, and I sat around a table and reviewed the problems we had that day and sought resolutions for the next day. Jean recalled, "These conversations were often heated, but the focus was always on optimal instruction for these children. It was a luxury to have these discussions."

During the second year, we continued with the children who had started in 1964, and also started a second group (cohort) of four-year-olds. The two groups were in different locations. The five-year-olds we had worked with were now in Hays School, in north Urbana. The four-year-olds were in a new facility purchased by the University of Illinois—Colonel Wolfe School—which housed our preschool, a somewhat traditional preschool under the direction of Merle Karnes, and a behaviorally oriented program for at-risk elementary school students operated by Sid Bijou. The building was set up so there was an observation room to provide a view of all the classrooms and small-group teaching rooms.

Starting with the second cohort of four-year-olds, our children would be part of a study that compared their performance with that of children in Karnes's preschool and those in a strictly traditional preschool. On the new schedule, Jean and I taught six groups a day—three groups at the preschool in the morning, and three groups at Hays school in the afternoon. Jean was scheduled to spend only two-thirds of her time on this project, and I was scheduled for half-time, but we both really liked what we were doing, so the work was not a hardship.

TRAINING NEW TEACHERS

If our project was to be further expanded, we needed to train new teachers. Carl first converted a very bright young research assistant, Valerie Anderson, into a teacher. She had been doing literature searches for the articles and reports Carl was writing. When he proposed converting her into a teacher in the preschool, she didn't seem to be excited about her new role, but the only question she asked was, "Will I get the same pay?" Yes.

I trained Valerie in teaching math, and the training dramatized the difficulty of teaching people to attend to all the variables that are important to teaching naïve preschoolers successfully. The routine was something like the ancient Japanese tutorial system. She would sit next to me as I taught a small group. Every few minutes, I pointed out something to her, about the pacing, the type of example, the sequence of examples, the correction procedure, or the reinforcement practices. Then I would turn the teaching over to her. Typically, she presented the same tasks that I had just presented, with the same examples. Slowly, I expanded what she did. When the expansion included making up appropriate examples, she had a very hard time keeping track of the details. She often lapsed into poor pacing and presented poor examples. For instance, early in math instruction, problems that have the same number twice, like 2 + 2, are poor. Here's why: You ask, "How many do you start out with? ... How many do you plus?" If children respond correctly, were they attending to the correct numbers, or did they think the first number is the one you plus? It's impossible to say. But if the problem is 4 + 3 there is no ambiguity because the first number is different from the second number. Also, 2 + 4 and other problems that have the first number smaller than the second are bad for beginners, because the problem tells them to plus four (count four places from 2), but children will say "four" when they count: "three four five six." Some children stop as soon as they say "four." If the problem is 4 + 2, there is no problem because children will not say "two" when they count from 4.

After each period, I gave Valerie feedback and practiced with her on details that were weak. Her improvement was slow, which was disturbing because she was very well read, knowledgeable, and witty. By winter, she was getting better about not repeatedly making the same type of mistake, but the number of details that demanded attention was so large that I was beginning to become skeptical about whether we would be able to train teachers.

By February, Valerie was working with the five-year-olds at Hays School, presenting large parts of each lesson. She cried on at least six occasions. Once, she was doing a part of a new exercise type that I had demonstrated. I signaled her to stop and I took over the group. When we took a break she said, "Why did you stop me?"

"You were leading the kids too much."

"I was not. I was doing *exactly* the same thing you just did."

"That was on a *correction,* not the basic presentation."

Tears.

Although the process was painful for her, by the end of the school year, she was quite good. But the training program I had used was clearly not good. She had to learn too many things by making mistakes—often repeated mistakes. Somehow we had to figure out a better way. We wouldn't put children through a program so ragged. There was no reason for using a ragged program with adults. But how could we make the teaching easier?

One of the other people Carl hired to learn to be a teacher helped provide the answer. Elaine (Cookie) Bruner was an energetic, inquisitive, and strong-willed young woman who was active in community affairs. She was to be the teacher of reading, and within a month after she was hired, she replaced Phil, who didn't have a great interest in continuing to teach reading but wanted to work on research. Training Cookie was not a problem. After two weeks she was up to speed.

The original reading program we used was different from the one my wife and I had used to teach reading to our preschoolers. The new reading program was designed to determine the extent to which children could learn to apply verbal rules to reading. Children learned to identify upper-case letters. They learned some sight words and learned to identify the same word from a sample of words that are similar. (For example, the word *HIM* is compared with *HIT, HILL, JIM, BIN.*) Children also did verbal exercises in which they rhymed with words that had a particular ending (*aper, paper, daper, laper*), and they worked with sets of three-letter words that shared the same ending and had different beginning letters.

The reading program had problems, and Cookie was quick both to point them out and to ask permission to change the program. She introduced a phonics program, but it moved far too fast for our children. Next she used a program called *Words In Color.* The basic design of the program was that any letter or combination that made a particular sound appeared in a particular color. For instance, any part that made the sound of short *u* would always appear in a particular shade of green, whether it was in the word *shove, hut,* or *color.* When sounding out a word, children recited the names of the colors then identified the word.

The problem was that it would probably have taken more time to teach the color names than it would to teach the children to read. Most of our four-year-olds didn't know the names of more than three colors. (Half didn't know any color names.) Before the program introduced work with words, children had to learn to identify over forty colors, including cyan, magenta, and puce.

Cookie dumped the program after trying to use it with the top group for a couple of weeks. She tried several linguistic programs that involved combining endings and beginnings, and she dumped those. The most promising program she tried was based on the ITA, the Initial Teaching Alphabet. Words are spelled phonetically, not conventionally. Was is spelled *wuz*, said, *sed*, and school, *skool*. The alphabet also had modified symbols for combinations *th, wh,* and *sh.*

The higher-performing children learned more smoothly than they did in any of the other programs we had used. The lower performers struggled. They had problems identifying the sounds (confusion of *b, d, p, t,* and of *a, h,* and *n*). They also had serious problems identifying the word after saying the sounds. They would sound out a word like *mat.* Then Cookie would ask, "What word is that?" The kids would say something like, "muh ah tuh," or just, "ah tuh," or "at."

The most serious problems with both higher performers and lower performers occurred after they had learned to read words in the ITA orthography and Cookie attempted to "transition" them into conventional orthography. Children were shocked to learn that they couldn't read or write with any certainty. They had enormous difficulty trying to learn words like *was* and *said.* They did a lot of guessing not only on these words, but also on many words that were spelled the same way they had been in ITA. Words that had *th* and *sh* were difficult because the letters were not joined and children tried to sound out words like *she* as sss h eee (suhee).

The transition was a disaster because the program had taught the children a set of rules and discriminations that did not apply to reading conventionally spelled material. When words appeared in traditional orthography, children had no guidelines about which of the things they had learned still applied. One fact was clear to all of them, however: You can't say the sounds for *all* the letters, and, for some reason, letter sounds don't tell you how to pronounce the word.

The problems children had implied exactly how the program needed to change. The problems they had in confusing letters implied that we had to introduce a font that made the letters more easily discriminated. For example, the font needed to show that *b* and *d* were not the identical objects in different positions. The letter *h* was modified so it had a long ascender and did not look as much like *n* as it did in conventional fonts.

The problems children had with transitions and in learning words that were irregularly spelled implied that the program had to introduce irregulars far earlier and alert children to the fact that they were irregular. Also, the transition to conventional orthography had to occur a bit at a time, starting earlier and involving smaller, less demanding steps. Cookie and I worked on a reading program that we hoped would avoid the problems with the ITA.

By spring, Carl had hired three more people to become teachers. Cookie and Jean trained them through the tutorial approach and encountered some of the same problems I experienced in training Valerie. When the new teachers presented material, they would often talk too much, use variant wording from one example to the next, fail to give clear signals to the children about when to respond or how to respond, and present series of examples that had technical problems (weak sequences of examples and poor examples).

We had to design the material so it avoided at least some of these problems. We didn't know how radically the procedures would change. At first, we thought it might be sufficient to provide trainees with a list of the examples they were to present. With this change, the trainees did not have to make up examples or create sequences of examples. They would just refer to the list and present the next example listed.

This change helped Valerie and Cookie a lot. However, it was not a sufficient remedy for the other trainees. Even with the list of examples, these teachers talked too much, used clumsy wording that was not consistent from one example to the next, and presented labored corrections. I observed one new teacher trying to explain how to read words from left to right. She referred to preferred hands. "Who is right-handed?" Blank stares. "Which hand do you throw with?" Children demonstrated their throwing behavior and argued about who could throw the best.

After restoring a semblance of order, she told the children whether they were left-handed or right-handed. *As she faced them*, she held up her right hand and told the group, "I'm holding up my right hand. Let's see if you can hold up your right hand." Naturally all children held up the hand that was on the same side as her hand, their left hand. At that point, I stopped the teacher. I gave all the children a poke on the back of their right hand and said, "The hand I poked is your right hand. Which hand? … Hold up your right hand." All did it. Later I worked with the teacher and told her that if she wanted to demonstrate right and left, she had to face the same direction the children were facing. Then left and right weren't problems.

Another new teacher presented objects of different shapes and colors. She gave the objects to children so they could "manipulate" them. Then she held up a red ball and said, "This is a red ball." She directed a child to

"Show me something that is not a red ball." The child pointed to a blue triangle and said, "That ain't no red ball." Even though the child was right, the response was ambiguous. It didn't indicate whether he knew either *ball* or *red*.

The remedy was to change the statement used to identify the red ball from "This is a red ball" to "This *ball* is red." If the child pointed to a triangle and said, "This ball ain't red," his response would not be true.

Hundreds of other details followed the same pattern. We would observe problems the teacher and children were having and we would provide a remedy. We would rehearse the teacher in how to present the remedy, how to correct mistakes the children might make, and how to revisit the newly taught skill or concept to make sure that children received sufficient practice in using it.

Because lists of examples were not sufficient, we programmed simple, consistent wording and consistent and manageable correction procedures. Jean and I wrote scripts for language; Cookie and I wrote them for reading. Even though the first scripts we developed were crude, they helped immediately. We no longer had to teach our teachers series of rules about examples, sequences, wordings, and corrections. We could train them in presenting the script verbatim, possibly memorizing the wording for the critical and frequently-used tasks, and teaching standard correction procedures that were tightly referenced to the script. When we tried out the scripted lessons, we discovered some basic rules for making the scripts effective across both talented teachers and those who didn't have an intuitive sense of communicating efficiently.

1. Keep the materials simple and direct. Don't present creative excursions, just mainline, basic instruction.

2. Always provide overkill in the scripted sequence. If it seems that something can be taught in two five-minute segments over two days, provide three five-minute segments over three days.

3. Keep wording to a minimum. The more wording a task has, the more the teacher has to refer to the script. If the wording is simple and applies to many examples, the teacher will rely less on the script and be able to focus more on the children and their responses.

4. Always put reinforcing activities at the *end* of a sequence, never at the beginning. Something that is entertaining or interesting should never function as a seduction to the first tasks presented, but as a carrot, a reinforcer that occurs after children have successfully learned some-

thing. Seductions don't work. They may pique interest, but what follows is a huge disappointment for the children because it is not entertaining. They've already seen the best show.

5. Design the material so that a high percentage of the tasks presented are responded to by the group, not by individual children. For this objective to be practical, tasks must be designed so that all children will be able to produce the same response, saying the same words. If the task admits to variant responses, the teacher will be unable to determine the extent to which individual children respond correctly.

The scripts were successful because they permitted the teacher to teach, not to be both an instructional designer and a teacher. Because the scripts relieved the teacher of the technical design details, the teacher was able to concentrate more on presenting the material efficiently and providing corrections. The introduction of verbatim scripts did not make the teachers flawless presenters; it simply limited the number of details they had to learn before they were effective.

With scripts, we were able to teach new trainees more in two weeks than we had previously been able to teach in more than four months. Possibly the biggest change was that trainees were now able to present examples at a much faster rate (8 to 18 a minute) compared to their former rate, which was often fewer than four examples per minute.

Most important, trainees were also able to concentrate on student mastery. Mastery is essential for lower performers. Unless the practice children receive occurs over several lessons, lower performers will not retain information the way children from affluent backgrounds do. Prevailing misconceptions were (and are) that children benefit from instruction that exposes them to ideas without assuring that children actually learn what is being taught. If you present something new to advantaged children and they respond correctly on about 80 percent of the tasks or questions you present, their performance will almost always be *above 80 percent* at the beginning of the next session. In contrast, if you bring lower performers to an 80 percent level of mastery, they will almost always perform *lower than 80 percent* at the beginning of the next session.

The reason for this difference is that higher performers are able to remember what you told them and showed them. The material is less familiar to the lower performers, which means they can't retain the details with the fidelity needed to successfully rehearse it. After at-risk children have had a lot of practice with the learning game, they become far more facile at remembering the details of what you showed them. When they reach this stage, they no longer need to be brought to such a rigid criterion of mastery.

At first, however, their learning will be greatly retarded if they are not taught to a high level of mastery.

This trend was obvious when I taught formal operations to preschoolers. At first, the low- and high-performing groups were close in learning rate. Later, there were huge differences. Group 2 was able to learn at a much faster rate, largely because it was not necessary to bring them to a high level of mastery. On several occasions, I purposely taught the children in Group 2 to a low level of mastery (around 60 percent). I closed the work on the topic with one model of doing it the right way, and I assured the children that this was very difficult material. At the beginning of the next lesson, almost all of them had perfect mastery.

Even though the project expanded during the second year, we continued to have our daily shakedown meetings after the children left. Our focus was on what went wrong and how we could do a better job of teaching. My descriptions may give the impression that our teaching sessions were grim. Not so. Laughter and humor were regular events in all the instructional groups. A visitor who had gone to all the voguish preschools of the day said that he came to ours expecting to see something very strict and serious. He said, "I heard more laughter and humor from teachers *and* children in your classrooms than in any of the other projects."

DISSEMINATING RESULTS

During the second year of the preschool, Carl and I wrote a book that detailed the procedures we used, *Teaching Disadvantaged Children in the Preschool,* which was published in 1966. The book outlined the programs and philosophy of accelerating children through an early intervention that addressed language and academic content. We labeled our approach "Direct Instruction." We wrote the book fast and tried to get it out in time to provide an alternative for the format Head Start had adopted. In 1964 Congress had passed the Economic Opportunity Act, which was to provide programs designed to win the war against poverty. The EOA acknowledged that education was one of the most direct routes to neutralize the effects of poverty on young children. The problem was that the EOA was ill-informed about what worked or what to do; it was influenced by the philosophy of early-childhood educators. The model they used for early intervention was the traditional nursery school, which had no evidence of effectiveness and did not address the fact that children of poverty were significantly behind.

Project Head Start began in the summer of 1965 as a play school, with a nutrition and health component, and with lots of compelling publicity—children smiling, eating healthy foods, playing, singing, and learning. The message the book that Carl and I wrote was that the preschool could provide a means of accelerating children so they would catch up to their middle-class peers. Accelerating performance meant simply teaching more each day than the children would learn if they weren't in the preschool. The gains attained each day add up. Furthermore, if at-risk children receive this instruction, they will achieve a head start simply because middle-class children are not learning reading and math as preschoolers.

If we had to do the book over today, we would have placed more emphasis on political correctness. We received a lot of bad press from the example we used for illustrating the steps for teaching children classification. The example was weapons. We could have used one of the other classes we worked with (vehicles or clothing, for instance) and avoided controversy over whether we were warmongers and advocates of violence.

Our approach was dubbed *the pressure cooker*. Originally, this designation was not negative. It was coined by Maya Pines, whose article in the January 1967 issue of *Harpers* referred to the program as a better way to teach four-year-olds. She wrote,

> In effect, Bereiter and Engelmann are operating an intellectual pressure cooker for children from the slums. They have totally rejected the standard, play-oriented nursery school, and made no attempt to reproduce a middle-class environment for these youngsters.

She described the interactions as "an intensely physical kind of teaching: rhythmic movements, clapping of hands, cheers like those of a cheerleader, lots of concrete objects related to the matter at hand, arm and hand movements to illustrate points."

Traditionalists picked up on the pressure cooker theme and spun it into a negative—unthinkable—feature, pressuring children to learn. Critics accused us of being everything from racists to uninformed pretenders. Several hinted that with names like Bereiter and Engelmann, we certainly had to be Nazis. Supporting this stance was the fact that our program was "authoritarian" and did not permit children to have any choice about what they were to learn. When a reporter asked Carl and me about the "authoritarian bias of our approach," we indicated that indeed we would not provide the children the opportunity not to learn. Carl pointed out that children may later choose not to use what they have learned, but at least they would have a choice in this matter, which could greatly affect their lives.

Subsequent publicity tended to focus more on the "controversial" aspects of our program than its results. For instance, the March 31, 1967 issue of *Life* carried an article on early learning, titled "The Big Debate—Teaching by Pressure or Discovery." Just as it is today, the good guys were discovery-oriented and the bad guys promoted direct and effective instruction.

The article indicated that Carl and I "horrify most of their colleagues with their hard-nosed approach. 'Discovery learning is phony learning,' scoffs Engelmann. 'One child is learning and five aren't.'"

The article had a full-page, close-up picture of me presenting a cracker to a child who looks intimidated. Indeed, I looked big and she looked small. The article contrasted our approach with that of Glenn Nimnict. The photos for his approach showed children talking on the phone, manipulating letters on a magnetic board, and listening to a jukebox through headphones.

My statement about discovery learning may have been politically incorrect, but absolutely true. Discovery learning does not work, which means that, at the time, there was no evidence that it was effective (just as there is none now, although discovery remains popular among educators). The ineffectiveness of Nimnict's program would be documented in 1977. The data showed that at-risk third graders who had gone through his discovery-oriented approach since entering kindergarten performed below the level of comparable Title I students.

During the same time that Carl and I wrote the book about the preschool, my wife and I wrote a book, *Give Your Child a Superior Mind* (published in 1966), which was based on the curriculum we used with our children. The premise of the book was that preschoolers' performance could be greatly accelerated through a program that taught academic skills early. The book sold over a hundred thousand copies and received good press. I was a guest on several talk shows, including *The Merv Griffin Show.*

The publicity on that book prompted me to consider where I should focus my efforts. I already had a pretty good sense that there would be more substantial rewards from working with higher performers because their parents are more literate and influential than parents of poor kids. On the other side, I felt strongly that the disadvantaged needed champions who would lessen the gap between their performance and that of advantaged children, not make the gap wider.

So I didn't pursue working with children who were potentially gifted because higher performers are able to learn from a variety of approaches. Although we could certainly accelerate their performance through systematic early instruction, these children do not present the serious social problems that failing populations present. Children who are not being taught well enough to become competitive in the more lucrative occupations present serious moral and economic problems, particularly if there is a cure for their condition. Our mission over the years has been to show that there is a cure; however, I greatly and repeatedly overestimated our capacity to change schools and districts in a way that enables them to be effective with at-risk students.

Ironically, one of the most prevalent misconceptions about the approaches we developed is that they work with low performers but are not appropriate for higher performers—children who are assumed to prosper from generically different practices. Yet, *Give Your Child a Superior Mind* is still in demand. Books in OK condition sell online for around $50. First editions sell for more than $100.

After the second year of the preschool, an independent evaluation showed that the first cohort of children was considerably ahead of the average child in math and reading. Only one child scored below the first-grade level, and the average was beginning second-grade level, a year above the norm. Also, their average IQ had increased from 97 to 121, a 24-point gain over the two-year period. Gains of this magnitude were unprecedented. They occurred, however, because children went into first grade as readers, competent performers of math operations; and children who had a fairly solid foundation in the basic language of instruction.

We were very excited about this data, particularly since no such gains had ever been reported before. Our enthusiasm was not shared by the field. The general response from professionals was that our perspective was "negative" and that we operated from a deficit model, which emphasized what children couldn't do rather than all the things they could do. Again, the criticism seemed to miss the point of what an intervention is supposed to do. There is no point in providing an intervention if there is no reason for it. Instruction obviously must address what children don't know, not what they already know.

Carl's 1967 final report on his grant for accelerating intellectual development in early childhood had this summary about the philosophy of the approach:

> We believe this study indicates that approaching early learning as a straightforward instructional problem, as later school learning is approached, is a productive and progressive way not only of developing effective educational programs for young children but also of identifying the constituents of those amorphous categories that now go by the names of "intellectual development" and "readiness."

WES BECKER—PRESCHOOL YEAR THREE

During our project's third year, we found out that Carl was leaving to go to Canada and become an investigator for the Ontario Institute for Studies and Education and a professor at the University of Toronto. He invited

Valerie and me to join him. Valerie accepted; I tentatively declined.

Carl's impending departure presented serious problems to the preschool project. The reason was that I was not qualified to head the project. The only degree I had was a BA in philosophy, and the position I held then was Senior Educational Specialist, which did not allow me to administer projects. Neither Jean nor Cookie could assume directorship of the project because they also lacked formal credentials.

The rumors were that the Institute for Research on Exceptional Children would take over the project and change it as soon as Carl left. I later found out that Jean and Carl met with Wesley Becker, a gifted professor in the Department of Psychology. Their goal was to seek his help in preserving the project. I had heard a lot about Wes Becker from my sister-in-law, Geraldine Piorkowski, who earned her Ph.D. at the University of Illinois. Wes was her advisor; from her descriptions of him I assumed he could even run on water. Among other achievements, he had set the all-time track record at Stanford for attaining a Ph.D., entering as a freshman and taking only six years to earn a Ph.D. in clinical psychology and statistics.

At the time he advised Geraldine, Wes was a cognitivist, but shortly after she received her Ph.D., he became an energetic exponent of Skinner's behaviorism, which is based on evidence that behavior may be changed by manipulating positive or negative consequences that follow responses. Wes abandoned his earlier orientation because it lacked data of effectiveness, a signature characteristic of Wes. The professional articles that Wes wrote in the '60s show his change in orientation from 1961 to '67: "Measurement of Severity of Disorder in Schizophrenia by Means of the Holtzman Inkblot Test" (1961); "A Circumflex Model for Social Behavior in Children" (1964); "The Parent Attitude Research Instrument" (1965); "How We Encourage Cheating" (1966); and "The Contingent Use of Teacher Attention and Praise in Reducing Classroom Behavior Problems" (1967).

I had met Becker only once. He had presented to our project staff and graduate students. He summarized his current research, which involved working with teachers in failed classrooms and teaching them techniques for using positive reinforcement with their students. His data showed that even though most teachers had to be instructed in how to give praise, and even though the praise some of them issued sounded contrived and unnatural, it changed students' behavior. The basic thrust of Wes's training was, "Catch kids in the act of being good." His studies were among the first applications of Skinner's version of behaviorism to humans and school settings.

After the meeting I told him about some of the observations we had made in the preschools. He listened, then asked, "Where's the data?"

I told him I didn't have any formal data related to the observations. He smiled and shrugged. The message this gesture conveyed was that if I wanted to demonstrate the validity of my assertions, I needed data.

Jean and Carl had set up their meeting to ask Wes if he would assume the role of director of our project. They didn't have a chance to ask him, however. As they entered his office, he greeted them, and said, "I know why you're here, and the answer is yes."

I count this as one of the more amazing commitments a person could make. The project was embroiled in controversy. The work was demanding. By saying "yes," Wes made an official break with the fortress of higher learning and moved to the trenches, the gritty realities of working with teachers and kids.

Wes brought some of his graduate and undergraduate students with him. Thirty years later, I still work with three of them: Doug Carnine, a shy undergraduate who had already authored articles that appeared in professional journals; Linda McRoberts, an adventurous and outspoken graduate student who later would become Linda Carnine; and Susan Stearns (now Susan Hanner), only nineteen years old but very smart and industrious.

MODIFYING BEHAVIOR

With Wes installed as director, we became involved in work that focused on behavior. The project expanded somewhat but the preschool and kindergarten continued without disruption. One of the expansions involved working with severe behavior problems in Urbana schools. One group had eight highly disruptive kids in grades four through six. A new trainee, Paul Tannenbaum, volunteered to work with the group. After his second day, he called for help. He wasn't able to attain even a semblance of control and didn't want to continue.

Indeed, the children were tough. The most feared (by both adults and the other students) was Kim, an African-American girl who was about five feet eight inches tall and totally unmanageable. Before she was allowed in the classroom, she had to remove her shoes to assure that she would not injure somebody with one of her brutal kicks.

Paul said, "It's hopeless. The classroom is a zoo."

I told him I would work with the group for a few days and get the behavior under control. Then I'd turn it over to him. He said, "I don't think anybody can work with that group."

The next morning, I set up a little table next to me, with a large bag of M&Ms on it. I presented tasks to the group. Paul stood behind the students to restrain them if they started to fight or attempted to leave the group.

The basic routine I followed was to tell the kids how much they could earn for doing a task, to present the task, and then to pay off those kids who performed acceptably. If they didn't perform acceptably, I ate their M&M, with a show of great relish. They frowned.

For the first task I told them to touch their head. Nobody performed. I touched my head, smiled, and said, "Thank you. I get the M&M."

"Next task. It's worth one M&M. Stand up."

One kid stood up. With a show of displeasure, I gave him an M&M. He smiled.

"Next task. Everybody, clap."

They all clapped. I showed displeasure as I gave each an M&M.

After about four more tasks, I changed the rules. I told them that I wasn't going to give out any M&Ms unless everybody did it.

They performed well on the next few tasks.

Still later in the session, I told them that I was going to present a task that was worth two M&Ms. I described this task as something very hard. I told them 6 plus 7 equals 13. "See if you can remember that. Anybody who can gets two M&Ms. Once more, 6 plus 7 equals 13."

I waited a few seconds and then asked, "What does 6 plus 7 equal?" All responded.

"Who can say the whole statement, 6 plus 7 equals 13?" All students responded, but one kid didn't say it right and didn't earn two M&Ms. The kids performed well on the rest of the lesson.

During the next session, I introduced more math. The kids were totally engaged, but after the group was over, Kim got in a scuffle with another student and was beating him up. I grabbed her and started to pull her away. She turned around and took a swing at me. I told her, "Sit down," and forced her down into a chair. Then I quickly said, "Stand up." She didn't respond and I pulled her up. "Sit down... Stand up..." On one of the trials, I tore a ribbon that she had around her neck. She cried, cussed, and assured me that her brothers would kick the shit out of me. After she complied with a series of stand ups and sit downs, I told her that I was sorry I tore her ribbon and I would replace it. She said, "You a fucking liar."

That afternoon I asked one of the trainees if she would buy a ribbon for me. I gave her 50¢. I had no idea how much ribbon you could purchase for 50¢ or how fancy it could be.

When Kim entered the classroom the next morning, I handed her a festoon of gold ribbon. I explained that this was the replacement for the ribbon I tore. She stared at the ribbon for a long time. Then she looked up with tears streaming down her cheeks and said, "Thank you."

The kids did very well that day. I had Paul present most of the tasks, and anybody observing those kids would not have any idea that the students had "severe behavior problems."

Paul presented entire lessons after that day. At first I checked with him after every session. As things continued to go well, I checked with him less frequently. The kids were in full-fledged academics and doing well.

After a month and a half, Paul showed me a problem. The top button of his pants was unbuttoned and his belt was stretched to the last hole. He explained, "I have gained more than twenty pounds since I took over that group. Every time they miss a task, I eat M&Ms. Some of the tasks are worth three M&Ms. I eat more than a bag of M&Ms a day."

I told him, "Stop using M&Ms."

"Are you kidding? I remember how they were. No way."

I explained that the M&Ms were now symbolic to them and that the kids would not revert to their earlier disruptive behavior. I told him I would teach the group the next day and demonstrate that they didn't need M&Ms.

I cut some small strips of yellow paper before the sessions and placed them on the table next to me. I started out the group by asking, "What's the most M&Ms you've ever earned for answering a question?" Three. I told them that the next task was worth four M&Ms "or one of these." I held up a strip of yellow paper.

I asked, "Do you know what this is?"

"Yellow paper," they said with curious expressions.

I explained that adults work for awards, not candy, because adults understand that pieces of paper are proof of their achievement. They have diplomas and other awards that show what they have achieved. I concluded by saying, "I know that you're kids, and you'll choose what kids choose, M&Ms. That's okay because you're still kids."

I presented a simple task; all answered correctly. I asked the first kid "You want the four M&Ms, right?"

"No. Yellow paper."

Everybody in the group except one kid picked the yellow paper. The holdout was a small boy, sitting between Kim and the second-toughest kid in the group. As he held the M&Ms in his hand, he looked up at Kim and smiled. She frowned. He looked at the boy on the other side. He frowned. The boy with the M&Ms said, "Well, I just going to save this for later." He put them in his pocket and worked for yellow paper for the rest of the period.

At the end I told them that I was really surprised about how grown up they were. Then I said, "Just remember, those strips of yellow paper show how hard you work and how smart you are." All the kids nodded in agreement.

Paul was shocked, particularly as he watched the kids leave the group saying things like, "I got 15 yellow papers."

"That's nothing. I got 18."

I explained to Paul that I treated the pieces of yellow paper as if they were worth more than four M&Ms, that's how important the students assumed the yellow paper was. They had long since stopped working for M&Ms, except as evidence of their achievements. They were working mainly to impress Paul, each other, and themselves. They were proud of what they were able to achieve in school, where they had always failed.

When we trained new teachers, we stressed the importance of their responses. If they treat something as if it's very important, that's the way children will respond to it. If they respond with indifference, the children will respond indifferently. We also stressed the idea that the reason for this phenomenon is that kids are logical. If they do something that is billed as being important or significant, they will conclude that they are capable of doing important and significant things.

This rationale leads to the ultimate description of teaching as acting, and of good teachers as good actors. To be good, teachers must say the right things at the right times. This formula assures that their children will receive positive evidence, even if the teacher is uncomfortable and clumsy at "catching kids in the act of being good." Some teachers balk at the notion of "acting" rather than being themselves. The counter argument is that they wouldn't want to do things that eroded the self-image of the children; they wouldn't think of treating something that is very hard for the children to do as worthless. Rather they would do things to meet the needs of their children. The only way to achieve these goals is to act in a manner that will provide children with the kind of practice and evidence about their performance that will stimulate healthy growth and positive attitudes about school. Act properly and the kids will learn better and like learning a lot more.

HIGH SCHOOL STUDENTS IN UPWARD BOUND

The difficulty teachers had praising kids was dramatically illustrated by the Upward Bound program at the University of Illinois. The project selected tenth-grade poverty students who were identified as having college potential and provided them with additional work designed to prepare them to go to and stay in college. Upward Bound was a program that paralleled Head Start. The director of the program at Illinois was J. Don Boney. I was in charge of instruction. J. Don also hired Greta Hogan (extremely smart, passionate, and effective at working with teenagers). I taught the math; Greta taught the writing.

The major effort occurred at the U of I during the summers. The students were from East St. Louis, one of the most depressed cities I had worked in. Almost all the 64 students in our first summer program were Black. They ranged from undoubtedly being capable of doing college work to highly doubtful. The selection criteria for the project seemed to be based more on their superficial classroom behavior than skill. All students were attentive. All took notes. All wrote "in a clear, round hand." The problem was that most of them didn't fully understand what you were telling them, and the notes that most of them took were completely inscrutable.

We used their teachers from the district as our assistants for the summer program. We trained them in how to respond to the students, how to praise them, how to pace the presentation, and how to give constructive feedback. The teachers had a lot of trouble learning to praise. Their M.O. was to be both nurturing and "strict" or "demanding." They were often demeaning, but they tried to help the kids and would be quick to respond to students who raised their hand or requested help.

After several sessions on issuing praise, I observed my assistant in the classroom going over a set of problems a student had just completed. There were only one or two small errors on the assignment. The teacher's remarks focused on flyspeck details that were wrong or sloppy. He was ready to go to the next student when I signaled him to praise the student for good work. He said, "James, that's a very good job, for a change."

The ethic of the teachers left serious scars on the students, who had internalized the message that form is far more important than function. If something is written in a book, it is law and must not be challenged. If the teacher says something in an emphatic way, one must take notes even though one may not have a clear understanding of the significance of the words.

The students' approach to writing was based on the strategy of psyching out what the teacher wanted. Students tried to make their writing sound proper, but it was often unclear and laden with empty verbiage. One day, after they did quite poorly on critiquing a story, Greta stormed into the classroom, held up a sheet of blank paper, and said in a loud voice, "What is this?" They answered.

Then she emphatically said something to the effect of, "That's how everything that was ever written starts out—as a blank piece of paper. And what goes on that piece of paper does not occur by accident or magic. It gets there because that's what somebody wants to put there. It may be good or it may be bad, but just because it's on paper does not automatically make it the truth and does not automatically mean you can't challenge it. You have as much right to put your argument on a piece of paper as the author has."

A related theme that Greta and I stressed was that there is no such thing as a general understanding. If you don't understand the details, you don't have a clear understanding of the whole. Most of the students were poor in math. Part of their problem was that they were not practiced in attending to the details presented in directions. During the first few days of the summer program, the students showed all the signs of attending; however, their later behavior revealed that they didn't pay attention to the directions I presented. Instead, they did what they assumed they were supposed to do. If I told them, "Copy the equation for the next problem, then stop," many would write the equation and continue working the problem.

For most of the students, written directions were not a specific guide about exactly what to do, simply rituals that accompanied school work. The typical approach students had was to ignore the directions and try to work the first problem the way they thought it should be worked. If they succeeded, they would work the rest of the problems in the set the same way. If this strategy failed, students would raise their hand. Their teachers would typically not refer to the directions but would show them how to work the problem. This demonstration served as a model for how to work the rest of the problems in the set.

The students' behavior implied that they needed direct instruction in following directions and that they needed a lot of practice. The program I created took the form of arbitrary and low-probability directions. The first example was a sheet with a set of simple two-digit addition-subtraction problems, and the following instructions: **Work the problems in this order: First work problem 5, then work 7, then work 3, then start with 1 and work the rest of the problems in order.**

I told the students, "Everybody, touch the directions at the top of the page. Read the directions to yourself. Read them carefully. Raise your hand when you've read them and understand them."

Hands went up. "Listen: Read the directions one more time. Raise your hand when you've read them and understand them."

Hands rose. I said, "Work the problems the way the directions tell you to work them."

The responses of the students showed how strongly ingrained their misconceptions were. Most of them worked problem 1 first, then 2. I presented questions to students who didn't follow the directions. Very close variations of the following routine occurred with at least eight students.

"Stop. Did you do what the directions told you to do?"

"What they tell me to do?"

"They're at the top of the page. Read them out loud."

After the student read the directions, I said, "Did you do that?"

"Do what?"

"Do what the directions told you to do."

"What do they tell me to do?"

"Read them out loud." The student read them again, and again I asked, "Did you do what the directions told you to do?"

"What do they tell me to do?"

"Read them out loud."...

Usually, after the third round, the student would look at me and say in disbelief, "You mean, you want me to do problem 5 first?"

"Yes."

Although most of the students had the same confusion, not one student in the class questioned the meaning of the directions before working the problems.

We continued to present arbitrary instructions for working problems until the students became quite reliable in following them.

There were other difficulties. A report that I wrote in 1968 described them:

> Some of the students in the project were shocked when they discovered that they were being held responsible not for merely attending classes and for taking notes, but for learning the material that was presented. They objected on three counts:
>
> A) Nobody is supposed to be forced to do anything.
>
> B) They did all that should be expected of them, namely, attend classes and take notes.
>
> C) They did not feel like learning the material presented.

According to their objections, learning was optional; the choice about learning the material was theirs; and students should be permitted not to learn if they wished.

When the students discovered that they would not go on a field trip to Chicago unless they passed a math test, they objected strenuously. For most of them the trip was the number one item on their wish list.

They worked very hard, once they accepted the idea that they had a choice about working hard enough to pass the test or not going to Chicago. All but one passed a test on the material. The girl who failed was pretty cavalier about her work. She pleaded for me to give her another test. She assured me that she could pass it. I told her that I'd have to give her a different test. She indicated that I could give her any kind of test I wanted; she'd pass it. I gave her the alternate test two days later, and she passed it.

A problem related to following directions was the difficulty students had in figuring out general rules from verbal descriptions of examples. The sequence below was taken from an audiotape. The goal of the instruction was to prompt students to derive a rule about all fractions that equal 1. (All have the same value in the numerator and denominator.)

$$\boxed{\frac{3}{3}}$$

"Look at 3/3. What's the same about the top and bottom number?"

"Huh?"

"Which is bigger, the top or the bottom?"

"You mean the top?"

"Which is bigger, this number...or this number?"

"They are both 3."

"So is one number bigger than the other?"

"No."

"And when they're both 3, you have a fraction that equals how many?"

"One."

"That's right. When the top and the bottom are the same number, the fraction equals what?"

"What do you mean?"

"We're trying to make up a rule about fractions. We see that 3/3 equals 1. Are there any other fractions that equal 1?"

"Yeah."

"Name some."

"You want me to name some? ... Some what?"

"Listen. 3/3 equals 1. So does 6/6, 7/7 and 12/12. Can you name some other fractions that equal 1?"

"You mean like two-halves and three-thirds?"

"Right. There are many fractions that equal 1. And what do you know about them? ... Which part of five-fifths is bigger, the top or the bottom?"

"They are the same."

"And which part of four-fourths is bigger, the top or the bottom?"

"They are the same."

"And which part of two-halves is bigger, the top or the bottom?"

"They are the same."

"Right. And they all equal 1. So what's the rule about fractions that have the same top and bottom number?

"Say that again."

"When the top and the bottom number of a fraction are the same, that fraction equals how much?"

"I don't know."

I concluded my report with the following observation:

> For the disadvantaged student, formal education must be a frustrating, mystic experience. The schools encourage a non-precise approach to learning by providing the student with a false sense of academic progress. When the student is in the fourth grade, he will do fourth-grade work—even if he lacks the skills that are essential prerequisites to the tasks presented. The teacher teaches material that appears on achievement tests. Going through the motions, putting something down on the paper, filling in every blank, producing the kind of marks that hopefully will satisfy the teacher—these become the important considerations for the student. They displace the need for mastery. The student settles for half-learning, for never quite understanding. He is not convinced that thorough understanding of something is possible because he has received very few demonstrations that it is.

We wanted to change the students so they wouldn't settle for superficial understanding. I would score Greta's efforts high. I would score mine as OK but needing work. Some things I taught through clout, not finesse. I repeated things until most of the students got it, but it was not an elegant sequence that anticipated the errors students would make and that preempted errors by teaching things earlier that would preempt the errors. When students had trouble I would learn why and learn something about what I should have done earlier in the sequence, but it was too late.

I was frustrated because I knew that there was a systematic solution, but I didn't know it. For example, I taught them rate problems using variations of the equation $H\left(\dfrac{M}{H}\right) = M$ (hours times miles per hour equals miles). The students didn't have much trouble with the math, but many of them could not apply the equation to word problems. For instance: A truck travels at an average speed of 52 miles per hour. The truck travels for five hours. How many miles does the truck travel?"

Most of them had serious problems writing the equation for the problem. They would write miles per hour as the term for distance, not rate. I told them, "The rate term names two units. Those are the other two units in the equation. If the rate term names miles and hours, the distance is miles and the time is hours." We did series of examples in which I said the rate term and they identified the other terms. "If the rate term is houses per week, what's the term for time? ... What's the term for distance?"

Whenever I think about Upward Bound, I wish that I could go back in time, knowing what I know now. I could have taught them the relationships quite easily, because we have a better system now.

Even though the program I used with Upward Bound students was sometimes crude, I kept the periods energetic and had kids responding at a good rate. During the first two weeks, we were in a non-air-conditioned unit, University High School, the only building on campus that could accommodate us. In the mornings, my classroom was fairly cool, but it was on the east side of the building. By ten, my shirt was soaked, and even with the windows open, the temperature had to be in the upper eighties. Starting with the third week, we moved to the second floor of Altgeld Hall, the Department of Mathematics building, a stately impressive stone structure with a bell tower that issued quarter-hour reminders of time, and with refreshing air-conditioned classrooms.

Some members of the math faculty looked at our group as a great curiosity. Clearly, they were not the kind of students the faculty was used to seeing. They were not only younger but more talkative and animated, particularly the girls. And although we worked hard during class time, we also had fun. An older faculty member stood outside our open door and observed the class every day for about a week. One day after class, he approached me and asked in a thick Slovakian accent, "Do you mind if I ask you a question? What is that you teach in there?"

I didn't know how to respond. I listed some of the things we were working on—rate equations, distribution ... He said, "No, I ask what subject that is you teach."

I said, "Math."

He smiled broadly, pointed at me and said, "I thought it was. I thought it was. I was not sure, but I thought it was math." His question apparently was motivated by curiosity, not malice. He asked why I presented the way I did, and I explained that the students needed a lot of practice and I needed to hear their responses so I could get information about whether they understood what I was presenting. He seemed satisfied, but he continued to observe the proceedings almost every day of the program.

Upward Bound projects were not permitted to report formal data or data that could be used to "compare" one program with other Upward Bound sites. This federal restriction was frustrating because we had an excellent project that taught the students a lot. I could not understand how the Feds could fund programs that ostensibly were designed to boost the performance level of at-risk students without securing data about which programs provided the most impressive boosts. I'm sure that our students would have greatly outperformed all the competition. About the only evidence we were able to publish had to do with the number of students who went to college and the number who later dropped out. We had a much higher rate of college entrants than a comparable population of students would achieve. The dropout rate was unfortunately high, but significantly lower than comparable Upward Bound programs.

AUTISTIC AND ESL CHILDREN

During the summer of 1967, my family and I lived in Toronto. Carl had invited me to work there with him. I spent most of my time at the Ontario Institute for Studies in Education (OISE), working with autistic children. This was my first exposure. They were clearly different from any of the lower performers I had worked with, and I tried to figure out their mental strategies so I knew what discriminations I had to teach to change their behavior. The first thing that struck me about these children was that they don't understand what causes what. For whatever contorted reasoning they use, they are obsessed with trying to figure out what causes what, and they don't succeed. The reason has something to do with whether things are relative or absolute. If they are relative, the outcome is influenced by the conditions that precede it. Many autistic children will do things that lead to punishment or painful consequences, and most of the four- to six-year-olds I worked with did not have a clear understanding of language and what information it conveyed. Typically, they did not understand *yes-no*, largely because the correct answer is not always *yes* or always *no*. Some were echolalic (repeating what was said) but they sometimes fooled their teachers. The teacher would say something like, "Do you want to go outside?" They would respond with the last words the teacher said, "Go outside?" and the teacher would assume they were answering affirmatively. Over the years, I have witnessed long conversations in which the child did nothing more than repeat the last part of what the teacher said, and the teacher thought the child was participating and sharing.

"Would you rather play outdoors or stay indoors?"

"Stay indoors?"

"But it's such a nice day. Wouldn't you like to play outdoors?"

"Play outdoors?"

"Yes, that would be more fun. Do you think you should wear your coat?"

"Wear your coat?"

"No, my coat is too big for you."

"Big for you."

"No, it's just right for me. But it's big for you. Isn't it?"

"Isn't it?"

At OISE I worked with a small group of children (four, sometimes five children) in the mornings. All were verbal. Most treated *yes-no* as a word game, not as information. For teaching these kids, I used a "shill," another person who would model responses the child was to make. I would first present the task to the shill, who would answer correctly, then to the children. This was particularly important with verbal tasks because it made corrections a lot easier for tasks involving *yes-no*, motor responses, and relative pronouns, like *my* and *your*. Without the shill the presentation would become quite confusing to the children. For example, the teacher says, "Touch your nose."

The child touches his nose.

The teacher says, "What did you touch?"

The child says, "Your nose."

Teacher: "No, my nose. Say 'my nose.'"

Child: "My nose."

Teacher pointing. "Remember, say 'my nose.' OK, touch your nose."

The child does nothing.

Teacher: "Come on, you know how to do it. Touch your nose." Teacher points.

Child touches his nose.

Teacher: "Good. You're touching your nose. What are you touching?"

Child: "Your nose."

Some of these children did not know the most basic language concepts that are used in teaching, such as "*Touch* ..." So we worked on tasks in which I would point to something on the table and say "Touch." Then I would move the object to another part of the table, point to it, and say "Touch." The reason for moving the object after each trial is that if you don't, some children will learn to touch the spot on the table where the object is, whether it is there or not.

The director of outpatients as OISE observed me almost daily as I worked with the group. After each session he asked many questions about what I did, and why I did it. My approach was the antipode of his thesis, which was that some fundamental change in the cognitive processing system had to occur before any type of true learning was possible.

I responded that we don't have much control over the processing system, but if we establish various behaviors that are functional and that lead to reinforcement, we automatically change something in the child's processing system. If we didn't, the cognitive system wouldn't be able to perform the new kind of processing.

One day he challenged me to teach a girl who was not in the group. She was a five-year-old who engaged in almost continuous self-abuse. She slapped herself in the face an average of over ten times a minute under normal conditions. When she was told to do something, the rate escalated. She cried, screamed, and hit herself with considerable force.

The staff had tried various restraining devices, but all failed. The first time I worked with her, we took off her restraining harness. I sat in front of her and talked gently to her. She started to slap herself about every five seconds. After she had slapped herself about twenty times, I waited until she was not looking at me, and I slapped her in the face—the same part of the face she had been slapping, with about the same force. Her eyes got wide and she looked around as if something very strange had occurred, something unpredictable. She didn't slap herself again for about twenty seconds.

Her behavior told me a lot about the way she thought. For whatever reason, slapping herself had a predictable outcome, so it wasn't really aversive, at least not as aversive as "unpredictable" things are; it was simply something that had to occur. I also understood that it would not be possible to use any common physical means to communicate with her and correct her behavior, because any type of restraint would probably suit her need for predictability. She slaps; you try to restrain. That's predictable. So that would be as far as the learning would go. Also, I couldn't slap her because she had probably been slapped before and had very confused notions about others slapping her (and about slapping herself).

To communicate with her, I needed something that was aversive, but nothing familiar to her. We used cold water in the face. When she started to slap herself, we would vigorously douse her face with about half a cup of very cold water. Her behavior changed quickly.

I trained the teacher who worked with her in the procedure for the cold-water treatment, particularly about being reinforcing when she stops slapping herself. The teacher did an excellent job. When the girl slapped herself, the teacher would issue the cold water then gently dry off the girl's face as she talked to her in soothing tones and praised her for not slapping herself. Following each dousing would be a latency period during which she did not slap herself.

In the next week, we taught the girl to touch things, including her face. She received special reinforcement for touching her face. "Yes, touch your face. That's good." With this skill in place, we could direct her to touch her face, which is incompatible with her hitting her face. Through the task, "Touch your face," we could provide a new kind of correction for slapping her face. Following a slap, the teacher would say, "No. Touch your face. Touch your face … Good. Again, touch your face …" This substitute behavior now served as an instructional replacement for cold water in the face. Instead of following slaps with cold water, the teacher would use the touch-your-face correction, praise the child for touching, and return to the activity in which the slap occurred.

A few days after the teacher took over the girl's program, I stopped observing every day. I dropped in a week later to see how the teacher was doing. I found her in the large classroom with four children, but I didn't see the girl who slapped herself. "Where is she?" I asked. The teacher pointed to a girl I had never seen. Her face was not reddened, her expression was not agonized, and her clothing was not wet.

We videotaped all the sessions. The director of outpatients observed regularly and asked me a host of questions about why this remedy changed the girl's behavior. Reluctantly, he accepted the facts that a behavioral remedy involving reinforcement and punishment could change basic feelings and cognitive-emotional processes.

Although the story had a happy ending for the teacher (who later did very good work with other autistic children) and the child who had slapped herself, the story for the director of outpatients had a sad ending, which I heard about months later. After observing the changes in the girl's behavior, he called a meeting of all the psychiatrists and psychologists on staff at OISE (a considerable number). He showed a videotape of the girl before the treatment, crying, screeching, and violently slapping herself. He then told the staff that the topic he wanted them to discuss was not theories of cognition or interpretations of the nature of autism, simply how to change the child's behavior so she is not in a constant tortured state. The staff launched into theories of why this behavior occurred. He kept reminding the assemblage that the topic was not to identify inner workings or to "diagnose autism" but simply to identify a process that a practitioner could use to change the child's behavior. The responses continued to be either very general descriptions of interactions or declarations that behavior could not be changed without the underlying processes being changed.

After about twenty minutes of discussion, he directed the teacher to bring in the child. The child walked calmly down the center aisle and onto the stage. The teacher presented a series of tasks. The girl performed on all of them. She smiled, was responsive to the teacher's praise, and did not slap herself once. The director announced, "The cure was cold water in the face."

Not long after this meeting, the director of outpatients was fired, possibly for forcing his staff to address an educational issue (changing the girl's behavior). Ironically the place that employed them, The Ontario Institute for Studies in Education, has *education* in its title.

The summer in Toronto was the first time I worked with disadvantaged non-English-speaking children. The work was at the West End Crèche, which was in a very poor Portuguese neighborhood. Most of the 35 preschool children we worked with had very recently immigrated to Canada and didn't know a word of English.

They were culturally different. Specifically, they were terrified by adult males. When they were in the presence of a male, they were very attentive, but also timid and afraid. At first, they would not laugh or say anything to me unless I presented a task.

Carl and I thought the crèche would be an ideal place to use language-teaching videotapes we had made. These tapes were designed to teach the same content presented in the beginning language program. We figured that this technology would make it easy for a teacher to teach language. The teacher on the screen did the teaching. The children in the classroom were to respond to the tasks the teacher on the screen presented. The classroom teacher did not have to teach, simply reinforce or correct the children who viewed the monitor and repeat any tasks the children missed.

When we tried out these lessons with the children at the crèche, we wanted to find out what kind of training teachers needed, so we initially provided the teacher with only verbal directions about what to do, not actual task practice and rehearsal. We spent about 15 minutes explaining the procedures to the teacher. The teacher was to reinforce children who responded correctly. The reinforcers were M&Ms. If the children made a mistake, the teacher was to tell them the correct answer and play back the last part of the video sequence. We showed her how to repeat tasks that children missed.

We then assembled a group of about 15 preschoolers, sat them on the floor in front of the monitor, and asked the teacher if she was ready. She indicated she was. Carl started the tape. The teacher in the classroom started to pass out the M&Ms to the children. No children were attending to the screen but were very attentive to the teacher.

After a couple of minutes, we stopped the videotape and tried to politely ask the teacher what she was doing. "Did you understand the directions?"

"Yes."

"Well, the narrator presented tasks but the children aren't responding."

"Oh, has it already started?"

We never did much with the videotapes that summer, but we recognized that they could have great potential if teachers were first well trained in presenting reinforcement and basic corrections.

Valerie and I used the regular version of the language program that Jean and I were developing, and worked with children in small groups. The children learned English at an amazing rate. Their performance, however, documented the difference between their learning and that of the at-risk children we worked with at the U of I.

In the class at the crèche were two disadvantaged African-Americans, whose native language was English. When the project started, these two children were the highest two performers in the group. Within a month, they were the lowest two performers, absolutely at the bottom of the group. The reason was that the Portuguese children knew the various concepts that we taught, and had a good idea of learning from adults. All they had to learn were the new conventions for expressing what they already knew. They had long since learned that if they were given directions and didn't follow them, there would be serious consequences. So they had effective strategies for learning new material from adults. The English speakers did not have either as thorough an understanding of their native language or the extensive experiences of learning from adults.

Before spending the summer in Toronto, I had toyed with the idea of moving to Canada and working there with Carl and Valerie. The work with children in the crèche convinced me to stay in the U.S. I believed that the U.S. had more serious educational problems and needed all the help it could get.

Although the stint in Canada marked the end of my work with Carl, I feel that I was incredibly privileged to have worked with him. Carl was considerate, concerned, and extremely smart. Not only was he a good friend, but like Becker, he had a healthy respect for data, and he used the data to guide the decisions he made.

DOWN SYNDROME PROJECT

In 1968, the Children's Research Center at the University of Illinois initiated a giant project involving Down syndrome preschoolers. It was an interdisciplinary approach involving the special ed department, the departments of psychology, speech and language, social work, and miscellaneous others. The project identified parents of preschoolers with Down syndrome from different parts of Illinois. The parents were screened extensively on the extent to which they would support the project and follow recommendations for interacting with their children when they were home on vacation from a residential facility at the Children's Research Center.

Through Linda Meyer, a smart graduate student who was involved in the preschool for disadvantaged children, I became involved in the project and more or less inherited the position of instructional director. Linda was my assistant. (I worked at the Children's Research Center in the mornings and at the preschool in the afternoon.) The Down syndrome project marked my first experience of working in a public health bureaucracy. For the other projects I worked on, the talk was short and decisions about what to do were quick. The focus was on carrying out the plans without a great deal of additional discussion. The Down syndrome project was designed so that it had many supervisors and precious few workers. In fact, there was reluctance, often resistance, for some of the participants to face the level of nuts and bolts—what the children would do on a moment-to-moment basis. Everything was painted with broad strokes—play, interaction, and learning.

After several agonizing meetings the group managed to define what seemed like reasonable roles for the various departments. At first, the plan was to have the speech people teach speech. I argued that the instructional "unit" needed to assume responsibility for teaching speech production, so it would be coordinated with the other instruction the children received. We really didn't need *pit, pat, pot* articulation games.

One of the more obvious problems was the coordination of what happened before school, during school, and after school. The department of psychology assumed this role. Linda and I pointed out that the skills taught during school time needed to be reviewed and applied to other situations. If we taught buttoning, the child should practice buttoning at other times, and the way children do it should be the way they were taught. Unless the person interacting with a child knew what she had been taught and how she was supposed to respond, much of the potential power of the instruction would be lost.

Later, the instructional unit pretty much took over the behavioral training that occurred throughout the day, including meal times, wake-up routines, and bedtime routines.

We worked with 10 children, who ranged in age from 3 to almost 7. The children varied greatly in their skills. A couple of them behaved in many ways like a 16-month-old infant. They were in diapers, had little receptive language and no expressive language. For these children, we rehearsed tutors in routines that provided opportunities for "teaching"—meals, dressing, moving around in the facility, and bedtimes. The tutors would generally spend all of their time with a single child.

For the others we had daily instruction in small groups, and we worked out routines that reinforced and built on what they were learning during school time.

We taught specific language skills as well as various motoric tasks. For those children who had no intelligible speech, we presented tasks that called for pointing, touching, or performing an action that was directed. We also taught them to respond to *yes-no* tasks by nodding or shaking their head. (For children who could make a pair of verbalizations that we could clearly identify as reliably meaning *yes* and *no*, we accepted the verbalizations.)

The children showed great improvement, particularly in things that they learned to do independently. The higher-level children learned to read, perform on math, and respond to a host of language tasks they had not been able to do when they entered the project. In many respects the program was a model of what could be done. It was poorly administered, however, and needlessly expensive.

Curiously, the parents tended to find fault with the program, including those parents who had had the highest "cooperativeness" ratings on the initial screening. The problems the parents identified were generally not well grounded. They had indicated earlier that they wanted their children to be more independent and require less maintenance. There was strong evidence that these objectives were met. After talking to some of the parents, I came away with the impression that they were disturbed mostly because their role had changed. My interpretation was that they had accepted the role of having a handicapped child and of being the central figure in meeting the child's daily needs. With the child's increased independence, the parents seemed to feel that their role had been usurped, that they were not needed as much as they had been, and in some ways, that their children were now like strangers.

Near the end of the school year, Linda conducted a study that compared the learning ability of the top five Down syndrome children with that of five high-performing children of the same chronological age. The study seemed like a good idea because the Down syndrome children had become very proficient at learning new material. The study documented how proficient by teaching a set of concepts to each child. These were concepts that no child would have encountered. The study showed the amount of time required for children to achieve mastery on the set of concepts and measured how well children retained the information a week after the completion of instruction. In preparation for the study, all children took the Stanford Binet IQ test. The children in the high group had an average IQ of 126. The average for the Down syndrome children was 42, a difference of 84 IQ points, which means that the high group had about three times as much knowledge as the DS children.

We made up six related "concepts" that each child would learn. These were six discriminable figures that had different subclass names.

All figures were labeled spree.

Here's an unadorned spree:

The children had to discriminate between five types of spree.

This spree is blick.

This spree is sote.

This spree is lat.

This spree is glabe.

This spree is cack.

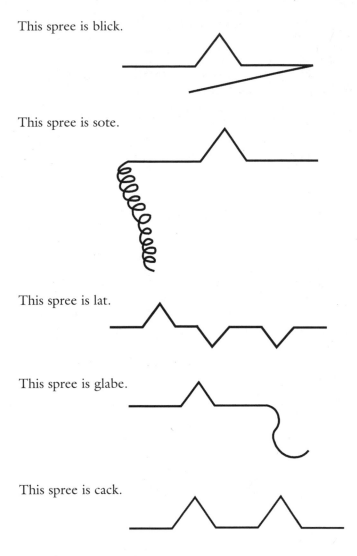

Children were instructed individually. The instruction occurred over three sessions. The rate at which the types were introduced depended on each child's performance. When the child identified a new type correctly five consecutive times, the next type of spree was introduced.

We assumed that the DS children would learn the new material at a good rate. We felt, however, that they would perform relatively poorly on the delayed test on all six classes of figures, which was presented a week after the last teaching session.

The results were very impressive.

The average amount of time required for children to learn the six discriminations was about 21 minutes for the high children and 23 minutes for the DS children—a difference of 2 minutes (9 percent).

The average retention of information a week later was 64 percent for the high performers and 56 percent for the DS children (a difference of 8 percent).

Statistical tests showed there were no significant differences in performance between the groups.

The performance of the DS children left no doubt that they had learned how to learn. They had also learned strategies for retaining information. We were very pleased over their achievements.

Both Linda and I quit the project at the end of the first school year, largely because it was becoming embroiled in politics. A new director came in with his ideas about the curriculum and the pecking order. These were not aligned with the approach that we had developed (which seemed to be very effective), and I thought some of his plans for reorganization were naïve.

I learned a lot about Down syndrome children from this work. Possibly the most unexpected fact I learned is that there exists great variability in their performance. (There is also a higher-performing variation that was not represented in our sample of children, mosaic Down syndrome, which is characterized by different physical characteristics.) I was not particularly surprised that the same kind of teaching that worked with preschoolers in the Bereiter Engelmann preschool worked with the higher performers. We extended the structured instruction to some children who performed lower than the children in our lowest group. I wrote up some of the strategies that we used in the project, including those for awarding token reinforcement and procedures for teaching following simple directions. This work would later become incorporated in the *Low Performers' Manual* (Zigsite.com), which provides specific information for working with children who are too low for our language program.

Our Down syndrome children definitely started lower than at-risk students. They needed more one-to-one interaction and careful instruction in yes-no, touching named objects, and other tasks than even the lowest at-risk preschoolers knew how to perform when they entered the project. Since working on the project I have never taught groups composed completely of Down syndrome children, but in the following years, we would have instructional groups that had a Down syndrome child in it. In fact, we have had these children in the top instructional groups.

DEAF CHILDREN

One of my assignments in working with Stephen Quigley at the Institute for Research on Exceptional Children was to analyze writings of deaf children in different residential institutions. I found the work both fascinating and frightening. It documented the magnitude of a typical deaf child's deficit not just in speaking intelligibly, but in being able to use the language as an effective communication tool. Upper elementary children in the better institutions were able to write coherent passages, making only a few word usage mistakes. The writing of children in average institutions disclosed that they had not learned the syntax of the English.

One of the tests used to evaluate their writing presented simple comic book sequences that depicted an event. Students were instructed to write a story to show what happened. The first picture of one sequence showed a boy and a girl playing catch with a ball, as a baby and a dog watched. In the second picture, the ball is going over the girl's head. In the next picture, the boy and girl are looking under the house, where the ball had gone, as the dog goes under the house. The last picture shows the dog emerging with ball in mouth. The children are delighted.

Below are four of the least sophisticated passages from fourth graders in one institution:

1. See ball boy girl baby and dog boy ball have girl. Dog ball boy girl baby. Baby ball girl. Boy baby.

2. Boy and girl play out. Baby is some look boy and girl game ball out boy and girl look house ball dog look. Boy and girl look & dog ball house happy.

3. He throws her a ball with head. Look baby see ball throw sit down look. The house look ball out under house dog saw ball get ball. Dog ball give him. She said Look come dog ball come here look dog last can go under.

4. The young tall boy said that you will try to how did you caught a ball. He says "please you caught it but if I throw it to yours hand make it fall on the ground between a house. I can't need it is on the ground between house. The young tall say that I can caught in all time. And he throw a ball to her can't caught it and it make under house. He say "oh that it under a house. Then he try to need it he fail to need.

Some protocols were better, but nearly all had serious usage mistakes. Here's one written by a high-average performer at the same institution:

> The boy tried to throw to the girl but the girl refused to catch the ball and tried to pick the baby. The boy threw her. She missed to catch the ball. The ball went under the house. The boy want the ball and he cannot reach the ball so he ordered his dog to pick the ball under the house. The dog did it. The dog gave back him the ball. The boy is glad that he has the ball.

Obviously, these children cannot learn about language the way hearing children can. In addition to their lack of understanding language usage is the fact that their speech is cacophonous. I had an idea for teaching the deaf to "hear" through tactual vibration. The idea was that if they could wear a prosthesis of some sort that would permit them to receive tactual messages that are perfectly parallel to those we receive through our ears, they would be able to learn speech and language the same way a hearing child does. Although most of the work I did on this project occurred later in Oregon, I had an opportunity to work with some outstanding people at the PLATO Lab (Programmed Logic for Automatic Teaching Operations) at the University of Illinois.

One of the men I played handball with after work was Don Bitzer (who forty years later would receive an Emmy for inventing the plasma screen). At the time, Don was a co-director of the PLATO Lab, two buildings on the engineering campus that housed one of the earlier computer systems. Don was upbeat, confident, and totally competitive. He loved a challenge.

One day, after handball, I mentioned my ideas about the prosthesis for the deaf, and he thought it was an interesting idea. He indicated that we might be able to do some research through his lab, but that he didn't think he could allocate funds to the project unless professionals in the field of the physiology of hearing supported the idea that the project was theoretically plausible. All this took place in probably less than 15 minutes (a sharp contrast with decisions in the Down Syndrome Project).

At the time, some of the most eminent physiologists in the world were attending a conference at the U of I, so Don contacted four of them and asked if they would give a verdict on the feasibility of the research. Two days later, they joined Don, an assistant, a secretary, and me at the PLATO Lab for what had to be one of the most amazing displays of function versus form I have ever witnessed.

We sat around a large conference table close to a chalkboard. Don quickly framed the problem: Does a person have the capacity to receive tactual information that is parallel to the information the ears provide? The first respondent went to the chalkboard and gave a somewhat detailed description of hearing, the organ of Corti, and some detail about the nervous system. The next respondent went to the chalkboard and added more information about speech, the different formants, and research on speech perception.

Then Don went to the chalkboard and said, "Let's get down to the main problem."

He drew something like a simple circuit from a finger to the head. He said, "OK, we start down here at the hand and send a message. So we need some facts about that message."

He pointed, "In the hand we have those things that fire. You know, the things that generate the message."

Our guests stared at each other before one said, "Do you mean neurons?"

"Yeah, those things. How many are there to the square inch? How frequently do they fire? And what's their recovery time?"

They told him what it would be for a finger, and he wrote a five-term equation on the board.

He pointed to the head in his diagram. "Somewhere along the route to the brain or whatever, there is a step up. Tell me about the step up."

They gave him the information; he put their numbers in the equation. He asked more questions. After no more than about three minutes, the equation was completed. He said, "There you have it. If the numbers you gave are correct, there should be ample capacity for the brain to learn whatever it is it has to learn from those messages."

They stared at his equation for some time. Then one of them said, "Bekesy has shown that the correct description is expressed by this equation." He walked to the chalkboard and wrote an equation. As soon as he completed the equation, Don said, "No, that's wrong and I can prove it."

He pointed out that the equation assumed that speech information could be transposed from one part of the speech spectrum to another. He said, "You can't do that without losing information." He rewrote the physiologist's equation with the correction and drew an arrow to his original equation. "You can derive the first equation I wrote from this corrected one."

Long silence. Then one of the other consultants said, "But that is at odds with what we know about the organ of Corti." He wrote an equation on the board. Don looked at it for no more than a second and said, "No. That's wrong and I can prove it." And he did.

This sequence of "No, that's wrong and I can prove it" occurred one more time. At the end of the meeting, the consultants were taking notes from information provided by a guy who didn't even know what a neuron was but who knew an amazing amount about electrical systems. I was struck by how different Don's approach was from that of academicians. He was not locked into the notion that physiology had its own brand of knowledge and electricity. If the phenomena are electrical, it didn't matter where they occur. They are governed by the same functions that govern other applications.

The group endorsed the research and we did some basic investigation through a set-up that didn't deal with speech, but with minimally different vibratory patterns transmitted by a small reed. The subject placed his finger in contact with the reed and indicated whether each pattern was high, medium, or low. The differences were very small. Furthermore, the trials were "discrete," which means that it didn't change from one level to another. It shut down after each trial, so the subject couldn't attend to how the pattern changed from one trial to the next (whether it became stronger or weaker).

One of the subjects was my oldest son, Eric. He achieved virtually 100 percent correct identification of the vibratory patterns. So we had preliminary information that it would probably be possible for the learner to identify more complicated vibratory patterns, such as those of speech that is transformed into tactual vibration.

We were scheduled to do more work on learning and recognition. But this never materialized because our project moved to Oregon. I didn't abandon the goal of working with somebody who could create a device for teaching speech information through tactual vibration.

An interesting event not related to anything I did at the lab occurred during the time I was there. One of the research projects analyzed responses to different stimuli. For this work, college subjects would sit in a chair and get wired for EEG, heart rate, breathing rate, and galvanic skin response. Then they would respond to various tasks.

When Don first reviewed the records of these subjects he noticed that just before the stimuli were presented, the subjects had a violent reaction, with their heart rate escalating and the other readings going wild. After a couple of minutes, the response patterns would return to normal.

Don checked the procedure they were using with the subjects and discovered the problem. The subject was on the first floor of the lab. There was a large open area to the basement, where much of the computer hardware was. Because this project involved linking different units together, investigators would wait until the subject was in the chair and wired with all the devices. Then, the person conducting the research would walk over to the open area and shout to the assistant in the basement, "Turn on the high voltage!"

CONSULTING

During the late '60s, we did a lot of consulting. I talked at many conferences. One that I remember as being significant was in Boston in 1966. Doug Carnine accompanied me. The audience responded to the message I delivered with boos. Most teachers and administrators were shocked or disgusted by what I said about teaching at-risk children. The discussants who critiqued my talk found nothing positive about the position I outlined, but much negative. In my final comment, I said that what they were doing with at-risk kids was failing, and if they ever looked inside the classroom, they knew it was failing. So they might be well advised to set their prejudices aside long enough to at least try out the Direct Instruction approach.

During the break, Doug and I went outside and sat on the steps. It was a warm spring day. I smoked a cigarette and Doug made various observations about how irrational the audience seemed to be. I told Doug, "It's discouraging, but we have to keep trying, even if we don't win."

He then said something I'll always remember: "I'd rather sink with you than swim with them."

Later, Doug worked with me in writing and field-testing the early math programs. He proved to be particularly gifted in organizational skills. He had the ability to work on half a dozen complicated things at the same time and had the work ethic to complete them on time. One of his most remarkable feats, however, was his ability to find things that he had filed. Everything he worked on and used as references was in piles—large, untidy piles that gave every impression of being nothing more than stacks of stuff. He didn't have a correspondence file. He had a few correspondence stacks. His office was filled with these stacks—on the floor, on shelves, and on his desk. Sometimes, before Doug could invite a visitor to sit down, he would have to remove piles from one of the chairs. Someone once commented, "I think he learned his filing system from a pack rat."

Doug's system was not as disorganized as it looked to me and other naïve observers. If somebody asked about a specific paper somebody wrote, a communication, a reference, a report, or information on a particular topic, he could go to the right pile and find it usually within less than a minute, often much faster than somebody could find such information in a conventional filing system.

All the piles looked the same to me, but somehow, he always knew what was in these apparently indistinguishable piles and where each pile was located. I don't remember more than a few times over 35 years that Doug was unable to find something within a few minutes.

Jean, Cookie, and I developed programs primarily for our preschool. We worked on these programs every day (not as part of any grant, but on our own time). We used them not only in the preschool but with a couple of other schools that were interested in our approach.

One of the schools we consulted with was in York, PA. The material it used was reproduced on mimeograph machines. We trained the primary-grade teachers and worked with them in the classrooms. The principal was a doer and clearly the instructional leader of the school. At one of the first meetings with his staff, he was instructing teachers in a form they were to fill out. One of the teachers asked, "Should we use pen or pencil?"

He said, "I don't give a damn if you use your finger nails as long as somebody could read it." Several members of the staff quit after that meeting. The ones that remained were very smart, and it was exciting to see the change that occurred in them and the school.

The success of this school generated interest in other places in Pennsylvania, including Pittsburgh and Harrisburg. One of my most memorable consulting trips occurred in Harrisburg. A large conference on our approach was scheduled. Phil and Valerie were already in Harrisburg training in one of the schools. I couldn't leave for Harrisburg until late afternoon on the day before the conference. I flew into Pittsburgh from Chicago. There, I was to transfer to an Allegheny Airline flight to Harrisburg. The plane was delayed. The gate attendant indicated that he didn't know how long the delay would last, then announced that if anybody wanted to go to any other city served by Allegheny, they could. I had heard about the picturesque train ride from Lancaster to Harrisburg. A flight to Lancaster was leaving in about twenty minutes, so I signed up for it. I figured I would get to Harrisburg before the flight did.

The folks who told me about the scenic train ride didn't tell me much about Lancaster, specifically that nobody there spoke English. When I got off the plane that night, the terminal was vacated. There was a cab on the street. I told the cabdriver to take me to the railroad station. He couldn't understand me. I knew that they spoke Pennsylvania Dutch in this area so I tried to communicate in German. *"Ich gehe zur Bahnhof."* He couldn't understand me. I couldn't understand him. At last, I pointed to myself, said "TOOT TOOT," and made some choo-choo noises. Aha.

The ticket office at the train station was closed. I went up to the platform and asked a couple of people waiting there if this was where I should be. They didn't understand me until I said, "Harrisburg." A woman nodded yes and gave a long explanation that was absolutely incomprehensible. At last a man who could speak English told me that I could buy my ticket on the train and that the right train had the destination sign: Harrisburg.

The train ride was spectacular, even at night. The track curved along the Susquehanna River and tunneled through hills. In Harrisburg, I went to the hotel where the others were staying, checked in, unloaded my stuff in my room, and went to Valerie's room. I knocked on her door. She opened it. She was crying. When she looked at me her eyes got wide and she yelled out, "Oh, my god. Oh, my god."

I asked her what was wrong.

She gave me a full-fledged bear hug and shouted in my ear, "You're not dead."

Phil ran to the door and looked at me with wide eyes.

I asked what was happening.

Valerie pulled me inside and told me the story she and Phil had just heard from somebody in the hotel. The scheduled flight from Pittsburgh, the one I was supposed to be on, crashed, and everybody on board was killed.

About an hour later, we found out that the report was false. No plane crashed and nobody died. During that hour, however, I believed that if I had been on the plane it would not have crashed. I understand that this attitude is perfectly irrational, but I had some reason for believing it. In the late '50s, I was on my way to New York. I had a layover of a few hours in Chicago, so I visited my parents, who lived on the south side. My mother was upset over the idea that I wasn't staying there overnight. She finally convinced me to change my flight to the following day. The flight I had originally scheduled crashed on its approach to La Guardia, falling short of the runway in the East River. Most of the passengers were killed. My mother tried to talk me out of going to New York the next day. I told her that the plane wouldn't crash.

PREPARING PROGRAMS

We knew that the programs we were developing in math, language, and reading would be published, although we didn't have a publisher yet. To make sure they would work well, we tried them out in places closer than Pennsylvania, where we could observe the progress of the teachers and children. Our objective was not so much to find out what was right about the programs (because we already had pretty good evidence that they worked with our teachers and children) but to find out what was wrong with them, what needed fixing. Cookie worked with several at-risk schools in Chicago. We mimeographed copies of the reading program and sent them to the tryout sites in ten-lesson batches. Cookie visited the schools regularly, worked with the teachers in the classroom, and noted (in copious detail) any problems she observed or that teachers reported. After each visit Cookie and I would revise the details of the program that didn't work well.

Jean followed the same routine with the language program. Not all the places we worked with tried out both the reading program and the language program, which was unfortunate because it became obvious that the children performed much better in the reading program if they went through the first part of the language program before starting the reading program. This language work taught them how to follow directions and taught the meaning of many of the words that the teacher uses in giving children specific directions.

The school in York, PA was one that used all the beginning-level programs we were developing. So did a school in Rio Linda, CA. In some ways, this school was quite different from the one in York. The children were Hispanic, not African-American. The principal was not as hands-on as the one in York. And the setting was very different. The two main aspects that were the same, however, were that the principals were the instructional leaders, and the teachers were very smart and committed.

One of the current myths about high-poverty, high-performance schools is that the way to create such schools is to give teachers time to collaborate and share what they have learned. This myth is based on the fact that high-poverty, high-performance schools have provisions for teacher collaboration and for stronger teachers to lead and train weaker ones. The problem with the facts about teacher collaboration is that they confuse a cause with an outcome. Both the school in York and the one in Rio Linda showed this relationship. When they were successful, they had provisions for teacher collaboration—teachers discussing specific problems and teaching techniques, teachers observing each other teaching. This kind of sharing is neither productive nor practical for failed schools, however. In York the teachers shared before they used our programs. The sharing did no good because, although the teachers were smart, none were successful; so sharing produced no results. The most they gained from sharing was consensus that what they were doing didn't work. This is the pattern for the vast majority of failed schools. It's not that some classrooms do well and others don't. The entire school is a failure, which means there is no teacher who has productive information to share.

In 1964, Orchard School in Rio Linda was the lowest performer in the district. The principal, Armond George, made a pact with his primary-grade teachers. They wanted to find an approach that worked well with their students. He agreed to support any program or approach they wanted to install, under two conditions. First, every teacher in the primary grades would buy in and participate fully in the approach; second, as soon as it became apparent that an adopted approach was not working well, not only would the school drop it immediately but the school would never revisit it.

During the next two years, the school tried out at least four approaches. The staff judged that they did not cause significant improvement. Direct

Instruction was the fifth approach. Cookie and I went to Rio Linda and trained the teachers.

We did some lecture-type format for the initial hour to acquaint them with the mimeographed material they would use. Then we did mock practice, mock practice, and mock practice, with pairs of teachers working together, one teacher playing the role of teacher and the other the role of child. Then they would switch off. We worked on all the details that we knew would give them trouble—the pacing of the presentation, the clarity and timing of pointing, saying the proper wording, signaling children to respond, and correcting mistakes. Following this training, we worked with teachers in the classrooms, demonstrating with children, providing specific feedback on what they needed to do to correct the problems they were experiencing, and later, rehearsing them on the techniques they were to use.

The teachers caught on quite quickly, partly because they were strongly committed to providing their children with successful instruction, and partly because our training procedures were getting pretty good.

Over the next four years, the school went from the lowest performer in the district to close to the highest. George kept huge performance charts in his office, mapping how far each class progressed through the programs and how each class performed on achievement tests. Performance improved each year.

Also, the interactions among teachers changed because now the school was armed with teachers who could walk into a classroom and demonstrate how to teach difficult skills. The school now had the capacity to train new teachers and to operate independently of input from Cookie or me. Working cooperatively was a byproduct of teacher competence and a system that made it easy for a teacher to tell another teacher, "I'm having trouble teaching _____. I don't know what I'm doing wrong. Could you observe me and tell me what's wrong?" Yes.

The staff never lacked the global notion of working together in an effort to succeed with children. That's what they did when they formed a pact to find out what worked.

EQUAL EDUCATIONAL OPPORTUNITIES

Some of the consulting I did in the late 1960s brought me in contact with racial issues in the South. A young civil rights worker who was involved with the United Negro College Fund set up some meetings with places that needed preschools. I believe the first place she and I visited was Holly Springs, Mississippi. As we drove from Memphis, Tennessee into Mississippi, she became pale. She told me how she and a couple of her coworkers were incarcerated in Meridian the year before. As we approached Holly Springs, she said, "I can't go through with this." She told me to stop at a gas station. She went into the ladies room and threw up. When she came back, she said, "Listen: Be goddamned careful down here."

On the following morning, we met with a minister who had expressed interest in making the church's preschool into an academic preschool. As we walked down the street, the sheriff met us. He spoke with a kind of sinister friendliness. "Well, Reverend, how are you?" The reverend looked down and said that he was well.

The sheriff looked at me and said, "You're not from around here, are you?"

I told him I was from Illinois. He said something like, "Well, you're walking with a Negro. Do you mind telling me what your business is down here?"

I told him that we were talking about setting up a preschool.

"My, that's fine. We certainly need preschools for little Negro children, don't we?"

He wished us a pleasant stay and we continued to the preschool. The civil rights worker was pale. She shuddered and said, "Be careful." The preschool never materialized.

Another place I went to was Southern University in Baton Rouge. I spent the night in the student union building. The atmosphere was strange. I didn't know at the time that on the following day, H. Rap Brown (famous for his radical slogans like "Burn, baby, burn") was speaking at the stadium.

The schedule for the next morning was for me to have a meeting with people associated with the preschool at Southern, then go to the preschool, spend a couple of hours there, then return to campus and meet with representatives from other Negro universities.

The route to the preschool went close to the stadium. It was a sight I will never forget. Just after the road crossed railroad tracks there were what had to be hundreds of state police cars, lined up on both sides of the road with two Black officers standing smartly beside each car. The road branched off toward the stadium after about a quarter mile and the train of stationary police cars branched with it, all the way to the stadium.

We continued ahead to a different world. The school was a playschool and the teachers did not seem very excited about providing academic instruction. They explained that they used enrichment activities to teach the children and that they felt that these were sufficient to stimulate intellectual growth in their children.

The meeting that I had later that day with administrators had to be among the most incredible meetings I had ever attended. The main issue was whether Southern University would have an experimental preschool. Probably ten administrators were at the meeting. Most were less than risk takers. But some were long on oratory and appearances.

After about an hour of skirting the issue of whether Southern would implement an experimental preschool that could serve as a model for other Negro colleges, one of the administrators suggested conducting a "feasibility study to determine the effect and practicability of such a preschool program."

I indicated that the proposal sounded reasonable, but how and when were they going to do it? After several comments about how that would require some thought and we shouldn't try to make snap judgments, a professor on the other side of the table said, "Well, I believe that we should first investigate the feasibility of such a study."

I said, "Wait a minute. Are you suggesting a feasibility study of a feasibility study?" Most nodded yes. I told them that my participation in the meeting was over, and I left.

Nothing ever happened with the Negro colleges. I thought that was a shame. On the one hand, H. Rap Brown was promoting frightening revolutions, but policy makers did not have sufficient commitment to install anything different to improve the performance of young children.

I'm not blaming them for being cautious, but it was unfortunate.

PERSPECTIVE

Before Project Follow Through commenced in 1968, we had learned a lot about working with young children. We had installed practices that were different from those customarily used. The biggest difference between our approach and traditional practices was that we tried to use honest statements of problems and information about solving these problems as a guide for measuring success. We did not start out with assumptions about how to teach effectively, or even what to teach. Our primary bias was simply that we believed the children were capable of learning if we were capable of figuring out time-efficient practices that would accelerate the rate at which they learned new material.

Virtually none of the things we did were adopted by the field. Even today, the overwhelming percentage of programs that are used with at-risk children have never been field-tested and shaped on the basis of problems that teachers and students have. The lack of regulations that demand field tryouts provides prima facie evidence either that the field of education does not really believe that there is any difference between good instructional material and poor material, or that the material should be tried out on a small number of students before it is adopted and installed in all classrooms of a school district or of a state.

Perhaps the most prophetic indicator of what would later occur with Project Follow Through was the educational community's reaction to data about our approach. In 1969, the Office of Education published a booklet, *Academic Preschool, Champaign, Illinois*. This was one in its series, *It Works* (Successful Compensatory Education Programs). The booklet was created by the American Institutes for Research (AIR) and provided a description of how we taught reading, language, and math. It also presented data on achievement of our later cohorts of children (ones who went through our more polished programs):

> The experimental group achieved significantly greater Stanford Binet IQ gains than the subjects in the comparison program, both at the end of the first year and two years of instruction. The comparison group showed an 8.07 gain after the first year of instruction, but had a loss of 2.96 points after the second year. The experimental group showed a 17.14 gain after the first year and an 8.61 gain after the second year.

The report also indicated that upon completing the kindergarten year, children in the program performed at grade level 2.6 in reading, 2.51 in math, and 1.87 in spelling. Although these gains were unprecedented, not one major school district made plans to install the program, even on a trial basis.

Over the next 35 years, there would be three more evaluations of "what works" by AIR, and three more endorsements that the programs and the full-school implementations that we had developed were effective. Yet, during the entire period, not one major school district administrator would seek our counsel, ask how we did it, or ask what would have to change in a district so it could fully implement the program. We had hoped that our work would spark interest in improving instruction for at-risk children. In 1968 there was no interest. This stance of urban school districts has remained unwavering but paradoxical. They were complete failures that postured themselves as unquestioned experts on instruction. No serious advances will be possible until districts learn that those who fashion failures are failures.

A final note: The discussions of data and programs are abstract and general, but they evolved from specific interactions with unique individuals. When I wrote this chapter, I had to search documents and contact people to reconstruct many of the events. For example, I didn't remember later preschool cohorts in great detail. I remembered some individual children, but I couldn't reliably match names with children. Not so with that first group. I remember the name of every child, and I remember much detail about every child—from athletic Dexter and his niece of the same age, Rene, to quiet Mark, beautiful Yolanda, and feisty Tony. I remember the incidents with them more clearly than I recall most events of ten years ago: I clearly remember the times I brought Owen and Kurt to the preschool and how they interacted with the preschoolers. The two years in which our lives intersected were long and rich in detail. Hopefully we played as important a role in the children's lives as they did in ours.

CHAPTER 2

Project Follow Through Begins

DEVIOUS LOGIC OF THE 1960s

Project Follow Through, a creation of the '60s, was the largest educational experiment ever conducted, the most responsive effort ever designed to find out what works well and how to serve at-risk children effectively. Yet, Follow Through is not recognized as a landmark study or a source of revelation about how to educate children of poverty effectively. It remains a secret, both to the public and to the educational community. In fact, its results have never been used to fashion even one urban school district, and the project has been all but erased from what serves as the current idiom of the "history of compensatory education."

To understand how this happened and why it could have happened, we have to examine the logic of educational reform and its disregard for data. The 1960s and '70s was the period when human values and the realities of the schools clashed, promoting guile designed to maintain the image of public education that was consistent with educators' prejudices. The primary enemy that educators had to fight then and now is evaluation because evaluation reveals the discrepancies between the educational rhetoric and the effectiveness of the schemes based on this rhetoric.

The Elementary and Secondary Education Act of 1965 established Title I as the main instructional intervention in the war against poverty. To qualify for funds under this title, a school had to have at least 40% of its students from low-income families.

There were serious debates about how to measure effectiveness of the program. Robert Kennedy believed in educational evaluations. In 1965, he asserted that if parents of at-risk children had sufficient information about what works in school and had a voice in educational practices, schools that serve at-risk children would become accountable and therefore improve. Toward this end he sponsored a plan for creating reports on the performance of Title I schools. At a Senate hearing, Kennedy argued for a testing system that would provide documentation "as to what progress had been made under this program."

Both the political sector and school administrations vigorously opposed this plan. Milbrey McLaughlin wrote about the predictable responses of educators to data in *Evaluation and Reform,* which provides an excellent summary on the futile reform efforts of the 1960s and early '70s. The book documents the repeated efforts of the educational system to institute reforms without using data to guide them. McLaughlin reported, "Educators argued that evaluation would stifle creativity and local flexibility." This argument is curious because how would it be possible to assert that creativity and flexibility have resulted in benefits unless there was supporting data? If the program had these virtues, it would seem that a rational person would be eager to prove that it promoted creativity and flexibility. Given that there was no evidence that Title I generated improved performance, the creativity and local flexibility that contributed to this outcome are phantoms at best.

McLaughlin observed that the fault educators found with evaluation was that it would create competition.

> Schoolmen contended that such competition was unprofessional and would result in less attention to specific local needs. Whereas Kennedy contended that parents should have something to say in how the schools serve the needs of their children, schoolmen argued that the professional knew best.

Again, the nature of the schoolmen's knowledge was elusive because there was no data that Title I resulted in measurable benefits. Schoolmen accepted the Title I funds with full understanding that the purpose of these funds was to improve the performance of at-risk students. Without comparative data, however, there could be no evidence of improvement.

Logically, the schoolmen's position is contradictory. It is not possible to implement any school well without providing intense attention to local needs—those of the children being served. Even more disturbing, how did the schoolmen possibly know what's best unless they had some kind of data to suggest the professionals' professed expertise? A person who had never built a house would not be categorized as an expert house builder. But educators with no evidence that their plans work ordain themselves experts who apparently have privileged knowledge that competition would result in less attention to local needs.

In 1965, something of a compromise evaluation plan came out of Washington, D.C. Each local Title I project was required to ensure that "effective procedures, including provisions for appropriate objective measurements of education, will be adopted for evaluation at least annually of the effectiveness of the program in meeting the specific educational needs of educationally deprived children." Unfortunately the term, *objective measurements of education*, admitted to many interpretations, as the later reports on Title I confirmed.

In 1967, first reports of this evaluation came in, and the results glowed with good news. Local educators were reportedly "moving quickly to devise effective compensatory strategies." These reports suggested that Title I had exceeded even optimistic expectations. The problem was the nature of the data presented. McLaughlin observed that it emphasized "impressionistic local reports, testimonial data, and photo journalism."

Furthermore, this evaluation was highly suspicious because it contradicted three important studies that suggested Title I was failing. One was GE's TEMPO (Technical Military Planning Operation), a kind of system analysis of Title I schools that had been identified as exemplary. The analysis was based on the idea that systems maximize their "outputs," which were improvements in student performance. Because the schools analyzed in the TEMPO analysis had been identified as exemplary, the outputs should have been obvious; however, the report concluded that whatever outputs the schools "maximize" had no relationship to student performance. In other words, there was no performance increase.

Two other studies that came out around the same time totally devastated the pretense that Title I was effective—the 1966 Coleman Report, which was followed in 1967 by the report of the U.S. Commission on Civil Rights. Both focused on Blacks, and both provided a frightening portrait of the inner-city student. The Coleman Report was based on performance data of 600,000 students. The general conclusion of the report was that a great performance disparity existed between at-risk Black students and Whites. Part of the report compared schools of equal physical characteristics and concluded that those schools serving Blacks performed far below those serving Whites. The report noted prophetically, "*The finding was that money spent on smaller classes, laboratories, counseling, higher teacher salaries, and higher teacher qualifications had no effect on academic achievement.*"

The subsequent report by the U.S. Commission on Civil Rights documented the fictitious nature of the Title I reports and concluded, "None of the programs appear to have raised significantly the achievement of participating pupils, as a group, within the period evaluated by the commission."

Title I procedures made it virtually impossible for schools to be successful. The key instructional provision was to provide students with two-program instruction. During one period of the school day, students used the regular reading program adopted by the district. During a second reading period, they would use some form of compensatory reading program to "supplement and enhance" the regular program.

This approach greatly confused children in the early grades who were trying to learn what reading is and how to do it. When engaged in the "regular" program, students were encouraged to guess about words they could not decode; students focused on whole words, and they referred to letter names. If they used a Direct Instruction program as the compensatory supplement, they would be discouraged from guessing; they would focus on parts that made up whole words before identifying whole words, and they would refer to letter sounds, not names. It shouldn't have taken incredible imagination to figure out that this lack of continuity would be very confusing, or at best, poorly designed to accelerate performance of the children.

Like hermit crabs who have lost their borrowed shell, educational policy makers were denuded by the Coleman Report and, like hermit crabs, scurried to find security, regardless of how bizarre the shelter was. Their effort resulted in one of the more inhumane programs ever initiated—bussing. For educators, however, bussing was an ideal solution because herding children into a bus did not require any kind of instructional expertise.

Because bussing was a non-instructional remedy to an instructional problem (the failure of the schools to teach children effectively), policy makers needed some compelling rhetoric to make busses symbols of progress. They fixed on history and *redefined the performance problems of poverty Blacks* as *a social problem, rooted in history and caused by discrimination against Blacks.* With this link established, policy makers could point to busses and declare, "There's your evidence that we are responding to the data. We are breaking down discrimination. Therefore, we are addressing the fundamental *causes* of the poverty Blacks' performance problems."

This redefinition of the instructional problem greatly benefited photojournalists and writers of moving prose, who showed and described the plight of Blacks and the terrible scars of discrimination on them. Although this causal explanation is accurate in one sense, it doesn't imply anything about what the schools can do to correct it. It suggests how society needs to change so that future generations will not suffer these inequities, but it doesn't directly address how a teacher is to work with Jackie and Alan and the rest of kids in a fourth-grade class of an inner-city school. Here, children are already far below grade level and are on schedule to fail in school, drop out, and fail in later life.

Bussing lacked one structural link to effectively disguise it as a vehicle of salvation. That link was data. What data was there that could compel liberals and possibly even conservatives to think that putting Jackie, Alan and the others in integrated classrooms would be effective in increasing performance? Thomas Pettigrew provided the keystone that could keep the non-educational plan from collapsing. He had reanalyzed the Coleman data and discovered that Black students attending mostly White schools had achievement levels much higher than Blacks in segregated schools. Also, in these schools, the White students' performance was no worse than that of Whites in segregated schools.

The conclusion drawn by a thoughtful person who was not racially prejudiced would probably have been, "So what? Just as there are middle-class Whites, there are middle-class Blacks. Middle-class kids perform at a high level whether their neighborhood schools are segregated or integrated."

Once more, policy makers confused correlation with causation and drew the conclusion that if Black children in integrated schools performed higher, putting Black children into White schools would create an integrated school, and the children in this integrated school would perform as well as the children in schools that were "naturally" integrated.

This reasoning is both romantic and cruel. Jackie and Alan couldn't perform on fourth-grade instructional material in any school. They had learned only about two years' worth of skills in four years. Putting them in a fourth-grade classroom with children who performed two years above them would constitute incredible punishment, not intelligent education that ostensibly addresses "the local needs of the children."

Yet, that's what happened to Jackie and Alan. They spent one hour and 45 minutes a day on a bus, which took them to a school in a strange neighborhood, where there were smart White kids who were not very tough or streetwise.

Ironically, someone could not draw the conclusion that bussing kids would work unless that person was blatantly prejudiced. Policy makers (and law makers) probably would not have taken kindly to the idea of taking White middle-class second graders, dropping them into fourth-grade classrooms, and letting them sink or swim, but through some contorted logic, this solution was okay for Blacks who performed on the second-grade level. That's prejudice of the highest order.

The most ironic aspect of bussing was that it was advertised as "equal educational opportunity." All policy makers had to do to obtain unquestioned data on the instructional problem bussing created was observe for an hour in an inner-city school. They would have had to do nothing more sophisticated than hand different students material that properly placed fourth graders would have no trouble reading, and say, "Read this out loud."

I've seen such demonstrations provided for community workers. And I've seen tough male adults get tears in their eyes after observing the painful performance of the students. Almost universally, they would later say, "I had no idea. I had no idea." That's unfortunate because the observations would take less than $1/1000$ the amount of time required to formulate the details of a bussing plan.

In 1970, evidence on bussing in Boston documented the inevitable—bussing failed not only for Blacks who went to integrated schools, but also for Whites in these schools. Performance dropped and many Whites migrated to the suburbs. A principal of a White school to which Blacks were bussed succinctly told me the reason for "white flight" from integrated schools:

> We're supposed to have standards here. We don't do social promotions. So if I place Black kids where they belong, more than 75 percent of them would be in special ed. If I put them in special ed, I'm a racist. If I leave them in the regular classrooms and flunk them, I'm either a racist or an ogre who doesn't understand affirmative action. So what do I do, close my eyes, sell out our standards and socially promote them, or go to another school?

He went to another school.

Bussing wasn't the only educational assault on the war against poverty. Before evidence on bussing came out in 1970, two "instructional efforts" became operational—Project Head Start and Project Follow Through. Head Start was implemented to give at-risk preschoolers a boost in performance. Follow Through was initially designed to maintain and extend that boost in grades kindergarten through 3; however, Follow Through was not implemented as a large social program because there were not sufficient funds. The first director of Follow Through, Robert Egbert explained:

> The early years of school had been omitted from the Economic Opportunity Act, but they soon attracted nation-wide attention when initial evaluation studies appeared to suggest that Head Start gains were being washed out in kindergarten or first grade. Concern over these studies triggered a complex series of events that led to a request for a program to "Follow Through" on Head Start—a program that, because of budget restrictions,

administrators were forced to change from one of service to one of social experimentation.

The expected budget for Follow Through had been $120 million; however, the project initially received only $15 million. Egbert pointed out that this might have been a blessing:

> With such limited funds, it seemed sensible to change FOLLOW THROUGH'S primary purpose from 'service to children' to 'finding out what works.'

Egbert introduced a design called "planned variation." The design was based on the idea that the National Follow Through Administration would make no judgment about what works, but instead would set the stage for selected investigators who believed they knew what works to prove it in the field, not in a laboratory experimental setting. This decision would result in the most carefully designed educational experiment ever conducted. It was not perfect, but the design features were certainly strong enough to provide voluminous comparative data about the extent to which different approaches were effective.

The overall plan was simple: Follow Through would identify proponents of different approaches and would set the stage for something like a horse race in which there would be a winner or winners, some also-rans, and some losers. The study would involve over 200,000 students, 22 sponsors of different approaches, and 178 communities, which spanned the full range of demographic setting variables (rural, urban) and ethnic composition (White, not-White; poor, not-poor; English-speaking, non-English-speaking).

Just as a series of meteorological events and human circumstances set the stage for a saga involving a "perfect storm," the conditions in 1967 set the stage for a saga involving the perfect conflict of ideologies and practices. Wes Becker and I would direct one of the approaches in the Follow Through horse race. Our approach would be based on our commitment to data and our belief that data was the primary guide for mapping our way. The prevailing educational context in which we would operate was characterized by thorough disregard for data and a prevailing philosophy that schoolmen know best and don't need data to make informed decisions. The question was not whether there would be conflict but how Follow Through could declare winners if the winning models were not approaches schoolmen endorsed. The history to that date showed that the establishment had both the power and the will to ignore and even disdain empirical evidence.

WELCOME TO FOLLOW THROUGH

I knew nothing about Project Follow Through until after I gave a presentation on Direct Instruction in New York in the fall of 1967. After the talk, a tall distinguished-looking man introduced himself as Dick Schneider. He told me that the Office of Education was planning a large educational experiment involving different educational approaches for full-school implementations for disadvantaged kids. I confessed that I had never heard about Follow Through, and he confessed that he had never heard of Direct Instruction, but my talk persuaded him that we definitely had an approach that worked with at-risk children and it seemed worthy of sponsorship in Follow Through.

Schneider informed me of an upcoming organizational meeting Follow Through was holding in December and indicated that if Wes and I were interested in becoming a Follow Through model, we needed to attend that meeting. I called Wes immediately. He said what I hoped he'd say, "Let's do it."

The meeting was held at the Office of Education in Washington, D.C. Dick Schneider opened it with an introduction and overview, which indicated how Follow Through was funded and specified the ground rules for the sponsors. He used the horse-race analogy to describe the project. All sponsors would start at the same point and have the opportunity to work with participating school districts for a sufficient length of time to fully implement their approach (eight years). At that time, all approaches would be evaluated. Until that time, no comparative data on sponsor performance would be published by participating sponsors. The reason was that some sponsors indicated that it would take years for their approach to mature and be absorbed by the school enough to change the ethic of how teachers and children were to interact.

In the end, however, the project would address the issue of which approach to instructing at-risk children in grades kindergarten through 3 produced the most substantial achievement gains in reading, language, spelling, math, and possibly other areas.

After the final evaluation, National Follow Through would not only disseminate information about effective models but would arrange for successful models to work with more schools, while models producing inferior results would be phased out.

Sponsors were to receive a sufficient amount of funds to do whatever research they needed and to service their participating sites. School districts would receive enough money and support needed to fully implement whatever approach they adopted—$750 per child, per year (over $2200 per child in 2007 dollars), which would be in addition to the districts' current maintenance of effort. The project would also provide liaisons, both from different universities and from the central office to help resolve problems and to facilitate the implementation.

Following the introduction, Robert Egbert took over the proceedings. My first impression was that he looked too young to be director of the project, and his attitude seemed cavalier. (I would later discover that my first impression was categorically wrong.) He first had all 18 sponsors in attendance briefly describe their approach. I was surprised about the way most sponsors responded. They seemed to try to talk the others into their viewpoint. That didn't seem very likely.

The description that Wes and I provided indicated that we would use behavioral techniques that had been demonstrated to be effective and instructional programs that were referenced to what the students needed to learn. We would simply extend what we had developed for grades K and 1 to grades 2 and 3. The goal of all instruction would be to teach more in less time and thereby accelerate the performance of the children.

A young Don Bushell from the University of Kansas seemed to have serious stage fright as he described the Behavior Analysis model. I was familiar with the model, which had solid data to support it. In fact, Wes's daughter Jill would later complete part of her graduate studies in Kansas with this group.

One of the sponsors I had met earlier was Dave Weikart. He seemed like a nice guy. He had an early intervention model in Ypsilanti, Michigan. Dave had visited our preschool several years earlier, and Jean Osborn had worked with teachers of Weikart's disadvantaged preschoolers, using a prepublication edition of the language program. Weikart conducted a study in which he compared this group with two other treatments, including one that he had designed. His approach was quite similar to the others based on Piaget's theories.

The horse's ass of the sponsors in this horse race had to be the spokesman of the British Infant School (Education Development Center, sometimes called, "open education"). His supercilious message was that we are misinformed if we try to impose learning on kids. The simple elixir is to set the stage for children to experiment and learn, and stay out of the way of nature. It seemed obvious that he had never worked with kids and had no idea of the bedlam that would occur if this approach were seriously implemented.

One of the sponsors was Lauren Resnick, then a behaviorist at the University of Pittsburgh, who wanted to use her site to develop an approach to teaching classification, which she seemed to think was the end-all of instruction and would permit children to do remarkable things. We had talked with her before the meeting. Wes thought she was great. I thought she was quite smart but lacked sensitivity to the problem of providing a service for these children. She seemed far more interested in her model for teaching classification (which was neither analytically nor practically very sound) than she was in considering Follow Through children as more than subjects in her experiment. She would later become a non-behaviorist, the flag bearer of a failed approach called *constructivism*.

One Piagetian-based approach was that of Ira Gordon from the University of Florida. His idea was to provide stimulation in school and use trainers to visit parents and instruct them in how to work with their children at home on the same Piagetian activities that were presented in school. I thought he was either misguided, or the kids in Florida were a lot different from the ones we worked with in Urbana, California, Chicago, and Pennsylvania. Gordon's strategy might have worked with the kids in Toronto, but not with kids who need more help. With the inner-city population, there is little likelihood of either being able to work extensively with the parents or of the parents working successfully with their kids. This is not to say Gordon's goals were ignoble, simply impractical. If it's not taught thoroughly in school, the parents of the kids most in need are not going to be successful at augmenting the program.

Several other models featured play as one of their major ingredients. One was that of Lasser (Larry) Gotkin from New York University. He was greatly different from the others. Although his model was based on games, it was very clear that he had worked extensively with kids in school. He understood how to communicate with them, their learning tendencies, what "motivated" them, and what essential skills had to be taught in school. One clue that he was different was that he had revised his games on the basis of student performance. Another was the details that he gave about kids and their problems with learning. He was clearly approaching the problem from the standpoint of data on how kids learn. He indicated that his approach was something like ours, but differed fundamentally with respect to how effective learning begins.

Several models were based on the traditional notion of "language experience" à la Sylvia Ashton Warner. Their format was to do something that engaged the kids and use the experience as a basis for teaching extensions, such as writing about what they did.

One language-experience model was TEEM, the Tucson Early Education Model, designed by Maria Hughes. The other was Bank Street College of Education, in New York City. The Bank Street representative gave an example of the kind of teaching that could accompany the real-life experience of children going up the stairs. The teacher observes, "We are going *up* the stairs." And the children would associate this language with the experience and learn about prepositions. It was obvious that the presenter didn't have any idea of either the kind of instruction or the number of repetitions that would be required to teach *up* versus *down* to low performers. Although both the Arizona model and Bank Street delivered some of the same rhetoric about Piaget and learning, the Bank Street approach seemed more disciplined and organized than the Hughes version of language experience.

A final group of models was based on the schoolmen's slogan that the local site knows intimately about the instructional needs of their kids and would be able to provide instruction that is more carefully targeted than some form of pre-packaged approach. All communities identified for participation in Follow Through would have the choice of either selecting one of the models or opting to be a self-sponsored program.

Egbert explained how the sponsors were grouped into three "categories"—models designated as focusing on basic skills, those that stressed cognitive skills, and those that addressed the affective concomitants of learning (how kids feel about themselves and their abilities). Both our model and the University of Kansas model were delegated to the "basic skill" category. I couldn't understand how someone could teach cognitive skills without teaching basic skills. Don Bushell, Wes, and I objected to the classification, but we were to remain with Lauren Resnick in the basic skills category.

Egbert expanded on some of the support features of Follow Through. For each site there would be an outside facilitator whose mission was to work with the sponsor and the National Follow Through office to assure that the sponsor's approach was being satisfactorily implemented in each site. These facilitators were recruited from various universities. In addition, there would be full-time liaisons, employed by the National Follow Through office. They would also work with sponsors and communities to settle disputes between sponsor and site and to verify that the terms of the agreement between site and sponsor were being executed. The designers of Follow Through felt that these provisions were important so that there was a lasting marriage between each site and sponsor. Sites would be discouraged from switching sponsors because such switching would contaminate the data. This marriage relationship would prove to be particularly problematic with one of the communities that later selected our model.

The level of funding for the project was above anything that had ever occurred in educational research before or since. Follow Through recognized that if sites were to implement particular approaches, they would need more funds for aides, material, travel (for meetings with the sponsor), and training. The $750 per Follow Through student, above the level of maintenance of effort that the district committed to the project, seemed adequate to meet this goal. In addition all sponsors would receive funds based on the number of schools served and the geographic distribution of their sites.

PICK A SPONSOR

Sponsors did not pick from the selected sites, nor were the sites assigned by the national office. Rather, the format was more like the one that Robert Kennedy proposed. Each site identified a Parent Advisory Committee (PAC) that would be responsible for selecting one model. Each participating district agreed to implement whatever model the parents selected.

Bob Egbert set up three meetings in which PACs would be able to talk to representatives of the various approaches and make an informed decision. Egbert scheduled one meeting in the east, one in the west, and one in New York City. Ostensibly the reason for NYC having a separate presentation was that the district was to have more schools than any other site and each school would select its sponsor.

The format of the meetings was fairly simple. Bob Egbert or Dick Schneider would give a brief overview. Then, sponsors would take about five minutes each to tell about the relevant details of their model. Finally, there would be a question and answer period.

Wes did the presentation in the West. I did both the Eastern one and the one in NYC. The presentations in the East and the West were uneventful. The one in NYC, however, had a great deal of fireworks.

At the time of the meetings, Black Power was in full swing in NYC. The teachers were on strike; an estimated 70 percent of the children were not in school. The district had recently been parceled into local districts so that parent groups would have control of the educational outcomes in local schools. Ocean Hill Brownsville (Bedford Stuyvesant) was the flagship of the movement for local control. The Urban Coalition asserted that community control was the only answer to the failure of public schools. The coalition took out a full-page ad in the New York Times, which carried the headline, "If It Works for Scarsdale, It Can Work for Ocean Hill." The coalition made the ambitious prediction "That by February 1, 1970, there will no longer be any student [in Ocean Hill] classified as a non-reader."

The exuberance over local control would later fade, largely because local schools would do things the ways they had in the past and would not provide any form of standardized testing or serious evaluation of the schools' progress. In 1971, when NYC did test students in junior high schools, administrators discovered that seventh graders did not score at grade level 7.7, as anticipated, but at 4.7, three years below grade level, a score students could achieve if they randomly chose a, b, c, d for each multiple-choice test item. Diane Ravitch (educational historian) reported in 1972 that not one school "recorded a higher score in 1971 than it had in 1967" which was before the strikes and turmoil.

Back in 1968, we had already been contacted by the PAC from Ocean

Hill Brownsville. Representatives indicated that they had investigated the credentials of the Follow Through sponsors and would select us at the upcoming meeting.

The educational bureaucracy in NYC despised us, probably because we stood for everything their philosophy of progressive education abhorred. The central office promoted the Bank Street college model and other soft approaches, and they were not very subtle about their position.

The meeting took place in Brooklyn at the district's central office (110 Livingston), a large old building in the shadow of the Brooklyn Bridge. The building had a lecture hall with a balcony, which accommodated possibly 400 people. Before the presentation began, all sponsors were assigned to tables on the mezzanine. Parent groups from the various NY Follow Through schools were to visit sponsors. Several NYC administrators actually herded parent groups away from our table, saying things like, "Oh, you don't want to go there. Go over to that side. That's where the good models are."

Just before the presentation was to start, Bob Egbert recognized that I was not in very good humor, pulled me aside, and told me not to use foul language when I presented to the assemblage. He cautioned, "Don't say 'bullshit.'" Apparently this was my signature characteristic. A year earlier, Carl Bereiter had been interviewed by a reporter who asked, "What was the most important thing you have learned from your association with Engelmann?" He thought a moment and then said, "I learned to say bull-shit. Earlier, if something sounded preposterous I would try to find some-thing good in it. Now, I just say 'bullshit.'"

I told Bob Egbert I would be well-behaved.

The place was packed with virtually no standing room and people blocking the exits. The audience was noisy. I was one of the later presenters. When my turn came, I gave my five-minute synopsis, indicating that the instructional practices in our model were not negotiable (unlike those of some of the other models that presented); that we accepted the responsi-bility of teaching all kids the skills that they needed for future learning; and that the practices we used were data-based. I gave a couple of examples of the small-step progressions in our instructional sequences, which assure that even the lowest performers will be able to learn.

There had been a few questions and comments following several of the preceding model descriptions. Following mine, there was an animated comment-question-answer period. A woman on the first floor said, "You talk about coming into our city and telling us about our problems. People outside New York don't know anything about our problems." Great cheers.

I told her, "No, everybody knows about your problems except you. Or if you know about them, you're sure not solving them." Boos.

Another woman said, "You think you have the power to come in here and tell us what to do. Well, you just go into a place like Ocean Hill Brownville, and you'll see who's got the power." Cheers.

A woman in the first row of the balcony stood up and said, "I'm a member of Ocean Hill Brownville Parent Advisory Committee, and believe me, we know who has the power. We also know how to use it responsibly, and we have selected the Becker-Engelmann model." Considerable rustling.

A distinguished white-haired man on the main floor stood up and gave a long, dramatic oration. He ended by saying in rising volume, "I hear talk of skills and sub-skills and sub-skills of sub-skills, but why is there nowhere in Mr. Engelmann's presentation one word about [pause and dramatic point toward the ceiling] **learn by doing and do by doing!"**

Explosion of cheers, shouts, applause, which lasted probably more than 10 seconds.

When the place calmed down, I said, "Well, I promised Bob Egbert that I wouldn't say *bullshit*, but I'll try to answer your question anyhow." I went on to explain that not only was the originator of slogans about learning by doing, John Dewey, dead but that there was nothing to suggest that his slogans had much relevance to the problems facing disadvantaged kids. As I talked, the man's face became so red I thought he would explode. After the meeting, Bob Egbert looked at me with a wry smile and shook his head. I later found out that the man with the long question was the director of math instruction in NYC.

I found the naiveté of proponents of progressive education shocking. If people knew much about John Dewey, they would have known that he and his wife operated two lab schools based on radical progressive education and both were unquestioned failures. The first was at the University of Chicago. It failed so categorically within three years that Dewey was forced to leave Chicago. He went to NYC where he and his wife founded his famous Lincoln School in Manhattan. This effort failed in two years. Yet, a hall full of grown, educated people from NYC found the slogan, "learn by doing," something of both a battle cry and religious experience, regardless of the amount of student failure it generated.

PREPARATION FOR FOLLOW THROUGH

When the results of parent group selections came in, we knew that we would have to work very hard during the next few years. The parent groups in 19 communities selected our model, which resulted in a total of **39** schools, making us one of the largest Follow Through models. We would work with African-Americans in: Providence, RI; NYC; D.C.;

Williamsburg County, SC; Tupelo, MS; Dayton, OH; Flint and Grand Rapids, MI; Racine, WI; and E. St. Louis, IL. Our non-English sites were Uvalde and Dimmit, TX and East Las Vegas, NM. Our schools that served Whites were in: Chicago; Smithville, TN; West Iron County, MI; and Flippin, AK. Our Native American sites were Mission and Rosebud, SD and Cherokee, NC.

If all the schools we were to work with were assembled in one place, they would be able to serve a community of more than 200,000. It seems ironic that our approach could be so distasteful to educators and so attractive to parents. The administrations in nearly all our sites were opposed to the model, and most tried to dissuade their PACs from selecting Direct Instruction. The districts' apparent reason for participating in Follow Through was the money it would bring to the district. Over the next 15 years, we would have many painful reminders of the gulf between the goals of parents and those of the participating districts.

Our immediate concern was to be ready to work in the schools by the fall of 1968. The pattern for the implementation of Follow Through in schools was based on cohorts. For schools that had a K, the first cohort was to begin in kindergarten in 1968. During this year, kindergarten and grade 1 would be implemented. The next year, a new cohort would begin in K. After three years, all grades, K–3, would be implemented.

This format was thoughtful. Most models had not worked in grades 2 and 3. In 1968, we were able to accommodate children in grades K through 2 because we had two levels of reading, language, and math in final form. Most of the programs would go out in mimeographed form; however, the first level of reading would be published during the '68-69 school year.

A year earlier, Jean, Cookie, Doug Carnine, and I had negotiated publishing agreements for the beginning levels of the language, reading, and math programs. As early as 1966, we had tried to find a publisher. The only one that showed any interest was Follett, but that venture did not materialize. It resulted in two language books that were printed but never published.

Ironically, the organization that ultimately published our programs came to us. John O'Keefe, a vice president of SRA (Science Research Associates), visited our preschool and later proposed a kind of back-door publishing arrangement. It was back-door because the programs were not to be published through SRA's educational publishing division, but through the Test and Guidance division. The reasons were that O'Keefe had control over the Test and Guidance division, and that the mainline educational publishing division found our approach unpalatable and refused to publish the material.

During the first year of Follow Through, the only option we had for providing our sites with math, language, and the second level of the reading program was to send out pre-publication mimeographed material, which meant that we would have to mimeograph a staggering amount of paper over the next couple of years—around a million single-sided sheets per month (10 pages per daily lesson for the teacher script and about 3 for the student material, for 3 programs of 180 lessons each).

To reproduce and ship this material, we rented an old house close to campus. A couple of our graduate students worked part time as supervisors, and we hired some neighborhood high school students as "collators." Each page was mimeographed and stacked in vertical compartments that were a few inches apart. Collators would take one page from each compartment in sequence. Some of them became amazingly fast. The second fastest was one of the supervisors, Carol Hunter, a graduate student (who would later be our on-site manager in Cherokee, NC). She was tall and had long fingers, so she could pick up pages from four compartments with one motion, which she did very fast. One of our high school students could beat her, however, using a different technique—taking one sheet at a time, but at an unbeliev- able rate. The shop had a nice atmosphere because everybody treated the work as fun and, lo, it became fun.

We also had to put in a lot of hours writing the new material that we would need, and we could not do this work during the time we were supposed to be working for the University or for Follow Through. If we did, the programs would fall into the public domain. So my routine when I was in town meant that I had to work after dinner until 10 PM every weeknight and from 8 AM to noon on weekend days. This bothered me, not so much because of the work, but because I felt I was shorting my kids. They were at the age when a good dad makes a big difference. I was prob- ably more of a stranger than a good dad. Our family would have dinners together, and we did a fair amount of joking around, but at 7 PM I went to the study and did something that I thought at the time was more impor- tant than being a good dad. The prospect of being able to help thousands of children was exciting, particularly because I had absolutely no doubts that we would win this horse race.

TRAINING AND ORGANIZATION

Although we had the instructional programs, we needed to have an organization and procedures for training and monitoring the performance of our teachers. The standard format for staffing grades K and 1 was modeled after the preschool. Children would be grouped by skill level, into three groups—high, middle, and low. We would have three teachers in the classroom, one for teaching reading, a second for language, and a third for math. Two of these teachers would be instructional aides. That decision created some good news and some bad news. The bad news was that this format would not be popular in some districts (but theoretically, we were to have waivers from standard district requirements). The good news was that this staffing format made it easier for us to train all the teachers because we wouldn't have to teach one teacher how to present material from three programs, just one.

The initial organization was a prototype of the one we still use. It is based on a model of nested responsibilities, which both simplifies the organizational problem and has clear delineations of responsibility. The teachers and aides were responsible for the performance of the children and for meeting projected performance standards. For instance, a top homogeneous group in a classroom would be expected to complete more than one level of the program during the school year; a middle group would be expected to complete a level, and a low group less than a level. Teachers were not to skim through the program but teach to mastery.

A project manager would be in charge of each site (the schools in a district). The project manager would be responsible for training the teachers, monitoring daily and weekly performance, solving whatever routine problems occurred, and making sure that students were meeting projections.

In terms of nested responsibilities, the teachers and aides were responsible for solving the various problems of weak-performing children; the project manager was responsible for assuring that teachers performed adequately (which means that a project manager was responsible for both the performance of the children and the performance of the teachers).

If a project manager could not solve a problem in a timely way, she referred the problem to Wes or me. Wes would tackle the administrative problems; I would address instructional problems. With respect to instruction, I would be responsible for the performance of the project managers and the various consultants they used to train and manage each site.

This nested responsibility is far different from the organizational patterns that districts use. In a typical district, the principal is supposed to serve as a conduit for what goes on in the school. However, there are multiple inputs from various departments and functions of the central office—input from Title I, from the superintendent in charge of elementary education, from those in charge of subject areas (reading, language arts, math, science, social studies), from possible area superintendents, from bi-lingual and special ed directors, and from other consulting agencies or special "projects." These inputs are often in conflict with each other, and there is no scheme for addressing these conflicts or for assessing the progress the school is making and the problems the faculty and staff are experiencing. Principals may know that they need to achieve some globally described harmony, but they have no assistance or guidance in the nuts-and-bolts details of how to do it or even how to find time to do it.

I have read some principal manuals, such as the one issued by Chicago Public Schools. It is more like a list of possible things that an omniscient person might do. As a Chicago principal put it, "If this manual describes a competent principal, I'm not sure Jesus Christ could make it in Chicago." Typically, the principal is expected to do everything from organize family support assistance to accelerate math performance. There are no regularly scheduled observations of each teacher and aide, or of each principal. About the only provision for identifying problems is through self-reports. (The exception is the classroom that is totally out of control because this problem is obvious to anybody who enters the school.) But self-reports have to be viewed skeptically because a teacher's reporting is going to be limited by what she knows. If she lacks knowledge of how to teach effectively, her self-report will provide a distorted view of the problems.

This traditional organization is an example of the districts' lack of respect for data. If data on performance of principals, supervisors, or teachers is not compared with the ambitious expectations of the system, there is no reality check. Our system of problem-identification and solutions had lots of reality checks. Unfortunately, it was as foreign to the districts we worked with as our data-driven approach to teaching.

STAFFING

By the end of the 1968 summer vacation, we had to be prepared to work with 20 districts (the 19 that selected us and Houston, which was a parent model that voted to work with us). We had to engage in an entirely new level of instruction—designing training procedures for teachers and school administrators. We estimated the number of "on- site" days trainers would have to spend at each site, and we worked on designs for packaging the training.

The most serious problem we had was our lack of personnel. Our most seasoned instructional people were Jean, Valerie, Cookie, and me. If we did nothing but train at the sites (which would not be possible) we would be able to provide only a small fraction of practice the teachers needed. To properly implement a school required a trainer to be on site at least 30 days during the first year. Most of the on-site time would involve working with teachers in the classroom, particularly those having serious problems. Also, we would need some provisions for obtaining information about teacher performance for times that trainers were not on site.

Over 20 University students we had taught expressed interest in working in the field, but only four of them had ever taught in a school, and none had trained others to teach. So the staffing problem we faced was that we would send inexperienced kids into the field, to train and monitor the performance of teachers in tough schools with hard-to-teach children. Obviously, the plan wouldn't work unless we somehow were able to inject credibility into the formula. We figured that the most solid basis of credibility was in the arena of working with children. All the people we considered using as project managers or trainers could teach and manage at least pretty well. Most were a lot stronger in presenting effectively than managing out-of-control children, but we would have people available to work on problems of behavior management.

One of the first things we did was to petition districts to see if any would hire one of our trainees as an on-site supervisor. We thought that if we had one of our people on site, we would be able to communicate with the district more effectively. We succeeded with three sites. Carolyn Jarvis would go to PS 137 in NYC, Gail Jackson to Dayton, and Mike Frontier to Racine, Wisconsin.

To arrange marriages of trainers and the other sites, we ranked the sites on how difficult we thought each would be to implement and ranked the students on how capable we thought they were. We then tried to wed the more talented people with the sites that we figured would be most difficult. Although we spent a fair amount of time teasing and cerebrating over this ranking, we would have done as well if we had assigned trainers randomly. The person we judged to be the lowest, because she seemed nervous and uncertain, proved to be at least as good as any other trainer we placed. Several of the trainers we judged to be strong proved to be relatively weak at making decisions and following up. Some compromised on details that could not be compromised. We apparently lacked important information about the work ethic that our trainers had. The best ones worked very hard.

Most of the people we identified as trainers would live in Champaign and fly out to their assigned sites. They would generally work at the site more than one week a month, at least during the first few months of the school year. At the time, it was pretty easy to get to most of the sites, particularly those in the east. Ozark Airlines had a nonstop flight to DC, with a flying time of 1 hour and 5 minutes. A nonstop Ozark flight went to NYC in 1 hour and 15 minutes. There were quite a few flights to Chicago, which took less than an hour. Wes and I had to go to a lot of meetings in DC, so we really appreciated Ozark's service.

PREPARING THE SITES

As soon as we knew which sites we would be serving, we set up meetings with the various sites. We wanted to see the schools, the teachers, meet the administrators, and try to set up a working relationship between our project manager, the director of the local site, and other administrators who would be involved in the project.

Serious political machinations were going on in some sites. Among the more serious were the Indian schools in South Dakota. The funding of this site was complicated because there were actually two different "districts." One was Todd County, which had five participating schools. The other was Rosebud CAP (Community Action Program), which had another five schools, four of which were in Mellette County, north of Todd County. Most of the communities served were tiny. The children in some were very low performers.

In late March of 1968, Susie Stearns, Charlotte Govanetti, and I chartered a University of Illinois plane—a small one—to Valentine, Nebraska, the closest airport to Mission, South Dakota, which was our first stop. The director of the project met us in Valentine and drove us the 30 miles to Mission. My first impression was, "What a cruel country." It was below freezing, snowing, and the wind was gusting more than forty miles per hour. We drove through treeless ranges and saw a lot of newborn calves either dying or lying dead in the fields.

We met with the administration of the two districts and listened to their problems. The Bureau of Indian Affairs (BIA) was openly badmouthing the program and vigorously promoting limp early childhood programs. The Rosebud CAP had a meeting set up in St. Francis that evening and wanted me to speak to the parents. After visiting a couple of schools that day, we drove to St. Francis. The priest at the Mission in St. Francis told us about all the tension between the Sioux Tribal Council, which supported the program, and the BIA. Even the facilitator appointed by Follow Through was openly opposed to our program and was trying to talk the Council out of using Direct Instruction.

I told the priest that I wanted to demonstrate to the audience with a group of kindergarten children. He said, "Oh, don't do it. That would be a terrible mistake." I asked why and he explained that they would not respond in public. I told him that if we had five or six of them, I could get them to respond. He was adamant in his prediction that they would not respond. He said, "Please don't do it. You'll be humiliated."

I told him I thought I should do it so the parents get an idea of what the instruction looked like, and they could judge whether it would hurt the children. Moments later, the local director repeated the same prediction about how the demonstration would go. "Don't do it. They will not respond."

The meeting was scheduled for 7 p.m. The hall was packed. Many of the men wore farmer apparel. I gave a brief introduction and then worked with six children who had been seated in a semicircle with their backs to the audience (their idea, not mine). I sat down in front of a small chalkboard and drew a rectangle with the letters N, S, E, W on the different sides. I told the children, "This is a map, and I'm going to try to teach you how to read a map. It's really, really hard. It may be too hard for you, but let's try."

I then pointed to the appropriate letters as I said in a rhythm, "North is on the top; South is on the bottom; East on this side; West on this side. That's hard to say. Listen to the first part: North is on the top; South is on the bottom. I'm good at saying that. Once more. North is on the top; South is on the bottom. Who can say that part with me? North is on the top. South is on the bottom." Nobody responded.

"I knew it was too tough for you. Once more, North is on the top; South is on the bottom." One little girl responded with me. I said, "Wow, she and I can do it. Listen to this." Together we did it two times. Then one of the little boys joined in. Within a couple of more trials, they all were responding. I acted totally amazed. And after a few more trials, all were saying the whole thing, with four directions, and it sounded good, almost like rap—North is on the top. South is on the bottom. East on this side. West on this side.

I told the children to turn around and look at all the people in the audience. "I don't think they can hear you. Let's see if you can do it all by yourself, good and loud, so everybody knows how smart you are."

I did the pointing. They did the talking. Most of the people in the audience were clapping in time with the pointing, and a lot of them were reciting along with the kids. It was great.

Next, I taught the children how to identify how something moves on the map. I said, "When something moves on the map, you look at the side it is going to. Watch." I started a line in the middle and moved north. "What side am I going to? ... Yes, north. So what direction am I going?" In a few minutes, the children were performing perfectly with examples of the chalk moving, and changing direction. They were shouting out the answers. "Going north ... Going east." When it was over, the audience clapped, including the priest and the director. I shook hands with the children and congratulated them.

After the children left, I explained the program to the audience. I expressed our dedication to teach all the kids the skills they needed. Following my comments, the Follow Through facilitator stood up and pointed out that sociolinguists and early childhood experts were opposed to our program because it was counter to how children naturally develop and learn. She went on for some time. The people in the audience were polite, but obviously disturbed.

When she had completed her message, a middle-aged burly Indian in overalls stood up and said something in Lakota. There was some discussion in Lakota with others. Then he walked up to the front of the hall and gave a talk in Lakota that lasted possibly three minutes. When he finished, he said, in perfect English, "I asked if anybody would translate for me as I talked. Nobody volunteered, so I'll translate. I said that we have seen two extremes here." He pointed to the facilitator and said, "Long Tongue uses many words and expresses great concern, but Mr. Engelmann shows us something with our children that we can see and believe." He went on to describe what the children needed from school, that Long Tongue was not very helpful in addressing these issues, and that the Tribal Council would support the DI model. The parents nodded in smiling agreement. I learned later that the man who delivered this proclamation was head of the Tribal Council.

As we drove back to Valentine that night, we mused over the fact that none of our consultants were very interested in going to South Dakota. Susie observed that if they had been at the meeting, they would be fighting over who could work there. Hell, I wanted to work there.

The moment was great, but the battles with the district, the BIA, and the state were not over. In the end we would have to work with school administrators, a group that did not share the Tribal Council's priorities or the commitment to make the changes that our model demanded.

CLOSE ENCOUNTER WITH HOUSTON

Bob Egbert contacted us about a month after I returned from South Dakota. He complicated our plans by telling us that the director of Title I programs in Texas was interested in installing behaviorally based and Direct Instruction intervention programs. Bob wanted to set up a meeting in Houston with Don Bushell, Wes, and me. The date we settled on was May 3, which turned out to be almost exactly one month after the assassination of Martin Luther King, and one month before the assassination of Robert Kennedy.

The meeting took place in Houston. It was productive and positive, largely because the Title I director was not a typical bureaucrat; he wanted to install programs to make a difference. I was impressed by how knowledgeable he was about what works. He was aware of the resistance the program would face but indicated that he was prepared to meet the resistance. We discussed the kind of training and supervision that would be needed. The plan involved starting in a couple of sites in Houston, implementing the program well and using these sites as training centers for directors and teachers from other sites.

Everybody at the meeting had flights that were leaving around 4 o'clock. So after the meeting the Title I director, Bob, Don Bushell, Wes, and I went to the Houston airport, chatted a while, and went to our respective gates. All of us were on Braniff flights. The Title I director and I were on the flight from Houston to Dallas, where I would get a connecting flight to Chicago. Wes was on his way to St. Louis. Don was heading back to Kansas.

The Title I director and I had seat assignments next to each other in the second row. We boarded. As we waited for the flight to get underway, I told the director how refreshing the meeting had been, and how much I appreciated his position.

The cabin door closed, then re-opened and Bob Egbert walked in. He said, "Ziggy, I have to talk to you about some other business."

"C'mon, Bob. I'm on the plane. I have a connection in Dallas."

He said that he had taken care of that, booking me on a Braniff flight that left 45 minutes later. He said, "You won't miss your connection. So let's go. I have to talk to you about something."

I could tell by his tone that there was no point in arguing. I shrugged, stood up, said goodbye to the Title I director, and followed Bob off the plane.

We talked in the gate area for about 20 minutes. Then I overheard somebody near us say something about a Braniff flight that left Houston and crashed. I got a sudden chill. We knew a person on every Braniff flight that had left within the last hour—Wes, Don Bushell, and the Title I director. We asked the gate agent if there had been a crash. He confirmed that a Braniff plane had crashed, but he didn't know which one.

My flight left on time, but was late getting into Dallas. The reason was that it had to circle 40 miles to the west to go around probably the most impressive cloud formation I have ever seen. I wished I had a camera with me. A cumulonimbus structure rose to about seven miles. It had knots of tight billows linked to swooping wings and swirls of silver. With the western sun on it, the clouds produced shadows of orange, blue, purple and dark gray, which contrasted with dazzling white as the billows churned in slow motion.

In Dallas, I found out that the awesome cloud formation had killed all the passengers on the earlier Braniff flight from Houston to Dallas. The plane had attempted to go through the formation, but never made it. The summary of the National Transportation Safety Board indicated that "Flight 352 between Houston and Dallas, Texas crashed approximately one mile east of Dawson, Texas about 4:48 C.D.T. May 3, 1968. The 80 passengers and 5 crew members aboard the aircraft died in the accident, and the aircraft was destroyed." In the last communications between the plane and air-traffic control, the crew asked permission to drop to 5000 feet, asked if there were reports of serious hail in the area, and asked permission to make a 180-degree turn.

I felt sick about the state Title I director, and I didn't know what to do about it. It seemed that we should try to carry out the plans that we had discussed in the meeting. I had a very strong suspicion that it wouldn't happen because it would be unlikely that the director's successor would share his zeal and willingness to engage in some serious battles.

The incident was confusing because I didn't have time to think much about it. We were so overwhelmed with trying to get programs, people, and plans in place for the Follow Through debut that we didn't have time to follow up the way we would have liked.

Even though I am not a theist and I don't consider myself superstitious or mystical, I puzzled over the great improbability of my experiences with planes that crashed. A rough estimation of the odds (one in many trillion) made me at least consider the possibility that I was here for some reason. Rationally, I reject this conclusion. Secretly, however, I wished I had stayed on that plane because I believed that if I had, it would not have crashed.

TRAINING

We approached the training of teachers with the same philosophy that we applied to teaching children. We had to change teachers' behaviors so they taught well, and we had to work efficiently. Although we had some experience in training, this new challenge was different because we would be training large numbers of people. In some of the sites we would be training over 200 people at the same time.

The plan was to schedule weeklong summer training sessions at each site. Their purpose was to provide teachers and aides with enough information and skill for them to work successfully on the first day of school. They needed to know about DI and understand why it had been designed the way it was. Also, they had to have skill in the various techniques and procedures involved in teaching efficiently. We felt it was important for them to see somebody teach parts of the program to children from their site, and to do at least some practice with children, so we arranged for children to be available during the summer training.

Teachers needed a lot more practice in presenting exercises from the program than we could schedule with children. So we needed effective practices for "mock teaching," in which teachers would practice in small groups, with one teacher presenting and the others playing the role of children.

Most traditional schools do not actually begin on the first day. The reason is that they have faulty understanding of how children respond. They believe that children need a gradual transition from vacation or home life to school. This slow introduction, which may take a week or more in some schools, is ineffective because school is first social, fun, and easy. Then it becomes structured, serious, and harder. Students are far more likely to act up if they go through this transition, but traditionalists use the fact that students have difficulty adjusting after a weeklong transition to conclude, "Imagine how they would have acted up if we had tried to force instruction on day one." In fact, the transition is easier if children understand from the first day what they are expected to do. They won't have to learn that school supports rowdy and social activities and then learn rules for the later "no fun" program. If instruction is well designed, they see that they are reinforced for meeting the teacher's expectations.

Starting on day one was important for us because our commitment was to accelerate children's performance. If we taught on ten more days than schools traditionally teach, we would achieve a small gain. We needed to realize as many small gains as we could.

Our plan was to train all teachers to become expert teachers. It's difficult for somebody to look at an expert teacher teaching a Direct Instruction lesson and appreciate the details she is controlling. The reason is that things look easy and natural. The children are attentive. They follow the teacher's directions and respond together with the same rate of verbalization—starting together and finishing together without droning or saying words in an artificial way. If the teacher directs them to sound out a word in the presentation book she displays, she says, "Get ready to say the sounds in this word." She points under the first letter and children say the sound for that letter. She points to the rest of the letters and the children say the sounds. The teacher says, "Say it fast," and the children say the word.

"Good reading," the teacher says and presents the next word on the presentation page.

When you watch this teacher, you'll probably recognize the timing. If you had a metronome, you'd see that the cadence of her talking, pointing, touching, and the cadence of the children's responses are all coordinated. That's the product of training. Nothing she does was any more natural than it was for Valerie when she began teaching. Certainly, two expert teachers are no more the same than two cherry pies baked by people who followed the same recipe. But in important, functional ways, they are exactly the same.

Each detail of the expert teacher's behavior can be demonstrated to make a difference in how the children perform. If the teacher speeds up the rate at which she touches under each letter, for instance, some of the children won't respond because they don't have enough time to look at the next letter and figure out what it is.

Good training has to address each detail of seemingly simple behaviors, like pointing and touching. Teachers point and touch when showing something on the board and when they direct children to read material displayed in the teacher's presentation book. Teachers have to point so that all children are able to see what they're pointing to. They have to observe the children to make sure they are looking at the word to be read. And they have to apply the basic rule, "Point first, then talk. Don't point and talk at the same time." Seems simple, but it is very hard for some teachers. It's important, however. If the teacher says, "What sound?" as she is in the process of pointing to one of three letters, some children won't respond because they don't have adequate time to figure out which letter the teacher will touch. If the teacher first clearly points to the letter, then says, "What sound?" the probability of children responding correctly is increased.

Another thing teachers have to learn is to have uniform timing. Teachers who haven't learned this rule speak at one rate but expect children to respond at another rate. For instance, the teacher says, "Listen: the ball is on the table. Say the statement. Get ready." The teacher then permits the children to produce a slow droning response: "thuuuuu ballll iizzz onnnn thuuuuu taybllll." Some children in the group are not initiating the response, but simply copying the verbalization of others. If the teacher requires children to respond with the same cadence that the teacher uses, there is far less likelihood that some of the children are simply copying responses of the "leaders" in the group and therefore are not benefiting much from the work.

Because very little of what teachers are to learn is intuitively obvious, they need more than practice. They need to understand why we require them to do things a particular way. One of the early problems we faced was trying to configure training so that it provided enough practice for teachers to learn critical presentation behaviors and also incorporated sufficient rationale on the various techniques.

We had to make a lot of guesses at first because we lacked data on basic presentation issues. For instance, is the most efficient way to go through the scope and objectives of the program, then explain what the teachers will do, then present task practice? Or is it more productive to first direct teachers to practice a task and then explain the rationale for the task? Or is it more efficient to present the rationale in snippets that occur between small block tasks that they practice? Over the following years, we learned answers to these questions.

In the summer of 1968, we staged two kinds of workshops—one on reinforcement and managing behavior, the other on program-specific training.

We held the behavior management workshop at the University of Kansas. The campus was far different from that of the University of Illinois. Entering the campus was something like crossing the border, where security guards screen vehicles and check passes. At the University of Illinois, there are no entrances, exits, or guards—just buildings and walkways.

We worked for two days with supervisors and directors of our participating sites and with people from some of Don Bushell's (Behavioral Analysis) sites. Bob Egbert and quite a few people from the National Follow Through office also attended. Wes and Don provided information about the behaviorist's orientation. Ironically, the format for the behavioral segment was more informational than 'behavioral.' There were lectures, but very little practice.

I demonstrated with some kindergarten children and explained the programs, but the presentation was informational and lacked a serious training function, although it may have had some educational value for administrators.

Here's part of what Bob Egbert later wrote about the workshop:

> Don Bushell had invited Ziggy to do a demonstration lesson. My image of that occasion is still crystal clear. Ziggy was at the front of the large classroom when a half dozen five-year-old children were brought in. They were shy in front of the large audience and had to be encouraged to sit in the semi-circle in front of Ziggy. "How in the world," I thought, "will this large, imposing man who has not been educated as a teacher cope with this impossible situation?" I need not have been concerned. Within three minutes the excited youngsters, now on the edge of their chairs, were calling out answers individually or in unison, as requested, to the most "difficult" of Ziggy's challenges and questions. By the end of the demonstration lesson, the children had learned the material that Ziggy taught; they also had learned that they were very smart. They knew this because they could answer all of the questions that Ziggy had assured them were too hard for them!

We had a memorable beer party one evening, and I think everybody enjoyed the proceedings *a lot*. If we evaluated the workshop on how much fun it was, we would have scheduled one every year. We never did another one like it, however, because it didn't seem to be productive in changing teaching behavior. The teacher doesn't parcel tasks so that some involve "teaching" and some involve "reinforcement." The components are part of the same routine. The teacher presents tasks to the children and responds to their responses. The teacher's response conveys both information and affect. If the teacher is pleased, the children's effort is rewarded. If the teacher is displeased, the children's effort is punished.

Workshops that provide general information are not very useful if the goal is for the participants to apply principles to specific concrete examples. Granted, making the perceptions of the behaviorist's position more favorable is important, but we had more than enough to do just trying to implement on the level of nuts and bolts.

In addition to the behavioral workshop, we tried to arrange a one-week training session for all teachers and related staff in each site. These workshops provided the best training opportunity we would have during the year. During the school year, we would schedule ongoing inservice sessions that focused specifically on problems teachers were experiencing, but the week-long summer workshop would have to build a strong foundation.

Each workshop focused on five areas:

1. Information about grouping children homogeneously, placing them appropriately in the instructional programs, and scheduling periods for teaching them.

2. Practice on component teaching behaviors—particularly pointing, touching, signaling, and confirming correct responses.

3. Practice on presenting "critical exercises" from different parts of the program.

4. Practice on corrections for basic skills and on corrections for related skills.

5. Overview and rationale about the sequence of skills presented in the program.

Although all components are reasonable, the way we initially configured them was not strong. The exercises we had selected for practice came from the beginning, middle, and end of each instructional program. The sequence showed the increasing complexity of the material later in the program and how the later exercises incorporate skill components that are taught in the earlier exercises. The sequence also showed the instructional-design principle that everything the children would need for later tasks is taught earlier, and nothing that is not needed is included in the program.

We treated the rationale as a priority, believing that teachers armed with knowledge of why the program was designed as it was would have a more positive orientation toward practicing how to present tasks from the program.

The session that taught reading started out with about one and a half hours on rationale, describing the scope and sequence and presenting illustrations. After the morning break, teachers would work on presenting exercises. For this practice, they would be working in groups of three or four teachers.

For each task that was practiced, the trainer would use a format similar to the one teachers would later use with children—model, lead, and test. The trainer first modeled how to present a particular task. For one of the early reading tasks, the trainer printed the letter *m* on the board and showed participants the procedure for pointing to the letter (with their finger below the letter and not obscuring the children's view of the letter). The trainer next said, "Get ready," paused about one second and touched just below the bottom of the letter, as the participants responded by saying the letter sound, "*Mmmm.*"

Next, the trainer led the participants by responding with them. All wrote an *m* on a sheet of paper and held it up so the trainer could see it. The trainer then signaled them to point and say, "Get ready," and touch under the letter. The trainer would first provide the cadence and lead them with proper wording, "Point, one, two, get ready, one, two, touch ... again from the beginning, point, one, two ..."

After participants seemed firm on this "lead step," the trainer presented the test step, directing teachers to work in groups of three or four, with teachers taking turns at presenting as other members of the group responded as children who made no mistakes and tried to follow the teacher's timing as closely as possible.

Most of the remaining time would be spent on task practice, including procedures for correcting mistakes the children made (from producing no response to responding late, early, or producing the wrong response.) The session also addressed recording data on the performance of every student.

A shipment that never reached one of the sites provided data on the major weakness of our first-year workshops. The material for reading that was sent to Tupelo, Mississippi didn't arrive in time for the workshop. Through recurring foul-ups, Tupelo did not receive these lessons during the entire week. All the trainers had were the first five lessons of the program. So the trainers provided some description of the later parts of the program, but the only exercises they could use for practice were from lessons 1 to 5. So teachers worked on presenting all parts of these lessons. Every teacher taught the entire sequence of lessons several times during the week.

When we observed the performance of teachers during the first few weeks of school, we discovered that those in Tupelo performed better than those in other sites. The reason had to be that teachers in the other sites weren't trained as well. They had spent too much time working on tasks that they would not teach to children for months. In contrast, the Tupelo teachers became quite familiar with everything they would present during the first week of school.

The project manager had to provide additional training during the first week so that teachers would be ready for the second week, but this training was not difficult because most of the exercises presented during the next five lessons were simple extensions of ones the teachers had already mastered.

We modified our original procedures, not so radically that teachers worked only on the first five lessons, but almost exclusively on the first 25 lessons. Also, we checked out teachers individually on presenting lesson 1 before they worked with children.

Over the years other details of the training changed as we discovered other problems with our procedures and tried to create practices that solved or avoided the problems. One important change had to do with presenting rationale. The rationale becomes a lot more meaningful if teachers first have a good understanding of what they will be doing. So the general format for later workshops put rationale in the cracks and seams between task-practice. The trainer opened with a bare-bones orientation and then launched into task practice. After working for about twenty minutes on presenting early tasks, the trainer took "time out" and presented a segment of rationale that related to what the teachers were doing. "You're probably wondering why we present these tasks and how they fit into what the children will be doing later in the program ..." For example, after working on sounds for the letters that are presented early in the program, the trainer pointed out that when children learn sounds for only seven letters, they start to read words composed entirely of these letters. Reading starts long before they have learned any letter names or all the letters' sounds. Yet, when reading is introduced, children have the tools needed to decode the words the program presents. Children say the sounds they have learned for the letters in the word and then identify the word.

This format positions rationale as a reinforcer, a payoff. Not only is it related to what the teachers know; they feel more comfortable listening to rationale than they do practicing task presentation. So the attention to rationale increases; the rationale provides a break from task practice; and teachers have a reference point for understanding how the rationale translates into concrete examples.

Over the years, trainers adapted the basic training template. Some first described a typical problem that lower performing children have in learning to read, then quickly sketched the solution and presented task practice on an exercise that addressed that problem.

NEW FUNCTIONS

The major problem we had in working with the sites was that we could not make observations of what occurred in every classroom every day; yet, we needed to receive ongoing, accurate information about every instructional group if we were to solve teaching problems. Our compulsion to obtain current data on the performance of every student stemmed from some facts about learning and relearning. The relationship is simple: The longer a student has misunderstood something, the longer it takes to teach the content correctly. If the teacher uses a good reading program, at-risk beginning readers will learn to discriminate the words *a* and *the* with perfect accuracy after about 40 trials. If the teacher uses a poor program and children confuse *a* and *the*, their confusion becomes solidly ingrained. When they are fourth graders, it takes about 400 trials to re-teach them so they are perfectly accurate at reading these words. If the remedy is delayed until the students are in high school, it will probably take more than 1,000 trials to induce the correct behavior.

Our initial plans for securing data involved both record keeping and frequent observations of teachers. We first set minimum expectations for every instructional group. The highest groups were expected to progress fastest through the program—about 1 and a half lessons per school day. The expectation for average groups was about 1 lesson per day, for low groups about 3/4-lesson per day. These projections were to be modified as we discovered more about the performance level of each child. Note that the projections were based on performance of the children, not the teacher. We used projections as a baseline for identifying teaching problems. If the projection for a group was achievable and the rate at which the teacher was going through the program was slower than the projected rate, there was probably a teaching problem. Information about the rate didn't tell us precisely what the problem was, just that something was out of place. So the next step was to observe the teacher and try to identify the reasons for the slower rate. (It was almost always *reasons*, not merely one reason.)

Each classroom would post lesson data every day for every group in reading, math, and language. Within less than a minute a trainer or supervisor could go into the classroom, look at the posted data and determine if there were serious problems. For example, a coordinator makes an observation in a classroom on the 60th school day. If one of the groups was supposed to be progressing at the rate of one lesson a day, it should be close to lesson 60. If the group is closer to 40, there's a problem. The teacher is taking far too much time to present each lesson.

Some problems don't have to do with how much material the teacher has covered but whether the children are taught to mastery. To provide information about mastery, we required teachers to test children every tenth lesson on what they had learned during those last ten lessons. Teachers would then post the pass-fail performance of all children on every program.

The interpretation of mastery test data is straightforward: If virtually all the children in a group fail the test, the teacher is not teaching to mastery. If most of the children pass the 10-lesson tests, but the same one or two children in the group consistently fail, those children don't belong in the group. They should be in a group that is proceeding more slowly through the program.

Even with posted information on lesson progress and 10-lesson test performance, the trainer would not be able to identify all possible causes of failure. Often the data serves only as a prompt for further investigation, which may lead to a wild variety of possible causes. Training teachers to be highly efficient would be easy if there were only one or two elixirs that could make failed classrooms successful. Unfortunately, teaching effectively is a technical enterprise. There are two broad classes of problems, those that involve the structural details of the classroom and those that relate to teaching behavior. For the classroom to be highly efficient, both the structural and the teaching details must be in place.

Here are the five most important **structural details.**

1. *The instructional sequence must be well designed.*

If the instructional sequence is poor, the only way the teacher will be successful is to ignore parts or all of the program. The problem is that the teacher may have no foreknowledge of which parts are poor. If the teacher follows the program, the children may not benefit greatly even if they achieve mastery. For example, if the sequence initially presents only three-sound words (such as *man, fit, bug*) day after day, some children will have serious problems when two-sound or four-sound words are introduced (*in, bent*). Many children will try to transform them into three-sound words, because from the information they have received, all words that are read are three-sound words.

The more compulsive the teacher is in bringing children to mastery, the harder it will be to later teach two-sound and four-sound words. So teaching to mastery makes sense only if the program anticipates and avoids possible mis-teaching.

2. *The physical setting must be appropriate.*

The setting affects both what children learn and the rate they learn it. If there are many distractions, the teacher must work harder and spend more time on maintaining the children's attention. The ideal location for a small group is in a quiet corner of the classroom, with the teacher sitting in the corner (facing the open classroom) and the children facing her, not facing the part of the classroom that has distractions. Many other details of physical setting are important. For instance, during small-group teaching with beginning children in K and 1, children should be within touching distance of the teacher. This provision assures that the teacher will be able to give them physical prompts when they have trouble touching symbols the teacher names or drawing lines to match objects.

The lowest performers in the group should be directly in front of her; the higher performers should be on the ends of the group, farthest from the teacher. If children are seated in chairs (not desks), there has to be a provision for children to write words or problems during the lesson. (The simplest solution is for the children to kneel on the floor and use the seat of their chair as a "desk.")

3. *Instructional groups must be homogeneous in performance.*

Given that children learn at different rates, children will benefit most if they are in groups composed of children who learn the material at about the same rate. If the teacher presents enough repetition of a task to bring one child to mastery, the chances are good that the same amount of practice brought the other children in the group to mastery. In other words, the teacher is capable of gearing the instruction to the needs of all children in the group if they are homogeneous in skill level. If the group is heterogeneous in skill level, it is impossible for the teacher to present practice that is appropriate for all children in the group. The lower performers will require three times the practice of the higher performers.

4. *All groups must be placed appropriately in the instructional sequences.*

Homogeneous grouping makes sense only if the children are properly placed in the instructional sequence. If they are in a well-designed program and are placed beyond their skill level, they can't learn nearly as fast as they can if they are placed in the proper lesson range. The reason is simply that they would have to learn much more to achieve mastery on everything in a lesson beyond their skill level. Placing children appropriately is difficult for most teachers because their idea of how to accelerate performance is to place children where the work is "challenging," which means it is difficult for children, and thus they make frequent mistakes. Teachers of low performers almost uniformly assume that if the children have an easy time learning the material, they are misplaced. Appropriate placement in a well-designed sequence means the opposite—that the children are able to achieve mastery on the current lesson by learning a relatively small amount of new material.

5. *Daily schedules must be coordinated and designed so they provide sufficient practice.*

The scheduling is complicated in K and 1 by the fact that there are three small instructional groups, which means that 1 and a half hours must be scheduled for each subject if each group is to have 30 minutes of reading instruction. Ideally three groups are being taught at the same time during this hour and a half, one in reading, one in math, and one in language. Every 30 minutes the children move from one subject to the next. In addition to being adequate, schedules must be coordinated across classrooms on the same grade level (so that some cross-class grouping is possible for children who don't fit into any group in their classroom). If schedules are coordinated, these children can go to a different classroom where there is a group more appropriate for them.

Adequate learning is not *guaranteed* if all the structural details are in place, but poorer performance is guaranteed if any are *not* in place. The structural details simply set the stage for effective teaching.

Here's a quick summary of the six primary **teaching variables** that make a difference in how well children learn.

1. *The teacher must follow the wording provided by the script for each lesson.*

2. *The teacher must pace the presentation appropriately,* going as fast as practical but providing "think time" before signaling a response that requires several mental steps. "Listen: 3+1. Tell me the answer."(Pause.) "Get ready." (Signal.)

3. *The teacher's signals for the children to respond as a group must be perfectly clear and consistent.*

4. *The teacher must be efficient in presenting tasks* to both the group and to individual children. (The teacher does not present tasks to individuals until the group produces solid responses.)

5. *The teacher must use effective procedures for reinforcing children* and

showing them through responses to their performance that she is impressed when they perform well.

6. *The teacher must use effective correction procedures.*

Learning corrections is more difficult for teachers to master than presenting the script. The reason is that when the teacher presents the script, the sequence of events is fixed and predictable. The teacher knows exactly what she'll say next. Following the script is something of a solo, rote performance. When children make mistakes, the events are not predictable because the teacher doesn't know which children will make the mistake or what kind of mistake they may make. So now the rules for a solo recitation don't work. The teacher must now play an interactive game with the children. Through this game the teacher gives children both the specific information and the amount of practice they need to achieve mastery. This game must be played immediately.

The only evidence that the correction worked is that if you presented the same task later, the children would respond correctly. The teacher must therefore present delayed tests of tasks that are corrected earlier. For instance, the children are lined up to leave the classroom. The teacher says, "Let's see who remembers those opposites we worked on today. Everybody, tell me the opposite of *open*. Get ready ... Tell me the opposite of *fast*. Get ready ... Good remembering."

Learning effective reinforcement procedures is difficult for teachers for the same reason that correcting is. Exactly what you will do is not scripted. It depends on what the children do. If they do something well, the teacher tells them specifically what they did that was good. Teachers have to learn to present brief statements of reinforcement after children respond to individual tasks in a series or exercise and present more elaborate reinforcement at the end.

When the teacher provides reinforcement makes a difference. For instance, if the teacher praises children for doing each step of an operation like reading the word *mat*, children will tend not to chain the steps together as quickly as they learn if the teacher praises them for doing *all* the steps. This pattern shows that the ultimate goal is to master the larger unit of work.

Also, teachers must understand that teaching to mastery is not plodding, ritualistic repetition; it is not picky carping or a focus on peripheral behaviors that are not relevant to the tasks they present; nor is it an attempt to turn instruction into something that would occur in military training. Teaching to mastery is simply the orchestration of structural variables and the teaching variables. It involves both finesse and clout—finesse with respect to how the teacher achieves efficiency, clout with respect to providing sufficient practice.

As noted above, if children are placed appropriately in the sequence, teaching to mastery is not difficult because children are not required to learn a great deal of new material to achieve mastery. If children are placed beyond their skill level, they will struggle, because they must learn a lot more to achieve mastery than properly placed children have to learn.

CLASHING PHILOSOPHIES

Our goal was to set up implementations that would control all variables that affected the performance of children. However, even today, the field does not recognize these variables. No urban school district has undertaken any serious effort to train teachers in the technical details of effective instruction. Recommendations are on the global level, not on the level needed to assure that this hour, this minute will maximize what children learn.

Just as children span a large range of individual variation, teachers in failed schools come in a variety of skill sizes, from teachers who demonstrate a lot of the component management behavior and try to present things so that children learn them, to teachers who have no expectations that children will learn much of what they "teach." Working with the full range of teachers was new to us. In our preschool, we could hire people who had verbal skills. We could work with a potential teacher for a while and if she didn't show signs of learning the teaching details, we could drop her. In the field, we had to work with all the teachers, including the ones that were seriously deficient in skills and those who were highly resistant.

The magnitude of the problem of implementing failed schools may be estimated by comparing the list of things that have to be in place for the school to become effective with the things that are not in place. If only a couple of things need to be added or changed, the problem is not as great as one that requires changing a school that has none of the pieces in place.

None of the schools we were to work with recognized that there must be a substantial teacher-training component. None had at least some of the structural details and effective-teaching practices in place. All were failed schools that ranged from those like Orchard School, in Rio Linda, which had a fair number of lively, concerned teachers who could quickly become superstars, to those that had few or no teachers with this profile. All failed schools, however, had an ethic that supported non-functional routines and roles, which is why the school was failing.

To succeed, we would have to reconstruct virtually all instructionally related details of a school, including its ethic. The school would have to become a teacher-training facility that supported an effective teaching machine. Teachers would have to learn new standards for evaluating what they did; the school would have to adopt a problem-solving orientation. The principal would be involved in instruction and would address issues of teacher and student performance. The teachers and aides would become specialists in one of the subjects and would later expand their expertise to other subjects. The management practices would change. And the school ethic would become one of professional pride, with the teachers recognizing they were able to teach any kid that came into the classroom. The school would need to exude academic pride about its ability to serve all children.

That was the plan, which may have been more accurately identified as a dream. Because our orientation ran counter to just about everything the failed school currently did, we encountered resistance on just about everything we required schools to do. In 2004, my son Kurt and I wrote a chapter for a Rand Corporation book, *Upscaling Educational Reform Models*. Our chapter presented the premise that the greater the number of demands that are required to implement a model, the less likely it would be for schools to make the necessary changes or accept the model. Both the editors of the book and the reviewers didn't find our position convincing.

Kindergarten was the most active battleground. We expected every child in kindergarten, even the very low performers, to learn to read by the end of the school year. We did not accept excuses like dyslexia or attention deficit disorder. Some children would certainly be harder to teach than others, but we were convinced that all children we would work with had the capacity to learn if the teaching was adequate. In other words, the problem was not that the children had dyslexia, but that the teacher had some form of *dysteachia*. Most of the schools we worked in were concerned with the children's "readiness" but not with providing instruction that would make them ready.

Kindergarten was particularly important to us because of our goal to accelerate student performance. The greatest relative performance gain is achievable in kindergarten. Unfortunately, not all the schools we worked with had kindergartens, so those schools did not have as great a potential to accelerate. For schools that had kindergarten, our expectation was that most of the children would enter first grade far ahead of their peers. If this pace of learning was maintained through first grade, the children would be a year ahead of the curve in reading performance. They would tend to stay ahead until around the third grade, when books that use adult language replaced the simple readers of the earlier grades.

When language-rich reading is introduced, children with strong language backgrounds have a great advantage over at-risk children. Even so, at-risk children who receive good instruction will remain a little ahead of the curve.

Another reason we saw kindergarten as being so important is that if children learn reading, math, and the language of instruction in kindergarten, it will make the teaching in all the subsequent grades much easier. The reason is that the children will be practiced in learning, will have a good repertoire of skills that serve as foundations for expansions, and will enter the following grades as "smarter" students than teachers on that grade have previously encountered.

A second grade will have very low students during the first year. The teacher may have to teach beginning reading to at least a third of them. The following year, the children who enter second grade will be different because they have gone through a first grade that taught them more skills than first graders in this school had learned before. In year 3, the second-grade teacher receives the first cohort of children who went through kindergarten and grade 1. Although the instruction they had received was not as good as it would become during later years, these children enter second grade with far more skills than any other cohort of children to date.

Because it's easier for teachers to be successful with children who are more skilled, the school can be successful even if the teachers in second and third grade are not as talented as the teachers in K and 1.

Quite a few of the schools we worked with objected to starting instruction in kindergarten. Furthermore, kindergarten typically had teachers who were the least talented and who had no sympathy for teaching. They had gone through early childhood education programs in college and came away with prejudices that made it difficult for them to learn about teaching. They saw themselves as some kind of cross between Captain Kangaroo and a facilitator who provided opportunities for learning. They didn't view children as having serious instructional needs or view themselves as teachers who should meet those needs.

So in the grade that needed the best teachers, we had the worst. We tried to replace those teachers. Often we had to buttress against a weak teacher by placing good aides in kindergarten and turning over the more critical teaching assignments to them.

Of course, we also faced the problem of aides teaching. According to many state laws, the aides are there to "augment, supplement, and complement the instruction the classroom teacher provides." So we had to work out bogus routines that met the letter of the law but that made it possible for aides to teach. One trick was for the teacher to read the introduction of a lesson to the children then turn over the teaching to the aide. The teacher theoretically "introduced" the content for that lesson.

The next problem was homogeneous grouping, and trying to explain to the teachers and the district that this grouping did not mean that children were locked into one group for their entire school career. It meant simply that they would be in a group where all children had instructional needs that were in the same range.

The unpopularity of homogeneous grouping stemmed partly from the psychological myth that if lower performers were with higher performers, they would be able to learn from higher performers and would have a sense of belonging to the "mainstream." This myth also holds that if the group contains only low performers, children will have negative feelings because everybody will know that they are in the dummy group, as surely as they would be dummies if the teacher labeled her groups the red birds, the blue birds, and the buzzards.

The *reductio ad absurdum* of heterogeneity is "full inclusion," which is inspired by the unscientific notion that at-risk children benefit more from being placed in instruction far beyond their ability. Virginia Roach, recently deputy of the Association of State Boards of Education, revealed how grotesque the myth of full inclusion has become among those who have influence on instruction. She indicated that if a student with an IQ of 50 wanted to attend university-level classes in physics, he should not be denied access. I think a marvelous demonstration would be to place Ms. Roach in a 300-level physics class and document how comfortable she felt, what she learned, and the grade she received.

The notion that the lower performers are humiliated if they are in a homogeneous group with other lower performers is actually backwards. They will suffer far more if they, like Alan and Jackie, are placed far beyond their level of skill and knowledge, because they will receive an uninterrupted flow of evidence that they are dumber than all the other children in the group (as Ms. Roach would be able to describe after her stint at full-inclusion physics).

If children in homogeneous groups receive evidence that they are learning important material and receive reinforcement for their efforts, there will be fewer management problems and a much higher percentage of positive interactions between teacher and low performers than there is in a heterogeneous group. The reason is that the low performers are able to play the role of good students in homogeneous groups but not in heterogeneous ones. In homogeneous groups, they receive ongoing information that they are smart and that they master everything the teacher presents. It doesn't matter that there are other groups on the same grade level that perform far beyond the level of this group. Kids can have fun playing basketball even if they know that there are others who play far better than they do. With homogeneous grouping, lower performers do not receive ongoing comparative information that the content is designed for higher performers.

Even some of the more innocuous features of our model became barriers and battlegrounds. One was projections of how far each group of children would be in the program at the end of the school year. Schools and districts strongly resisted, on the grounds that we were telling teachers what they had to do. Some districts took issue with our practice of observing teachers as they taught and providing teaching assignments based on observed performance. Teachers felt that they were being "evaluated" (which meant to them that they would be punished if they had "problems"). Our goal was not to grade the teacher in some way, but to work on the teacher's weaknesses to make the teacher more skilled.

LET'S IMPLEMENT

In 1968, I tried to get to as many of the one-week workshops as I could. The performances were not bad. In some cases, our trainers were not facile in answering questions about the program and why we did things as we did. But some trainers were very polished. One was Sue Rice (who would later marry the Prince of Ponopa and become Sue Moses). She was organized and very sensitive.

On one trip, I met with the superintendent of De Kalb County, Tennessee. He was a large man who spoke in a slow drawl. We got into a fairly heated discussion on the use of programs other than the ones we specified. After I pointed out that this issue was not negotiable, he turned red and said, "If you keep goin' on like this, you and me are going to have to go outside and rassle."

It didn't come to that and we worked things out. But some of his comments pointed out a basic flaw in the Follow Through design. It divided the school. Grades funded by Follow Through had the advantages of increased funds, aides, smaller groups, and better material. Other classrooms in the same school had no aides and had classrooms with 32 children. Understandably, this division of the school created a great deal of ill will.

The training in Uvalde, Texas (about 85 miles from San Antonio and the same distance from Mexico) revealed one of the recurring problems we would face throughout the Follow Through years and beyond. At least one of the aides did not speak English well enough to teach in a classroom. This problem was linked to an even bigger one, which was that our proposed program for teaching language was at odds with the mandates of the federal guidelines for teaching English as a Second Language. These mandates called for presenting instruction in Spanish, then slowly introducing English. I pointed out that this plan made no sense, particularly since we could easily teach enough English in K and 1 to permit children to learn whatever else the programs taught through presentations in English.

Therefore, from day one of school, all instruction was to be in English. The only exceptions were emergencies or situations in which no English explanation would communicate adequately. Not only was this plan seditious in 1968, it is still contrary to legislation in some states. New Jersey, for instance, still has a 1974 law that "was enacted to ensure that students of Limited English Proficiency (LEP) are provided instruction in their native language in order to develop academic skills while acquiring English language skills." The problem is that there are no requirements or schedules for how they "acquire" these skills.

A second rule we followed was that children were never to read something they did not understand, which meant that the teacher might have to read it aloud and explain some words before children read the selection. Over the years, I've seen hundreds of non-English-speaking students who could decode English texts and not understand one sentence of what they read.

The rule for our children was that language was the first priority. We tried to set up classes in which the aides would play the role of children and go through at least the first part of the language program before they taught it to the children.

The children in Uvalde had a large range of skill variation. The lower performers were lower than any of the Portuguese children I had worked with. Teachers felt that these children were progressing slowly because instruction was in English. I had a teacher test some of the lower-performing children in Spanish on their knowledge of prepositions, colors, and words like *left* and *right*. Not one of the children knew more than a third of the words the teacher tested. I tried to make the point that if children don't know the "concepts" in either English or Spanish, the most efficient practice is to teach in English. We knew that they would need understanding of them in English to perform on tasks the teacher would present later.

The children we worked with in Tupelo, Mississippi were overwhelmingly Black, but the schools weren't as segregated as some of the other sites, like Williamsburg County, South Carolina, where the question of discrimination was more like a question about people from different worlds. The Blacks were in places for Blacks and went to schools for Blacks. In Tupelo, there was discrimination, but White and Black teachers taught together, without a lot of posturing and pomp. Most of the teachers were African-American.

During the workshop, the small groups of teachers were doing their mock teaching on exercises. The classroom was not air-conditioned. As I was observing, one group broke into uncontrolled laughter. They were practicing an exercise that demonstrated to children that continuous sounds like *r, s, m,* and *e* could be pronounced for a long time—*mmmmmmmm* (compared to stop sounds like *b, g, t,* and *c,* which cannot be pronounced for more than half a second). The laughter resulted because the woman presenting the exercise got one of the lines from the script backward.

The line: "When I touch it, you say it. Keep on saying it as long as I touch it."

She said, "When I say it, you touch it, keep on touching it as long as I say it."

The others in the group howled. The presenter tried again but again said, "When I say it, you touch it ..." Howls.

The presenter tried two more times and finally got it. A few minutes later another person in the group made the same mistake. Howls. The more members of that group made the mistake, the more likely they were to make it again. When the practice was over, I told them, that's just what happens to kids when they're trying to learn. If they tend to make a lot of mistakes, they have more things in their memory—all the correct responses and all the mistakes. The likelihood of them remembering which ones are the correct ones and which are not is reduced. If they tend not to make many mistakes, the memories of the correct way are far stronger. I didn't mention it to them, but this is why discovery learning is ill conceived. Even if a child finally learns a solution to a problem type, the chances are reduced that he'll remember the solution steps rather than some of the abortive strategies.

In Providence, Rhode Island, there was a different kind of laughter issue. One of our trainers laughed when a participant mentioned something about the program robbing teachers of their individuality. The trainer told me, "I thought she was kidding and it seemed funny to me. Her school is a total disaster." Apparently some of the other participants and administrators in attendance took the trainer's reaction to be evidence of malice and our disregard for the individual teacher who thinks on her own.

After the summer training, we had ideas about which sites would make the greatest progress, and of course we were almost as consistently wrong as we were about predicting which trainers would be superior. We felt that New York would do well because of the strength of the parent group and the on-site trainer. We felt that East St. Louis would not do that well because the city had been decimated by riots. There was no downtown, simply an area that looked like a war zone. One of the sites we were sure would do well was Grand Rapids. It had very strong leaders. The city was in transition. Parts were populated by White Europeans with strong work ethics. Large areas, however, had become low-income Black neighborhoods. The strength and commitment of the administration seemed strong enough to prevail. The first summer workshop in Grand Rapids went smoothly. There were a few problems later, but it seemed that the kindergartens would be strong and the support from the central office unquestioned.

INTERACTING WITH SCHOOL DISTRICTS

One of the pandemic problems we had in working with districts was district guidelines. This issue was particularly sensitive for Follow Through schools because any exemptions from district policy would not apply to the entire school, only the K-3 classes. In most cases, districts did not believe that Follow Through classes should be exempted from any district policies. This meant that the school would have dual standards for evaluating the principal, the teachers, and the children. The district would use one set of standards. We would use another. There would be dual training that pitted the district in-service against our in-service, dual teacher evaluations that pitted our evaluation against the district's, and so forth. The result at some sites was that aides we ranked as the highest were fired; some of the teachers we ranked as too low to teach were retained, without any required "assistance program"; some of the principals we judged to be resistant and effete received commendations; and some of the children we rated as showing great gains received low grades on their report cards.

From the standpoint of political realities, I can appreciate how the district interpreted our position as being both insulting and arrogant. Districts had adopted programs that we would not use. As one assistant superintendent put it, "What the hell are you people thinking of? It's a perfectly good program that is used in the rest of the school. Why can't you use it?"

Districts attempted to schedule subjects that were not in our curricula, such as district science programs, labs, and literature programs.

According to the districts' agreement with Follow Through, they should have waived these requirements; however, they didn't. So we had to fight each of these attempts to diminish our program's integrity. If we hadn't and permitted the program to be sifted through district requirements, it would have been no better than the ones that were currently failing in the districts. In other words, if we had acquiesced to district pressure and complied with the districts' requirements, we would have failed.

We pointed out that we were not opposed to any of the content the district required, simply to how it was delivered. For instance, we showed that we teach science and social science within the context of our reading program. The first two levels of this program focus on learning to read, the third and beyond, on reading to learn. In the third and fourth levels students would read about the oceans, galaxies, dinosaurs; they would learn geography, geology, anatomy, and more.

Many districts did not believe that our programs were worthy replacements for the district programs because our programs weren't designed as spiral curricula, which were popular at the time. A reading program that had a spiral design presented a parade of topics like main idea, supporting detail, cause and effect, and fact versus opinion. A classroom might spend three or four consecutive periods on main idea, then move on to the next topic and spend a few days on it. The parading topics were sequenced so that after possibly 60 school days or more, the cycle would start over with the first topic followed by the other topics arranged in the original order.

This design has no empirical validation and no practical endorsement as a sensible strategy for teaching anything. If you teach something, it is supposed to be for a reason, which hopefully means that you will use it. So if the sequence were designed sensibly, it would teach main idea to mastery and then use it from then on. The periodic revisiting simply sends a strong, but inappropriate message to both teachers and students: "This material does not have to be mastered. It will go away after a few days." The teacher knows that there is little hope that students will master it, and the students learn that this kind of exposure is just another of the school rituals.

Of course descriptions of a spiral curriculum sound appealing: "It revisits each topic and expands and intensifies student understanding with each cycle." Even worse than the revisiting, however, is what is revisited. Main idea is taught as a reading skill. Why? Main idea is more reasonably taught as a writing skill. The directions for writing typically provide the main idea: "Write about a time you did something that embarrassed you a lot." The student identifies the incident then gives supporting detail.

Some of the other reading topics have serious logical problems. Fact-versus-opinion, for instance, creates a false dilemma, which is that either something is a fact or it's an opinion. Not so. Somebody could have an opinion that is supported by fact. The unit typically treats any value words like *pretty* or *better* as opinion words. The statement, "Car A has better performance than Car B" is not a value judgment but one based on evidence.

The only paradigm that would rectify the confusion would be one that distinguished between facts that were true and those that weren't, and that presented statements of value as being neither true nor false. ("It's pretty" is a value statement; "It's green" is a true-false statement. "It's better than that one" could be either fact or value.)

We tried to point out to the districts that the purpose of Follow Through was to determine what worked, and the treatments therefore had to be kept "uncontaminated," but if the district wanted information about a serious alternative, it could conduct its own experiment, which seemed like a good thing to do. It would permit the district to obtain data on how well the content of one of its spiral curriculum was transmitted to the students. It would also permit the district to discover which program taught more information, the DI program or the district program.

The districts rarely appreciated our logic or explanations.

One of the more irritating positions was that the school had to teach what's on the achievement test. Our position was that the achievement test does not determine what is appropriately taught. If we do a good job of preparing what the children need to know to take the next steps in their education, they will ultimately learn enough to do well on achievement tests—if not on the second-grade tests, then probably on the third-grade test. Simply because the first grade achievement test has math items involving estimation of what the answer should be, we don't treat these items as a sufficient endorsement for us to devote instructional time on it. The children are not prepared to learn it yet. Possibly by fourth grade, estimation might be a reasonable topic, but not in first grade.

IN-SERVICE

One of the most serious problems we encountered during the first year in Follow Through was the in-service training put on by the districts. Our teachers were required to attend these sessions, even though the content and procedures were in obvious opposition to what we were trying to teach teachers to do. We told our teachers that the district in-service content did not apply to Follow Through; that our model was supposed to have waivers to do what we do; and that we would do our own in-services. The formula that we used was as different from the districts' procedures as our instructional techniques were from theirs. Our plan for in-service was to identify common problems that teachers were experiencing in the classroom and focus in-service sessions on these problems. If teachers were having problems teaching something in the second level of the reading program, we would schedule a session, not for all teachers, but for those who were using the second level of the reading program. Because there were problems in all grades and with all levels of the programs, we had to design teacher schedules so there would be periods on one or two afternoons a week that could be used for in-service.

We introduced an operating philosophy that was counter to that of the district, our notion that problems are simply information. We need to know about problems teachers experience because we want to solve them immediately. For the district and the teacher new to Follow Through, problems were associated with some form of punishment. If an authority figure identified the teacher as having a problem, there would probably be some form of "consequence."

In contrast, our goal was to identify all problems teachers experienced. When our trainers were on site, they were to spend at least 75 percent of their time in the classroom, not in meetings. Their objective was to see as much of the instruction as possible and fix up problem areas as quickly as possible.

Following each classroom observation, the trainer would leave each teacher who had been observed with a "teacher performance summary"' that indicated specific presentation problems (pacing, corrections, reinforcement, and so forth) and indicated a remedy (an assignment the teacher was to follow). At a time later in the day, the trainer would go over the teacher performance summary and point out what the teacher needed to do differently. The trainer would rehearse the behavior specified in the assignment with the teacher.

Here is a copy of one of our earliest teacher-performance forms. Notice that the various categories cover the full range of variables described above—both the broad ones and the teaching behaviors.

Teacher Performance Form

Subject: _____   Teacher: _____
  Level: _____   Supervisor: _____
 Lesson: _____   Date: _____
                                    Group: _____
              Number of Children: _____

Strong areas:

_____ Following formats   _____ Reinforcement

_____ Signals   _____ Watching children

_____ Pacing   _____ Corrections

_____ Mastery teaching   _____ Setup/Mechanics

Assignment: Date Due: _____

Comments:

Dates checked: _____   _____

_____ Checked out

_____ Re-do

The trainer would fill out the form (indicating the areas in which the teacher was performing well) and would provide only one remedy (one assignment), even if the teacher was doing many things wrong. The trainer would try to select the area most critical to the teacher's progress. The trainer would rehearse the teacher on exactly what behaviors the trainer expected to see and indicate a date at which the trainer would return and check on progress (often the next day). A firm rule was that if the teacher had questions or needed help, she could call the trainer.

During Follow Through, we did some manipulation of observation forms to determine the extent to which the teachers' performance needed to be monitored and how important the Teacher Performance Form was in providing teachers with a yardstick for them to measure their performance. Actually, our investigation of teachers' reliance on the Teacher Performance Form stemmed from an accident. Near the end of the first year, we reorganized the categories on the Teacher Performance Form, but by accident, the second edition of the form had a category missing—pacing. Before we noticed its absence, we observed that teachers who'd had pretty good pacing were not pacing their presentations well. We corrected the form and the teachers again tended to have better pacing.

We later did it purposely with another category—corrections. We made up a Teacher Performance Form that didn't list it and observed the extent to which teachers' behavior changed. It changed a lot. We were distressed over this fact. We had hoped that the teachers would see the importance of all the criteria in the performance of their children. The fact is, however, that while teachers are still learning how to be effective, they need clear performance markers. If the markers are absent, their performance slides.

BECOMING SCHOOLWISE

Trainers and project managers had to become effective in working with all the teachers, not just with some of them, which meant they had to learn effective strategies for observing and solving problems. The first trap they had to avoid was spending almost all of their time working with lower-performing teachers, sometimes at the expense of observing teachers who were judged to be high performers. Often, trainers who focused too much on the lowest teachers were shocked when they finally got around to observing teachers who were supposed to perform well. In most cases, these teachers had problems and needed help. So trainers couldn't devote more than about half their time to their lowest performing teachers.

Because some of the teachers were performing below minimum acceptable standards, trainers had to implement interim solutions to assure that the children were being taught as the training with the teacher occurred. For instance, the trainer might combine classrooms with a good teacher and arrange for the problem teacher to team-teach with the good teacher.

A second problem was the prevailing suspicion of teachers being "evaluated." Some schools argued that only the principal was empowered to evaluate. In these schools we tried to arrange for the principal to indicate that the trainer was the principal's surrogate. In other schools, we tried to work through the local Follow Through director to establish guidelines that permitted our people to work productively with teachers.

In some places, the issues of evaluation and assignments were never settled, which meant that for the duration of Follow Through we continued to fight battles over observing teachers and giving assignments.

Even if schools officially permitted observations and assignments, teachers were very clever about concealing problems and distracting the trainer. One of the more common ploys of teachers who did not want to be observed was to greet the trainer with praise. "The program is wonderful. I'm amazed at how well all the children are doing. What a delightful program." The message was, "Things are great in this classroom so there is no need for you to observe." We taught trainers not to believe this kind of endorsement without first directly observing performance of teachers and children. Trainers who did not heed this rule were often disappointed later when they observed that the teacher had serious problems.

Another teacher ploy was to take the trainer out of the observation mode. For example, as soon as the trainer entered the room, the teacher would stop teaching and say something like, "Oh, I am so glad you are here. I'm having some real problems with parts of the lessons. Could you demonstrate for me?" The ploy was clever because while the trainer taught the group, the trainer was not observing the teacher. We had cases in which teachers actually left the room as the trainer demonstrated.

We cautioned trainers about this strategy and told them to respond to the call for help by saying, "Okay, why don't you teach the exercise you're having trouble with, so I can see firsthand what the problem is."

Our early attempts to design effective in-class training procedures were not without fault. Initially some of our trainers undertook the job of shaping teacher behaviors by focusing on form, not function. They would focus on the teacher's behavior and try to change it so it looked more like that of a good teacher. We provided a fair amount of training that there's a problem if the children are not performing as they should. That's where the observation starts, and that's where the remedies focus. If the teacher is sloppy with her signals but the children perform well, there's no problem. In contrast, if the children are not responding well in response to whatever signal the teacher uses, there is a problem.

We worked on interactions between teacher and trainer so the emphasis would be on specific details. That training started with the teacher reconstructing part of what occurred during the lesson. Any excellent teacher is able to provide detailed information about what she did and what the children did. An important step in shaping beginning teachers' abilities is to model what they are to do and what questions they are to ask themselves.

For instance, the trainer would ask the teacher questions about problems.

"Tell me how the kids performed when you reviewed the sounds of letters."

"What do you mean?"

"Did students respond well to all the tasks?"

"Well they're a little weak."

"Which sounds did they have the most trouble with?"

After the teacher identifies the sounds, the trainer asks, "Well, what do you think is needed to make them stronger on those sounds?"

This kind of routine not only shapes the teachers' attention to specific details, but also shows what training is all about—identifying specific problems and providing the kind of practice that fixes them.

Overall, teachers became more trusting after they learned that the purpose of observing was not to "grade," "compare," or "punish" the teacher but simply to identify things that needed to be fixed, and to make the teacher more effective at diagnosing problems and solving them. If we could have implemented by working directly with teachers (without the detour through the district's administrative processing machine), I'm convinced we would have had far fewer problems with teachers. We would simply go about the business of teaching them how to teach children content they had never been able to teach before.

I consider teaching a noble enterprise. What I miss the most over the last 20 years is teaching regularly and observing teachers. I find it flat thrilling to watch an expert teacher hold children on the edge of their chairs, fully engaged in learning and completely committed to showing the teacher how smart they are.

Furthermore, I sympathize with the commitment demanded by an uncompromised effort. I know how long the school year feels around March, how tiring the daily grind becomes, and how much harder it is to hype yourself into not slacking off and taking it easy, particularly because nobody would know the difference—except you. It is a tough job and only a few recognize whether it is done well or how well the expert does it. I consider those who do it heroes. Their recognition is minimal but their impact enormous.

Finally, I am amazed at the raw talent that exists in failed schools. Often, four or five teachers in an ordinary failed school located in an unattractive neighborhood will emerge as undisputed superstars. These teachers were there all the time. They were ineffective, but they, like Alan and his classmates, had the capacity to become highly competent performers when they were taught effectively, through a program that started where they were and systematically worked on what they needed to know to achieve a remarkable metamorphosis.

One reason our approach to training teachers was so different from traditional approaches was that we were concerned with the performance of every child, which implied that we had to be concerned with every teacher and aide assigned to teach children. If a logical person started with the notion of monitoring the performance of teachers so that problems could be identified and solved in a timely manner, the person would derive all the features of our approach. The first question the person would have to address is, "What are the expectations for each child by the end of the year?"

The next question would be, "How do you respond to problems the teachers are experiencing?" In the traditional school, there are no provisions for responding to problems in a timely way. Even if problems are observed early in the school year, nothing usually happens until the next school year.

Identifying problems in a timely way is not possible with programs that permit teachers latitude in what they teach or how fast they proceed through the program. A trainer couldn't walk into the classroom, view posted data and conclude that there's a problem. Instead, the trainer would have to get more information about specifically what the teacher has been teaching, then try to determine what the problem is and what caused it. Because the problem with traditional programs is strongly rooted in the poor program design, about the only way the trainer would be able to help the teacher is to redesign the program and the tasks that are relevant to the problem. This kind of remedy not only requires considerable amounts of time but also has limited benefits. If it takes a trainer 12 hours to redo the program and then train the teacher in using it, the trainer would not be able to work with more than a small fraction of teachers that could be serviced if the program were designed more carefully.

School districts do not encounter these problems because they have never taken the first step of making projections for the performance of every student. Until recently, children who were clearly not learning to read were not even identified as having a problem until the end of third grade, when they would take the state test, fail it, and earn the label of "learning disabled."

Note that strategies of blaming children have characterized liberal education for decades. During the reign of "whole language," school and district administrations used lies to assuage concerns of parents whose children were not reading. In California, for instance, teachers were told to tell parents not be concerned if their first grader was not learning to read because the child would catch up by grade 4. This was not a white lie, but a whopper. Performance at the end of grade 1 is the strongest predictor of performance at the end of grade 4. And grade 4 performance is the best available predictor of school dropouts, teen pregnancies, felony arrests, unemployment, and so on.

Reid Lyon, of the National Institute of Child Health and Human Development, gave testimony in 2001 before the House of Representative's Subcommittee on Education and the Workforce, in which he gave some numbers.

> Of children who will eventually drop out of school, over 75 percent will report difficulties learning to read ... Only 2 percent of students receiving special or compensatory education will complete a four year college program. Surveys of adolescents with criminal records indicate that at least half have reading difficulties, and in some states, the size of prisons a decade in the future is predicted by fourth grade reading failure rates. Approximately half of children ... with a history of substance abuse have reading problems ... It is for this reason that the NICHD ... considers reading failure to reflect a national public health problem.

The best place to start solving that problem is in grades K and 1.

CHAPTER 3

Follow Through Continues

HOUSTON REVISITED

About a month after the plane crash, we had a second opportunity to work with schools in Houston, not through Title I but as part of Follow Through. The Houston Follow Through program was a parent-directed model. The Parent Advisory Council (PAC) indicated that it wanted us to work with several schools. The initial training would require two of our trainers. We wanted to install good people, but I believed that the only pair of trainers who were not already assigned would not work well together. These trainers were Margo Fitzgerald and Corinne Coselle.

Margo had recently completed our graduate program at the University of Illinois. She was a young, attractive teacher recommended by Barbara Bateman, a colleague who would later become a leader in special education. Barbara told me, "She'll be a handful, but she's worth it."

Margo was one of the funniest people I have ever known, a terrific mimic who could do faultless Black dialects, southern drawls, NYC accents, Swedish, and others. This skill, coupled with her ability to tell foul jokes and satirize events, made her the number one entertainer of our group. Once, several years after she left our project, she and I were in an Irish deli in San Francisco. There was a line at the counter and we were at the end of the line. A customer in front of us commented that one of the women preparing sandwiches wasn't putting enough corned beef on them, and Margo said loudly in her best Irish brogue, "Ah, don't be scrimping on that corned beef. Lay it on thick." Everybody smiled, and Margo launched into a running commentary that would have shamed George Carlin. Everybody in the place was laughing. One of the women working behind the counter had tears in her eyes.

When we were getting our orders filled (amidst Margo's commentary and directions about how to fix the sandwiches), a woman behind us asked Margo, "Are you for real?" She spoke with a heavy brogue. Margo responded, "And what about herself here? Is she for real?"

After some bantering, the woman explained that she had just come from Ireland and couldn't tell whether Margo was from the Emerald Isle. Margo explained that she had never been abroad, but that her parents were Irish and that she had known lots of people who spoke "in the mither tongue with foin diction."

Margo's talent stood in stark contrast with her teaching, which was just this side of terrible. She had been a teacher for a couple of years before coming to the U of I, and she was like a human reference book on bad teaching habits. She approached teaching sternly. When children made mistakes, she behaved as if they had insulted her. She had poor pacing and indecisive responses to what the children did.

I tried to talk her into a new frame of mind, and treat the whole thing like telling a joke and setting kids up for the punch line, but she couldn't seem to let go of her bad teaching habits, and she went through her labored teaching routine for months, until at least one of our trainers was ready to give up on her. One day early in the spring, I observed her putting on a pretty poor show. After the period I told her that she just didn't get it and that with her sense of humor and timing, she should have those kids on a string. I told her, "Whatever they do, you should have a comeback." I asked her why she made such hard work of teaching when it's just like joking around. They do something, you make a joke about it. I told her, "With your skills, you should be having fun out there."

I don't know the extent to which my bawling her out influenced her, but shortly after it she emerged from her cocoon—a totally different teacher. She had her opening routines in which she would read something and the children had to catch her mistakes. "Which you're not going to do because it will be too hard for you."

"No, it won't...You can't fool us."

She did things that were technically sound, but did them with the Margo touch. She became as good as I guessed she would be.

The other trainer available for Houston was Corinne Coselle, a young Black militant. She had been a teacher in Carver Primary, one of the Chicago schools that field-tested the original reading program. She later moved to Champaign and became Cookie Bruner's assistant. Corinne taught well and managed well, but she intimidated a couple of the trainees. When I told Cookie that I needed to talk to Corinne about her behavior,

Cookie tried to discourage me. She indicated that Corinne would quit, leaving Cookie without an assistant. I talked to Corinne anyhow. I told her I didn't care what she thought, and I didn't care what she did on her own time, but when she was on Project time there were no racists and no agendas other than working well with each other to get the job done. If she couldn't work amicably with the others, she couldn't work with us.

She agreed to the terms, and I was very glad, because if she had left, I would probably still be hearing about it from Cookie. Corinne was never very "friendly" in the sense that she didn't initiate interactions with others, but she was good with the people she trained.

The problem with putting both her and Margo on the same project was that a clash of personalities seemed inevitable. Margo (who had never worked with Corinne) was not tolerant of the militant aspects of Black Power. I cautioned Margo about Corinne. Margo rolled her eyes and indicated that she understood.

Margo and Corinne had been in Houston working in the school for two days before attending a meeting at the school with Wes, me, and district officials. Before the meeting began, Wes and I were outside smoking when the women approached. Margo said in Black dialect, "Say sister, what do you say we talk to these honkies a while?" Corinne laughed and playfully pushed Margo aside. I had worked with Corinne over two years and I had never seen her laugh.

It turned out that Margo and Corinne had attended the same high school in Chicago (Hirsch) and they knew a lot of the same people. By the time they met us that morning, they were already good pals, sharing the same hotel room.

If anybody had told me that somebody could joke around with Corinne I would have been skeptical. Apparently, Corinne had done her share of joking, too. When she and Margo had arrived by cab at the Holiday Inn, onlookers stared at a White and a Black riding together in a taxi. As they walked to the hotel, Corinne balanced a stack of books on her head. This was 1968 and Houston was heavily entrenched in segregation.

Shortly after the women met us at the school, Margo said, "Oh shit. I left my notebook in the room. I'll be right back." She returned about half an hour later with a curious report. When she went into her room, she found the manager of the Holiday Inn and four others in the room. All of Margo's and Corinne's belongings had been removed from their luggage and the interlopers were examining them, an item at a time. The manager gave a limp excuse about training staff members in security, but to Margo it was clear. No self-respecting White would share a room with a Black unless something very seditious was afoot. The possibility that the two women could be colleagues or pals could not account for such an outrageous disregard of the color line. They had to be dangerous people, and the staff was bent on proving it.

This chapter of our close encounter with Houston ended suddenly and mysteriously. The training was going well. The participants were working with children daily. According to both Margo and Corinne, the children were learning well, and the teachers realized that the program really worked; however, the director of the Houston Follow Through Project informed us that Houston would not install Direct Instruction. The reason was that the PAC did not feel that the approach would benefit their children. According to Margo and Corinne, the reason was that the program obviously worked, and the dominant political forces in the community and the district did not want a program that put Blacks on an equal footing with Whites. I don't know what the truth is, but— based on what happened in other urban district—I would lean toward the Margo-Corinne interpretation.

I was disappointed about losing Houston because I wanted to provide something of a living memorial for the former Title I director. That plan was now dead. Another unfortunate aspect of Houston was that the termination of the project left Margo and Corinne without a site to manage, so neither continued with us in Follow Through. Margo went to Seattle, where she became instructional director for CAMPI, a preschool program for at-risk kids, funded jointly by the Seattle School District and the community. Corinne went to Las Vegas, where she operated a tutorial service for failed students.

IMPLEMENTATION FACTS

Implementing failed schools takes time. The time requirement is not based on amorphous factors, but on the nature of the teacher-training problem. In an ideal teaching situation, you would teach a concept by presenting positive examples of the concept and negative ones. The positive examples clarify what the concept you're demonstrating is; the negative ones, what it isn't. If you had to teach something using only negative examples, the process would be far more difficult. Consider trying to teach what a shoe is using only negative examples. You could present socks and say, "This is not a shoe," and you could present slippers and say, "This is not a shoe." But you couldn't present a shoe and say, "This is a shoe." It would be some time before the average learner figured out what a shoe is.

Implementing a failed school from scratch poses the same kind of problem in the sense that the trainer can't show positive examples of how the school should look, how it should operate, or how teachers should teach. These examples are not available because the school has failed and has no positive models for teachers to observe. Aside from the demonstrations and snippets provided by the trainer, teachers can't observe others teaching the right way because there aren't any.

The standard learning pattern is, therefore, that teachers learn a lot from the mistakes they make. They do something wrong; the trainer corrects them and shows them how to do that snippet correctly. And they learn a new bit of information. They don't see the big picture, however, or get a clear notion of how this bit fits in with other bits.

Teaching teachers in a school that is well implemented is much easier because there are ample positive examples—teachers who manage well, who attend to the picky details of presenting content efficiently, and who are articulate in explaining what they do and why they do it. Training teachers who are new to the implemented school is easier because it is possible to show them exactly what is expected, and how it looks and feels when the program is well implemented. The trainer may arrange for a teacher who is having problems to team teach with one who is proficient. In this setting, the apprentice teacher receives information about the details and the big picture (the overall expectations the teacher has about how children will perform and the overall strategies of how to achieve the details). This option is not usually available in a first-year implementation, or possibly even a second-year implementation that has a hard-to-teach population.

The documentary film, *The Battle of City Springs*, shows the difficulty of implementing through negative examples in one of the lowest two schools in Baltimore. One scene took place during the middle of the implementation's second year. Kindergarten was thoroughly unimplemented and the teachers were completely untrained.

In the scene, the trainer is trying to organize a small instructional group. The children are crying, leaving the group, and not attending to the teacher or the trainer. The trainer is mother-henning the teacher and children, trying to establish some positive behaviors so there is a basis for reinforcing the children with little treats (which didn't entice the children).

The trainer's efforts are punishing to the children because the children have been reinforced for doing pretty much whatever they wanted to do. They didn't want to sit in a chair or watch the teacher so they cried and used other techniques that had worked in the past to reestablish their freedom.

The teacher and aides in this situation must learn something from this negative example. Understandably, they are not convinced that the trainer knows what she is doing. (It obviously is not working.) They don't have any reason to believe that the children will behave any differently than they are behaving now because nobody has ever seen them sit in a group and attend. The trainer doesn't have the option of taking the teachers into a classroom that has the same population of children who are engaged in academics and enjoying what they are doing. Nor does the trainer have the option of exchanging the teacher and aides for those who know how to manage children effectively.

In the film, the trainer tells the teachers, "It will get worse before it gets better, but it will get better." Several teachers have skeptical expressions. The trainer was right, however. It did get better. By 2003, the school had progressed from possibly the lowest in Baltimore to at least one of the top three. There were no behavior problems in kindergarten. The mid-year performance of the children who went through the well-implemented kindergarten program did not resemble the children in the film. Every child in the 2003 kindergarten class who had been in attendance at least 90 days could read. A year later, this group finished first-grade reading on the high second-grade level. They performed at the 99th percentile in both reading and math, compared to all first graders.

During Follow Through, we kept records about how long it took a new teacher or aide to achieve what we considered minimum acceptable performance—basic presentation behavior; knowledge of placing children; and skills in teaching to mastery, correcting and reinforcing children. The numbers were pretty uniform across various sites. Teachers and aides who began in unimplemented schools required about one and a half years to achieve this base level of performance. In contrast, a new teacher in a well implemented school achieved the same performance criteria in a little over three months. There were no significant differences between the rates of teachers or aides.

This information has serious implications for how to implement more efficiently. If several classrooms of a school to be implemented are "seeded" with experienced teachers and aides, those classrooms can serve as training centers that provide models of how to execute details of the program.

In a 1976 Follow Through technical report, we documented the change in performance of children going through kindergarten. The second cohort of kindergarten children (1969–70) achieved the 47th percentile on the Wide Range Achievement Test by the end of the school year. This score was slightly below the average of all children but quite a bit above the performance level of children not in the program (which was around the 20th percentile). The sixth cohort of kindergarteners (1973–74) achieved the 73rd percentile, which is far above average. The difference had nothing to do with changes in demography. We noted in a technical report:

> In the early years, kindergarten teachers were not prepared to believe that their children could be taught to read, so they did not always follow through with sponsor suggestions. After a

number of demonstrations of what could be done, and a real targeting by the sponsor on kindergarten-level performance of teachers and aides, improvements were made in the number of lessons taught and in the quality of the teaching.

TROUBLE WITH THE U OF I

In 1969, things were going fairly well in the field; however, we had two problems with the University of Illinois. One was that the University would not permit us to have an undergraduate teacher training section that taught Direct Instruction principles and techniques. The University had a traditional undergraduate program that presented broad and often bogus principles. The teachers who went through the program were expected to incorporate these into their unique styles. If medical schools taught surgery according to this format, surgeons would receive only general principles about anatomy and surgery before giving them six weeks in the surgery room and then licensing them.

We had a graduate program at the U of I, but with the number of people we would need to service our sites, we felt that it was very important to train undergraduates. Wes petitioned the University twice for a section of students who would be specifically trained to work with at-risk students. Both petitions were soundly rejected.

The second problem was that the University had unreasonable regulations for purchasing material needed for our grant. Our mimeographing operation used paper at the rate of 42,000 sheets (84 reams) a day. The university purchasing department charged our project the same price for each ream that it would have charged if we purchased one ream.

We checked and discovered that with the amounts we purchased, we could purchase reams at about one-fourth the price that we were paying the University. We asked the purchasing department to simply let us treat paper purchases as an office cost and we would send the bills to the university. No.

After several rounds of trying to work out a reasonable arrangement, I contacted the person in charge of the purchasing. He remained firm in not giving us a quantity discount on paper. I told him, "That's bullshit." He sent letters to my various superiors about my lack of decorum.

Before the Christmas break, our group had a meeting about possibly moving to another university, where we could have a section of the undergraduate teacher training and reasonable overhead procedures. Wes was the primary instigator of this plan. The group agreed that if the majority of our people voted in favor of the move, all who could go would go. The vote to move had a strong majority. Cookie and Jean voted no because their husbands were professors at the U of I (Ed Bruner in anthropology, and Howard Osborn in math), and both husbands were satisfied with their current situations. I voted no because I was in the process of finishing my "dream house" on Lake Iroquois, about 35 miles from Champaign. It was located at the end of a peninsula, a plank-and-beam construction that had Douglas-fir beams 30" x 4" x 28' (which you probably could not buy for any price today), over 3,000 square feet, and lots of glass, which provided views from just about every room in the house.

Almost everybody else voted yes, so it wasn't a question of whether we would move from Illinois, but of where and when. Wes compiled a list of places that had expressed a commitment to serving disadvantaged populations and contacted them. Of the list of 16 places, only two expressed any interest in our project: Temple University and the University of Oregon. The lack of interest was curious because one of the carrots the project had was that we would bring our Follow Through grant with us—$1 million year, which translated to around $4 million in current valuation. The overhead on the grant should have been attractive to any university, particularly one committed to helping disadvantaged kids.

I objected to the notion of even considering the University of Oregon because it was geographically so remote from our sites. Temple had a far more desirable location, in Philadelphia, quite close to 12 of our sites. So we first pursued Temple. We negotiated with a university level administrator who was quite excited about having us move there. Things seemed to be falling into place. Then possibly three weeks went by without any word from Temple. Finally, we received a short letter from the administrator. After apologizing for not communicating sooner, he wrote, "I don't feel that I can invite the project to Temple because the faculty of two departments, education and psychology, voted unanimously against this proposal."

Unanimously? That seemed hard to believe, but it was something we had to accept. We now had just one choice, the University of Oregon. I hoped that Oregon would also turn us down. Wes did the negotiations. He took two trips to Oregon. Near the end of the spring term, he announced that the deal with the U of O was a go. That meant I had to get a lot of personal things in order—sell the house, finish the place at Lake Iroquois and sell it, get rid of my work car (a black-and-white '55 Olds four-door hard top, the first model Olds built), and attend to what seemed to be an endless string of details. Fortunately, my wife was as well organized as I was disorganized, but she shared my reluctance to move. She was a lawyer and would not only have to quit her practice, but take another bar exam and find a suitable position in Oregon.

Every day after work during that spring, I drove up the back roads to Lake Iroquois and worked on the house. It had 2,400 square feet of decks, cantilevered on the massive beams. The decks had to be finished, and there was still a lot of detail work inside (installing door frames, varnishing, and painting). I had decided that the best scenario for my car would be to drive it so hard it would break down. Then I wouldn't feel bad about leaving it in Illinois. (There was no way I would have time to drive it to Oregon.) The back roads had very little traffic so I drove over 90 mph for most of the run. After more than a month of this routine, the car ran just as well as it had on the day I started. But the house was still not completed.

Our Champaign house was in a modest development on the northwest side of the city. When we had bought it, it had about 960 square feet. We put on three additions, giving us plenty of room for a family of six (mom, dad, and four kids). We sold the house to a Black family, the first in the neighborhood. I know that some of our neighbors were probably upset about it, but we figured that we should do what we could to offer housing to middle-class people who were stuck in a nasty ghetto on the north end of town because of prejudice.

I sold my car to a 17-year-old kid who lived across the street. He had asked about buying it several times earlier. I sold it for $140, which was far less than it was worth, but I was glad it was getting a good home.

Before we moved to Oregon, I went there to buy a house. With the insane schedule I had that summer, I was able to spend one day in Eugene. An associate dean, Dick Schminke, had contacted me, indicated that he dabbled in real estate, and said that he would show me some places when I got there. Dick was the liaison to our Follow Through site in Racine, Wisconsin, but I had never met him. He and another man I didn't know, Bob Mattson, greeted me at the airport. Bob, a large, bald, jolly guy, was the primary engineer behind the invitation from Oregon. He was an associate dean, in charge of special education, and he was in the process of assembling a department of talented mavericks at the University: Jerry Patterson, Hill Walker, Barbara Bateman (who had been at Illinois), Rob Horner, and Tom Bellamy. Bob was familiar with our model and felt the same way Wes did about data.

Dick Schminke showed me several houses that day. One was on Fairmount Boulevard, close to the university. It was a large corner building (3,300 square feet) with two levels, two lots, and a two-car garage, located in one of the "more desirable neighborhoods" in Eugene. Building prices in Oregon were substantially lower than they were in Illinois. The house cost $48,000, which included the second lot.

I bought the house that day, had a couple of beers with Dick and Bob, and flew to Chicago, knowing that I had some common interests with

Mattson and Schminke. All of us played handball and we were all interested in trees and agriculture. I didn't know then how close I would become to these men over the next 30 years.

I hired a carpenter to finish the Lake Iroquois house and we moved to Oregon. We put the house up for sale, but it did not sell by the next summer. My family went on a long road trip that summer and spent about a week at Lake Iroquois. I joined them and spent a weekend there, the only two nights I ever spent in the place. Unfortunately, when I arrived, I was sick with a fever and painful strep throat. I went to a specialist in Champaign who indicated that he could drain the large sack in my throat either in his office or on the following day in the hospital. He indicated that if he did it in his office, he could not use an anesthetic. He told me that it would be painful and that I couldn't move during the procedure, which he said would take only ten seconds. I told him to do it. He sliced the sack and spread it. Within two minutes after the surgery I felt better than I had in days.

The following morning was the last time I saw the Lake Iroquois place. I looked back at it as we drove away. The sun was reflecting from the huge windows on the second-story living room. I felt uneasy about leaving the structure unattended.

OUR NEW HOME IN OREGON

Eugene didn't have a lot in common with Champaign-Urbana. Champaign is flat; Eugene is hilly. Champaign was intellectual; Eugene was folksy. It didn't feel like home, and I was not at all sure that we had done the right thing, but I was fascinated with Oregon. For years in Illinois I had planted exotic trees. The Midwest winters tend to be cruel to a lot of them, but there are some that survive. The two huge trees south of the Student Union building at the U of Illinois are bald cypress. When I first identified them, I couldn't believe that they survived and did not suffer the same fate as car radiators, frozen house pipes, and ice-covered electric wires. I had planted some exotics on the Lake Iroquois lot, including bald cypress.

Oregon trees dwarfed anything in the Midwest, with forests of Douglas fir that were taller than 18-story buildings. I figured that as soon as we sold the Lake Iroquois place, we would buy some land in the country, where we could raise exotic trees.

One of the professional benefits of the move to Oregon was that I became an associate professor. At Illinois I had the rank of Senior Educational Specialist. Wes engineered my promotion. I hadn't asked him to do it because I figured that it might not be fair for somebody who did not go through graduate school to assume regular-faculty status.

I met with the dean of education shortly before the fall term began. He didn't seem very pleased with the deal he had made with Wes, and he indicated that there was absolutely no way I would ever advance beyond associate professor. I told him that I could live with that.

The crew that came to Oregon included Doug and Linda Carnine, Susie Stearns, Don Steely, Glenda Hewlett, and Jessica Daniels.

Jessica would be Wes's administrative assistant. The project was housed in two large prefabricated buildings (trailers) next to the Clinical Services building, which served as a very large bathroom for our project. The administrative functions were carried out in Trailer 1. Wes, Jessica, and the project coordinators resided here. The project coordinators performed a support function for project managers. Each of the two coordinators (initially, Carol Morimitsu and Linda Carnine) worked with ten sites. The role of the coordinator was not to boss the project managers or manage them, but to support them in a way that allowed them to maintain reasonable working relationships with site administrators. The formula was simple. If a battle over an implementation requirement occurred, and if the project manager could not solve it in a routine manner, the project manager would report the problem to the coordinator, who would then take over and become the designated combatant. In this way, the project manager would not be the one who battled the district, simply the one who was trying to do her job and get along with others. The project manager could assume the stance, "I don't make the rules. I just try to carry them out. The project coordinator is the person who has the authority to negotiate on this matter."

If the problem compromised the implementation, but the project coordinators could not solve it in a timely manner, they would refer it to me or Wes. That meant that Wes and I spent a large proportion of our time working on nasty disputes that had not been solved on the school level or district level.

Trailer 2 housed people who performed data-processing functions, which included analyzing videotapes from sites. We arranged a schedule for each teacher to be regularly taped teaching a whole lesson in reading, math, and language. The site would send each tape to Eugene, where trainers would view it, identify serious problems, and tape a remedy in which the trainer demonstrated how the problematic parts of the lesson should be presented.

There were serious technical problems associated with taping a teacher in a way that would provide the analyst with information about both teacher and children behavior. The first tapes could have been entered in an impressionistic film competition. When the children were responding, the visual might show a close up of the teacher's face, or possibly a close-up of her hand. The typical pattern was for the taper to try to "follow the action." If the teacher was talking, the camera moved to her in the best home-movie, hand-held tradition. The camera would swing toward the children when they responded. Of course, the swing was always late, so that much of the information about the children's responses was lost.

We tried to specify guidelines about where to place the camera and both what to do and what not to do. Apparently, those doing the taping did not share our quest for specific information about the teacher's performance and the children's responses. For them, human interest consistently outweighed a need for information, and we continued to see tapes that focused on a word on a worksheet that a child was erasing followed by a wide-angle shot of the entire classroom.

In the end, we marked the classroom floor to show exactly where the camera tripod was to be placed, and we showed frames of what was to be in picture—the teacher and all the children. The aide who did the taping was to set the tripod on the marks, set up the microphones so they would record both teacher and student responses, focus the camera, make sure that the machine had ample tape, start the machine at the beginning of the period, and turn it off at the end. This procedure yielded tapes that had the information we needed.

The taping provided us with good information about common problems teachers were having. We used a lot of this information to correct specific mistakes and to revise specific parts of our instructional programs. For instance, when the first students started the third level of our reading program, they had serious problems. Unlike the earlier two levels of the program, level 3 focused heavily on comprehension. Although the first lessons of this level did not have challenging syntax or vocabulary, they presented "rules" children were to learn and apply. The tapes of teachers teaching the program showed clearly where the program was weak and needed additional instruction.

The main problem with the taping format was our time. The tape of the teaching was mailed to our shop on the same day it was recorded. We were supposed to review the tape and return it on the same day we received it. In practice, tapes were not mailed on the day they were recorded, and they often sat for several days in our shop before they were analyzed. Several project managers insisted that they needed to see our responses to the teachers' problems before the tape was returned to the teachers. (On a couple of occasions, the trainer who analyzed a tape provided a remedy different from one the project manager had specified. Not good.)

A related problem was that project managers were on the road a great deal of time and often didn't review tapes for more than a week. We tweaked the process a bit so that if the tape analysts observed a severe problem, they would call the project manager and describe the problem. This procedure worked reasonably well.

By 1973, Trailer 2 had an enormous archive of tapes from our sites. They showed hundreds of teachers and aides teaching hundreds of small groups of children. We cut down taping activity in the following years, using taping for special occasions or for documenting specific problems.

The strangest problem we had in the trailers was the relationship between Jessica Daniels and Wes. Jessica was very talented and a good teacher, but did not get along well with Wes. The problem was partly the times and partly the backgrounds of the two. Jessica, who had recently received her Ph.D. from Illinois, was Black. She felt that Wes was a racist, and she was able to find racial allusions in the most innocent things he said.

Wes definitely was not a racist. He hadn't had the kind of contact some of us had with Blacks, but never, in any of the private conversations we had, did he say anything that suggested he was a racist.

Still, he managed to say things that could be misinterpreted or stretched into a misinterpretation, and Jessica pounced on them like cat on mouse. Possibly the most outrageous example occurred following a long dispute about something that Wes had said. I was picking up papers from the trailer, and I could hear them arguing in the back room. Wes was trying to defend his comment. As the volume of the argument increased, Wes said, "But, Jessica, I'm just trying to call a spade a spade."

"That," she shouted, "is exactly what I'm talking about!" She stormed out of the office as Wes, sputtered, "I didn't mean it that way and you know it ..." Wes could not find words to mend the fence, and he was marked the same way as the sultan in the Arabian Nights tale was after he farted during his wedding ceremony. Within less than a day, everybody on the project had heard the story and tittered over it.

I never had any problems with Jessica, but she wasn't happy in Eugene, where there were very few Blacks at the time. After working on the project for three years, Jessica went to Boston College.

COLLEGE TRAINING

One of the major jobs for the summer of 1970 was to set up our teacher training program at the U of O. Our undergraduate program was far different from the traditional teacher-training program in which students attend lectures and take courses that provide some information and an intro-duction to the teacher's traditional role. Only in their senior year would traditional students actually teach—a six-week session in a classroom, monitored occasionally by a graduate student who carried a clipboard, but who knew very little more than the students did.

Our program was designed so that after the first week of school, the undergraduates would spend two hours a day teaching in a classroom. During the part of the day that they were not teaching, they would take courses that explained the content they were teaching (reading, language, math) and the instructional techniques they were using. They would also learn about management practices and some theory of instruction. The program expanded greatly during the school year of 1971–72.

Because our program had such a heavy emphasis on daily teaching, we needed to have local classrooms that were set up so that our student teachers would learn what they had to learn. Carol Morimitsu and Sue Rice inherited the job of finding local schools that could serve as practica for our students. The classrooms not only had to teach Direct Instruction, they had to be managed according to the rules we expected our student teachers to apply. The carrot that we had for schools was that a teacher who had two or more of our trainees did not have to train them. All training would be done by Carol and Sue. So the teacher would have a lighter teaching load and fewer responsibilities.

Our first schools were Park Elementary in Springfield and Whiteaker, one of the two lowest schools in Eugene. Our coordinators and trainers spent a lot of time working in the classroom, grouping and placing children appropriately in the program, and working with the participating teachers on the details of their presentation and routine. In some classrooms we placed three trainees.

The lure our undergraduate program had for candidates was that students who did well were guaranteed employment in Follow Through. Our first cohort of trainees had four promising teachers. One was Linda Youngmayr, who grew up in Eugene. She was taciturn during the first couple of years she was involved with the project, but she was one of the most incisive diagnosticians of instructional problems I had ever seen. She later became quite loquacious but remained a sharp diagnostician. Initially, I got the impression that she lacked a strong commitment to accelerate the performance of children. I observed her conducting an activity that had nothing to do with reading during the reading period. I later told her that she had to think of the children she worked with as her own kids and provide them with uncompromised instruction that would accelerate their performance. Another rule that Linda and many of the other trainees had to learn was that during working hours, there were no favorite children. All of them needed the teacher's best effort.

Linda became an excellent trainer and project manager. She worked with us throughout Follow Through and beyond.

Another first-year trainee was Millie Schrader, who would work with us throughout Follow Through and then become an indomitable principal in California. The student population in her school spoke 13 different languages. Millie provided a model of what could be achieved with this diverse population, but neither the state nor her district paid much attention to her results because what she did was not consistent with the California state and district guidelines, called *standards.*

PARENT TRAINING

The national Follow Through program required all models to have a parent training component. The articles and chapters that we have published about Follow Through tended not to discuss this component; however, we had what I would judge to be the best parent program of all Follow Through models. Millie Schrader was in charge of it. We wrote several manuals for the various grades, K through 3. The manuals had a dual emphasis. The first was to explain the instructional sequences the children were going through and provide parents with specific instructional materials they could use to help their children. We also wrote a 182-page manual, *Parent and Child Home Practice Guide,* which had examples from the preprogram editions of the first level of the reading, math, and language programs, with instructions on how to present the material and work in a reinforcing manner with the child.

The second emphasis of our parent program was to provide parents with some tools they could use to do battle with the district. The publication that created some controversy was *Guidebook for Parent Workers,* a manual that articulated the various functions of our Parent Advisory Committees. It stressed the importance of parents reinforcing the instruction the school provided, but it also spelled out some of the survival techniques the PAC would need to assure that schools were implementing good instruction and that the district was facilitating or at least not interfering with the implementation.

We believed that this emphasis was particularly important because our parent groups supported us and what we were trying to accomplish; however, almost none of our participating districts would have chosen us. For us to survive, we needed informed parent support; that is, support that was directed at school and district administrators and made it clear that the parents had a voice that the district was obliged to recognize.

The *Parent and Home Practice Guide* articulated this function.

In Follow Through parents have both the right and the responsibility to share in deciding the kind of education their children receive. Parents must be given opportunities to take a role in all parts of Follow Through ...These interactions can (1) help parents learn how they can best support and have a say in the program, and (2) help staff become more aware of the needs and goals of the parents...

The manual encouraged parents to visit the classroom.

Usually, parents are welcome at any time. In some schools, the number of visitors wanting to observe experimental programs is high, and it has become necessary to schedule regular visiting times. Check with your principal. If you are not happy with the answer you get, go to a PAC meeting and give your views.

The guide for parent workers echoed the message that the parent group was not a supporter of school policies, like the PTA, but a group that was to have an active voice in the quality of the services the school provided.

The PAC ensures that parents will have a voice in the education of their children, and it serves as a link between the parents and the school. It is the responsibility of the PAC to respond to the needs of the parents, involve them in vital decisions, and attempt to ensure that the school system meets their needs and the needs of their children. The Direct Instruction model supports giving parents a major role in judging the effects of school programs for their children.

Another part of the guide put the issue more bluntly:

A well organized PAC can be responsive to the needs of the parents, involve the parents in decision-making and make every effort to see that the school system meets the needs of the children. Based upon the rights of parents to have control over their children's education, it is the PAC's function to see that the parents responsibly exercise this control.

The orientation of our parent program was not popular with at least one teachers' union and some bureaucrats in Washington. The criticism was that we were referring to the "control" the PAC had, but the PAC was designated to be an "advisory" committee, not an organization with any real power or control. Wes and I responded that a clear assumption of Follow Through's design was that the parent group indeed had control, from the beginning. The PAC, not the school district, selected the model. The school district agreed to permit that model to be implemented and would not impose its prejudices on the kind of instruction the children were to receive. (That's why Follow Through was referred to as an experimental program.) The responsibility of the cooperating district, therefore, was to cooperate with the model and the PAC, which means that the PAC had an obvious power base and had every right to challenge the district when it had information that the district was interfering with the implementation of the model.

We pointed out that our parent program was neither revolutionary nor seditious, but a logical extension of the basic premises of Follow Through.

A bureaucrat in Dayton was particularly adamant that this focus was not in the spirit of cooperation, which for him meant that it questioned the district. I wrote him, "Can you imagine the amount of shit that would hit the fan if a middle class school tried to get away with a tenth of the stuff that goes on in a poverty school? Parents need to know how to butt heads with the school and get what they were told they were supposed to get. Period."

NEW YORK CITY

Our zeal over empowering informed parent groups was tempered by the history of one of the best parent programs—the one in New York City. Our disappointment (and enlightenment) resulted from the district's decision to decentralize and create local school boards. The school boards were empowered largely in the peripheral aspects of the school, not the instruction; however the local boards were able to make decisions about hiring local people and companies to work with or in the school. They hired, fired, and placed aides; they were in charge of the food service, janitorial and other school functions. In other words, they made decisions about millions of dollars.

It didn't take the Black mafia long to figure out that if it controlled the local board, it could make a killing in the local district. That's what happened in the Oceanhill-Brownsville district. The procedures were not very subtle. We had serious problems in the 1971–72 school year. After the summer training, our trained aides were reassigned to other schools. School had started and we didn't have aides in K and 1. We protested and told the district we needed our aides. At first the PAC supported us, but suddenly, it became mute.

One of the PAC members told me the reason for her policy change. Her husband worked for the school, and if she didn't support the district her husband wouldn't have a job. She said, "I don't have any choice."

I set up a meeting with the local superintendent to convince him that we needed action and that without aides in the classroom, children's progress would slow considerably. His office was a modestly refurbished store about a mile from PS 137. I told him and his assistants about the difference an implemented program would make in the lives of kids who lived in that neighborhood. I told him how precious time was and how we couldn't wait months or even days to correct the problem. I told him he had the power to serve kids in a way that nobody else could at this time. By supporting the project he would serve humanity in ways that were not available to many people.

When I was done, I could tell that he was moved, but it took about two weeks to get the problem with the aides straightened out. Part of the reason it took so long was that about a week after I met with the superintendent, he was shot and killed. I never met with his successor.

The work in NYC reconfirmed the realities of big city politics and power. It revealed the foolishness and vulnerability of the local boards. Our school never achieved stardom or became a model of what could have been achieved. It remained an implementation that was "okay," but not outstanding. Over half the teachers were very good and some were awesome, but the school also had at least a couple of teachers and aides who should not have been in the classroom.

Even though the school did not achieve close to its potential, it outperformed all the other Follow Through schools in NYC. Follow-up studies showed that a significantly higher percentage of the kids went to college, and a higher percentage of those who did, stayed in college for more than two years. Unfortunately, the school did not serve to change a single policy or assumption of NYC school administrators. For them, our school in Oceanhill-Brownsville was either a foreign body that was to be removed or something that never existed.

PROVIDENCE

In 1968, Karen Davis and her husband, Gary, enrolled in our graduate program at Illinois. Gary ran our production shop. Karen was already a good teacher who was skilled at reinforcing children. She became better during that year and the next.

As I observed earlier, there are some teachers who are technically precise and very sensitive to the feelings of the kids. I find watching them teach thrilling. Karen is one of those. She could do things very fast, without hurrying. She could control children well, without raising her voice. Several times, we used her as a model. Gary was also an interesting guy: a 6' 5", straight-talking, jovial redhead, who was very smart and taught well.

Gary and Karen didn't come to Oregon with us, but moved to Providence to be on-site project managers hired by the district. At the time, Providence was a spotty implementation, initially involving four schools and later expanding to six. The project was not well coordinated. The local Follow Through director was an older woman who was very supportive of the model; however, she wasn't good at translating her support into actions.

Gary and Karen stayed in Providence for five years. During their Providence tenure, Gary kept a log of the various issues and problems that he and Karen had to address. In 1980, he wrote a long article with a title that pretty much said it all: *DI Follow Through in Providence—the History of a Failure.*

Even though that summary is true, it doesn't mean that failure was absolute, but relatively more extensive than it should have been. There were a lot of teachers and aides who did very well. The schools did relatively better during this period than they did either before or after Follow Through. The failure was created by the lack of convergence between our side and their side. Our side consisted of the project, national Follow Through, and the local parents; their side, the administration. Evidence of convergence would have involved change in the administration, provisions to institutionalize the project, recognition both that the results achieved by the project far exceeded those of comparable schools, and that far greater benefits were realized where the program was implemented with fidelity. The ultimate result of convergence would have occurred if the district used the program in other failed schools.

Gary's article provided ample evidence of how and why convergence and institutionalization never occurred. One caveat to the Providence project outcomes was that although both Gary and Karen were excellent teachers and trainers, they were not prepared for the politics of schools.

The following recap addresses only some of the more critical issues recounted in Gary's article.

During the school year of 1969–70, the schedule used in the schools provided periods of only 20 minutes, which meant it was not possible for many teachers to complete a lesson a day (which would require a 35-minute period). The result was that the children's progress through the programs was about 2/3 the rate they could have achieved.

Only one of the schools had a fulltime principal, which meant that there wasn't adequate time for a principal to follow up on problems. Instead of hiring the specified number of aides, the district hired half the number. Instead of aides, the district hired full-time teachers. Because there were not a sufficient number of teaching personnel for all classrooms, designated teachers (called swing teachers) would work in several classrooms. Gary described the operation.

> Implementation of the swing-teacher concept resembled a circus clown act at Berkshire Street School. At an exact time, teachers would stop teaching, grab their books and rush off to another room for another 20-minute group. As supervisor, I ended up running alongside trying to give them feedback concerning the lesson they had just taught. After the first day, I wore sneakers.

Swing teachers did not provide adequate follow-up because the teachers who checked the children's written work were not the ones who taught the children.

One school (Fogarty) performed better than the others because Karen spent more time in Fogarty. The school also had a fulltime principal who ran an organized school. This is not to say that he supported the program, but it was easier to implement in the school because it was organized.

During 1971, the National Follow Through office pressured the school district to get rid of the swing teachers and hire aides; however, "... the person doing the hiring had not the remotest concept of what we expected aides in the program to do ... Some were functionally illiterate. Some were illiterate." It took weeks before these aides were replaced.

There was a high turnover of aides because the district started aides at what was then a starvation wage—$1.80 an hour. The superintendent would not budge on aide salaries, even after considerable pressure from the Director of Federal Programs.

The Fogarty principal filed a grievance against aides teaching. Two years later, the state board ruled that the teacher had to introduce new concepts and the aides could only "reinforce them." Gary noted,

> By now, we had learned the game. We ignored the state ruling. No administrator in Rhode Island was ever going to go into a classroom and see what was happening. The ruling was quickly and quietly forgotten by all.

The most poorly implemented school in 1971 was Our Lady of Lourdes. During the first part of the year, there were no chairs for the children. Materials were not distributed to teachers on time, and the teaching was atrocious. The schedules of teachers and buses were at odds with the regulations. Buses arrived over 15 minutes late and left at least 15 minutes early. Teachers arrived at school when the children did and left when the children did, so the school effectively lost at least half an hour a day.

Bus drivers in the district followed a plan of "suspending children from the bus" for loud or disorderly conduct. When suspended from the bus, the children were effectively suspended from school and therefore preempted from learning. The disruption was compounded when the children returned to the classroom because they were behind in skills that children in attendance had acquired. So the teacher had to spend time to bring the returning children up to the level required by the current lesson.

Gary quickly corrected this problem. A basic fact of instruction is that behavior problems are very easy to fix, compared to problems of teaching new skills and concepts. Gary implemented a ticket program. He first rehearsed the children on the behavior that was expected on the bus. Then he set up a system for awarding tickets to children who followed the behavioral rules on the bus. Virtually no children were suspended from the bus after this intervention. Gary observed,

> The administrator in charge of transportation was impressed. He told me he had never seen anything like it. (He continued to suspend and harangue kids at other schools because he didn't understand the importance of positive reinforcers.)

An ongoing theme with all city schools is turnover, not only of children, teachers, and aides, but also of administrators, starting with the principals. Our rule for principals is that they need to spend most of their time in classrooms, observing. For these observations to make sense, the principal has to know what the program teaches and what the expectations are for teachers and children.

Gary noted,

> We worked very hard this year to have principals become involved in what was happening in the classroom. We had two workshops designed to explain the program. We designed a principal observation form and worked with them on how to use it. It was never used by most principals. The new Jenkins Street principal responded to it. He observed every teacher and aide in his school. The classroom observations visibly made a difference at Jenkins. Out of the nine principals we had in Providence, he was the only one that was supportive and interested in the program.

In 1972–73, supervision became a serious problem. There was a drop in enrollment of Follow Through students, and money had to be returned to Follow Through. This meant that two supervisors and Karen Davis were assigned to the classroom. The assistant superintendent later interviewed people for the vacant supervisor positions. He selected a Follow Through teacher who was extremely disorganized and poor at teaching, and a non-Follow Through teacher who knew nothing about the program. He rejected Karen Davis. After a considerable amount of pressure from Oregon, Karen was reinstated, and the poor teacher was rejected.

In 1973–74, Gary and Karen attempted to set up some kind of accountability system. The plan was for teachers to make projections, based on the performance level of each group, not just in terms of how many lessons would be presented to the children, but also with respect to their level of mastery. Every six weeks the projections would be compared with student performance on tests that measured the content presented in the program during that time span.

The teachers' union objected to the plan because it involved accountability for children's performance. Gary observed,

> We could keep coded graphs on teacher progress. Teachers could not be identified by name. We could also suggest to teachers that they move the children faster, but could not require them to do so.

At every site, we tried to set up a program that provided college credit for aides, so they could become certified. (Courses were also offered for teachers.) One of our consultants would supervise, critique, and tape the performance of participating aides. We arranged with several participating colleges to accept their daily classroom work and the performance of their students as their "student teacher" work, and as their evidence of teaching proficiency in subject matter areas.

The University of Oregon provided up to 18 quarter credits per year, at a total cost of $16. Typically, a local cooperating college would provide summer classes or night classes that would satisfy the additional credit requirements necessary for certification.

Wes was the prime mover of this program. He devoted a lot of time engineering it through the University of Oregon and coordinating it with local colleges of education.

Providence implemented this certification plan. It led to some very worthy people getting certified (several within two years). During the school year of 1973–4, the district administration showed disdain for our aide-training program. Gary observed,

> There were seven teacher openings in Follow Through. Several excellent aides that just completed their degree work

through the Career Development Education program were eligible for the positions. The former aides had at least three years teaching experience in the classroom ... None of the aides was hired. Ranked above them were five teachers with no experience except student teaching. The rationale given was that the former aides had no experience in the regular classroom and, when Follow Through folded, they wouldn't be able to hack it. The message was clear to the aides—your skills and experience count for nothing.

In June of 1974, all non-tenured elementary teachers in Providence were suspended because of a shortfall in funds. Sixteen Follow Through teachers were in this group. At the summer training session for the next school year, "teachers did not know their schools, grades, or even if they had a job. Most were eventually placed in the program."

Further contributing to the chaos was the closure of two Providence Follow Through schools. The children were disbursed to five schools, which meant that Follow Through now had to work with seven schools, but not with all the children in K through 3. This move created serious logistical and supervisory problems. Two of the new principals expressed great interest in the project but, . . . neither set foot in the classrooms or observed a group. Neither followed up on problems; both took Follow Through aides out of their assigned classrooms and used them for non-Follow Through purposes.

The original Providence director of Follow Through was replaced by one who was sporadically supportive, destructive, and indifferent. In 1975, Gary discovered that two years earlier, the central office had told the director that "he was supporting the program too strongly, and 'outsiders' were dictating too much of what was happening in the classroom." This perspective had led the director to implement some wild plans that crimped the implementation. One was a poorly designed time-allotment schedule. Others were picky attempts to change Follow Through procedures. All resulted in spirited hassles. When the director acquiesced to reason and suspended these plans, he received abuse from his supervisors. So he was caught in the middle of two forces that viewed the schools, teachers, and children from grossly different perspectives. One was passionately concerned with the status quo and providing very little evidence of concern with either the children's welfare or how schools could be improved to serve children better.

Despite the problems, the supervision and performance of the schools improved. Fogarty remained the flagship. It now had some teachers who were in the top one-fourth of good teachers I have observed. They were fun to watch. Even the lower schools were doing a lot better because they had fulltime principals, which led to more order and continuity.

In the spring of 1975, Providence announced a plan to phase out Follow Through. The proposal, which called for funding only second and third graders, was motivated largely by financial considerations. The administration felt that children in K and 1 could be disbursed throughout the system, and that this placement would alleviate the high cost of aides.

One of the last disruptions in Providence involved the directorship of the program. To save funds, the administration replaced our director with the director of early childhood education, who continued to retain early childhood education. The new director turned out to be both more cooperative and competent than the former director, but the former director filed a protest with the state board, pointing out the director of the project had to have principal certification, which the new director did not have. So the original director was reinstated. He resigned in June of that year, and the exiled director was reinstated (even though he still lacked his principal certification).

In 1977, the parents voted to end the program because it had deteriorated greatly. It wasn't that the parent group was not supportive of Follow Through. It was that the PAC knew the district would never accept it as anything but a foreign object that must be transformed and absorbed by the current system. Although the National Follow Through office tried to support a full implementation of Providence schools, the district was now preoccupied with a K–4 program the curriculum department was developing. I have never seen a district-developed program that is better than sophomoric. The one in Providence was no exception. It proved to be a complete failure.

The point is not so much that Providence didn't institutionalize Direct Instruction and didn't learn anything from the amazing performance achieved in Fogarty and some classrooms in the other schools. The point isn't that there was no fact-finding, no perspective that the district was a thorough failure and needed serious organizational change. The point is that Providence didn't respond to Follow Through as a way of serving low-performing kids because it couldn't. It was (and still may be) a non-responsive, non-functional operation that does what it does for one reason: That's what it does. Providence had neither the organization nor the accountability standards that would force administrators to go into classrooms, look at children, look at data, and follow a simple scientific mandate that if something shows better results, adopt it, institutionalize it, monitor it to assure quality control, and nurture the hell out of it.

In the last two years of the project, the district hired a new superintendent, who had received his Ph.D. at Harvard. Wes and I met with him shortly after he had been installed. His expressed philosophy focused on the strengths of children of poverty, not their deficiencies. He indicated that he didn't agree with the Direct Instruction focus. He was the primary force behind the Curriculum Department's development of the abortive K–4 program that would never be field tested before it was installed. After an hour of trying to convince him to look at the data about what was happening in Providence, Wes and I left the meeting with the impression that we had met with somebody less informed of what the children needed than just about any 16-year-old kid in the neighborhoods we serviced.

I have some fond memories of Providence, but they are bittersweet because the bottom line was that the program wasn't implemented. One fond memory was eating the food served at the Fogarty cafeteria. It was not only the best of any school cafeteria I had frequented; the Italian dishes, particularly, were as good as those at the finest restaurants. When I went to Providence, I tried to fudge my schedule so I would be at or near Fogarty when the noon whistle blew.

Another positive incident occurred at a cocktail party Wes and I attended during the third year of the implementation. The senior reading teacher and guru in one of our schools instigated an argument with me about reading— what it was, and how best to teach it. In the best cocktail-party style, we were polite, and the small group surrounding us was intent. The teacher's premise was that the creativeness of teachers should not be trammeled by a lockstep program like DI. She was well read, and quoted the literature with flourish. After the discussion went on for possibly ten minutes, one of our first-year teachers from the same school interrupted and ended the argument. She said,

> Angie, you know more about reading than I'll ever know. You know linguistics and all those theories I don't understand. All I know how to do is follow the program. I do what it tells me to do in black type, and I say what it tells me to say in red type. But Angie, my kids read better than your kids, and you know it.

SOUTH DAKOTA

The administrations of Providence and Todd County, South Dakota were different in many ways but curiously similar in others. The trappings and how people were arranged were different, but the functions were the same. In other words, Todd County had the same kind of implementation problems we experienced in Providence. In South Dakota, there were two projects. One was the Todd County School District. The other was the Rosebud Tribe CAP (Community Action Program.) The CAP was a parent group. The difference in directorship did not create black-white contrasts between the two agencies, but they certainly created clear differences. The Rosebud parent group supported the project to the end; in Todd County, there was no convergence, no support from the parent group, and no attempts to institutionalize the project. Many decisions in Todd County seemed to be motivated by the rule, "Make no waves with teachers or the BIA."

According to a summary written by our project manager about the progress and problems of our schools in the 1969–1970 school year, Todd County had very bad teaching at He Dog. Some of the aides couldn't read. There were no screening procedures for the hiring of aides. There was a big move on the part of some parents to get rid of the program. We'd been through various parent rebellions and, to the best of my knowledge, every one of them had been instigated by the administration. In this case, the BIA engaged in an active lobbying effort to get rid of the program.

The summary indicated that in Rosebud CAP schools during 1970–71, "There was virtually no director. Norris School had bad teaching. The principal was also bad. Two teachers were to be fired next year." We argued that if these teachers are failing this year, the remedy should occur this year.

The report indicated that in another school, "Next year, over 50 percent of the staff will be new or are presently having serious problems teaching."

In 1974–75,

> There was essentially no director. Because of this there was continual confusion about materials—where they were to be sent, who got what, and so on. A morale problem developed among teachers and aides because there was nothing tying them together, helping them solve problems, except our consultants.

At one school, "High absenteeism among aides developed. No consequences for being absent were specified and many teaching days were lost." One of our consultants observed, "In defense of absent aides, some who worked at He Dog had to walk 10–12 miles to school. Snow storms were a big problem."

The last of our project managers to work in South Dakota, Randy Sprick, wrote the following summary in 1976:

> Rosebud CAP has maintained a fairly high number of

consulting days and has continued to implement the program well.

St. Francis has had a fair number of days but weak local supervision and weak administration. The result is a questionable implementation.

Todd County has operated with very few consulting days the last couple of years. The relationship between Oregon and the local administration has not been good, and the program has suffered.

The reason Todd County and St. Francis received fewer consulting days was not that we were lax in providing them, but that the administrators refused them. The administration also tried to implement techniques that could not work. In 1971–72, Todd County received 360 consulting days. In 1975–76, Todd County had only 12 consulting days. It probably needed five times that number. Randy wrote:

The major problem was that Todd County staff did not want Susie or I to work directly with teachers. We felt that this was unreasonable and that our jobs dictated that we would be able to work directly with teachers in the classroom.

It would be unfair to characterize the administration as being the only cause of Todd County's administrative stance. Sometimes our consultants and our communication created problems. The director of the Follow Through program in Todd County was probably not to blame because he was in the same position as our directors in Providence—pressured by our project to do one thing and by the administration above him to do another.

Randy is very talented, direct, and at the same time, diplomatic. Years later I told him I believed that if he had been project manager of the site from the beginning, we might have been able to solve some of the problems in Todd County.

He told me that he appreciated the vote of confidence but that I was giving him more credit than he deserved. He said, "That administration was very intractable."

He was right. We had assigned good people to the site. They worked hard and had credibility, but the battle line was drawn from the beginning and it remained uncompromised at the end, which came in Rosebud CAP in 1976. The parent group voted to terminate the Follow Through project. They still supported our goals and efforts, but they recognized that the program was so poorly implemented that its continuation would be a travesty.

Like the other sites, however, our South Dakota schools outperformed comparable schools.

GRAND RAPIDS

Our work with schools in Follow Through raised a serious moral question: "How much do you compromise the fidelity of an implementation?" If the project is doing poorly because it is purposely not being implemented but is working with some children, do you continue because you're serving those children? Even if it's only a third of the 300 students in a school, you would serve 100 children with a quality of instruction that would not be provided if you dropped the project.

The problem with this solution is that you are not serving 200 children well. Compounding this problem is the fact that if you're not doing well, your potential for serving other schools diminishes. The reason is that if there is no data that your approach works well, there's no very compelling reason for other schools to adopt the practices. In the context of Follow Through, the model with the best data would be designated the winner. The only way we could hope to win was to implement with fidelity. Even if we did well in other sites, critics would point to the "low performing" school and conclude that DI did not work well with some school populations.

We had to face this dilemma with several schools and districts during Follow Through. The ultimate challenge was Grand Rapids, Michigan. Initially, it had an administration that supported the project, and although it had growing pains during the first two years, the project was on schedule to do well and have at least two model schools.

In 1972, Grand Rapids Follow Through got a new director, a woman with the reputation of being a mover and shaker. Shortly after she assumed leadership of the project, our project manager and consultants reported serious changes in schedules and procedures. Some schools were using instructional material that greatly interfered with the skill development of our program. It wasn't long before the list of unsolved problems was so long that the implementation was a sham.

The site was being managed through National Follow Through by Susan Green, a smart, dedicated young woman who had a passionate interest in seeing to it that her sites were well implemented. She was one of the bright spots in the often-bleak South Dakota landscape. She observed that the program worked where it had been implemented and did everything she could to implement the schools better. She never stopped doing battle with the intractable administration. Susan later traded sites with other facilitators so she could work exclusively with DI implementations, including Grand Rapids.

After Wes called her about the director problem in Grand Rapids, she made several calls and tried to work out a resolution, but the director was firm in her presumption that she knew what was best for the children, and she would act accordingly.

When Susan told Wes and me about the director's stance, I said, "We'll have to drop the project."

She said, "Oh, no, you can't do that. Think of the kids you will let down if you quit."

I told her that I felt for the kids, but I also felt for all those kids who could be served if our model won the Follow Through horse race. I said, "If we do poorly in Grand Rapids, we'll be providing educators with evidence they'll use to show that DI doesn't work."

Susan didn't budge. "You can't quit."

Several days and phone calls later, Wes told me that Susan had set up a meeting in Grand Rapids, where we would present the issues to the parent group. It would be like a debate, with the parent group making the decision about the direction the project should take.

Black Power was in full swing in Grand Rapids. The meeting was scheduled for 7 o'clock in a packed assembly hall at one of the larger schools. Susan moderated the meeting. Those who were to present sat on the stage. When Susan introduced Wes and me, the crowd booed. When she tried to articulate what some of the problems were with the new director's stance, the crowd booed. When the director was introduced, the crowd cheered. The first speaker was a Black minister who gave a passionate endorsement of the director. Following were endorsements from several teachers and a statement of unquestioned support from the director of the PAC, who looked at me and Wes during his speech and said, "You should get down on your knees and thank God for having Lola as the director of your Follow Through project." Great cheers.

During the meeting I turned to Wes and said, "I don't think we have any choice."

He said, "Neither do I."

After a couple of abortive efforts by Susan to focus the issues, I presented. There was a small smattering of applause mixed with grumbles. My message took no more than a couple of minutes. I said, "We came to Grand Rapids to support the parent group. The PAC selected our program and we promised that we would implement that program. Just as we were committed to the parent group then, we are committed to it now. If the parents no longer want their kids in our program, we will honor that mandate. This meeting makes it clear that the parent group wants to go in another direction, so we will resign as sponsors of the program." Grumbles.

Susan said, "Wait. That doesn't have to happen. I believe we can work something out."

I said, "We will support what the parents want to do."

That was it. We dropped the site. We kissed off the hundreds of hours we had spent working, the hundreds of kids we knew would go down the drain. We did this with a sense of being guided by cold rationality, but it hurt. After the meeting Susan, Wes, and I had a couple of beers at our hotel. Susan cried. She said, "It was working. Isn't there something we can do?"

I said, "No, I don't think so." I tried to keep my voice from cracking as I got flashes of some of the good teachers, the children, and the brutality of our decision.

YEOMEN SITES

A few of our sites achieved some degree of institutionalization, not on the level of regulations, job descriptions and established practices, but on the level of people. So long as key figures remained active, the project performed well. Typically, when the key people (yeoman types) left, the performance of students regressed.

Tupelo, Mississippi was one of the sites that remained fairly strong throughout Follow Through and even beyond. Part of the reason was that it had a strong director, Juliet Borden, who worked hard and attended to details compulsively. She was positive, active, and result-oriented. One of the program's star teachers, Julie Green, was also instrumental in keeping the project on an even keel. She was very attractive and technically solid. After the first year of Follow Through, Wes went to Tupelo far more than I did. The reason was that he was in love with Julie. In 1972, he married her and she moved to Oregon but continued to work with the district. The project remained active and fairly productive until the schools were forced to integrate. Juliet Borden left and the performance of the Black children sank back to baseline.

Our schools in Dayton, Ohio were pretty good. One reason was that the district had hired one of our students, Gail Rowe, to serve as the on-site supervisor. Gail was committed and hard working. Also, the Follow Through director, Willetta Weatherford, endorsed DI and did what she could to implement it. Although she worked closely with Gail, the higher administration was "intractable" and didn't actually pay much attention to their suggestions or to the gains that were occurring in the schools.

In the fourth year of the implementation, the administration wanted to adopt a format for teaching math that was less sophisticated than the card game *War*. I sat through two meetings on this proposal, which was finally rejected. Like in other districts, however, so long as Willetta and Gail supported the project, it remained in place. When they left, the project tended to fold.

Flint, Michigan had a profile similar to Dayton's. The project had two very talented classroom supervisors, Arzetta Johnson and Georgina Hosmer. They were quite different from each other in the way they taught and supervised. One tended to be curt and strict; the other approachable and very accommodating. Both were thorough and hard working, and both taught very well. They trained some of the better teachers I have seen.

Flint remained active and fairly well implemented for more than ten years. Then, when the supervisors left, the performance of the schools slid back to what it had been before Follow Through. Even though Flint, Dayton, and Tupelo had good people in the Follow Through project, they stumbled because they could not get the basic procedures in place, such as ordering material, establishing and following schedules, hiring literate aides, getting rid of teachers who obviously were not following the program specifications, and providing monitoring and training.

East St. Louis was another Yeoman site that had a strong leader and some of the best teachers I have seen. Because of the work I had done with at-risk high school students from East St. Louis, I was particularly interested in working with the Follow Through children. I compared the performance of the Follow Through children with that of students in Upward Bound on things like following complicated directions and being able to draw implications from what they read. Interestingly, the third level of the reading program presented some of the tasks that had challenged the high school students, but the children in Follow Through had fewer problems with the material.

For some reasons, the East St. Louis Follow Through project had a high percentage of teachers who thoroughly understood teaching to mastery.

I went to East St. Louis quite a few times with the project manager, Jean Osborn. The city, which is in Illinois, lost most of its industry and most of its White population in the late '50s. In the '60s, the city had the second-highest violent crime rate of any city its size. During the early Black Power movement, rioters devastated the entire downtown area. It remained rubble during the period we worked there.

The city had one legitimate hotel, the Holiday Inn. The last time I stayed there somebody was intermittently firing 30.06 rifle bullets through the building, which did not promote sound sleeping. There were no reports of people being injured or killed that night, but I was pretty punchy the next day.

On a later occasion, Jean had a room on the first floor, facing a patio. In the middle of the night an intruder picked up a piece of patio furniture and crashed it against the glass sliding door of the unit two doors from Jean's. The thief walked in, took the guest's valuables, cautioned him not get out of bed or call for help, and left, via the defunct patio door.

During the third year of Follow Through, we worked hard with all our sites on teaching to mastery. East St. Louis needed far less work than the other sites because most teachers there had an intuitive grasp of why teaching to mastery was essential. They understood that you have to make sure students know something if you're later going to build on it.

Doug Carnine and I made a tape of second graders in East St. Louis. The children were in the classroom of one of the coaches, Mrs. Beard. She was not flashy and not effusive in her reinforcement. She demanded near perfect performance from her students, but they knew that they could meet her expectations.

For the demonstration we taped, I worked with the second highest math group, the orange group, as the other children in the classroom observed the teaching from their desks. The idea the demonstration was supposed to convey was that if children have learned to mastery, they have learned how to learn, so it is possible to skip ahead in the program and teach them something that is completely new and requires far more learning than it would if it were presented as part of the program sequence.

I skipped ahead in the program to the introduction of carrying or regrouping for addition problems like 35 + 48.

Before teaching the orange group the operation, I pointed out to the other children in the class that the top group, the purples, had not yet reached this part of the program. The orange group learned very fast, and it was evident that they had strong strategies for retaining new material. It was also obvious that Mrs. Beard had taught them to mastery on everything the program introduced. After I demonstrated the carrying procedure with a couple of problems, I took the orange group through three problems a step at a time, with the children telling me what to do next. From time to time, I waved goodbye to the purple group and said something like, "Goodbye, purples. The orange group has just passed you up." The purples frowned and watched intently.

The teaching took about 10 minutes. After the orange group worked two more problems with very little structure, I said to Doug, "They've got it."

Doug said, "Shouldn't we test them?"

We did. Doug and I wrote a unique problem for each member of the group (a problem they had never seen during the training and one different from those presented to the other children). Students worked the problems with no assistance. Every member of the group performed perfectly.

I said to the rest of the class, "Are they impressive or what?"

A boy in the purple group said, "Well, we could work those problems, too."

I said, "How could you do that? You weren't even taught how to do it."

"We watched," a girl said. "We can do it."

A kid from the red group (the lowest group) said, "We can do it, too."

"Get out of here," I said. "You can't do those problems."

The children disagreed and insisted that we should test them.

Doug said, "Raise your hand if you think you can work those problems." All students in the purple group and the red group raised their hands.

The room had chalkboards on the front and the door side of the room. We wrote a unique problem for every student. After they completed their work, they stood next to their work. Every student but one did it correctly. Mrs. Beard said nothing, but walked over to the student whose work was wrong and stood next to him. He looked at her, quickly looked at the problem, spotted the calculation error, and fixed it. Mrs. Beard nodded without saying anything. Doug said, "All 28 of you got the right answer. Give yourself a hand." They clapped vigorously and wore broad smiles. Even Mrs. Beard clapped a few times but without smiling. A couple of the children in the purple group threw kisses to the children in the orange group and said, "Goodbye, orange group."

Even the lowest performers in that classroom had been changed by the excellent teaching they had received. Their strategies were far different from most of the Upward Bound high school students. The older students had an amorphous approach to learning; those in Mrs. Beard's classroom had a very precise way of pinpointing what was to be learned and learning it. Mrs. Beard, and the teacher in grade 1 had done a superb job with these children. When I later told that to Mrs. Beard, she nodded and said, "Thank you." Without smiling.

The East St. Louis site was good because the director, Geraldine Jenkins, who was soft-spoken but had an iron will, insisted on staffing the project with good teachers. Geraldine's sister, Ruby Hudson, was possibly the strongest of the group and the strongest I've ever seen. Whenever I watched her, I couldn't help but think how lucky those kids were to have such an awesome teacher. I would have loved to have had her as my first-grade teacher. I wanted to get a tape of her teaching, and asked her several times, but she didn't want to be taped.

Despite all the good aspects of the program, there were continuing problems. One was that although the teachers were generally good at teaching to mastery, some progressed through the program at an unnecessarily slow rate. In a 1977 summary, Jean Osborn listed the implementation problems.

1. The site initially had no kindergarten. In 1972 a half-day kindergarten was installed, but not all children went to it, which meant there were groups of beginning readers in first grade and groups of continuing students.

2. The teaching in kindergarten was weak and children were not at mastery on parts of the program they had covered.

3. Some classrooms had over 35 children.

4. Garfield school burned to the ground in January. The classrooms were moved to another neighborhood school, but a high number of teaching days were lost.

5. One of the schools had very low rates of progress through the program (far below projections).

6. Children in various schools had serious problems with the beginning parts of Reading 3, largely because they were not brought to a high level of mastery at the end of Reading 2.

7. The model school that had been set up as a training-dissemination center (Robinson School) was not very useful because "It is very difficult to get teachers out of one building and into another, and I would say that the model classroom is not truly functional for East St. Louis."

8. Former Follow Through students in grade 4 and above were not placed in programs that built on their skills, and they were not showing the kind of gains they had achieved in Follow Through. Part of the problem was the extremely high turnover rate of students and the small percentage that completed the K–3 sequence. (Most completed a 1–3 sequence.)

Jean noted some good news. "In Dunbar School there are three Follow Through teachers who have become teachers in the fourth through sixth grade." Not only did their students make good progress. The three teachers agreed that the best students they had, by far, were the ones who had gone through the Follow Through program.

At least one famous person went through the East St. Louis Follow Through program—Jackie Joiner-Kersey, renowned track star. She was a very good, determined student.

I generally did not feel threatened by the neighborhoods we served. Sometimes, working late in Brooklyn was a problem. More than one taxi driver at the airport refused to take us to our school. Furthermore, the only taxis we could rely on to take us from Brooklyn were gypsy cabs, often run-down heaps that gave the impression they weren't going to make it. Taking the subway to Manhattan late at night was sometimes intimidating, depending on who was on the train.

Some neighborhoods in East St. Louis were intimidating. One time, Geraldine Jenkins wanted to meet with Jean and me at the end of the school day. She gave us the address of the meeting place, which was close to the school where we were working. The place was a corner bar, and there were lots of rough looking men in and in front of that bar, some decorated with prison tattoos and scars. As Jean and I waited on the corner for Geraldine, I felt outrageously White and out of place, even though none of the men paid much attention to us. When Geraldine showed up, we went inside, sat in a booth and ordered something to drink. The place was crowded and loud, but not raucous. I made the observation that this seemed to be a pretty tough place.

Geraldine shook her head and smiled. "Ziggy," she said, "do you have a reason for being here?"

"Yeah, I'm meeting you here."

"You know that as a fact?"

"Yes."

"Well so do they. As long as you have a reason for being here, you have nothing to worry about."

Our only school in DC (Nickles Avenue) had some excellent teachers and, overall, it outperformed all other schools in DC that served disadvantaged children. But it relied on a central administration that was remote, obtrusive, and absolutely disorganized. One reason was that the school was in DC and was, therefore, governed by Congress. The result was not simply that one department didn't know what kind of input another department was giving the schools. It was that one department sometimes didn't know that the other department existed. Hiring and assigning aides was a continuous problem. So was scheduling even routine functions. During one year, some material that was needed at the beginning of the school year was not ordered until the following April.

The school never completely bought into the model. In a 1975 report, the director commented, "We have always fought the way they structure our whole day. We feel kids in this community need other things along with Direct Instruction."

Other comments were fashioned from the theme that only people who live in the community understand what their children need. The site was reluctant to look at the data, which showed good performance gains were achieved when schools followed the schedules the model required.

Some of the gripes the teachers and the director had about us were quite reasonable. We made mistakes there, and we tried to learn from them. We tried to streamline the summer training program, but it didn't work, and we went back to the old plan. The director commented, "I feel this entire program suffered when Oregon stopped having workshops for everybody. I'm glad they're starting them again."

One complaint the director had was that I didn't go to the site often enough. That was probably true. On several occasions, I wanted to go to the site after a meeting in DC, but either the meeting ran late or something else took precedence over the school visit. I disliked that situation because I felt the school was the most important business we had in DC, but time was a serious problem. In most cases, I couldn't afford to spend another night in DC, so if I couldn't cram the school visit in before catching the last flight that could get me home, I didn't go to the school.

One event that kept me from going to the school was a meeting that SRA had scheduled at the new IBM facility in DC. (Our publisher, SRA, was a subsidiary of IBM.) On that day, we met with National Follow Through until almost three. Then we were scheduled to go to the IBM facility, where I was to give a two-hour workshop on Direct Instruction.

I am very compulsive about being on time. We were almost running late that day, which meant that I was getting edgy. An SRA manager picked us up at the Follow Through office and drove us to the new facility. We hurried into the lobby, where we were met by two IBM executives. One of the men who greeted us was a VP. I don't remember his name, but I clearly remember what he said after his name. It was something like "Greg Tiller, IBM."

As we shook hands, I said, "Zig Engelmann. So do I, but I don't advertise." As soon as I said it, I knew I shouldn't have, but it just came out. I told him I was just joking, and he chuckled politely, but my wise crack was in bad taste. IBM had been very gracious to let SRA use its facility.

THE PAIN OF TRAVELING

I think the amount of travel people on our project did drove some of us a little crazy or crazier. Back when I had been in advertising, I loved to travel. I loved it all, going to the restaurants and ordering strip sirloin, staying in a hotel, even going to the meetings. It was a nice change from the daily grind. In Follow Through, however, travel was the daily grind, and by the third year of Follow Through, I hated every part of it, from those pretentious restaurants that had the same tired menu and the same lousy service to the damned hotels, with the heating units that defy attempts to regulate them and the showers that surprise you with abrupt changes in water temperature. In the evening, you're not only lonely, but too tired to work and too tired of being around people to do anything social.

For me, the routine for going to DC involved finishing up the day's work, spending a few hours with Therese and the kids, driving 120 miles from Eugene to Portland, departing at midnight for DC, arriving around 7 a.m., spending most of the day in meetings that started at 8:30 or 9, and trying to get home that night.

The most hideous part of a trip was a delay on the way home. Delays on the way out often created problems, but those on the way home destroyed the dream of what you wanted to do more than anything else at the time— go home. Spending another night away from home was torture, not only psychologically but productively. You'd have to do things to make up for at least some details of the lost day.

Different people in our group had different strategies for getting home. Mine was: "Get as close to home as you can." If the closest place is Denver, go to Denver. Once there, you can probably get a flight to Seattle or Salt Lake City. Once there, you can probably get to Portland. And once there, you're as good as home. Rent a car; drive like the wind; and you're home in an hour and a half.

Once, when the project was still in Illinois, Jean and I were trying to get home from San Antonio. O'Hare was closed, but there were rumors that it would open at some undisclosed time referred to as "soon." Jean was leaning toward waiting, but she was concerned because she was hosting a social function at her house later in the afternoon. I applied the get-as-close-to-home-as-you-can rule, and said, "What the hell. Let's fly to St. Louis, rent a shit box and drive to Champaign." We did that. We flew to St. Louis and drove like the wind. (There were no highway speed limits in Illinois.) In a little more than two hours, we had completed the 180-mile trip (mostly on two lane roads—no freeways). Jean walked up her front step only a few minutes after the party had started.

In her role as faculty wife of a mathematician and classical musician, Jean followed rules of decorum different from those on the project. Specifically, she didn't swear when she was wearing her faculty-wife hat (which she wore graciously and unpretentiously). When she arrived home she was still somewhat excited from the ride. As she related the story about the harrowing trip home, she told her guests, "I wasn't sure what to do in San Antonio, but Ziggy said, 'Oh, what the hell. Let's fly to St. Louis and rent a shit box.'" Whoops.

Carol Morimitsu held the record for the worst sequence of delays. She was trying to get from Grand Rapids to Racine in the middle of the winter. It took her three days. She spent most of the time in Chicago or Indianapolis, back and forth. The person who may have had the best record of getting home on time was Linda Youngmayr. She made it every time. I asked her how she did that. She said, "I don't want to tell you." After a few "Oh, c'mons," she said, "Okay, I cry."

"What do you mean cry?"

"I mean make a scene, wail and sob loudly, as I relate all the reasons why I absolutely have to get home tonight. The agent gets his supervisor, and sometimes the supervisor's supervisor, but they always manage to find a seat for me on a plane that gets me home."

"How many times have you done that?"

She said, "I'm not telling." And she never did.

To insulate myself from the realities of travel, I worked, both in the airports and on the planes. At the time, people didn't type on planes. I did. I had an Olivetti super thin portable. As soon as I hit the terminal, I found a place to start working. (In major cities, I went to the United 100,000 Mile Club, of which I was a member.) On the plane I would start typing as soon as our tray tables no longer had to be in the upright and locked position. I always sat on the aisle. I would ask the person in front of me if it would be disturbing for me to type. In about 99 percent of the cases, they'd give permission. I never asked permission from the person next to me because my typing wasn't going to rattle that person's seat. I typed faster then than I do now. I could probably do over 100 words a minute, with many mistakes. And I composed relatively fast. On several legs from Portland to NYC or DC, I wrote more than 15 pages.

In addition to trying to get as much productive work done as I could, I tried to be efficient. Even if I was going to be gone for a week, I never took more than two pieces of luggage, the typewriter and a regular-size carry-on. I never checked any bags because the track record of the airlines was probably almost as bad then as it is now, and even if there were no screw-ups, waiting around in a baggage area was not my idea of a good use of time. By Friday, I was still wearing the same pair of pants I wore on Monday, but I had clean shorts, socks, and shirt. It worked.

One of the worst experiences I had trying to get home occurred in DC, following a winter snowstorm. The airport had been closed for over 24 hours, but opened around noon on the day I was to return home. My flight was scheduled to leave around 4 o'clock and arrive in Chicago around the same time. National Airport was a terrible scene. People were everywhere. Every chair was occupied, and there were hundreds of people on the floor, sleeping, reading, snacking, and waiting. In some places I had to walk around them or step over them. I felt sorry for them, but I also felt a little smug because I had a confirmed reservation. All I had to do was present my ticket at the counter, and I would be out of this war zone.

The ticket agent blasted that dream. He looked at my ticket and said, "This flight left an hour and a half ago."

I presented my itinerary to show him he was wrong. But he wasn't. The time of the flight had changed, the flight had already left, and my only option was to get on the waiting list. I called my travel agent to see what he could do. Nothing.

There was another option. If I could get to New York in a couple of hours, I would be able to catch a flight to Chicago and make my connection. I called the train station. No seats available until the following afternoon.

I went to the commuter flight area. Passengers didn't need reservations for flights to New York. When I first saw the double line of people outside the area, I thought, "There is no way that this is a line for people hoping to go to New York." The line looked to be over two blocks long. I asked a man in line, "Where are you going?"

"New York, if I can hold out that long." I found this situation desperate. It seemed that Washington was about as close to home as I could get, unless I did something that was on the low-budget side. I didn't think it would work for me to go to a ticket agent and cry. So, I thought of a desperate plan, bought a couple of colas, walked to near the front of the line, until I saw a guy that looked mellow. I handed him a cola and said in conversational voice, "Thanks for saving my place." Under my breath, I said, "Don't blow my cover. I've got to get home." I wasn't proud of myself. But I felt as if I would explode if I had to camp out in that airport. I offered to pay for my benefactor's fare to New York, but he said the cola was payment enough.

The plane left on time and arrived on time at the commuter terminal at La Guardia. I grabbed my bag and typewriter and ran to the main terminal (which was pretty far away). I made it in time to catch a plane to Chicago and make a connection to Portland. I made it all the way home that night. (By now, Oregon definitely felt like home).

THE MODEL CLASSROOM

I have stated a couple of times that watching an excellent teacher at work is thrilling. It's like watching any highly skilled person do something that requires considerable skill and practice—the skilled bricklayer, the circus acrobat, the hibachi chef, the star basketball player, the concert pianist. They make it look easy, but you know it isn't. In fact, the more you know about how to do it, the more you appreciate the skill of the expert. The star teacher in the early grades controls details of her interactions in a show she puts on every school day—not simply during the small-group instruction but from the moment the children enter the classroom. Everything is engineered to be productive.

Consider a scene in one of the star classrooms in Providence. It takes place in kindergarten during January.

As we walk into the classroom, the children are beginning to arrive, small knots of very small children, seemingly buried under coats and hoods, dragging boots and galoshes.

A teacher and two aides greet each child at the door. Each adult asks a series of questions. "Hello, young lady. What's your first name?"

"Angela."

"And what's your last name?"

"Johnson."

"Well, Angela Johnson, do you know your address?"

"Eighteen-forty-six Fulton."

"Good remembering, Angela. And do you remember which group you're in?"

"Yellow group." (The yellow group is the lowest group.)

"Good." The aide pats the youngster on her shoulder. "Are you smart?"

"Yeah, I smart."

"You sure are. Go hang up your coat and see if you can do that hard writing sheet on your desk."

The children take their seats and carefully copy four rows of letters, then copy the word "it". The teacher and the aides circulate from child to child, asking different questions:

"What's this sound?"

"*Ssss.*"

"Good. Do you know that word you're going to copy? ... Sound it out."

"*iiit...It.*"

"Good reading the word *it*. Remember to say that word to yourself when you write it."

As soon as the bell rings, the teacher says, "Everybody, you can finish your worksheet later. It's time for our morning warm-up. So get those thinking engines ready to go. The blue group is ready ... so is the yellow group."

The aides are positioned on each side of the room. The teacher walks to the chalkboard. "We're going to start with the days of the week. Tell me what day it is today ... Get ready."

The teacher claps. As she does, nearly all of the children respond, "Tuesday."

"Good. Once more, what day is it today?" The teacher claps. Everybody responds.

"Thinking big. What day was it yesterday?" Clap.

"Monday."

"Yes, yesterday was Monday, so what day is it today?" Clap.

"Tuesday."

"And what day will tomorrow be?" Clap.

"Wednesday."

"You're terrific." The teacher smiles. About half of the children smile broadly. Some of the others are wearing semi smiles.

"Everybody, say the days of the week ... Get ready." The teacher claps once. In unison, the children recite: "Monday, Tuesday, Wednesday, Thursday, Friday, Saturday, Sunday."

"Blue group only. Say the days of the week ... Get ready."

The blue group names the days. The task is repeated with the red group and the yellow group. The teacher says, "I'm not sure who did the best job. Everybody looked pretty good."

One of the aides points to a boy in the front row. Her signal indicates that he hadn't responded appropriately on the last task. "Let's try Rodney. See if he can say all the days in the week. Do it, Rodney."

He did it. The teacher says. "Let's give him a hand."

The review continues. The children indicate the number of days in a week and the number of months in a year. Some children mix up the responses to these two questions. The teacher repeats the two items, mixing up the order of the tasks and presenting them to all the girls, all the boys, the children in the yellow group, and everybody.

"I think you've got it now, but if you don't, ask Carol. She does such a good job on those questions. She really knows the answers."

"So do I," one child and then another observed.

"Let's see. This is the last time. Everybody, tell me how many months in a year. Remember, *months* in a year ..." A long pause follows before the teacher says, "Get ready ..." and claps. Every child answers. One of the aides smiles and says, "They've got it."

"Let's see you name the months of the year. Get ready ..."

Some children have trouble with October and November. "My turn," the teacher says. "SepTEMBER, OcTOBER, NoVEMBER, DeCEMBER. My turn once more." The teacher repeats the four names then directs the children to do it with her.

"All by yourselves, starting with SepTEMBER. Get ready ..." Clap.

"From the beginning, say all the months of the year. Get ready ..." Clap. This time, all but one girl performs. One of the aides points to the girl and says quietly, "I'll get her during the worksheet period."

The large group-work ends with the awarding of points. All children receive two points.

For the next activity, each group goes to a specific area of the classroom, one for reading, one for math, and one for language. Each area has a divider on each side, so that it is somewhat shielded from the noise created by children in the other areas. The children sit in a semi-circle with their backs to the classroom. The teacher faces them, sitting on a small chair.

During the first period, the teacher works with the yellow group, which consist of five children. As the teacher presents reading to this group, each aide works with one of the other groups. At the end of the 35-minute period, the groups switch places, the teacher now works with the red group, and the yellow group goes to the arithmetic area.

"Today, we do Lesson 56," the teacher explains as she holds up the presentation book so that the children can see the display on the first page of the lesson. The display consists of different "sounds": **th, ī, c, o, d, i, r** and **ē.** "This is a treat," the teacher says, "because Tom gets to be the teacher. You're on, Tom." As the teacher positions Tom so that the members of the group can see the book, she explains. "Tom is going to touch the sounds. When he touches a sound, you say *it*."

Tom glances at the teacher, points to the "*th*" and touches it. The children respond, "*thththth*," (as in *the*, not *thing*.)

"Yes, *thththth*," says the teacher.

Tom glances at the children, points to the next symbol (t) and touches it. Three children say the sound. One boy responds late.

"Good," the teacher says.

Tom presents all the sounds. The response of the group is weak on *i* and *o*. After Tom presents the last sound the teacher says, "Tom, you're quite a teacher. That was good." She gives him a quick tickle on the ribs and he squirms and smiles.

"Let's do some of those sounds one more time." Moving fast, the teacher points to *t*. Everybody, think big now ... Get ready." The teacher touches under the sound and the children say the sound. Next, she presents the sounds *o* and *i*. Finally, she calls on different children, and each child identifies two or three sounds.

"Good job on that page. Close your eyes and don't look."

The children close their eyes and the teacher quickly turns the page. The display on the next page is another group of sounds. "Open your eyes. I'll cross out the sounds on this page when you can tell me every sound. Remember, when I touch it, you say it."

The children identify the first six sounds without error. The teacher covers the page with an acetate sheet. She says, "This time I'll cross out each sound when you tell me what it is." The teacher points to the first sound and pauses. "Get ready ..."

She touches under the first letter as the children say, "*ēēē*." The teacher quickly crosses out the letter and says, "Goodbye, $\bar{e}\bar{e}\bar{e}$." Two of the children say, "Goodbye, $\bar{e}\bar{e}\bar{e}$" with the teacher. Another waves goodbye.

By the time the last sound has been crossed out, five minutes of the period have elapsed. The teacher instructs the children to close their eyes as she turns the page. The display consists of a column of words: *fit, on, at, mat, nat.*

fit
on
at
mat
nat

The teacher instructs the children to open their eyes. She then explains, "Remember, if you can do all the words on this page, everybody gets two points. It looks tough, but here we go." The teacher says, "Sound it out ... Get ready ..." Using the same timing that she uses for other signals, the teacher quickly loops under the *f* and pauses; then under the *i*, and finally under the *t*. The children say the sounds in time with the touching. "*fffiiit.*"

"What word?"

"Fit," the children say loudly.

"Yes, that coat does not fit," the teacher says, already touching the ball for the next word, *on*. Two children respond weakly to the *o*. The teacher says the correct sound an instant after the weak response. "Again," she says, touching the ball. This time the children sound out the word firmly and answer "What word?" correctly.

The last three words on the page (*at, mat, nat*) are presented as rhyming words. "These words rhyme," the teacher explains. The children sound out and identify the word *at*. The teacher then quickly touches the ball for the word *mat*.

"This word rhymes with ... *at*. Get ready ..." The teacher quickly moves her finger right, along with the arrow, as the children say *mat*.

"Yes, what word?" The procedure is repeated for *nat*.

"Those rhyming words are tough," the teacher says, "and you did that page. So what does that mean?"

The children laugh. "We all get two points," the little girl on the end of the group says.

The next page is another column of words: *is, it, fit, sit*. The teacher says, "These words have a hard new sound. See who gets fooled by that new sound."

The children have no trouble with any words on the page.

"Now you get a story." The teacher hands each child a worksheet that has word-copying tasks, several tasks involving pictures, a cross-out game, a matching exercise, a story, and (on the reverse side of the sheet) a picture for the story. The children read the story before looking at the picture. The teacher instructs the children: "Finger on the ball of the top arrow." She checks to make sure that children are touching the arrow, which runs under the first line of print. "First word," the teacher says. "Sound it out. Get ready ..."

The teacher claps three times rhythmically, as the children touch under the appropriate letters and say the three sounds, *nnnŏŏŏt*. They say the sounds again as the teacher claps. Then she says, "Say it fast."

"Not," the children say in loud voices.

The procedure is repeated for the next word, *me*. The teacher claps for each sound as the children sound out then identify the word.

"We're going to read this story the fast way."

The teacher points under *not* and says, "Not." She moves under *me*.

"Me," the children respond.

The teacher says, "In the picture you will see somebody who is ..."

"Not me." The children's response is weak, so the teacher repeats the task several times.

"Turn your worksheet over and look at the picture of somebody who is not me."

The picture shows a dog. The children giggle and comment, "That ain't nobody. That's a dog."

The teacher asks, "Is that me? ... What is that? ... What's he doing? ... Does he look mean? ... What would you do if you met a dog like that?"

The teacher listens to the comments, agrees, and spends about half a minute chatting with the children. "Miss Hunter, Miss Hunter, I got a big cat. My cat named Turk ... I see a dog just like that one out there ... I see him all the time ..."

Finally, the teacher gives the children instructions for the work that they are to do independently on the worksheet. They will complete the worksheet after their next period, which is language. Before the children leave the group, the teacher says, "Let's see, everybody earned two points on those hard words today. And everybody earned two points for reading that story. Let's see what that does. Go find your ribbons."

The children dash to the corner of the room. There are name cards for every child in the group. (The names are written in the same font used in their reading program.) Beneath each name is a spool of ribbon. About two feet of exposed ribbon hangs from each spool. The exposed ribbon is marked off in units about a half-inch long. Inside each unit is a star. The teacher passes out five stars to each child, and the children paste the stars on the next five units of ribbon. As they do this, the teacher says, "We're going to run out of stars the way this yellow group is working. Look at that. I don't ever think I've seen kids earn so many stars."

A boy holds up his spangled ribbon. "My ribbon going to be bigger than me."

The teacher says, "Maybe you want to slow down so we don't run out of stars."

"No," the boy says sternly, "we going to keep getting stars."

The teacher shakes hands with the children, tickles one of the little girls. "Time's up," she says, and the children go to their language class.

The aide who teaches language talks louder and faster than the reading teacher. As soon as the children are seated, she pats the two children closest to her. "It's time for an action game. Everybody, touch your *chin*." The aide signals with a loud finger snap. "Good. What are you touching?"

"My chin," the children say.

"Everybody, touch your cheek." Snap. "What are you touching ...?"

"Let's try a harder game. I'll get you on this game."

"No, you won't," the children say.

"Here we go. Everybody, hold your hand IN FRONT of your nose." Snap. "Where is your hand now?" Snap.

"Put your hand ON your nose." Snap. "Where is your hand now?" Snap.

"Listen carefully. Where WAS your hand?"

"In front of my nose," the children say.

"Oh," the aide says, frowning. "I couldn't fool you. Say the whole thing about where your hand *was*."

"My hand was in front of my nose."

"Again ..."

After doing several other actions, the children work a concept application problem. "Listen to the rule. The wet bird will fly. Everybody, say the rule with me ... Again ... All by yourselves. Say the rule." Snap.

"Let's look at the birds on the next page." The aide turns the page and displays the presentation book. The picture shows three birds, one of which is drenched. The other birds are looking at the wet bird with dull expressions. The aide asks a series of questions about each bird. The aide has the children say the rule about which bird will fly, then calls on two children. "Show me the bird that will fly." The children point to the wet bird.

"How do you know that bird will fly?"

"It's wet."

"Let's see if you are right."

The aide turns the page and displays the picture. The children laugh. "He's flying," one of the boys shouts.

"We was right," another boy says.

"You sure were," the aide says. She then presents the other tasks on the page.

The rest of the lesson goes smoothly. At the end, the children get more stars then do their independent work. The children complete the language worksheet (coloring in the objects, drawing lines to join the objects that go together). They then complete their reading worksheets. They copy the story ("Not me"). They work independently, talking to each other from time to time but remaining quite engaged in the activity.

The remainder of the day's schedule calls for recess, work in arithmetic, singing, a period of writing and drawing, PE and a short firm-up period, during which the teacher or one of the aides works with the group on specific skills that have not been taught adequately.

Things are organized and regimented in this classroom, but not along the philosophical lines of a traditional school that has "high standards." The undercurrent in these schools is that the students are responsible for their education, and unless they apply themselves, they suffer the consequences of not learning. The organizational assumption of the classroom we observed is that if the teachers and aides are trained in effective practices and behave in ways that will both motivate the children and communicate clearly with them, the children's performance will accelerate and they will achieve at higher levels.

The day usually passes without a tear. The children are eager to go to their groups, eager to show their teachers or any visitors the skills they have mastered, and quick to show their stars—symbols of their achievement. They also demonstrate in many ways that they are quite fond of their teachers.

The children we observed entered school with an average IQ of less than 85. At the end of the year, all these children will be reading. All will be proficient in basic arithmetic operations, and will have a good grasp of the basic language of instruction. They will be facile, not only with the concepts that are referred to in a teaching demonstration (such as "in back of" and "was") but also with the statements that are used to express those concepts. Now, their IQ will be closer to 100.

The behavior of the teacher and the two aides seems quite natural; however, they are adhering very closely to rules and practices, not just for what they do during the lesson, but how they schedule the children's time from the moment they enter the classroom. As noted earlier, the teachers and aides followed set procedures for seating the children, for pointing to the letters or pictures, for signaling with the claps or the snaps and for correcting errors—all these procedures were taught. So were the reinforcement practices, and the large-group activities. The teacher and the aides were not pieces of clay that were transformed by the training program. They were very bright people, and they contributed a great deal to the classroom. For example, the writing sheets that the children receive in the morning were constructed by the teacher and one aide. Addition practice sheets were created by the arithmetic aide, and the language aide developed a series of games and activities that involve the various language concepts that have been taught.

When it's all put together, it's an awesome show.

HOW MUCH TRAINING?

Several critics have suggested that our program is impractical because it requires too much training. Our orientation is that if teachers and aides cannot perform adequately without training, they need the training, and the success of training is measured by how well they perform after training. Teachers go through at least four years of college education and learn few, if any, technical skills. If they were trained properly for $1/4$ this amount of time, we wouldn't have to do any additional training, simply supervise them and help them solve any problems they experienced.

The traditional assumption is that if teachers do not perform, they lack either motivation or intelligence. The suggested remedy for the motivation is to provide something that will turn them on—higher salaries, shorter working days, merit pay—or something that frightens them—the state taking over the school. A remedy for assumed low teacher intelligence is to hire teachers who are more highly qualified, teachers with more education.

The Coleman Report had shown that increased salaries, shorter workdays, more prep time, and similar provisions did not work. It also showed that teachers who had received more education or had more experience did no better than the others. Something more than motivating teachers, threatening them, or hiring others is needed—effective training.

The first step is to provide a frank assessment of teachers' technical skills. In 1976, we presented a questionnaire to eight project managers. The items addressed the competencies of the average teacher in an unimplemented poverty school. Respondents were to rate the teacher's performance on a scale of 1 to 5 and write a brief rationale that explained their rating. Note that each of these project managers was not only a model teacher but an experienced trainer of teachers who became high performers. Below are the items and sample answers for each. I selected only two responses for each item. These were typical of the other six responses.

1. Before training, how proficient would you rate the average certified teacher in working with lower performing children?

Response: Teachers are not trained either by college courses or inservice to work with lower performers. In fact the opposite is true. All types of labels are used on kids who are "not normal," and specialists are paid extra to work with kids that have these labels.

Response: The typical teacher has not been taught how to work with children who do not learn readily. They do not know how much repetition it takes, how to be consistent, how to analyze tasks and structure the teaching of skills. They do not know how to motivate these children.

2. **Before training, how proficient is the average teacher in correcting specific mistakes that children make?**

Response: Teachers are punishing or simply unable to make clean corrections. They have a tendency to draw out the answers by using a lot of verbiage. Corrections involving any sophisticated procedures are a wipeout.

Response: They often don't even identify an error. If they do, their corrections are often sloppy and confusing. Primarily, however, they blow it by failing to give the kids anything near sufficient repetition. They never repeat tasks.

3. **Before training, how proficient is the teacher in providing effective remedies for deficiencies in students' skill and knowledge?**

Response: If teachers are able to pinpoint deficiencies, they usually have no idea how to remedy the deficiency. If they try to provide remedies, they usually have no concept of evaluating whether a remedy has been effective or not.

Response: The critical problem here seems to be the inability to teach one isolated skill rather than a hodge-podge of semi-related skills and failure to provide sufficient practice. There is an additional difficulty here—attitude. Often teachers are aware that specific problems exist, but simply don't like putting the time or energy into remediation.

4. **Before training, how proficient is the teacher in identifying "reasonable or acceptable answers" to items that have more than one possible correct answer?**

Response: Most teachers either accept too wide a range of responses (e.g., "Where is the sky?"—"It's blue.") Or accept only responses specified in the teacher's material.

Response: Teachers tend to fall into one of two categories. Either they have an answer in mind and will not accept any deviation or reasonable response, which confuses the children who give reasonable responses and get punished for it, or they accept anything, including wrong responses.

Just as at-risk children have serious skill deficiencies, their teachers have serious deficiencies. And just as it would be difficult to design effective instruction for children without addressing their deficiencies, it would be difficult to teach teachers effectively without identifying theirs.

Throughout our work in Follow Through, we tried to provide training remedies for observed shortcomings in teacher responses. We did this by assembling our trainers and coordinators from the various sites and addressing specific problems they were experiencing. We staged a workshop in Providence, another in Chicago, and one in Grand Rapids. The most extensive one was in Racine, Wisconsin. The primary problem we addressed was management, both within the classroom and in other parts of the school—lunchroom, bathrooms, playground.

One of the more serious training problems in our Black, urban schools was behavior management. Most of our schools that served African Americans had serious behavior problems and teachers who were not skilled at solving them. Typically, students were well behaved during the instructional periods, but were often rowdy in the lunchroom, hallways, bathrooms, and on the playground. In some schools, beginning teachers tried to maintain control by doing a lot of yelling and berating. In others, they simply ignored the bad behavior.

In the summer of 1972, we brought all the directors and on-site coordinators to a school that had serious control problems. For one week, they spent part of each day working in the classrooms. During the rest of the day, they went to "classes" that reviewed what they were learning, addressed specific problems they were having, and previewed their next assignments. The goal was to demonstrate how radically a school environment and ethic could be changed with effective and consistent practices.

The classroom experience was a shock for participants who worked in Native American and Spanish-speaking sites. The directors and coordinators had never experienced the kind of rowdy behavior they encountered in Racine. On the first day, the director from one of our Texas sites was working with a group of third graders. While she was presenting, one of the boys observed, "You the ugliest bitch I ever did see." (She was actually quite attractive, but at the time, the Black Power movement had moved from the East to the Midwest.)

The director from a Spanish-speaking site was completely unable to manage her group of five third-grade boys. They were laughing, jostling each other, and ignoring her directions.

I told Carol Morimitsu to work with the group for the rest of the period. Carol had worked with us since we were in Illinois and was one of our project coordinators. She had an extensive repertoire of skills for teaching children and teachers. She had one problem, however: she looked very young. How young was demonstrated on a flight from Chicago to Portland. Shortly before we landed, a flight attendant handed her a "kiddy kit," which contained some puzzles and a set of gold wings, like those worn by the crew. Carol wore the wings proudly.

She was shorter than any boy in the rowdy group in Racine. She sat down, picked up the presentation book, and started presenting in a fast paced, very positive manner. None of the boys responded to her first question. She repeated the question. None responded.

She shouted in a loud, angry voice, "STAND UP."

All stared at her with wide eyes.

She grabbed the biggest boy by his arm and again shouted, "STAND UP." All the boys stood up. Carol said, "WHEN I TELL YOU TO STAND UP, YOU STAND UP. DO YOU UNDERSTAND?"

They nodded. She said, "SIT DOWN."

They sat down. She said, "ARE YOU READY TO WORK?"

They nodded and said, "Yes."

She picked up the presentation book and switched into her pleasant teacher mode. "Okay, let's start over ..." She presented the tasks positively, and the boys responded.

"Good job," she said and went on to the next task.

At the end of the period, I asked three of the boys, "What did you think of that teacher?"

One boy said, "Oh, she mean." The others agreed.

"Well, is that good or bad?"

"Good." All agreed.

"Would you like to work with her again?"

All said, "Yes."

I said, "Well, do a good job with your other teacher and I'll see if Carol will work with you again. Remember, do a good job." They did and she did. They performed well with their original teacher, received a lot of praise, and had a good time during the rest of the week.

Understand that when Carol yelled at them, it was not out of anger. She was simply applying a technique to change their behavior the fast way. And it was fast. She turned those boys around in less than one minute. As soon as the behavior changed, she returned to her positive mode.

The biggest problem in the school was the behavior in the halls and on the playground. On the second day of the training, we targeted that problem with techniques designed to change the children's behavior quickly.

The technique we used was a ticket game, similar to the one I used with behavior-problem students in Urbana. The rules for making the game work are simple, but they must be precisely executed or the technique won't work. The game, like most well designed management games, is based on

Wes's rule about catching kids in the act of being good. Teachers and aides are stationed at different places of the school and playground during the times children are not in classrooms. The teachers monitor the children's behavior but say nothing until a student does something that is either considerate, such as helping another child, or consistent with the rules, such as walking quietly in the hallway. The monitor gives the child a small strip of paper and tells the child what he did that was good. (Good holding the door open for that boy.) The monitor reminds the child to hang on to that ticket and give it to the classroom teacher for a reward.

That's all the monitor was to say to the child. Furthermore, the monitor was not to respond to other students who asked for a strip, or asked questions. The monitor was simply to walk away to another spot and stand silently until she observed another good act. At the end of recess, the monitors gave occasional tickets to children who were standing in line without pushing or arguing as they waited for the doors to open. Monitors also gave occasional tickets to children who walked properly in hallways.

Within five minutes after the procedure had been implemented on the playground, groups of kids followed the monitor around, asking for tickets. The monitor ignored them, identified occasional children who were behaving well while engaged in a playground activity, and awarded them a ticket. Very quickly, the students caught on that they couldn't get tickets by asking, but they could if they behaved in a different way on the playground.

I wish we had taken videotapes to document the changes in the children's behavior. By the second day, the children's playground behavior had changed completely. Teachers were not yelling at children and children were not misbehaving. The school seemed to have a different population of students—no running in the halls, good cooperative behavior on the playground, good waiting in line to enter the building, and good behavior in the lunchroom and bathrooms.

The procedure sounds easy but was actually hard for many teachers because teachers didn't understand the purpose of the various details. On the first day of the implementation, some teachers were talking to children who asked questions about what they were doing. I observed one teacher who was handing out tickets to the children who surrounded her.

Even on the third day, we had to remind teachers not to yell at the children and tell them what not to do, like, "Lester, DON'T RUN IN THE HALL."

We told teachers to give a ticket to another child who was behaving acceptably. (Naturally, if an offender is doing something that is dangerous either to himself or another, the teacher is to intercede immediately.) So long as the technique was monitored, it worked. After the training was completed and the regular aides and teachers worked full time with the children, some regressed to their traditional nagging and the children reverted to behavior that predictably causes nagging. Behavior management, like instruction, must be institutionalized as rules and procedures that are understood and followed by everybody in the school.

LARRY GOTKIN

The results on Follow Through drizzled in over a three-year period. These results were not for publication but were simply information for the various sponsors. The earliest data showed that some of the traditional approaches were doing well. The DI model was far from the top performers. We were not particularly concerned because we knew that the sites were improving.

During the first year of Follow Through, both Larry Gotkin and I had presented at the same symposium in New York (Education and the City Child). After the symposium, we had a couple of drinks and talked about our educational strategies. After that meeting, we talked from time to time about specific language concepts and how to teach them.

Larry's orientation, like ours, did not stem from abstract and unapplied principles or vacuous metaphors, but from experience and a solid perspective of what the children didn't know and needed to learn. Also, he passionately believed sponsors had a strong ethical responsibility to see to it that their programs effected this change. For him, Follow Through was not a game, but a mission. I didn't agree with his instructional strategy. The prospectus on his approach presented his rationale.

> The game-like nature of the structured learning situations adds greatly to the children's sense of challenge and involvement. Not only are they challenged to master the subject matter themselves, they are challenged to direct other children in learning the same material. To direct others, children must also master the language of explanation. The sense of importance derived from leading or teaching others, and the verbal transitions between pupils intrinsic to the process, act as direct stimulants to language development.

We disagreed. This starting point assumed that teachers knew how to teach well, respond appropriately to what the children did, and reinforce skills children were to derive from the games. We had no disagreements with Larry about the problems the program addressed—the deficiency in language skills, particularly the area of "the language of explanation."

Larry's program was one of the better performers. Over the next two years, the performance of his two schools slipped, even though he spent extensive amounts of time in the schools, working directly with the teachers and kids.

After some of the results revealed that his teachers were not moving the kids forward as well as he did, and that his attempts to train teachers was disappointing, he became morose. Jean Osborn, who had become his friend and confidant, prompted me to call him and see if there was something we could do to lift his spirits.

I called. He indicated, "You were right in your analysis of what these kids need. I was wrong, and I misled people because I thought I was right."

I told him that he shouldn't look at it that way. I said, "Why don't we work together?" I indicated that we could take one of his schools, install the basic language and reading stuff and keep the games, the music, and the pantomime activities that he had developed. I told him I believed this would be a successful approach. Larry thanked me for the invitation but wouldn't commit to doing something. He said, "I don't know. I just don't know."

I tried calling him a couple of other times, but I never got through. Jean indicated that she had had the same experience. About two weeks later, she was in New York working on evaluations of our sites. She went to Larry's place and met with him. She later learned that she was the only person he had met with in weeks. He was gaunt and unshaven, but seemed very glad to see her, and they talked for a long time. Jean tried to interest him in working with us, but he wouldn't commit to doing it.

Shortly after Jean met with Larry, we received the shocking news that he had committed suicide. I felt guilty because I believed that I could have prevented that tragedy by being more persistent and going to see him, rather than calling. I hadn't thought that the problem was so serious, but obviously I was wrong. What a shame that a creative person like Gotkin, who was concerned and dedicated to better the lot of kids, had such an unfortunate fate.

Wes and I wanted to set up one of Larry's schools as a memorial to him by combining his games with DI. There was great confusion and red tape associated with the status of his schools. In the end, nothing happened.

EYE DEVELOPMENT

One reason school districts had such low regard for our program was that it rejected what districts assumed were truths about learning and performance. For instance, the traditional belief in the 1970s was that reading had to do with the eyes, and that early reading would do damage to eyes because they were still developing. Traditionalists believed that attempts to teach younger children to read would result in later failure. The July 1972 edition of *Harpers* carried an article that many of our sites later quoted and used as evidence that our approach was destined to fail. The article, "The Dangers of Early Schooling," stated, "We argue that children probably shouldn't attend school until they are seven or eight years old."

The authors cited research. One researcher reported that one group of matched children began reading at six, the other at seven. "In two years, the late beginning group had caught up with the early beginning group ... at the end of their seventh school year, the children who began a year later were one year ahead of the early beginners." Another study found the same results with four-year-olds versus six-year-olds.

One researcher asserted, "Not more than 10 percent of five-year-olds can perceive the difference between *d* and *b* or *p* and *q*. Not until children are eight are their eyes mature enough to avoid such confusion."

These were insane views, which could be discredited with even casual observations of children, but school psychologists and administrators considered them more authoritative than our practices. During this time, I presented at a meeting where the first speaker brought up the "evidence" about the eye and its slow development. Before I worked with a group of pre-kindergarten children on the stage, I said, "If only ten percent of five-year-olds have sufficient visual development to see the difference between *b* and *d*, probably less than one child in this group will be able to learn the difference. Let's see."

I wrote the letter *b* on a transparency. I held it up and told the children, "This is *b*. What is it? ... But when I move it like this, [tilted 90 degrees to the left] it is not *b*. When it's like this [upside-down] it's not *b*. [In original position] Remember, if it's like this, it's *b*. If it's not like this, it's not *b*." I then presented a series of examples with the transparencies in different positions. For each example, I asked, "Is it *b* now?"

The children performed without making a single error.

I told them that I would now make it harder. I wrote a series of about 20 letters on the board—*b*, *d*, *p*, and *q*—in random order. I told the children, "This is really hard. Some of these are *b*. I'm going to call on different children to tell me if I point to *b* or something that is not *b*."

I called up each of the five children. I pointed to the letters from left to right and asked each child about four letters. The children made no mistakes.

After the demonstration, I pointed out that the *b–d* problem had nothing to do with the eyes. It had to do with what children have learned about objects from the time they were infants. A toy car is always a toy car, regardless of its position. All other objects children have ever encountered retain their identity regardless of spatial orientation—blocks, bowls, spoons, crayons, pencils, papers, parrots, and people. Then, a well-intentioned but naïve teacher expects children to learn the difference between *b* and *d* without even informing them that these symbols are weird because they are actually the same object. If it's turned one way, it's *b;* turned the other, it's *d.* I pointed out that if the earlier speaker was correct about the eye development, a child would not be able to recognize his toy car or his teddy bear unless it was in a particular position. I concluded by pointing out that children have the eye power necessary to learn this discrimination, but that traditional programs don't have the communication power necessary to demonstrate what the symbol is and what it is not.

By now we should have had at least some credibility, but we didn't. The U.S. Department of Health, Education, and Welfare had published a 21-page report titled *It Works,* which described the Bereiter Engelmann preschool and cited performance data and follow-up data: children graduating from kindergarten had realized an IQ gain of 25 points during the two-year program, while the control group of matched children in a different preschool format gained 5 points. Our children performed on the middle second-grade level in both reading and math. Their spelling performance was about beginning second-grade level. These achievements placed our children more than a year and a half above the norms, and more than two years above the performance level of comparison children from the same population.

Despite this validation and another endorsement by AIR (the American Institutes for Research), which also confirmed *It Works,* districts and agencies did not conclude that we must be doing something right. Instead, they espoused soft theories of the brain and development and concluded we were wrong. We had frequent confrontations with our sites over whether our program would damage children. This concern was ironic because all the schools we worked with were initially failures. It would seem that when schools had information that first graders were now performing higher than third graders had performed several years earlier, educators would conclude that there had been obvious improvement and no apparent damage. Educators, however, did not reason that way.

THE BRONX

A meeting that showed the gulf between the perspective of educators and those of parents occurred in the Bronx. Don Bushell had a Follow Through school in the South Bronx. He was having trouble implementing the school and asked if we could use some of our people to help out. We did that. One of the biggest problems the school had was that the central administration was making it hard for the implementation to move forward. The parent group wanted a meeting in which they could raise issues about the administration and Direct Instruction. I was to present at the meeting.

The timing was bad. The meeting was scheduled during blustery wintry weather. The city was in the third week of a garbage strike. Mountains of garbage in the streets overflowed onto the sidewalks. The wind was gusting, scattering papers and nondescript stuff across the streets and sidewalks. The meeting took place in a school gymnasium and was scheduled to begin at four.

The meeting did not begin on time because of traffic snarls and scarcity of parking places. The garbage and the weather made people edgy. The audience was noisy. By the time the meeting started, the gym was crowded with parents, teachers, and at least five administrators from the central office. People were standing in the back of the room. The principal kept reminding them not to block the exit.

The stage at one end of the gym had bleak overhead spotlights that illuminated circles and created heavy shadows on the stage. I had arranged to demonstrate with a group of low-performing children. They walked in and sat in their chairs. I told the audience that I would first assess the kids and then teach them something from the program.

I presented tasks from the beginning language program. The lowest child was a shy little guy who could not repeat sentences like, "This is a ball," or phrases like, "under the table." He didn't know prepositions or colors. As I worked with him, I had a sense of how surreal this situation was—the unfortunate kid sitting in bleak surroundings under the stark lights. Before testing the other children, I presented the boy with a couple of tasks he could do— "Touch your nose." Clap. I praised him. After I showed some of the things the other children couldn't do, I worked with the group on several language tasks, with emphasis on saying sentences. Then, I called on different individuals to perform on one of the tasks we had practiced. I congratulated the children, shook hands with them, and gave each of them a little treat. The audience clapped and the kids smiled. I thought it was a good demonstration for showing why we had to start with basic language skills if we hoped to accelerate these children.

After the children left, I gave a brief synopsis of their performance and the method of teaching that we used. I stressed the idea that we have to be realistic about what the children know, and be scrupulous about starting where kids are and pacing our expectations to what they show us they are able to do. I concluded with the message that if we do not provide a good start in K, we jeopardize the kids' chances of catching up, and that a good start involves heavy-duty instruction.

The principal asked for questions or comments. The first few asked about the program and teaching techniques. They were followed by one that addressed the poor performance of kids in grades 3 and beyond. I pointed out that they have deficiencies that can be traced to deficiencies in K. After I answered the question, a White woman in the front row stood up and said, "Teachers in the third grade and beyond can't be blamed for not teaching well if the children who come to us have not been taught the basics. We could be successful if the teachers in the early grades prepared the children." Some spirited comments came in the form of catcalls. The principal reminded the audience to be orderly.

A woman from the central administration stood up and said, "Our early childhood program is appropriate for *all* children and it has been shown to prepare children very well." She suggested that the problem was not with the design of the program but with the unwillingness of the schools to implement the district program.

The moment she stopped talking, a Black woman several rows behind her stood up and shouted, "That's a goddamn lie! You don't do a goddamn thing to prepare children." Other people started shouting. The principal shouted, "Settle down! We'll have an orderly meeting or it will be over."

People settled down. A woman from the board raised her hand and gave a saccharine account about why everything would be okay if we simply had more faith in nature. She pointed out that children are individuals who grow and develop in different ways and at different rates. She ended with the observation, "I think we all need to recognize that children learn in strange and mysterious ways."

I got very angry. I pointed to the empty chair where the lowest little boy had been sitting. The chair was spotlighted, surrounded by the dark stage. I preached to the empty chair, "Oh, yeah, why didn't I think of that? *You* don't need careful instruction. *You* don't need somebody who will structure your experiences so you learn the things you'll need for grade 3. *You* don't need carefully designed practice in what and how to learn. How could I fail to see that we don't have to worry about you because *you will learn in strange and mysterious ways?*"

It felt like a bolt of electricity went through that gym. As soon as I felt it, I knew I shouldn't have delivered that sermon. People were on their feet, yelling. Some had clenched fists. Most of the yelling was directed at the people from the central administration. The principal tried to quiet the crowd but the yelling continued. He shouted, "This meeting is over!"

He went to the light-switch panel and turned off all the lights, returned to the mike and shouted, "This meeting is over! Go home!" I sat in one of the chairs on the stage in that dark gym as the shouting and arguing continued. After a few minutes, groups of people left the gym, still arguing. The central administrators were surrounded by swarms of vocal critics.

When the last people had left the gym, the principal turned the lights back on, looked at me, and said, "Damn."

CHAPTER 4

During Follow Through

THE EB LEARNING CENTER

Throughout Follow Through, I worked on different projects that had nothing to do with Follow Through. The combination of Follow Through work, my university duties, and these other projects resulted in a work schedule that was challenging if not insane. I received half-time salary for my role as faculty member of the University of Oregon. The other half of my salary was paid by Follow Through. We were developing programs during this period, so I wanted to make sure that there was no question that either Follow Through or the University of Oregon were paying for program development. (The rule at the time was that if the Feds paid for any part of the development, the material would be placed in the public domain. This meant that no publisher would be interested because anybody could reproduce the material.) I protected the programs by carrying a full-time teaching load with the University, not a half-time load. Furthermore, my commitment to Follow Through demanded full-time work on the project, which meant a fulltime load with Follow Through.

For the program-development work, we needed a shop that was independent of the University. Wes and I formed Engelmann-Becker Corporation. During our first two years in Eugene, "The Corp" hopped to three locations. It outgrew the first two, and in 1972, it landed in its current location on the fringe side of downtown Eugene, a 10,000-square-foot building, which had been a beauty college with a beauty parlor and a suite of offices rented to what some called "the mad dentist." His "lab" was in the basement. In the middle of it was a post covered from ceiling to floor with wax that held hundreds of teeth—rotten, unrotten, front, back, big and small. One of his upstairs "closets" concealed his project, which was to dig a downhill tunnel from his upstairs office to the lab. He apparently carried the dirt out in buckets, but he didn't make it even halfway to his lab.

The building cost $125,000 and was a serious investment. We converted the basement into offices and built a row of small rooms on the main floor that could be used to work with small groups of students. Following the remodeling, we opened a learning center, which was designed to serve hard-to-teach children and school failures. One of the earliest groups, however, was not low, but was composed of six preschoolers whose parents were professionals or professors. One student was Wes's youngest son. We worked with these children as four-year-olds and five-year-olds. They went through the reading and math programs as fast as they could go at mastery, which was frighteningly fast. (There was no need for the language programs because these children were very bright.) Even though they worked for only a little more than an hour a day, they went through all four levels of the programs we had for Follow Through classes. Before they entered first grade, they performed on the fourth-grade level in both reading and math. And they loved school.

We never published anything about the performance of these children, largely because the group had only six children, which meant that experimental purists would "question" the results. (Usually, at least 15 experimental children are needed for establishing outcomes that are recognized as valid.)

Although these children were awesome, their performance showed a critical difference between their potential and that of the at-risk child. When these advantaged children came to the third and fourth levels of the reading program, where the material becomes entrenched in and decorated with sophisticated language, they did not slow down. The profile for the at-risk child is different. Performance slows considerably when they reach the vocabulary-rich transition. They have parallel problems with math when the word problems become more substantive than a few pared-down sentences that present necessary information in a "familiar" format.

The performance of the high preschoolers pointed out the terrible paradox of effective instruction. If we accelerated the performance of all students in a district that had a full performance range of children, the outcomes would suggest that we were not serving the at-risk children well. Their gains would be far less than those of the higher performers. So we would actually be widening the difference in one sense. In another sense, we would be narrowing it if the at-risk children learned a sufficient amount to become "competent learners," which means that they would have the information, the background knowledge, and the learning skills they needed to quickly learn anything we wanted to teach them.

Viewed a third way, we don't have to worry as much about the performance of higher performers. High performers will tend to learn from teaching that is hideous (as many programs for the talented and gifted demonstrate). These programs provide instruction that appears to be purposely designed to teach, explain, and develop skills in the most circuitous and confusing manner possible. Certainly it's cruel to subject students of any skill level to such instruction, but in the larger scheme, far less cruel than subjecting at-risk children to certain failure. Although it would have been possible for us to work with both populations, we reconfirmed the decision not to work with higher performers but rather to show the degree to which at-risk children would catch up to higher performers with careful instruction. We figured that teaching higher performers effectively is so easy that in time, those who educate them would learn how to do it effectively. It certainly hasn't happened yet. But we felt that we needed to work with the lower performers simply because it is not easy, and teachers don't know how to do it. In fact, we believed that if we didn't do it, it wouldn't happen because nobody in or out of Follow Through (with the exception of the University of Kansas) was close.

Somebody could make a strong argument that it is more important to assure that higher performers achieve their potential because they will be the leaders that advance science and technology. To us, it seemed to make more sense to assure that at-risk populations generated their share of leaders. Even though this is a far harder job, it may be a far more important one.

NO TENURE

When I had been hired, the dean told me that I would never get beyond the level of associate professor, but I applied for promotion each year. (After the first year, the college had a new dean.) And I was rejected the first three times. On the fourth (1974), I was promoted to full professor.

I accepted the appointment on the condition that I would not receive tenure, which I thought was an unreasonable practice that didn't really function well to protect academic freedom. I figured nobody should expect more than possibly a five-year contract. I later changed my mind when I became aware of some of the abuses the system would possibly commit, like sending older, higher paid professors out to pasture with not much likelihood that they would be hired by another institution.

IQ AND LEARNING

There were some high-IQ children in Follow Through. For the 1976 Technical Report to National Follow Through, Wes did an analysis in which he plotted the achievement performance of children from different IQ ranges and correlated it with their progress through the program as measured by achievement tests. The study involved over 5,000 children; 700 of them had IQs of 80 and less (the average, 73). The analysis showed that the lower performers and average performers progressed at about the same rate through the programs. The difference was where they started. The average performers started quite a bit beyond where low performers started. Clearly, however, the low-IQ students learned how to learn.

High-IQ children progressed at a faster rate than the others. The progress of both lower and average IQ children slowed when they reached grade 3. The highest performers performed the same way the advantaged high performing preschoolers did; they maintained a fast pace.

The higher performers in Follow Through were definitely not accelerated as fast as they could have been. This was largely a result of our classroom format. A classroom with a teacher and one or two aides was able to accommodate three groups, occasionally four. Fewer than 15 percent of its students, however, were in this high-IQ range, which meant that fewer than two would be in a classroom. So they were placed in the top group, which did not move through the material as fast as this minority group could have proceeded.

To show the degree of acceleration that was possible with students at or above average, Doug Carnine and I did a formal study, which appeared in our 1978 Technical Report to National Follow Through. Thirty children in a Springfield, Oregon elementary school went through our reading program at an accelerated rate. These were not children with extremely high IQs; however, all but two met the district's criteria for "higher performer," which was that they performed at or above the district average when they began the first grade. (The district had no kindergarten.) The two exceptions were low performers who were added because the teacher felt they could benefit from the program. During grades 1 and 2, the children had daily reading lessons of about one-half hour per day and devoted another half-hour to independent work. The teaching was conducted by trainees in our practica. The classroom teacher was a star, but she did very little of the teaching. She made sure, however, that the trainees performed very well.

At the end of their second grade, children read at the middle fourth-grade level according to the Stanford Achievement Test. They performed on the fifth-grade level of an oral reading test. The top ten children received a fourth-grade test that measured speed and accuracy. (We could find no test for the second or third grade.) Students performed on the seventh-grade level.

The children were not taught science as a subject, but level 3 of our reading program has stories that are heavy in science content. The class performed at the fourth-grade level in science.

On their rating of themselves and the program, most indicated that they didn't consider themselves exceptionally smart, but 75 percent of them judged that they would be very smart when they grew up.

MORE PIAGET

During the years we participated in Follow Through, I did work on several other projects. One was another experiment designed to discredit Jean Piaget's theory of development. This theory was popular among educators, but it was dangerous because it suggested that critical knowledge could not be taught, but had to be acquired through amorphous interactions of children with their surroundings, a process described as self-regulation.

The experiment I did involved teaching six at-risk five-year-olds some of the rules they would need to pass various Piagetian tests, including the test of specific gravity, which is generally not passed by children under 12 years old. Like the earlier experiments I did, the teaching was designed to violate every principle that Piaget asserted is necessary for learning to occur. Because Piaget assumed that his principles are universal, one five-year-old passing the test of specific gravity would discredit his theory.

The instruction for all the topics took a total of 3 hours (distributed over 6 sessions). Part of the instruction presented rules about the floating and sinking behavior of objects. There were no demonstrations involving sinking and floating, and no activities in which children manipulated anything—just the rules and verbal examples.

After instruction, children were tested individually by a recognized Piagetian researcher. We added some items to the standard Piagetian tests so we could evaluate the extent to which children learned generalizable strategies. For example, in addition to the standard Piagetian tests of whether objects will float or sink in water, we added a test involving mercury. Steel balls float like corks in mercury. The tester presented two steel balls, one small and one large. The tester asked whether the smaller ball would float or sink in mercury. After the child responded, the examiner would put the smaller ball in water and ask why the ball floated. The children in the study had been taught that if something floats in a medium, that thing is lighter than a piece of the medium the same size as the object.

The examiner next asked what the larger ball would do when it was placed in mercury. The children had been taught that if two things are made of the same material they would behave the same way.

Another test involved a candle. The examiner asked whether the candle would sink in water. Then the examiner proceeded to cut the candle into a small piece and a large piece. She asked about each piece.

Most of the children passed the test of specific gravity. One of our graduate students was outside the door of the examination room, monitoring the proceedings. When I saw her during the break, she said, "Oh, that mercury test is amazing. After the little steel ball floated in mercury, the tester asked David what the big ball would do, and he said it would float. I knew he was wrong. That big ball is so heavy. But he was right. It floated!" It seemed that our graduate student did not have a generalizable notion of specific gravity.

One of our subjects showed great generalizability of what had been taught. Before the examiner cut the candle into two pieces, she asked the girl what the candle would do in the water. She said it would sink.

The examiner started to cut the candle, then stopped and asked what the big piece would do (sink) and what the little piece would do (sink). The examiner started to cut again when the child announced, "It will float."

The examiner stopped and said, "First you say it will sink and now you say it will float. What will the little part do?" (Float.) "What will the big piece do?" (Float.) "What will the whole thing do?" (Float.)

"Why do you now say they will float?" The child pointed to a flake of candle that was floating on the water. "That piece came off when you cut the candle. It's floating. So the whole thing will float and all the other parts will float."

In contrast to the generalizations that the children produced were the responses of Piagetian researchers to a simple (but tricky) problem of conservation. I presented the paper on the experiment at a symposium held in Monterey, California sponsored by the California Test Bureau and titled, "Conference on Ordinal Scales of Cognitive Development," which means simply what knowledge emerges first and next, and do they always have to occur in the same order? The audience consisted of around 200 people. I told the aside about our graduate student not having a generalizable notion of specific gravity and pointed out that at least some members of the audience didn't have a generalizable notion of basic logical structures, like understanding conservation of number.

To illustrate, I presented the following problem. You have two identical glasses, both filled to exactly the same level. One contains whiskey, the other water. You take exactly one spoonful of whiskey and put it in the water glass. Then you take one spoonful of the mixture from the water glass and return it to the whiskey glass.

Question: Is there more whiskey in the water glass than water in the whiskey glass? Or is there more water in the whiskey glass than whiskey in the water glass? In other words, the percentage of foreign matter in each glass has changed. Has the percentage changed more in one of the glasses, or is the percentage change the same for both glasses?

I asked for those who thought the percentage changed more in one glass than the other to raise their hands. Considerably more than half the people in the audience raised their hands, which means that they did not have logical operations that eight-year-olds are supposed to acquire, according to Piaget.

I pointed out that this problem is interesting because it presents a situation that is rarely encountered. But if one had an understanding that liquids are composed of fixed numbers of counters or parts, the answer is simple.

Instead of water and whiskey, think of red balls and white balls. Each glass starts out with 100 balls of a single color. We remove three balls from the red-ball glass and put them in the white-ball glass. Then we return three balls from the glass with the "mixture" and put them in the red-ball glass. If we return three white balls, one glass will have 97 red and three white; the other glass will have 97 white and three red. If we return two white and one red, one glass will have 98 red and two white. The other glass will have 98 white and two red. No matter what combination of colors is returned, the change will be exactly the same for both glasses so long as three balls are moved. If a person had a logical operation involving fixed units, the person should have no more difficulty with this problem than our graduate student should have had in figuring out that the big ball should float in mercury.

Neither my experiment nor the presentation (which was published in the book, *Measurement and Piaget*, 1971) had any effect on the popularity of Piaget's theories. Educators still felt that if children failed to learn, the problem was largely developmental and could not be greatly influenced by instruction. This was a convenient stance because we can't blame the teacher for a child's poor performance if that performance is supposed to be governed by the child's self-regulatory mechanisms. With this formula, children are clearly assumed to be the cause of their failure.

DEAF CHILDREN

Another area that I worked on during Follow Through involved a device that would help deaf kids hear through tactual vibration. This was an extension of the early work at Don Bitzer's lab in Illinois. The reason I was interested in this device was that it was very difficult to teach speech and nuances of language syntax to children who are profoundly deaf. If children are only partially deaf, they are relatively easy to work with by using some form of amplification system or hearing aid that transmits at least a low-grade version of the auditory signals. The profoundly deaf are different. Lip-reading is very hard because only about 30 percent of the speech sounds are discriminably different when presented in isolation. When the sounds are in the context of words, the probability increases, but it's far from 100 percent.

Teaching speech sounds to profoundly deaf children is tedious. When you try to work on individual sounds like the short-*o* or the short-*u* sound, you try to prompt the learner to produce a response you can reinforce. If you reinforce the child for approximations, you're sending a mixed message. Your reinforcement indicates that the learner has done something that is correct. At the same time, you know it is not correct and will not be reinforced for that approximation later. You hope that if the learner gets in the right ballpark, she'll produce sounds that more closely approximate the acceptable sound.

Yes, there are tricks to prompt the proper sound. If you put the child's hand on your throat, you can feel a little difference between the tension pattern for the short-*o* sound and the short-*u* sound, but it's a pretty small difference. For teaching more global discriminations, like the difference between sounds that are voiced (produced with the vocal cords activated) and those that aren't (produced sans vocal cord accompaniment) the throat prompts are useful. For instance, to show the difference between the sounds for *v* and *f,* take a deep breath and let it out with no pauses as you turn the vocal cords off and on. You'll produce a string of sounds that alternate between *f* and *v* (the *f* sound without the voice and the *v* sound with it). The child can feel that difference. She can see how your lips are formed and feel the stream of air that comes from your mouth.

With patience and much practice, you can teach most sounds. You can even do some corrections. One pattern is frequently not corrected and it characterizes the speech attempts of many deaf children who become relatively proficient in speaking. They have a nasal component to their vowel sounds (particularly short-*i* and long-*e*). You can create this sound by holding your nose closed and saying the long-*e* sound so that you feel a lot of nose vibrations on your fingers. If you say the sound properly there will be no (or very little) nose vibrations because there will be no nasal component. If you don't know this trick, you can work for weeks on vowels, and the child will sound something like a child with a cleft palate. If you use the trick, however, you may create some unintended problems. Some children will over-generalize. They learn that if you talk without letting very much air out, they can produce sounds that don't have the nasal quality, but it gives them a robotic sound, and often an absence of the *n* and *m* sounds.

The characteristics of their speech that are most difficult to change are their inflection and their patterns of expelling air as they talk. I can tell whether deaf kids who can speak pretty well have 15 percent hearing in the speech range of voiced sounds or zero percent just by attending to two things, their inflection and their patterns of expelling air as they speak. The profoundly deaf speaker's inflection ranges from monotonal to cacophonous. When we say the word *ball,* our voice has significant pitch variation and goes down at the end of the word. A German saying *ball* would not have this pitch pattern, but one much closer to the way some deaf persons would say it. Teaching proper pitch variations is difficult.

Also, the inflections change for different sentences. If you say *Vern,* at the end of a yes-no question and at the end of a statement, the inflectional patterns are different: That boy is Vern. Is that boy Vern? It is possible to teach the difference in these extremes. One technique is to present sentences that have the same word inflected two ways. (Say the sentence, *Vern is Vern* and the sentence, *Is Vern Vern?* You can hear the differences in *Verns.*) Although it is possible to teach these inflectional differences by working with such sentences, the instruction must be delivered one-on-one; the teacher has to be very good; and the priority of working on inflections must be balanced by all the other things about language the children must learn.

The most serious problem facing most profoundly deaf children is that they don't learn the language we use—not just the vocabulary but the syntax and the myriad of idiomatic ways that language is used. For example, if Ted is winning the race, he is *in* first place, not *on* first place or *at* first place. This information and thousands of comparable bits must be taught to the deaf child compared to the blind child, who has no trouble learning or using language.

My hope was to work on a device that could transform sound into some sort of corresponding vibratory pattern that provided the same information that hearing children receive through their ears. If the machine were designed ideally, the child using the device would experience vibratory patterns that could be "louder" or "softer," slower or faster, higher or lower, and that would present information about the sounds in words. Deaf students who used the device would learn hundreds of times the amount of information about spoken language they currently receive and would not need teachers to teach all of it a laborious step at a time.

One of the things I did after we got settled in Oregon was to try to find somebody like Don Bitzer to work with. Don was an electrical engineer, so I talked to several electrical-engineering candidates. The first four I contacted had very conservative viewpoints. One argued that such a device had not been invented; therefore, it couldn't work. The others simply concluded that it wouldn't work. The most educated of the group (a Ph.D.) cited a study in which somebody had tried using such a device. The article indicated that they tried it out for a couple of hours of training. The kids didn't seem to learn. So the experimenters concluded that it didn't work.

I pointed out that the training was incredibly inadequate. I told him about some of the studies with deaf and blind kids that hinted at the amount of practice that would be required for children to learn key discriminations. One of the studies involved adults who'd had cataracts removed and were able to see for the first time. The experimenter (Senden) worked with these subjects for months and reported how difficult it was for them to learn even the simplest discriminations. One of his subjects finally learned to discriminate between a ball and a box on the nightstand next to the bed, but the subject could not identify either when they were moved to a different location. After the patient became more proficient, a familiar object was placed on the nightstand and was illuminated with a colored lamp. The patient could not identify it.

The engineer was not impressed by this information. As he put it, "It won't work."

Fortunately, a colleague introduced me to Bob Rossov, a talented electrical engineer who was also a really nice guy. He had ideas about how to design the device and was not convinced it wouldn't work.

We tried to get some funding to build the device and conduct the experiment, but our grant applications were unsuccessful. So my wife and I provided the major funding, and four Oregon-based trainers in the Follow Through project volunteered their time. Oregon Research Institute and the Collins Institute also provided some funds. I was particularly grateful to the trainers—Linda Youngmayr, Laurie Skillman, Millie Schrader, Carol Morimitsu—because they volunteered their time although they didn't have spare time.

The project started in 1972 and continued into 1974. Bob constructed a device called a vocoder, which took speech sounds and divided them up according to the frequency range of the components. The device had 23 channels, which spanned the auditory spectrum from sounds that are very low in pitch (85 hertz) to very high frequency sounds like the sounds for s and f (10,000 hertz). Each channel was connected to a vibrator. The greater the amount of energy the vibrator received the more vigorously the vibrator responded. The final prototype device consisted of five metal boxes, each with four vibrating reeds. We strapped the boxes to different body parts.

Our first experiments were with hearing subjects, our trainers. We didn't want to start with deaf subjects until we were certain that our device and training practices were at least good enough to teach hearing subjects. We expected hearing subjects to learn much faster, because they already knew the language and its phonological structure.

Our trainers worked in pairs, one being the trainer and the other the subject. The trainer wore a microphone, which transmitted speech sounds to the boxes.

The subject would have earplugs and wear headphones that transmitted 85 decibels of white noise. So they were rendered deaf. During most of the 20- to 30-minute period, the trainer would stand more than six feet behind the subject and talk into the microphone. This format provided the subject with no visual information about lip movement.

The subject would try to repeat everything the trainer said. When the trainer was behind the subject, the trainer attempted to correct mistakes the subject made with no visual contact.

Trainer: Get ready.

Subject: Get ready.

Trainer: Fan.

Subject: Fan.

Trainer: Yes.

Subject: Yes.

If the subject made a mistake, the trainer would use a verbal format that compared the word the subject made with the correct word.

Trainer: And.

Subject: Hand.

Trainer: Not hand.

Subject: Not hand.

Trainer: And.

Subject: And.

The same format was used to present sentences that the subject would repeat. To test the capacity of the vocoder, we introduced tasks that required the subject to match the trainer's inflection. Using the same set-up for words and sentences, the trainer would say one of the familiar words with unique inflection, such as a name, like Laurie Skillman, with each of the four syllables a different musical note, such as, *b, e, c, b,* or *f, a, d, e.*

The subject was to match the pattern exactly, with respect to pitch and timing.

The two subjects who received 60–80 hours of instruction had mastered 60 words in isolation and were 88–90 percent accurate when these words were presented randomly. Their performance in identifying words in unique sentences (composed entirely of words they had learned) was over 95 percent accurate. Their ability to match tonal inflectional patterns was virtually 100 percent.

So we had enough information to begin with deaf children. This work was very interesting.

Our first subjects made so many mistakes on the first words presented that we adopted the practice of using a "throwaway" set of 6–8 words. We would try to bring them to a high criterion of performance on these words, but the children would often develop such serious mistake patterns that it would have taken thousands of trials to bring them to an acceptable criterion of performance. So we just brought children to a modest criterion of performance and then threw the words away, never using them again.

If the nay-saying electrical engineers had observed the children at the beginning of the sequence, they would have concluded that their judgment had been right, and the device could not possibly work. The first two words the children learned after the throwaway set were *man* and *elephant*—words totally different from each other. Children could not identify them reliably after possibly 400 trials. For each of the subsequent words, the children would not only confuse it with one or more of the other words but would also regress to mistake patterns they had not produced for days.

The pattern with the "keeper" set was that children learned the first ten words very slowly then learned the next ten faster, and then hit a wall. Whatever strategies they had used for the first 20 words didn't work when their repertoire exceeded 20 dissimilar words. Typically, children struggled at this 20-word plateau for almost two months. Then they accelerated. By week 40 they could learn new words as fast as we could introduce them. One subject went from a vocabulary of 80 words to 150 words in eight weeks, performing at a high criterion of performance.

The kids we worked with were interesting. One was an out-of-control behavior problem who proved to be one of the fastest learners after he decided to try to learn what we were trying to teach. He was the first person I ever saw who gave you the one-handed finger if he was pissed off with you, but the two-handed fingers if he was really pissed off.

One time I was presenting words to him as he faced the other direction. I asked him a series of yes-no questions.

"Are you sitting?" "Yes."

"Are you a boy?" "Yes."

"Are you reading?" "No."

"Are you a girl?"

He didn't respond. I repeated the question. No response. I repeated it again. He wheeled around in his chair and with perfect inflections said angrily, "I am not a girl!"

The fastest learner we had was a deaf girl of 12 who was not retarded but had spent most of her life in an institution for seriously retarded children. She was very happy, very accommodating, but very naïve. She had to be taught basic social behaviors, like not scratching her crotch in public.

She didn't have good strategies for learning from adults because she had been taught very little from adults. She knew possibly a dozen signs but not much more.

During instruction, children wore the vibrator boxes on their thighs, three boxes on the left, two on the right. This arrangement left children free to use their hands. We started her instruction with a relatively simple task. We would say speech sounds. Her task was to point to the box where the vibrations occurred. A box that processed the sounds *mmm, rrr,* and *nnn,* was on her left thigh; the box for *sh, fff,* and *t,* was on her right thigh.

She made a lot of mistakes. I figured she was probably trying to figure out some kind of pattern of which thigh to point to. (Am I expected to point to my left leg next or my right?) Her responses were at a chance level and remained there for two complete sessions. On the third session, we simplified the task by removing the vibrators from her right thigh. Now the test was simple. The only leg you point to is the left. The only time you point to it is when the vibrators start buzzing. I stood behind her and said *rrr* into the microphone. A shill prompted her to point to the vibrators. After one more model, she did about three trials without prompting. On the next trial, I said *rrr,* and the girl pointed to her right leg, which didn't even have vibrators on it.

We were presenting the simplest task possible, so about all we could do was give her feedback and keep presenting blocks of tasks until she caught on.

After she had learned the first three words, her performance was amazing. She had some of the same problems the other subjects encountered when the set of words reached 20, but her difficulties were not severe. After two review sessions, she was back on track. She continued to learn at a very fast rate, almost equal to that of our hearing subjects, through the end of her program. Within less than a year, she passed up all the other subjects, learning more than 120 words at over 90 percent accuracy.

So this vocoder worked. Two qualifications emerged from the experiments, however. These took some of the luster from the children's achievements. One was that the information provided by the vocoder might be achieved for some children through hearing aids only. One of our subjects could hear slightly if he wore his hearing aid. For his program, he learned the first 20 words using both the vocoder and the hearing aid; for the next ten, he used only the vocoder. His performance was initially so bad on the vocoder-only words we had to start over. He quickly relearned the 20 words. For the next part, he used both hearing aid and vocoder. He performed well. At the end of the program, we tested him on all the words, presented in random order, using only the vocoder then using both, then using only his hearing aid. He performed almost as well with the hearing aid only as he did using both inputs, which means that we possibly could have used the same program to serve some students who have sufficient "hearing" to learn rudimentary speech discriminations, but who have not received anything approximating the kind of training that teaches how to translate these weak auditory receptions.

The second luster remover was the lack of interest the field had toward the results. Education runs on tracks that are forged from tradition. The traditional scheme does not have a category that addresses highly unfamiliar learning. That's what our study was all about. We wrote several papers, and I made a presentation on the study at a conference sponsored by the Council for Exceptional Children. Nobody seemed very interested in the research.

I also presented the data at a conference on deaf education. After I talked, a panel gave an amazing critique. Panel members did not address the potential use of information or the pattern of learning that the children exhibited, which has serious implications for the kind of practice it takes to teach speech discriminations. The major focus of their responses was that we did this research without consulting the deaf community. The deaf community, according to this scenario, would make its own determination of what research should be conducted and how that information was to be used.

I pointed out that we had made the determination of what was needed on the basis of the deplorable instruction profoundly deaf children receive. The panel indicated that this was not a sufficient basis for conducting experiments with deaf children without consulting the deaf community.

That was the last time I tried to address the speech problem of deaf kids. Several years later, Rossov went to the University of Kansas, where he did some work with a model of the vocoder that children could wear during other activities. Apparently not much came of it.

Although we abandoned the vocoder, we continued to teach deaf children language, using our beginning language programs. In most settings, children use a signing system that has provisions for indicating word order, tense, and number (American sign syntactical). In other words, children are generally not responding with verbal responses, but with signs that convey the syntax of the language. The beginning language program sets the stage for teaching writing and extended vocabulary. One of my associates and co-authors, Don Steely, was involved in several experiments that showed the enormous performance differences between middle school and high school classrooms that use the Direct Instruction approach and those that follow the traditional recommendations of deaf educators. With a good language-instruction sequence, we can obviate many of the problems children have in writing passages that are syntactically acceptable.

OREGON RESEARCH INSTITUTE

During the '70s, Wes and I became involved with Oregon Research Institute. The Institute had been prosperous and very traditional in the '60s. When I became a research associate, it was on the decline because of a great exodus of principal investigators who took their grants with them. Jerry Patterson (a really good guy) had problems with the director and the priorities of the Institute. Jerry and several colleagues established Oregon Social Learning Center, which prospered. Other PIs who had problems with ORI set up the Eugene Research Institute (which prospers).

I worked with ORI largely because of the tactual hearing device. The Institute was about the only handy home that could accommodate both Rossov and me.

The long-time director of ORI left in the early '70s, following a nasty insurrection. Wes had been peripherally involved with ORI and accepted an appointment to the board of directors. I was one of the few investigators left, so I also became a director. Within a remarkably short period of time, what had been a multi-million-dollar operation was reduced to virtually one and a half researchers. I was one and Hy Hopps, a behaviorist and also a good guy, was the half. His predicament was that his grant was running out and he was submitting applications for another grant to various agencies, but the proposal was rejected again and again.

The once-flourishing Institute was reduced to three board members and Hy Hopps. The third board member was a physicist from Oregon State University. Wes engineered a move from ORI's original facility, which could accommodate a staff of more than 40 people, to a three-room office that accommodated two. The three board members met regularly, and I found the meetings futile. On most issues, Wes and I would agree; the physicist would disagree. On some issues, Wes and the physicist would agree; I would disagree. I could not see that the Institute was going anywhere, particularly after a strategy meeting that turned into a rather heated disagreement. This was one of the few times I was really angry with Wes. Following the meeting and a report that another funding agency had rejected Hopps's research proposal, I resigned as a director. ORI seemed to be a ship that was sinking with great resolution.

My vision could not have been cloudier. Wes prevailed. He worked with great persistence, trying to interest principal investigators to relocate at ORI, trying to interest different funding agencies, and trying to keep the Institute financially afloat. Hy Hopps was funded. In fact, he was funded for several minor variations of the same proposal. New PIs came to ORI, and within a year after my resignation, the Institute had to move to larger quarters.

Three years later, the politics of the burgeoning Institute left Wes in a minority position on the board and he resigned. He never received much recognition for nurturing the all-but-dead Institute. Today, ORI is far different from the crystal-ball image I had when I resigned from the board. ORI has an operating budget of $16,000,000, 60 research grants, 40 principal investigators, and 300 employees.

LET'S VOLUNTEER

I'm particularly proud of the people I worked with in Follow Through because, on their own time, they helped teachers and schools in need. As I indicated earlier, four of our trainers spent considerable time training deaf children on the vocoder project. Much of our trainers' volunteer work occurred where they lived. Those who lived in Eugene worked in local schools. Our local districts are cut from the same template that describes districts in other cities, which means that they are characterized by the same indifference, confusion, and inability to respond to data.

The local districts were not interested in or supportive of DI. Several principals, however, were. The principal of the lowest-income school in Eugene, Whiteaker Elementary, believed that his students could perform a lot better than they were performing, so he arranged to have a large number of practicum students from our university program work in his school. He also wanted to train his teachers. Several of our trainers spent a lot of time working at Whiteaker as volunteer trainers.

The program extended to all grades. This was timely because we were developing corrective reading programs for older students who read poorly. The achievement level of students in Whiteaker rose significantly and stayed high for a long time; however, the district took issue because the school was not using district-adopted programs. The fact that the students in all grades were performing higher than they had historically did not seem to matter to central-office bureaucrats.

The program could not have survived without the support of the principal, Walt Berges. I liked him not only because he had a lot of common sense but because he lived out in the country and shared my interest in trees. As long as he stayed at Whiteaker, student performance was good. His departure created some good news and some bad news. The good news was that he wanted to install DI in all grades of his new school; the bad news was that Whiteaker inherited more typical principals over the next few years and began the slow slide back to baseline. The first new principal supported the program somewhat, but not as well as Walt Berges had. We tried to convince the next principal to continue the program, and he actually issued some verbiage that could be construed as supportive. As one of our trainers later described him, however, "He talked the talk but definitely needed a walker." Once ranked as one of the top Title I schools in the state, Whiteaker slowly decayed as skilled teachers left or did things more consistent with the district's current concept of how to teach at-risk students.

The changes affected the early grades first. New programs were introduced in K and 1, and students in these grades immediately performed far below where the DI cohorts performed. The performance curve in the higher grades was different because these students had been taught a lot of skills and knowledge. If a student performs well in grade 4, he will predictably be a relatively high performer in grades 5 and 6. He might not learn as much new material as he would in a well-designed sequence, but even if he learned nothing in grades 5 and 6, his sixth-grade level performance would be higher than that of children who were low performers in grade 4. So several years after the school had returned to traditional curricula, Whiteaker was among the highest fifth- and sixth-grade Title I performers in the state, in both reading and math. Then the performance in these grades dropped, as children who had gone through the current curricular sequence reached grades 5 and 6.

In the meantime, Walt Berges went to Coburg Elementary, a semi-rural school that had low achievement levels and a fair percentage of Title I students. One of our trainers, Phyllis Haddox, had already been working as a volunteer trainer in the school. Also, one of the best teachers from Whiteaker went to Coburg. She was a product of our teacher-training program at the U of O.

In a couple of years, Coburg became a model school, from K through 6. Imagine: just about all the teachers in a modest, "country" school being super stars; able to handle the lowest kids and all behavior problems; able to accelerate the performance of students far beyond what the same student population had ever achieved. Coburg was that place. We used it to cut videotapes on specific training and performance techniques. We used it as a tryout site for new programs we were developing. And I used it as a place to provide some reassurance that I was not going crazy. Being out there for a couple of hours was definitely an elixir.

That school gave us reassurance that solid, schoolwide implementations are possible. I was always impressed by the talent of the teachers. The group varied, politically, religiously, demographically, and personally. But they worked well together; they knew that they had something special and that everybody played an important role in the school's achievements.

A good DI school has a unique sound and rhythm. During the morning periods, you can hear the groups in the early grades responding verbally— the language groups, reading groups, and math groups. You walk into a classroom, any classroom, and you're greeted with a warm atmosphere. The teacher is positive with the children, who are proud of their status as good learners.

One of my co-authors, Bob Dixon, moved to Oregon. His wife, Susan, was a teacher but knew little about DI and was philosophically opposed to it. Bob thought it would be great if Susan could teach at Coburg. He asked Phyllis if she could find time to work with Susan. On just about every day that summer, Phyllis practiced with Susan. They would wear their swimsuits, lather tanning lotion on each other, and practice presenting exercises from the program. Jerry Silbert also worked with Susan.

The work paid off. Susan was good when she went into the classroom. She had a couple of presentation problems, but she learned fast and by the end of the year she was quite good.

Ironically, she and Bob moved to Champaign, Illinois the next year. Susan got a job in the school our kids had gone to, Garden Hills, which adopted DI and had Susan as one of their star teachers. I visited her classroom during her second year in Illinois. She ran a flawless math lesson with a low performing group, then asked the children, "Would you like Ziggy to teach you?"

Yes. I did the best I could, but compared to her performance (which I would rate about 9), mine stunk (5). Neither my timing nor rate of presentation was close to hers. I believed that if I had worked with that group for a couple of days, I could have given her a challenge, but without some practice, the scorecard showed that I was not in her league.

Before we started working with Coburg, it had been among the lowest three schools in the district. When it was fully implemented, it was among the top three. Yet the population of children and most of the teachers had not changed. Not only was the district unimpressed by this improvement, Coburg had to go through extensive "waiver" procedures (more accurately described as hassles) to permit the school to use programs that were not adopted by either the district or the state. Several times, teachers and Berges had to go to Salem, Oregon and defend the decision to use material not on the state or district-approved list. In other words, the principal and staff were systematically punished by the system for improving a failed school. In contrast, the later principals at Whiteaker didn't have to defend the fact that students' performance had tumbled toward the bottom of the scale during the time the school used approved material.

The State and District posed as rational organizations that had provisions for accommodating some variations from the "procedures." This stance was a sham. In effect these agencies were saying something like, "You want to show us up by rejecting the material that we, the experts, have designated? Do it, and we'll have you jump through so many hoops you'll be bowlegged. We'll see how your negative attitude feels after a couple of rounds of this action."

Also during this period, rumors about the subliminal details of our reading program flourished. A recurring one suggested that the program promoted belief in Satanism and various kinds of voodoo magic. The evidence was a story about a genie, one about a ghost named Boo, and various references taken out of program context. We had to write several explanations to "prove" that we were not leading children into the underworld.

The program in Coburg began to die when Walt Berges retired. Like Whiteaker, the death seemed both tragic and unnecessary; and like all the other school deaths, it saddened us, leaving us with knowledge that it could be done, with happy memories, and with great pride in the people we worked with.

Another trainer who undertook a significant volunteer effort was Glenda Hewlett. She lived in Rochester, New York and worked as project manager with schools in Las Vegas, New Mexico. She was probably the most meticulous of all our trainers with respect to intricate details of interacting with children. Several teachers in a failed Title 1 school in Rochester contacted her about learning DI. She worked with them the same way she did with teachers in her Follow Through sites.

Over the next year, she provided me with many unsolicited progress reports and repeated the message that I needed to see for myself. She judged that the classrooms in her Rochester school were as good as any in our Follow Through schools. After about a year of telling Glenda that I would visit her site the next time I was on the east coast, I did it.

Children in a second-grade classroom were working in the third level of the language program. Glenda introduced me to the class, told me where they were in reading, math, and language and said, "Ask them anything about anything they've studied in any of the programs. Anything." I asked questions about story characters, the movement of liquids and gasses, and the solar system. Glenda threw in some math problems and a few questions about trivial details in the stories children had read. The children answered all the questions correctly.

Then Glenda said, "We've got ten minutes left in this period. The next thing they will learn in language is subject-predicate. See how much you can teach them in the next ten minutes." (I had recently done a workshop on this material so I didn't need to review the material to go through the steps.)

I first told the class that all sentences have two parts, one part that names and the other part that tells more.

"What does the first part do?" ...

"What does the other part do?" ...

I modeled a series of progressive examples:

"Listen: We went fishing. Say it." ...

"The part that names is *we*. The part that tells more
is *went fishing.*"

"What's the part that names?" ...

"What's the part that tells more?" ...

"Listen: Tom and his uncle went fishing.

"What's the part that names?" ...

"What's the part that tells more?" ...

"Listen: Tom and his uncle went to Grand Lake.

"What's the part that names?" …

"What's the part that tells more?" …

"Listen: Three lazy dogs went to Grand Lake.

"What's the part that names?" …

"What's the part that tells more?" …

I presented possibly 15 more examples. The last one was, "They are very smart students."

Glenda pointed out that I had only four minutes left.

I explained:

"The part that names and the part that tells more have names.

"The part that names is called the *subject*.

"What's the part that names?" …

"The part that tells more is the *predicate*.

"What's the part that tells more?" …

"Listen: They are very smart students.

"What's the subject?" …

"What's the predicate?" …

"New sentence: Mr. Briggs drives an old car.

"What's the subject?" …

"What's the predicate?" …

After I presented four or five more examples, Glenda said, "Let's see how well they learned subject-predicate. Take out lined paper and copy this sentence." She wrote on the board, "Her dog followed her to school."

"Circle the subject. Underline the predicate."

Every student performed correctly. (Some of them made a circle for each word in the subject rather than one circle for both words.)

Glenda tested them with two other examples. One was, "Ted's sister and her friend did not watch TV often." Two kids screwed up. One didn't copy all the words of the sentence. The other circled *Ted's sister and her friend did not*. For a ten-minute drill, however, their performance was very impressive.

Before we left the classroom, Glenda asked me, "Well, what do you think?"

"I think they're as impressive as any classroom I've ever seen."

Glenda said, "True."

BRAIN-INJURED SUBJECTS

Starting in 1973, the Corp began working with juveniles and adults who had suffered traumatic brain injuries, caused by accidents or strokes. The primary reason for this work was to try to learn more about how much of what they lost they could relearn. The literature was vague, primarily because the amount and type of practice provided during rehabilitation was probably less than 1/100 of what some victims would need to relearn which pathways produced which words or ideas. The learner who has a stroke or suffers from a head injury tries to say something like, "Hello," but instead he may say "Merry Christmas" or "Good." These responses are positive, versus something like "Go away," which is negative. So somehow, the basic classification system may still be intact (with the good things grouped and distinguished from the other things). The problem is that the pathways for accessing the right words are not working. Depending on how severe the problem is, the learner may or may not know that the response "Merry Christmas" is wrong. We wanted to find out how much of what is lost can be recovered by an intensive instruction that is closely referenced to the learner's current status and focuses on the specific problems the learner has.

Some victims lose their ability to do math. Some lose almost everything—both their receptive knowledge and their ability to express what they want to say. Some have losses in only a few specific areas, like memory of people's names.

Our operating assumption was that there might be enough redundancy in the brain to accommodate relearning in the non-motor skills. The disabilities resulting from neurological damage to motor areas do not improve as a function of practice. The cognitive aspects of the brain are different. They are not clearly wired to specific areas (but the language center is usually on only one side of the brain). The problem a victim has, however, may not be easily dichotomized as either a "motor" or "non-motor" problem. A person who has obvious mechanical problems trying to speak and who has lost cognitive functions has a combination motor and cognition problem. Ultimately, whatever improvement the subject makes is limited by whatever capabilities the injured brain has. Our goal was simply to test some of the limits.

Our strategy was to start with the assumption that all could learn. This was just a working hypothesis that could be discredited by the data we would gather. We had knowledge from working with very low performers and deaf children about ballpark numbers for the amount of practice required for initial learning, and about the trend of requiring less practice for subsequent items that are in the same class as those initially taught to mastery. So we anticipated that the subjects would need enormous amounts of practice during the early instruction.

The basic procedure we used was based on the idea that it's possible to make a task relatively easier or more difficult by manipulating the context of the task. By adding increasing amounts of distraction and manipulating the time interval between trials of the targeted tasks, we can create a continuum of tasks with increasing difficulty. The simplest task is a repetition of a task that was presented just a moment ago. "Your name is Darby. What's your name? (Short pause.) What's your name?" The second task occurs in the easiest context possible. It requires the least amount of memory, only a moment's worth, and the context presents no distractions that could divert the learner's attention.

The next easiest context is one in which some time elapses between the presentations of the same task. For instance, the task "What's your name?" becomes more difficult if there is a five-second pause between presentations of this task.

We can make the task still more difficult by introducing a "distracter" between the presentations of the targeted task. "What's your name? ... Yes, Teddy. Teddy, touch your nose ... Good. What's your name?" The task is harder because attention has to be mobilized to respond to the distracter-task then redirected to the targeted task. The result is that a learner may be quite reliable at answering a sequence of the same task with pauses between trials, but often will fail when the distracter task is interpolated.

The basis for judging when to move from a simpler context to one a little harder was the learner's performance. After the learner got a specified number of consecutive examples right on the simpler level of context difficulty, we presented items from the next level. The teacher always reviewed everything the learner had mastered. The review format simply presented items the learner had mastered in random order.

The review occurred at the beginning of each training session. The teacher greeted the learner and presented tasks. "Hi there, young man. Listen: What's your teacher's name? ... How old are you? ... Show me where your shirt pocket is ... Shake hands ... What's your name? ..."

Note that it's very important for these questions to be presented in a random order. When I was working with Alan Hoffmeister at Utah State University, we saw a great example of why items must not be presented in the same order. A graduate student had been working with a seriously retarded subject. He showed us what the learner could do. He presented a series of 15 tasks and marked things off on his clipboard as the learner performed. The first tasks in the sequence were, "Henry, go to the sink ... Pick up the glass ... Fill it with water ... Set the glass on the counter ... Go to the bathroom ..." The learner performed perfectly, but did one thing that showed he had not really learned to discriminate the commands but had simply learned the order. He started to reach for the glass as the trainer was saying, "Pick up the ..."

After the learner had completed the chain of directed behaviors, I asked the graduate student if he always presented the tasks in the same order. He said he did. I demonstrated the problem by playing the role of trainer. I took the clipboard and presented directions with the same tone that the graduate student used but the directions were different for all but the first task. "Henry, go to the sink ..." He did. The following task was something like, "Dibble de grop on the goozer." He picked up the glass. "Cram a lizard into a shloom." He set the glass on the counter. I continued to say nonsense phrases and he ran the entire routine as flawlessly as he had for the trainer.

Just as we varied the order of tasks we presented to the learner, we varied the place where the tasks were presented and varied the presenter. Unless this is done, the learner may not generalize what is learned. There's a phenomenon called the *magic aide* effect. A particular instructional aide is very effective with a seriously retarded student. The child performs on everything she presents, but she is the only one he responds to. The reason is not that she is magic, but that she used a poor program. She should have regularly had others present the review material that she presented.

Also, there's the magic room phenomenon. A seriously retarded child performs flawlessly in a particular room (the room in which all the training occurred). The learner does not respond in other places. The reason is that the learner has never been required to respond in these places. In other words, the program should have been designed so that the learner responds to the various tasks in different settings.

Our work with traumatic head-injured subjects incorporated provisions for reviewing material in various settings and for various people to present the material to the learner. The first couple of victims I worked with didn't have serious impairments six months after their trauma, and they completely recovered their functions after a couple of weeks of training. They probably would have recovered the functions without the training.

To work with more serious problems, I trained two exceptionally bright people. One was Ann Glang, who was in the Ph.D. program at the University of Oregon. She was a polished teacher and trainer. Ann later wrote several papers that documented great improvement of several head-injured subjects she had taught. The other person I trained was one of our Follow Through trainers, Linda Garcia. She was not interested in writing papers. She was a free spirit totally immersed in the work with her students and very astute.

We worked out procedures for providing a quick appraisal or diagnosis of each learner's capabilities. Part of the assessment was based on the idea that in highly emotional situations, impaired learners have more access to their "lost" verbal skills than they do in less emotional situations.

We exploited this fact by presenting an emotional situation and observing the learner's verbalizations. The procedure we used most frequently was to find something a learner disliked and then purposely do things that provoked the learner. For instance, one of the subjects we worked with was

Cheri, who almost died three times from anoxia. She was in her late teens when she had a serious car accident in which her jaw had been broken and cut off her breathing. Next, medics put her on a respirator that failed. Finally, there was a mix-up at the hospital and she was not on a breathing device for several minutes.

The first time we saw her was a year later. She was in a wheelchair. Her face was partly paralyzed, her mouth crooked, and she had very limited use of her left arm. Her mother indicated that Cheri had not uttered an intelligible word since the trauma.

I asked the mother what Cheri disliked, and she indicated that Cheri did not want anybody touching her things, particularly her purse. Cheri had a shoulder-strap purse. I asked Cheri a couple of questions that required verbal answers. She shook her head, no. Then I said in an aggressive way, "Hey, I want that purse. Give me that purse."

She shook her head. "Come on. Give me that purse." I grabbed it and started to tug on it. As she resisted, she said quite clearly, "Don't ... touch ... my ... purse." I thought her mother would faint. I told Cheri I didn't really want her purse. I just wanted to see if she could talk. She smiled.

We knew that she had some kind of residual core, which if aroused could lead to coherent and situationally-appropriate speech. But we had a long way to go for her to recover speech and concepts in situations that did not have strong emotional prompting.

One of the tricks we used early on to help her recover pathways was to present a string of tasks that didn't require verbal responses in quick succession. Following the last non-verbal task would be one that required a verbal response. If a person performs well on the non-verbal tasks, the probability is greatly increased that she'll perform on the verbal task. "Touch your head ... Good ... Clap your hands ... Good. Again, clap your hands ... Touch the paper ... Good. Are you touching a dog? ..." A response is more likely on the end of the chain because the earlier tasks require the learner to be in a "following direction" mode, which increases the possibility that she'll somehow access whatever pathways are needed to perform on the last task.

Within a week or so, Cheri learned a couple of things. Linda taught her to say, "I don't know," and "I can't" and required her to say it if she didn't know the answer or couldn't say something. Within four months, Cheri had had learned half a dozen more words and had recovered some of her functions (like being able to touch an object that was named), but her progress was slow.

The learning pattern for head-injured learners is not the same as that for "normals" because they already have much information stored somewhere; they simply don't know how to access it. During the early learning, they characteristically develop what we called "negative ghosts." For every new word or skill the learner masters, some of the words or skills that had been learned earlier become confused. The outcome was predictable with every learner we worked with. (We saw this same phenomenon with the deaf children learning new words.) When Cheri was reasonably firm on responding to a task like "Touch the top of the paper," and we introduced, "Hand me the paper," not only did she lose the ability to respond to "Touch the top of the paper," she lost responses to some tasks that had no apparent relationship to the new task, such as, "What's your name?"

The explanation we came up with was that the healthy mind has everything classified by "multiple criteria," including those that are very broad, such as "Things I don't like," "Things I did when I was younger," and "Things I learned in school." After the trauma, these connections are somehow obliterated, or confused. So the new instruction requires the learner not only to relearn a name but to reestablish this item so it again is where it belongs in the classification system. The task, "Touch the top of the paper," needs to be grouped with other tasks that call for touching, and other contexts that refer to paper. The system that is relearning pathways makes an "approximate" adjustment. The introduction of the next item (Hand me the paper) requires a more precise approximation and throws the post-trauma categories out of whack because they are not precise enough.

The more a learner learns, the fewer and less severe the negative ghosts become. The problems the learner now has may require only a half dozen trials to restore the information the learner had mastered before the latest disruption.

The ghost process is something like someone walking up one side of a hill and down the other. At the top of the hill the negative ghosts are all but gone. Starting down the other side takes us into the domain of positive ghosts. For every new thing you teach, you will observe spontaneous recovery of things you did not teach. For example, the learner has trouble performing basic counting tasks.

When the learner masters these basic operations, specific operations that are not closely related to counting or identifying numbers may spontaneously emerge. For instance, the learner may now know some subtraction facts he hadn't been able to recover before. Also, the learner may recover some skills that are only remotely related to math.

If the program can take the learner about 2/3 the way down the positive-ghost side of the hill, the learner will be able to learn a great deal without your help; but sometimes the traumatized learner's problems are not easily identified through casual encounters. Nicki was an example. She suffered a ruptured brain aneurism in her early thirties. If you carried on casual conversations with her six months later, you probably wouldn't even notice that she had a problem. "How are you doing today?"

"Oh, fine."

"What do you think of this weather?"

"It's terrible. I'm really tired of the rain. I want to go outdoors without getting wet."

And so forth.

But there were hundreds of basic things she didn't know. We had a tape of one of her training sessions. Linda was seated in front of her and asked a series of casual questions as they smoked. Everything Linda asked was something that Nicki had not known when we started to work with her. Some items still needed work.

"What's your first name?"

"What's your whole name?"

"How old are you?"

"Where are you right now?"

"What did you have for breakfast?"

She answered these items correctly.

"How many kids do you have?"

"Huh? ... I don't know."

"Three. You have three kids."

"Of course, three. I should know that."

"What are their names?"

"Their names? Um ... I'm not sure."

Nicki's performance was about a third of the way down the positive side of the ghost hill. So she still benefited greatly from work that would target things she couldn't do.

Some of the people we worked with were very different from either Cheri or Nicki. What struck me about all the victims was that their personalities seemed to be "exaggerations" of what they had been before the trauma. The young victim of a motorcycle accident was happy-go-lucky, even though he couldn't walk and had serious loss of knowledge and skill. A librarian was fussy and complained a lot both about things outside the learning center and about her training. "You're pushing me too hard. I can't think when you keep asking those questions." A juvenile named Darby was probably autistic in addition to being brain-injured. His behavior was both bizarre and unpredictable.

We even worked with a 64-year-old woman who had suffered brain injury three years before her son brought her to us. Both her age and the length of time since the trauma militated against high expectations of recovery. I told her son that the elapsed time since the injury made it a lot harder for her. During the time since her injury, she had learned to adapt to her post-trauma realities. Most of what she did to adapt would create great interference with what she had to learn. She learned to avoid things and to distort them so she could operate with the limited skills she had. The situation is parallel to teaching a sixth-grade student who failed at learning to read effectively. Trying to establish appropriate reading behavior requires at least ten times the number of trials required to teach the same kid as a first-grader.

Our 64-year-old student learned some. In terms of the ghost hill, she may have made it about 3/4 the way up the negative-ghost side. Virtually all of the others we worked with for more than a couple of months made it farther. Cheri reached the top of the hill and started a little way down the positive-ghost side. Nicki made it all the way down the positive side. An engineer Ann worked with could initially produce endless lectures on things like the economic conditions of Europe and the future of engineering. In contrast, he couldn't name four things that were vehicles, or add 12 plus 13. Through training, he made it all the way down the hill. Darby made it over the top and slightly down the positive side.

We took our subjects as far as we could within the time constraints we had. We tried to work with them five days a week for an hour a day. The work did not go beyond this group of subjects, however, because the professional community lacked interest in both our findings and our practices. Ann Glang tried without success to get several articles placed in respectable "journals." Nobody we contacted in the area of therapy, rehab, or neurology seemed to have any interest in what we had shown. A prominent neurologist who had diagnosed one of the boys we worked with indicated that the boy couldn't be doing some of the things we reported he was doing. He came down and observed Billy, and he was shocked at the performance. He said, "I had no idea that such improvement could occur through training."

Nothing else happened.

A postscript on Linda's students is sad. Nicki's sister had died of a ruptured aneurism when she was 36. Nicki also died of a ruptured aneurism at 36. Darby moved away and died a year later from some unknown cause. Cheri had a shunt removed from her head. The operation was very involved because the shunt was now solidly embedded in her brain. Following the surgery, she lost everything she had learned. She moved away, and we never heard more about her. These outcomes really upset Linda because she had strong emotional attachments to all the people she worked with.

Three decades later, a colleague from Chicago told me about a friend who had a brain tumor and was terminal. He wanted to recover some of his mental functions and wasn't satisfied with the "speech and language therapy" he was receiving. Did I know of anybody in the area that could work with him? I called Linda, who lived in the area, and asked her if she wanted to work with the patient. For nearly a year, she worked with him daily. He had completely lost all language, both receptive and expressive, which means he couldn't understand any words and he couldn't speak. He could understand non-verbal communication. So Linda communicated with him non-verbally. They joked, played games, and pantomimed. Linda became strongly attached to him and was very saddened by his death. After he died, she told me she didn't want to work with any more brain-injured learners.

CHICAGO'S EXPANSION OF DI

I was particularly interested in having a good project in Chicago, because that's where I grew up, on the south side. The Follow Through school we worked with in Chicago (Ogden Elementary) was interesting, but not the kind of school I thought we should be serving. It was 75 percent White and far from rock-bottom low in performance. In fact, it had some students from quite high income levels. The students were easy to manage, and the teachers did a relatively good job because they were not overwhelmed with a large percentage of children who were hard to teach. By 1973, the second-grade children finished the year performing at the beginning fourth grade level. This was higher than the performance of the three highest-income schools in the Chicago area.

Although Ogden was not what I would call a high-risk school, it was a catalyst for us to work with other Chicago schools and child-teacher centers. Joe Rosen was a maverick superintendent of District 10 (the third lowest in the Chicago area) who deserved his reputation of being tough. He believed that systematic instruction could elevate the performance of students in his schools. In 1969–1970, he observed at Ogden, met with us several times, and mapped out a plan for installing DI with 3,300 students in District 10.

Joe tried to implement schools as close to the model at Ogden as he could, using only Title I funds and working with Child Parent Centers. This goal presented challenges because his schools didn't have as many aides as Ogden, but he played with the budget and focused his primary effort on grades K through 3. On the average, his schools performed significantly above those of the same demography. The performance of second graders in 1972 was only a tenth of a grade level below the norm. By 1974, his second graders performed at grade level, a remarkable achievement considering the demography of District 10. The average Title I school performed more than half a year below this level.

In 1976, J. S. Fuerst, Assistant Director of the Graduate Program in Urban Studies at Loyola University, Chicago, wrote a detailed summary of the project, which appeared in *The Public Interest*. Fuerst summarized the results and reported the reactions to the program's success. His summary showed that the DI schools' second grades scored above the average of the city, and about 30 percent higher than the City's at-risk population.

Fuerst listed the same criticisms to the program we heard in other cities:

- Too much academic orientation
- No attention paid to psychological and developmental factors
- Requires hard work
- Teaches what is measured on achievement tests
- Mechanistic and stifles teachers' creativity
- Is not racially sensitive
- Requires more money
- Not appropriate for higher performers
- The results aren't lasting

Fuerst dealt with each criticism, pointing out that some of the best results were achieved by Olive Child Parent Center, which was housed in temporary structures and had a very low per-child cost. Also, he noted that some of the Ogden parents, " ... who are among Chicago's highest-income group, say that they could easily afford to send their children to private schools but prefer Ogden, with its Direct Instruction program."

A key point Feurst made was that DI could serve as a successful alternative to integration for segregated schools and indicated why the performance of these schools was actually higher than the data suggested: "1) ... Direct Instruction children rarely, if ever, have to repeat grades; 2) children rarely require special classes after being 'mainstreamed.'"

In 1974, Joe Rosen wrote a summary on the implementation and maintenance of the DI system. He made two basic, but rarely stated, observations about the program.

> One thing is certain and that is that where the principal has made his position in support of using DI materials and consultants unequivocally clear, consultant-teacher problems do not appear. Another certainty is that the best in-service occurs within the classroom when the consultant observes the teacher and speaks with the teacher about what she observed and may leave her with a notation as to what aspects of her teaching may need strengthening.

Judith Maillis did a master's thesis on teacher attitudes toward DI. She sampled 150 teachers. One of her conclusions was that teachers who had taught longer before using DI tended to be more positive about the program: Of first-year teachers, 88 percent liked the program or liked it very much; 95 percent of the second-year teachers gave this rating; 98 percent of the teachers who had taught 3 or more years gave this rating.

The experience I remember most occurred in the early '70s, during the riots. Two trainers and I went with Joe to a school within a housing project. We parked east of the project and followed a sidewalk through the wide corridor between buildings, as Joe gave a running commentary on the project. It was fairly early in the morning, but we were the only people outside. From time to time, the sound of gunshots echoed through the corridor. The consultants and I had wide eyes, but the shots didn't seem to distract Joe. Before we reached the school, I asked him, "Don't you feel kind of uneasy with all that gunfire?"

He said, "Oh, hell, they won't shoot me. I'm their friend. They're shooting at their enemies."

I asked who their enemies were and he said, "Each other."

The effort in District 10 had abundant data with large numbers of students. It documented that the program could be implemented in low-income schools, using only Title I funds and other sources that were available. The data revealed significant benefits the program produced; however, instead of the program format becoming institutionalized and expanded to thousands of other students in Chicago, the program was encouraged to wither and die, replaced by fuzzy attempts to focus on human values, not academic skills. Joe's effort was thoroughly erased from the Chicago Public Schools' memory banks.

MORE AUTISTIC CHILDREN

We did a considerable amount of work with autistic children during the 1970s. I had a great deal of input on a residential facility that opened in Vancouver, B.C. The plan was similar to the one used at the Children's Research Institute at the University of Illinois. We would arrange the day so the children learned academics and engaged in a variety of reinforcing activities.

During the summer of 1970, I spent a week at the facility, trying to smooth out some of the rough spots. I planned to visit the school regularly, but the most I could hope for, following the initial surge, was one day every couple of months. So I needed other trained people to work on the project. The problem in 1970 was that there weren't any. In 1971, however, we had some trainers who could spend more time in Vancouver. The person who did most of this work was Jerry Silbert, a maverick who suddenly appeared on the Follow Through scene at the Jack Tarr Hotel in San Francisco during a training session for our consultants and project managers. SRA representatives from the west coast also attended some of the sessions. Jerry asked me a list of questions the first time we met (before our first session). He had another list of questions after that session.

I answered the questions and gathered that he was somehow associated with our project, but I didn't know his story or exactly what he was supposed to be doing (except asking questions). He had come to Eugene on a ruse. He had been studying elementary education at the University of Minnesota and secured a small grant to "study Direct Instruction." The application had indicated that he would go to Eugene, observe, take notes, return to Minneapolis, and write a report. He never returned to Minneapolis.

I later learned that he had an unusual background. He grew up in New York, a Jew in a predominantly Italian neighborhood, spent time working all over Europe, including three months in a kibbutz on the border of Lebanon, and working for social agencies as a caseworker in New York City.

He had actually been in Eugene for several weeks before I met him. Jerry had somehow managed to talk Wes into giving him a job at the trailers doing clerical work and enrolling him in our master's program.

Just after I spent my first question-and-answer period with Jerry, several SRA representatives and I were standing in the lobby, chatting before the first session started. One of the SRA men asked why we chose the Jack Tarr Hotel.

I said I didn't know and asked what was wrong with the Jack Tarr.

"It's a hangout for hookers."

"You're kidding."

"No. They're all over the place."

"Well, I don't think I've seen any. How do you spot them?"

One of the reps started to list characteristics when the other interrupted and said, "Look, there are two of them right there, coming down the stairway."

He pointed to two attractive blonde women who were talking and laughing.

I said, "Are you sure they're hookers?"

"Hell, yes. Not a doubt."

When the women reached the bottom of the stairway, I waved and beckoned them to join us. They did.

I said to the SRA men, "I'd like you to meet two of our trainers, Linda Youngmayr and Glenda Hewlett."

Jerry proved to be a worker. He quickly became a pretty good teacher. His strength was management. That strength was the reason I began to work with him on training autistic children. EB Corp worked with a small group of autistic children. We were able to succeed with children that the county Educational Services Division could not handle, but our success was marginal with children older than 10. I felt that the greatest promise for success was with younger children. The younger the better.

I believe the most critical problem autistic children have is trying to figure out what causes what, and the more they try to figure it out, the more confused they become. I think the reason is that their mind is not linked to attention the way it is in a normal child. If autistic children try to attend to something, their mind doesn't obey, but instead attends only to peripheral details.

According to current classification systems, children who are labeled autistic comprise a far greater range than those who are actually autistic. According to current labeling, any child who is a little strange or shy is "autistic." Hard-core autistic children typically have trouble learning relative relationships. For instance, they have trouble learning the appropriate uses of the words *yes* and *no*. The reason is that the answer to the same question is not always the same word. The answer to "Are you brushing your teeth?" is sometimes yes and sometimes no.

The newly formed residential home in Vancouver accommodated 18 truly autistic children from ages 5 to 12. The facililty was located in an otherwise quiet residential neighborhood. The first group had some fascinating children. We made tapes of their responses to various questions. One child, Ben, seemed to be normal. After asking, "What's your name?" "How old are you?" and several other questions, I asked, "Are you a tiger?"

He laughed and said sarcastically, "A tiger."

I said, "Well, are you a tiger?"

Again, he said sarcastically, "A tiger."

I said emphatically, "Tell me: Are you a tiger?"

"Yes." (Emphatically.)

Aaron was a 9-year-old who had great trouble learning to carry out plans. He lived in Vancouver, but after much rehearsal and verbal drill about where to get off the bus, he rode the bus to the end of the line on more than one occasion. Although he had great difficulty learning the order of the four bus stops before he was to get off the bus, he could tell you the day of the week of virtually any date. If the date was recent, he would have almost no hesitation. If the date was 20 years earlier, it took him about 5 seconds to figure out the day of the week.

Wayne was another unique child. He could read well and perform on various language tasks, but while he was doing the tasks, he said more than the right answers. He verbalized much of what he was thinking, and his thoughts took many circuitous routes at the same time. Once, I was working with him in following directions that require no verbal response. I told him the rule, "Don't say anything, and you'll get to watch TV."

As he performed the actions, he gave a running commentary that referred to tasks that are in the language program, the rule I gave him and miscellaneous thoughts and impressions. As he did tasks like "Touch your nose," "Stand up," and "Clap," his commentary was something like this:

"Touch under picture. What is this? Listen to what I say. Watch TV. Stand up. Don't say anything and watch TV. Touch your nose. Go to a hockey game. Where have all the good times gone? To correct: repeat task. Praise correct responses. Don't say anything."

Wayne memorized commercials on TV and memorized TV schedules. His favorite activity was listening to hockey games on radio. One time, he was seated in the living room reading *TV Guide*. An aide was playing with three of the younger children. She pretended to chase them, and they ran squealing through the house. As they went through the living room, the aide shouted, "Run for your life."

Without looking up, Wayne said, "At the YMCA."

One of the children was Henry, who probably spent at least a third of his waking hours crying. He would say "*Bitte, bitte,*" but he wasn't German and didn't speak German.

An interesting event occurred in the facility's fenced backyard on the first day for an eight-year-old, Jimmy, who had come to the facility from the Northwest Territory. Jimmy was standing next to the swing set staring into the distance. Two aides were playing with four children. Another aide was working with Henry in the sand box. Henry was wailing.

A neighbor from across the street, an older man, came to the gate and called to me. He said, "I would like to talk to Henry."

I shrugged. "About what?"

"I hear him crying all the time and I know how unhappy he must be. I want him to know that I love him. I want him to know that somebody cares about him."

I opened the gate and the neighbor walked over to Henry, who now had sand in his mouth and was crying, spitting, and sobbing, "*Bitte, bitte.*"

The man bent down, patted Henry's sandy head and said, "I love you, Henry. I love you, Henry." Henry continued to wail.

As the man walked back toward the gate, he passed Jimmy, who was still in a statuesque pose, looking into the distance.

The man said, "Hello, young man. What is your name?"

Still looking straight ahead, Jimmy said, "Fuck you."

The neighbor never came back.

What was interesting about Jimmy was his capacity to learn. He didn't know how to read and didn't know a lot of language concepts. On his first day, we taught him *yes-no* in only a few minutes. At first he slapped himself every time he said either "yes" or "no." We got that problem at least partially under control on the first day and started him in the language program and reading program.

At first, he wasn't completely compliant, but then he got into the role of learner. The next time I saw him was about a month later. They had started the arithmetic program and his performance was unbelievable. Before the instruction began, he couldn't count, identify numbers, or do even the simplest arithmetic.

I could tell that he was catching on faster than the program presented new information. He wasn't making any mistakes. I took over the teaching and accelerated the pace to see how fast he could go. I presented the information as fast as I could read, point, and talk. He didn't make any mistakes. I moved about ten lessons ahead in the program. He made a couple of mistakes because the program had introduced things he didn't know. I corrected the errors he made talking as fast as I could and continued. The corrections took only a few seconds. After the lesson, I tested him on the new information. He knew it all.

In a few months, Jimmy learned more content than children would typically learn in two or three years. Jimmy's father later wrote the director of the facility a long, biographical letter that expressed the parents' frustration, grief, and joy.

After describing how he and his wife slowly accepted the idea that Jimmy (who was born prematurely) was not normal, the father listed the parents' unsuccessful attempts to get him into a treatment center. The father had just about given up. Here are excerpts from his letter.

> In the summer he roamed the town. He left home at sunrise and came home at sunset. He upset the whole town, by playing with garden tools, lawnmowers, cars, ... He was a public pest, but ... Jimmy was no longer my responsibility. Society was now responsible ...Then came the day. Susan, Jimmy and Anna left for Vancouver. Finally, nearly five years after we were told that there was nothing wrong physically, he is retarded, finally he was on his way to the treatment that was to allow him to live like any other boy lives.

> ... Susan phoned from Vancouver. But how do you explain over the telephone what Laurel House is like! ... Just after one day, Jimmy could say yes and no, and he knew when to say yes and when to say no. After just one day, and for five years, we have lovingly explained to him, we told him, we yelled, we hit, we did just about anything within the range from loving care to

desperate anger to get him to say yes or no. And you did it, in just one day.

In August, I had an opportunity to go to Vancouver. I was very anxious to see Jimmy. We missed him ... When I entered Laurel House, Jimmy was doing some reading lessons in the kitchen. I could observe him through the one-way mirror. It seemed unreal, he was actually reading, was sitting quietly, he was paying attention, and oddly, he seemed to enjoy it ... After he finished his lesson, his teacher sent him to the back yard to play, and I was told that I could now go to see him. I went to the veranda and watched him. I had to say something nice to him, but how do you call him lovingly if you have never experienced tender feelings with the boy. I have always loved him, but to him, Daddy, Mommy, a lamppost, the garden fence, it was the same, no difference.

... I had to act casual, as if this is what I expected. So I just called, "Hello, Jimmy." He turned around, he looked at me, and very gradually a happy sort of grin came over his face. In his hop-skip sort of manner ... he came towards me. "Hello, Daddy." ... He was just eight years old; how long I had waited for this one line ... I did not know what to say. I was not prepared to answer him. I just stood there ... stunned and perplexed.

Jerry witnessed this reunion. He told me it was a powerful experience.

Two people who lived in the Toronto area, Peter Lormier and Jeff Sherman, became interested in our approach. They worked with Thistletown, a mammoth facility near Toronto that served children of all ages. Jeff was in charge of House 17, which had the more severe autistic children. I went to Thistletown a few times and worked with some of the children. We put most of them in the beginning language program and moved as fast as they could go. We introduced other subjects when they were fairly solid in language.

At a session, I presented information about our approach to the entire staff and some outsiders. I put on the best demonstrations I ever did to show the problems autistic children have with directing their attention. A teacher from the project first demonstrated how the children were taught in the language program. She worked with a child I had never seen before. He was clearly having trouble with parts of the lesson and did not show much improvement after the teacher corrected mistakes and repeated parts of the lesson.

After she finished, I explained that there are two ways to work effectively with these children. One is ponderous, to plow through the program. The other is to trick the learner. To illustrate the trick technique, I asked the teacher to name some objects the child could not reliably identify. She listed six things, including a watch, a ring, a book, and a pencil. We got examples of all six objects from the teacher and people in the audience and put them on a table. Then I worked with the child. I did not review or even say the names of any of the objects on the table. I presumed that he actually knew the names of these objects. I tested that presumption with tasks that emphasized something other than the object name.

For the first task, I pointed to a woman in the front row and said, "You're going to give something to that person right there. Look at her." I told the woman to raise her hand. "That's the person, right there. Listen: give the watch to that person. That one, right there."

The child picked up the watch and gave it to a man sitting three seats from the woman.

I did the same thing with all the other objects. For each task, the child picked up the object I named incidentally and gave it to the wrong person. I pointed out that he did know the names of these objects in some form but he didn't know how to mobilize his knowledge or link it to tasks that required him to focus attention on that object and the relationship of object to name. (If I had changed the task so that I acted as if the name of the object was important, and the person in the audience was secondary, the child would have picked up the wrong object and given it to the right person.) The child's problem was not one of compliance but of not being able to control his attention. When he attempted to attend to something he experienced something like a blind spot. Things on the periphery were clear, but the thing he tried to attend to wasn't accessible.

The point was that the child needed work in plowing through the program so that he learned how to mobilize attention. At the same time, there were ways to accelerate the child or correct mistakes that did not involve repetition, but trickery. I demonstrated with a second child. For this one, I acted as if I was very concerned with his hands, which moved nervously. I kept reminding him to hold his hands down by his sides. I reinforced him for this behavior, and presented tasks from the language lesson with no particular reinforcement as if I was interested in his hands, not the tasks from the program. I made frequent comments about his hands. He performed flawlessly on material that he hadn't been able to do when the teacher had demonstrated with him. I skipped far ahead in the program. He performed flawlessly.

I combined trips to Thistletown with some work in Bellevue, Ontario, where I worked with first graders. After work one day, we went to a teacher's house for a social get-together. The teacher had a large, playful German shorthaired pointer. One of the guests tossed a small pillow across the room and the dog retrieved it but wouldn't let go. When the man tried to wrest it from the dog, the dog hung on, hunkered down, growled, and apparently thought this was the best part of the game.

The dog's master said, "It's no use. We tried everything, and we can't get him to let go of whatever he fetches." He listed some of the things they had tried—twisting his ear, swatting his butt. "Nothing works."

One of the guests said, "I'll bet Ziggy could teach him to let go in three trials."

I said, "I don't know. I think it would take four." (This was after a couple of drinks and my confidence level was high.)

At the time, I didn't smoke, but I knew from when I had smoked that dogs do not like it if you blow smoke in their face. So I lit up a cigarette and threw the pillow. The dog fetched and returned to me for the wrestling match. I grabbed the pillow, and he started his routine. I took a long drag from the cigarette, said, "Drop it," bent over, and blew smoke at the dog's snout. The dog let go of the pillow and vigorously turned his head away.

I did the same thing on the second trial—said "Drop it," bent over, blew smoke.

On the third trial, the dog let go of the pillow as I was bending over, before I blew smoke.

On the fourth trial, I said "Drop it." Before I started to bend, the dog let go.

One of the guests said in a half-joking way, "I get it now. You use behavioral techniques that work with dogs, and apply them to working with children."

I told him that wasn't exactly right. I assume that kids and dogs are smart. All of them are capable of learning what predicts what, which is what you do when you're teaching appropriate behaviors. So I just made it clear to the dog that "Drop it" predicts that I'll bend over, and bending over predicts that he'll get an aversive blast of smoke in his face. The simplest way to avoid the aversion is to let go of the pillow, which he learned to do.

LAND

I wanted to buy a few acres in Oregon and plant trees on them. The prices of land listed in the local paper were shocking. In 1970, parcels were selling for over $1,000 an acre, which was as high as the price of super land in Illinois (where the top soil may be over ten feet deep). On a flight back home to Eugene in 1971, I sat next to a man who worked in the timber industry. I told him I was shocked at land prices in Oregon. He pointed out that Oregon has a fairly small amount of private land because of the state's extensive national and state forests. Then he added that large parcels were not extensive. He said that his mother had a place for sale. It was 120 acres, fenced and cross-fenced. It had a house, an apple orchard, and barn. He said, "She's asking $325 an acre. But you have to remember, it's just cutover timberland."

Actually, it wasn't all cutover. It had groves of mature Douglas fir, and it had a knoll in the middle of it that rose up about 400 feet and provided spectacular views—the Cascades to the east, a large reservoir to the northeast, and Crow Valley to the south and west, fringed by the coast range to the south. Most of the land was grass, with stumps of trees that were harvested in the 1950s. On the top of the knoll was a remnant of a giant, a stump about 20 feet tall and more than 7 feet in diameter.

The place was only about 18 miles from our home. I was completely smitten with it. I bought it and spent part of weekends each winter planting exotic trees in the rolling fields—redwoods, giant sequoia, cedars (from Africa, Lebanon, and India), pines, firs, and spruce from different parts of the world. My three young boys helped me plant. I dug the holes with a mattax. They planted seedlings in the holes and tamped down the loose dirt. During each winter we would plant at least 1,000 trees (in some years, more than 4,000). The place now has more than 100 varieties of trees. Some of the ponderosa pine that we planted are now 70 feet tall. Some of the redwoods are even taller.

The place has always been a sanctuary for me. During the Follow Through years, my days were hectic and filled with problems. On a cloudy winter Saturday, all the tribulations would fade as we drove out to the land. We would work hard; we'd sweat. But we'd also walk around and admire this amazing place. We realized how lucky we were to have it.

Some of the other people on the project also bought country property. Bob Mattson had a picturesque farm about 15 miles from campus. Coyote Creek runs through it, and in two places along the creek are "trading areas," where different Indian tribes counciled and traded. These areas have lots of arrowheads and other artifacts.

Wes bought a small ranch close to Bob's place. Wes had three or four horses, three riding paths, and lots of poison oak. He had an old Ford tractor that he used to cultivate large garden areas. He grew the produce that he used to make his special salsa, which is still a gourmet item in a couple of local circles.

I told some of the people I worked with what the man I met on the plane told me. You can get acreage at a low price by putting an ad in the paper. Tell how much you'll pay, and if it's not less than $300 per acre, you'll get some takers.

Following this formula, Susie Stearns (now Hanner) bought 60 awesome acres, on which she and her husband built a "progressive" structure, which grew from about 1,500 square feet to over 5,000 square feet. Randy Sprick bought a 40-acre parcel that had a nice house. Don Steely bought 40 acres just outside Cottage Grove, where he and his wife built an amazing house that broke various "structural rules." For instance a three-story house cannot have discontinuous posts. Don's house was built with discontinuous posts. Posts went from the ground to the first floor. They stopped. The first floor was put in place and posts were set on top of the floor for the second floor. Don's plan worked because the posts were Douglas fir logs about two feet in diameter. When the house was finished, it was one-of-a-kind with secret rooms, narrow staircases to the top floor, and a lot of open space and windows. Don also planted over 30 varieties of trees on his land.

After Wes married Julie, they sold the ranch and bought a smaller parcel that fronted Fern Ridge Reservoir and that had an attractive house. Wes put on an addition of more than 1,600 square feet, making it an awesome estate.

Randy sold some of his land and bought a larger parcel. Like Don and Susie, Randy built an incredible house with very little outside help. The house is on a viewpoint high above a stream, pond, and mixed forest of Douglas firs and ponderosa pine.

The last of our folks to get into land purchasing were Doug and Linda Carnine. They bought a small place on the McKenzie River. Recently they purchased three large, scenic parcels near Eugene, more than 700 acres of land, which they are in the process of restoring to natural habitat, historical ground covers, and forest-savannah patterns.

During the latter years of Follow Through, Therese and I bought some land in Arkansas, near one of our sites, the town of Flippen. The children in the Flippen Follow Through program were White and smart. The local coordinator and trainer was Rosealee Wade, a very good teacher who was skilled at working both with children and her teachers. The project did well and had a relatively small number of crises, compared to our average site. In a 1976 summary of the project's history, Rosealee Wade wrote,

> There has been continued local support for the Follow Through program—mainly because of the excellent learning gains made by the children. Nearly all of the teachers and aides really believe in the program and they all claim that they are better teachers because of it.

Rosealee's husband was Chris Wade, a realtor. He showed us various parcels and we bought three of them. One had frontage on Bull Shoals

Reservoir (or more accurately about 60 feet above the reservoir). Bull Shoals is a massive lake of over 700 square miles that spiders and spreads through the valleys of the White River north of Flippen. The word was that the land would become developed as soon as adequate roads (which Arkansas tended not to have) were constructed along the southern part of the reservoir.

The parcel we bought was over 200 acres. It was very inexpensive, but was covered with valuable hardwood trees: ash, black walnut, and red oak. Most of the trees were not mature, and there was no market for the hardwoods because there were no sawmills to process them. I figured that someday, when there were roads and sawmills, that land would be worth a fortune.

As it turned out, this parcel and the two others we had along the White River became Therese's property after our divorce in 1982. She quickly sold the land, but her timing was poor. The Whitewater incident involving future President Clinton and Hillary was going on in the Flippen area. Chris was Whitewater's real estate broker. In 1982, the lots for Whitewater were not selling, so the company made a trade with Chris—20 lots for a Piper Seminole airplane and some cash. During the Whitewater trials, Chris pleaded guilty to not declaring contributions to Clinton's campaign. The deal involving the 20 lots later cost taxpayers $13,000, but cost Chris a large slice of his good reputation, which I believed he had earned. He struck me as a straight arrow, but I'm pretty naïve about politics, development companies, and roads.

CORRECTIVE READING

In Eugene's Whiteaker School and in some of the Follow Through schools, I did some work with children in the upper grades. I first went to different fourth- and fifth-grade classrooms, asked the teachers which students were the lower performers, and had them read some fairly simple material I brought with me—selections second graders should be able to read without making many errors. Their performance was tragic. They guessed at words, skipped words, added words that weren't there, did a lot of rereading, and asked about some words. They read no better than a lot of our third graders read when we began Follow Through. Our Follow Through strategy was to put them in our beginning reading program and teach them from scratch. For those students who had virtually no reading skills, this remedy was effective. The students were able to move through the program at a relatively fast rate and experience success in learning to read. For some of the other students, this solution was not highly efficient because these students had some reading behavior, and they also had strong habits and routines that led them to make decoding mistakes. They needed a program that targeted their abortive strategies and that discredited and replaced them with effective strategies.

I was curious about the performance of higher at-risk students in grades 4 and above, so I tested their performance with the same selections I used to evaluate the lower performers. A high percentage of them confused words like *a* and *the*, *what* and *that*, *of*, *to*, *for*, and others.

So I started making an outline of a program for correcting the reading behavior of these kids. I also thought about who would co-author the program with me. I do programs with a co-author for two reasons: two (or more) heads are better than one, and writing a program requires organizational skills that I don't have, which means that unless the co-author has and uses these skills, the program will not happen.

The way we write programs is not to develop them a lesson at a time, but to write "tracks" and later combine the tracks so that each lesson has activities from 3 to 10 tracks. A track is a series of progressive exercises that involve the same skill. For a program like *Corrective Reading*, one of the tracks would involve irregularly spelled words that are first introduced in word lists (not in sentences). Another track would involve stories. The stories would have to be decodable, which means the student would know how to read all the words that appear in a story before the story is presented. So the story track would have to be coordinated with the words presented in isolation. Another track would involve the teaching of "rule governed" features of the reading code, like words that end in the vowel-consonant-E (*home, shape, smile*).

When we develop a program, the tracks are in separate folders. We chart all the information about the program to show which exercises and examples appear on every lesson. Lessons are then assembled and field-tested. The results indicate where the first version of the program was weak. The specific types of mistakes the students make during the first field test imply both what has to change and how it has to change. To obtain this information, we need copies of actual student work and annotated scripts that teachers used, with their comments about specific problems (including problems of a lesson or part taking too much time).

To verify that we have adequately addressed the problems, we have to do a field test of the revised material. When all work is finished, we have enough charts to paper a 12-foot wall from ceiling to floor, enough copies of student material to fill four standard filing cabinets, and probably more than 2,000 pages of manuscript for each iteration of the program.

A final fact relevant to the organizational skills needed to fashion this kind of endeavor is that we must know about problems in a timely manner and be able to provide immediate remedies for serious problems.

Because there are mountains of material to write, revise, analyze, classify, and have available, I desperately need to work with co-authors who are both highly skilled and organized. If I had to work alone, I might have been able to complete one program during my lifetime. With organized people like Jean, Cookie, and Doug, we were able to do more than one program a year; however, for every hour we work together, the co-author must spend about four hours organizing and making sense out of what we just wrote.

When we work on a program, the coauthor sits next to me at a desk. I do the typing and talk out loud as I compose. The co-author points out wording problems, keeps track of examples and rules, and makes suggestions. We generally do not spend a lot of time dealing with loggerheads. If we can't quickly come up with something that satisfies both of us, we compose something and move on. We know that we will revisit everything we write several times before the program is ready for the first field tryout.

As it turned out, I inherited a lot of co-authors for the *Corrective Reading* program. One day, Linda Carnine was telling me about how things were going at her site, Cherokee, North Carolina. She mentioned that her first graders were doing better than students in third grade or above. Then she said, "So I've been talking with Wes about doing a corrective reading program for older kids."

I asked how far along they were, and she indicated that they were about where I was, aware of the problem and doing preliminary planning to write a program.

I said, "Well, why don't we work together?"

She thought it was a good idea. We asked Wes what he thought. He agreed to the merger, but he had to check with his wife, Julie, because she planned to work with Linda and Wes. Linda Meyer had also expressed interest in working on the program. So within a short period of time I had five co-authors—Wes, Linda Carnine, Linda Meyer, Julie Becker, and Gary Johnson. Gary was a talented teacher from Chicago who has super organizational skills. He was a Follow-Through trainer who would later receive his Ph.D., do extensive work with us in non-Follow-Through sites, become a highly successful assistant principal in Arizona, and work with me on several challenging projects.

We divvied up responsibilities and started work on the program. The plan was to run field-testing concurrently with the writing of the program. We'd keep writing tracks and lessons. A field-test group would be about 10 lessons behind us. We'd send material to this group, receive the feedback quickly, and send out the revised version to a second field-test group, which would be about 40 lessons behind the first one.

Before we started, we knew that this venture would not make anybody rich because the royalty pie was cut into seven pieces. The seventh was the

Corp. The Corp became involved because SRA was not interested in the program and didn't think there was a need for it. So the Corp funded the development, field tryouts, and publishing. These were not prosperous times for the Corp. Educators had rejected emphasis on teaching math and science because this emphasis had proved to be the great failure of the 1960s and was now replaced with concern over humanism, freedom, individuality, and self expression. This formula had little tolerance for "basic skills." Instead, emphasis focused on the open classroom, which was seen as an expression of humanistic goals. Of course, there was no data that open space would have a salutary effect on student performance, but this fact did not discourage the construction of hundreds of noisy, unmanageable schools that had insane traffic patterns.

A final problem was that designing a program to correct specific mistakes and strategies that poor readers exhibited was inconsistent with the prevailing interpretation that the problem with the poor reader was largely visual. The current remedy was to give them eye tests and glasses. When that didn't work, give them a label, like dyslexic.

Our position was one that still has not gained general acceptance: the problem is primarily that failing students were mistaught. All of the mistake types they made may be directly traced to ill-conceived teaching. The program they went through in the early grades wouldn't necessarily misteach *all* students, only those who had insufficient background skill. Kids who knew how to rhyme, create series of words that alliterate, and who had a lot of experience in being instructed could learn from basal readers like *Dick and Jane*. The learners who did not have strong language backgrounds failed from day one. They needed explicit instruction about specific details they didn't understand well, like the fact that the combination *th* makes a different sound than the letters *te* for instance. Students became progressively more confused as the material they read became increasingly more demanding.

In the teacher's guide for the first edition of the *Corrective Reading* program, we provided explanations of the corrective reader that generally are not accepted or understood by the field today. The guide stated the problem this way:

> It may be true that there is a percentage of children who have some form of neurological impairment. However, the vast majority of disabled readers are not 'dyslexic,' are not impaired, and do not suffer from some sort of trauma. They merely have not been taught how to read.

In another place, the guide addressed the question, "Why can't the poor reader read consistently?" This question followed some descriptions of the poor readers' inconsistencies when reading texts. Students sometimes identify a particular word correctly and sometimes incorrectly.

The answer the teacher's guide provides:

> His strategy is fragmented and fragile, so fragmented that the poor reader can easily 'lose the handle.' Let's say we give a poor reader a passage that he can read with relatively few errors. Now, let's change the passage so the first sentence is so tough that the child will make at least three errors. What happens to his performance on the rest of the passage? Typically, he makes over twice the number of mistakes he would make without the modified first sentence.

These are testable assertions. We made them because we investigated the effects of the first sentence on errors for the rest of the passage. Yet, I know of no formal investigations that systematically picked up on this line of reasoning to refine information about the poor reader. This line of investigation would not focus on the reader's "illness" or on parts of the brain that are overactive, but on the causes—the material used to teach the learner. Through the 1970s until the time of this writing, the traditional emphasis has not been on avoiding practices that induce confusion and should be scrapped, but on poorly articulated principles of learning and motivation.

We had no illusions about the potential acceptance of the program, but we all agreed that it was something that was needed. Also, I had more fun writing this program than any other. When we wrote stories, instead of two people gathered around a typewriter, we typically had four—the Lindas, Gary Johnson, and me. Each worked with teachers and kids on some of our preliminary stories and sequences, so each had specific information on error patterns and problems with the exercises we developed. Gary and Linda Carnine taught the program and had very precise information about details.

We generated useful information about student mistakes faster than we had for any other program we developed. It was also more fun to write stories for the program because although they appear to be fairly simple (or simple-minded) they were designed with great care—shaped by suggestions and rebuttals from all the co-authors, as the stories were developed a word at a time. I looked forward to these sessions.

Because corrective readers make more mistakes on specific words when they are in the context of a story than when they are in lists, we wrote stories that followed the maxim for correcting mislearning: present the information that students tend to confuse at a high rate. The goal is not to frustrate students, but to give them high rates of practice in applying what they have learned and high rates of examples that contradict their abortive guessing strategies. We designed stories so they would set the learner up to guess. But guessing would lead to mistakes.

For example,

Fran and Fred said, "Let's go to the lake." So Fran and Fred went _____.

The corrective reader would guess at the missing words, saying "... went to the lake." The text, however, might say ... *went to that place*. This kind of manipulation helps to unify the corrective reader's emerging strategy by providing repeated examples that decoding words in stories requires the same steps as reading them in lists.

The students did daily practice with different kinds of word lists. The lists were used to show students the relationship of individual letters to the whole word. For instance, one type of list was a buildup. The teacher starts with a base word like *at* written on the board and changes it to *rat, frat, flat, fleet*. These buildups reinforced the basic theme that if part of the word changes, the sound for that part changes, but the sounds for other parts of the word don't change.

Another goal was to write stories that prompted some kind of reaction from the students. Many of the stories that we wrote were burlesque. Students often responded with comments like, "That's stupid." But for possibly the first time, their reaction was based on what they had read, not what they heard others read.

For example, one of the early stories involved Tim and his Thin Boat. This story was designed to reinforce the short-*i* sound and several other combinations that had been taught—the difference between *oa* and short-*o*, and the difference between *th* and *t*. The events in the story are fantastic. One of the things Tim did to make his boat go faster was to dump rocks in the front part of the boat. The nose of the boat was now lower than the back so the boat was now going downhill and went very fast.

After reading this part, some students in the field tryout would say things like, "That's stupid. That boat ain't going to go fast." Right you are, but you responded to what you read.

Some of the stories we wrote had a variation of word lists in them. One involved a dog named Chee. The Chee stories targeted minimally different words like *she* and *Chee*. Chee was a talking dog who spoke in nonsense utterances when she became excited or angry. The words that she uttered were those that the students had trouble reading accurately in stories— *this, his, of, to, for, no, so, go*, and others. At first, students had trouble reading what Chee said when angered, but the stories helped them see that written words are the same words in lists and in stories.

A kid in one of the local tryout groups provided an incisive summary of the basic confusion corrective readers have about reading connected text. This kid was reading a passage composed of words that could be analyzed by sounding them out. During one of his turns to read a couple of sentences from the story, the kid missed a word. The teacher said, "No. Sound it out."

The kid said, "Tell me the word and I'll sound it out."

At first I thought the kid was being a smart ass, but then I recognized that he had said it all. From day one of his instruction, reading stories was billed as a special kind of "comprehension activity." The teacher would prepare the children by talking about the characters and the setting before the kids read the story. The pictures showed what the "reader" was supposed to say when "reading" the words. If the picture showed Fran and Ted falling on the ice, the story words would tell about Fran and Ted falling on the ice.

In all cases, the discussion that preceded a story and the story illustrations indicated what the reader would say when reciting the story. The student's observation that he could not sound out the word unless he knew what the word was is a succinct description of what he thought reading was all about—somehow knowing word *meanings* before saying the words. The misguided primary-grade teacher feeds this confusion by encouraging children to guess. "What could that word be?" The child responds, and sometimes guesses correctly. Regardless of the outcome of the guess, the strategy reinforces the false idea that to read, you somehow have to know what the words could mean before you can pronounce them. A large percentage of teachers still use and defend these techniques, apparently without any understanding of how they are crippling some children.

To wean students from the idea that you have to refer to some context like a picture when reading a selection, we designed storybooks with no pictures. The format therefore makes it clear that you must use the words that you read as the guide for the details of your mental picture. This orientation is closer to the one we expect children to learn about reading. The words you read provide the fuel for creating images and understanding.

READING COMPREHENSION

Several years after the Corp published the *Corrective Reading* program, SRA bought the exclusive publication rights. We expanded the program to have more levels of decoding and a parallel program that focused on comprehension. Initially, we assessed the comprehension of at-risk high school students in four cities, with a 100-item test that asked open-ended questions like, "In what year did Columbus discover America?" and "How many days are in a year?"

The results were frightening. Fewer than 25 percent of the students correctly answered the question about Columbus. (Several responded, "1942.") About the same percentage didn't know the number of days in a year. Their answers ranged from 360 to 12.

The ideal goal for these students is to provide them with enough information to permit them to pass courses. This is an ambitious goal. Because students lack so much information, it would be impossible within one or two years of densely packed instruction to fill all the gaps that have developed over more than ten years.

Following the first tryout of the initial level of the corrective comprehension program in Springfield, Oregon, the director of our high school project called me and indicated that the program was a failure. Why? Because students did not comprehend the history textbook scheduled for 10th graders.

I tried to explain that there were lots of concepts and knowledge of language that these students lacked and that we focused on central skills they needed. He didn't seem convinced, so I arranged to meet with him and the students. I indicated that I would give him concrete examples that showed the extent of their lack of comprehension.

When we convened, I directed the 20 students in the class to open their history book (*United States History for High Schools*) to the first chapter, "A New World and a New Nation."

I read the first sentence of the text and then asked them questions about it. The sentence:

> **Today, few Americans think of their country as having been a part of a British Colonial empire, but America's colonial history lasted over 150 years, and Britain's influence upon America was fundamental.**

I asked them about the sentence, a part at a time. Over half the students missed each of the following questions:

- The sentence starts with *Today*. Does that mean this day or something that would be true today, tomorrow, and yesterday? The consensus: only today.

- The sentence refers to *few Americans*. Is that a small number or quite a few? Quite a few.

- The sentence refers to *their country*. What's the name of their country? Britain.

- The sentence says their country was *part of a British Colonial Empire*. Which country was part? Britain.

- The sentence says that *few Americans think of their country*. Whose country was that? Britain.

- Was a *British Colonial empire* something owned by England or America? America. (Most students didn't know that Britain was England and that colonial referred to colonies, or exactly what colonies were.)

After asking about several other phrases, I indicated that the last part of the sentence says that *Britain's influence upon America was fundamental*.
"What does fundamental mean?" Long pause. One hand goes up.
"Tell me what it means."
"Dumb, stupid."
"Like what?"
"You know. Learning fundamental skills."
Comprehension is billed typically as *reading* comprehension, but it has very little to do with reading. Students don't understand a host of concepts and relationships involving any academic pursuit. It's not that they can't extract them from what they read. They can't extract them from what they hear.
During the following years, we extended the *Corrective Reading* programs so there are three levels of decoding programs and three parallel levels level of comprehension programs. The lowest level of the comprehension strand teaches skills and information taught in the second and third level of the language program that we use with children in grades 1 and 2.
An amazing phenomenon is that a lot of high school students who are considered pretty good students place in the highest level of the decoding sequence and the lowest level of the comprehension sequence. These students lack basic knowledge of how to draw a conclusion from evidence, how to apply simple rules to concrete examples, and how to identify contradictions.
The corrective reader is still not understood well by most states and school districts. This fact is evident from the criteria that states and districts use to rank and adopt programs. The criteria that California and Florida apply to corrective reading programs are the same grade-level criteria that apply to any reading program used in that grade level, like grade 8. In other

words, the corrective reader in grade 8 is supposed to enter the grade greatly deficient in reading skills, but is expected to learn whatever skills students who enter the grade with no reading problems are expected to learn.

This position not only flies in the face of reasonable expectations for a student who has a history of reading problems, but clearly documents that the states are extremely naïve about corrective readers and what kind of special instruction is needed to correct the habits and misunderstanding these students have. If the National Assessment of Educational Progress shows that in some schools the average students in grade 8 perform below the fourth-grade level, the students would be expected to learn more than five years' worth of skill and knowledge in one year to pass the test for grade 8. The unlikelihood of that occurring should be evident to all educators.

The teacher's guide for the first edition of the *Corrective Reading* program provided a formula that takes into account the nature of the instructional problem.

> A great deal could be done with the disabled reader by using either carefully designed programs or reinforcement principles. Success has been achieved by simply paying children for improvement. However, greater success can be achieved if a) the program is designed specifically for the children who use it and b) reinforcement principles are tailored to the instructional program.

CATSKILLS VERSUS SKILLS

One of my more memorable plane trips occurred shortly before the Follow Through evaluation. In February, I was scheduled to give an evening address in London, Ontario, and one the following day in the Catskill Mountains (Monticello). At first I declined the invitation to speak at London because I could see no way to get from London to Monticello overnight. A day or two later, an administrator from London called me and explained that he had been a professional pilot before going into education and that he could take me from London to the Catskills and then to Toronto where I could make a good connection on a flight to Seattle.

So I agreed to the arrangement, but when I met the pilot in London, I was disturbed by his appearance. He had a patch over one eye and walked with a heavy limp. He explained that he had crashed testing an experimental plane.

Valerie was also presenting at the conference. I told her my plans and she thought it would be fun to join me on the trip to the Catskills and then fly to Toronto with us. So I asked the pilot if she could come along. Yes.

The plan was to leave at 5 a.m. Valerie saw the pilot the first time shortly before we left. She took me aside and said, "No way. I'm not getting on a plane with that guy at the controls. He's only got one eye." I assured her that everything would be fine.

That morning, the wind was blowing snow from the north at about 30 miles an hour and the temperature in London was in the low teens. I sat next to the pilot in a shivering cold, single-engine plane. Valerie was in the seat behind me. The runway went from east to west and was entirely glazed over with ice. Our run down the runway was more like a slide. When the plane reached about 40 miles an hour, it abruptly shifted about 40 degrees to the north, which prompted me to grab the door handle and Valerie to grab my shoulders. But the plane didn't go north. It continued sliding straight down the runway, and the pilot didn't act as if anything unusual was happening. We took off smoothly and circled to the south. By now the cabin was starting to feel warm.

By the time we reached the border, the eastern sky was already tinted with light. We landed and spent over an hour waiting for the plane and passengers to be inspected. During this time, we received the weather report, which was that serious storm activities were expected in the area to the east (which was our scheduled direction). The inspector said, "I would advise you to wait until this afternoon."

We didn't wait. About half an hour after we took off, we were in the middle of a snowstorm. We bounced around in the clouds for over an hour. When we were only about 50 miles from the Monticello airport, we discovered a further problem. The airport at Monticello was not sending out its VOR radio signal. So we couldn't hone in on that signal to find the airport. Our pilot indicated that he could probably make a pretty close determination of where the airport was by using the ever-changing directions from two neighboring VOR signals.

It was no longer snowing, but we were still in dense clouds with no view of the ground, and with Valerie frequently tapping me on the shoulders, asking me what was going on and lamenting that she had gone on this crazy trip.

The pilot had a map on his lap as he switched the radio dial back and forth and checked his instruments. This activity seemed to continue for a very long time period. At last, he said, "We're close," and started to descend to see if we could get below the clouds. We remained in the clouds, and as our pilot pointed out, we were already below the altitude of some neighboring peaks. (I did not share this news with Valerie.) Finally, our pilot pointed down and a little to right as he hollered, "As close as I can calculate, the damn airport should be right there." And like a scene out of a cheap movie, a hole in the clouds opened in front of us a moment later and there was the damned airport, right where he had pointed.

Valerie clapped and cheered. I congratulated the pilot on a super job, and we landed without incident. A couple of SRA sales representatives drove the three of us into Monticello, where we had lunch. Then I did an afternoon training session on DI. During that afternoon, the weather changed in two ways; it got a lot warmer and dropped about four inches of snow. Around 4 o'clock the SRA crew took us on a wheel-spinning drive through slushy snow to the airport. By now, it was no longer snowing, and Valerie had completely bonded with the pilot, convinced that she would fly anywhere with him.

The wings and tail of our plane were covered with deep slushy snow, which we cleared off with our arms as we engaged in intermittent snowball throwing. Our pilot entered his flight plan, and we took off on a runway that had been partly cleared. The first thing that struck me after we took off and started to climb to our cruising altitude was that I should have gone to the bathroom before we took off. I reminded myself that this trip shouldn't take more than two hours.

The next thing I noticed as we were climbing was that the pilot had a grim expression and was holding the steering wheel tightly. "What's wrong?" I asked.

He explained that the cable to the tail of the airplane was frozen and the elevators would not move. The result was that he couldn't make the plane go down or straight ahead, only up. I asked him what we were going to do. He explained that he could use his flaps to slow the plane and keep it moving in the right direction. There would also be a problem landing the plane, but he believed he could do it. He pointed out that the big danger was that the cable would thaw when we were close to the ground. That might result in a crash.

So as my bladder continued to distend, we moved slowly north, soon in darkness. At one point we came to an area that had a deep valley with mountains on either side. The pilot slowed the plane more so it would descend, and we went through the valley with the hope that the air would be warmer here and it would melt the ice that was keeping the cable locked in the uphill position. It didn't work.

About the time I was ready to use an air-sickness bag as something of a urine container, we approached Lake Ontario. Our pilot informed us that the lake offered our last hope of freeing the cable. The air just above the water would be warmer than the air higher up. Our pilot cautioned, "We don't want to get too close to the water because when the cable busts loose, we could take a nose dive."

He called the traffic controller at Toronto and reported our situation, then we went down to less than 100 feet above the water. The buildings in Toronto grew larger, and this tour across the lake seemed shorter than I would have imagined. The pilot took us down to about 50 feet and shook his head.

Suddenly, the plane gave a little jerk, and the cable was free. No nosedives or even a jar great enough to spill coffee from a cup. The pilot smiled and gave us the thumbs up. Valerie shouted, "I knew he could do it!"

With the crisis over, I was very relieved, but I was in serious need of additional relief, and I wasn't sure I could wait much longer. Our pilot told the tower that we were okay and got landing instructions. The landing process seemed to take as long as the trip across Lake Ontario. The good news was that the plane parked only about 100 yards from a men's room. I might not have set any speed records for running that 100 yards, but I tried, and soon after the sprint I felt as triumphant as Rocky after he had run up the steps in Philadelphia. I was also thankful that our pilot was as skilled as he was.

SUMMER DI CONFERENCES

From the onset of Follow Through, Wes had concerns about communicating with allies and providing training. I agreed with the training part, but I didn't see many allies out there. The behaviorists were certainly in our ballpark, but they didn't have and still don't have procedures for analyzing what is to be taught. They simply analyze the behavior, which results in some of the worst programs and crudest techniques I've seen. The behaviorists who worked on the Down syndrome project were liabilities, not resources.

Training others made sense to me because we could do it. We had programs that would work if they were presented correctly. We couldn't do the kind of training possible with Follow Through, but if we staged a one-week workshop (with the emphasis on work and practice), we could go a long way in teaching motivated teachers what they needed to know to do a far better job than they were currently doing.

In July of 1974, we staged our first summer DI conference, a one-week training session in Eugene, sponsored by the Corp. The four main sessions were for reading, language, arithmetic, and reinforcement practices. This description may elicit images quite different from the actual event, which was not held in a hotel or conference hall, but in a large high school gym, with the acoustics of a large gym. That July was particularly hot for Eugene and the gym was not air-conditioned. So we propped the outside door open and set up several large, industrial-grade fans blowing cooler air into at least part of the gym.

About 120 participants attended the conference. When they were divided into three separate groups, each rehearsing the lines of critical exercises in the three programs, that gym was very noisy.

Earlier, when people had asked about training, we tried either to sneak them into the Follow Through summer training for a nearby site, or to put on a two-day workshop in the area. SRA also provided what it referred to as training, but it was pretty hokey, often scheduled for only two hours. Some of the SRA trainers were very good, but seriously handicapped by the half-day format.

We staged our workshop in Eugene, not because of its accessibility but because that's where most of our trainers lived and because they were tired of traveling. We wouldn't have to eat in restaurants, and we'd be able to go home at the end of each day. So the workshop was a treat for us.

The schedule was about the same as a regular teaching day—start around eight, be done by three. The workshop that summer reminded me a lot of working in University High during the summer. By noon, my shirt had very few dry spots. By the end of the day, I was very ready for a couple of cold beers.

We ran the next few summer workshops in another Eugene high school (Sheldon), which not only had air conditioning but allowed us to use some of the classrooms. This was a definite step up in class. After about the sixth year of holding the conference in high schools, we faced two problems: We projected that there would be a larger number of people than there had been for the earlier conferences; the school needed some of the space that had been formerly allocated to the workshop. So we faced the choice of keeping the summer conference in Eugene or going to a larger, more accessible place like Portland. Without a lot of discussion, we agreed that the workshop was very reinforcing for the trainers. To keep the conference reinforcing, we decided to keep it in Eugene. We moved it to the Eugene Hilton, which had conference facilities and could accommodate a thousand people.

The conference has been an annual event there ever since the early 1980s. The numbers continued to grow each summer, making the conference the second largest annual event the Eugene Hilton holds (trailing only the loggers' convention). Each year, nearly half the participants have attended earlier conferences; some even attended the first one. One of the scheduled events after the Monday session is a picnic in a park on the Willamette River, walking distance from the Corp. The bill of fare consists of burgers, hot dogs, potato salad, corn on the cob, watermelon, beer, wine, soft drinks, pies, and ice cream. There are no events like sack races, but there are people from all over the world who share an interest in providing good instruction to kids who would otherwise fail.

CHAPTER 5

Follow Through Evaluation

DI, UNDISPUTED WINNER

The formal evaluation of Follow Through sponsors and Follow Through's overall performance came out in April of 1977. At that time scientists had recently discovered the cause of Legionnaire's disease; Jimmy Carter had become President and had pardoned Vietnam War draft evaders. The worst air collision to that time had occurred when two planes collided over the Canary Islands killing 583 people.

The Follow Through evaluation did not make headlines because it had not been officially announced or interpreted by the Office of Education. The design of the evaluation was careful. To assure that the analysis was experimentally pristine, two organizations dealt with data. Stanford Research Institute collected the data; Abt Associates, on the other side of the continent, analyzed it. The evaluation cost $30 million.

At the time of the evaluation, Bob Egbert was no longer the national director of Follow Through. He had been succeeded by Rosemary Wilson, who shared neither his vision nor his conception that if Follow Through permitted sponsors to implement in a conducive context, the evaluation would clearly identify winners and losers.

The analysis centered around the third-grade performance of the later cohorts that went through the various Follow Through programs. 40,000 third-graders were tested. Part of the evaluation did not involve all of our sites, only most of the sites that started in kindergarten. Grand Rapids was one of the sites included in this part of the evaluation, although we had not worked with the site for three years and had received no money from national Follow Through for sponsoring the site. Yet, the analysis treated Grand Rapids as if it were one of our sites. Even so, we were confident that the data would show that we had won the horse race.

This confidence was in defiance of the educational community's consensus that there would be no clear winners or losers. Although sponsors were not permitted to publish data that could be construed as comparing performance of different models, National Follow Through analyzed the data and reported comparative data to sponsors as early as 1973, when a conference in Brookings, Oregon presented results from 1971. The book *Planned Variation in Education—Should We Give Up or Try Harder?* drew the conclusion, "It already seems highly doubtful, however, that the results will provide clear-cut indications that one model is best."

This conclusion was based on the 1970–71 cohort, but there was data on the 1971–72 cohort, which generated a far different picture. Kansas and our model were far ahead of the others. Also, the director of Follow Through research, Gary McDaniels, wrote, "Several sponsors looked very strong after the first year, while others did not. The strongest were those that emphasized short-term achievement effects [in other words, Kansas and us]."

The first published reports on the Follow Through performance were based on an analysis of sponsors conducted by Stallings and Kaskowitz, which appeared in *Behavior Today* in 1975. After making extensive observations of the various sponsors' classrooms, Stallings concluded that there were different winners that corresponded to different program emphases. According to Stallings's calculations, those approaches that focused on reading and spent more time on reading had better reading performance (DI and Behavior Analysis). The main problem with this conclusion was that we did not spend more time teaching reading than most of the models. In fact, we probably spent less than half the time provided by the Bank Street model and several others.

Stallings also concluded that different programs were creating children who were different in problem solving, responsibility, question asking, and cooperation. She concluded that children in High Scope and Open Education were high in these traits. She wrote: "Cooperation was marked in classrooms where a wide variety of activities occurred throughout the day and where children would explore and choose their groups." The problem was that she defined cooperation in terms of the activities. If children spent more time in activities that apparently involved cooperation, Stallings concluded that they were "more cooperative."

She also defined responsibility in terms of activities—a child or group engaged in any task without an adult. The definition has nothing to do with the amount of responsibility children learn. (Of course she assumed that if children spend time unsupervised, they must be learning more about responsibility.) If institutionalized children had been included in the evaluation, they probably would have had "responsibility" scores even higher than Open Education or High Scope because they often have no supervision.

During the period before the Abt Report came out, I was not concerned with what the analysts said about the data. I didn't have either time or interest to debate whether the fat lady was singing yet.

The fourth volume of the Abt Report presented data on Follow Through sponsors. It came out in 1977 and left no doubt about whether the fat lady had sung. The volume provided arias involving winners and losers, based on performance data. The report confirmed what we knew all along. No other model was close to ours in sophistication.

The achievement-test data and that of other tests were analyzed two ways, "adjusted" and "unadjusted." The adjusted data were expressed as positive or negative outcomes. If a particular site had a score that was a standard number of points higher than the other sites, the site received a plus (+). If the site had a score that was a standard number of points lower than the other sites, the site received a minus (−). If the site was somewhere between a + and −, the difference was considered educationally insignificant.

For analyzing performance of sponsors, Abt threw out performance comparisons if the Follow Through site and the comparison groups differed by more than 50 percent on their entry scores. Several comparisons involving East St. Louis were thrown out, which was unfortunate because East St. Louis children were initially more than 50 percent lower than the children in the comparison groups but still outperformed them by enough to earn a +.

There were other ways the analysis was bent to be unkind to DI, including the way some of the data were "interpreted." Even so, the numbers didn't lie.

The evaluation had three categories: basic skills, cognitive (higher-order thinking) skills, and affective responses. The graph on page 226 shows the outcomes for the nine major sponsors.

Number of Significant Outcomes for Basic Skills (B), Cognitive Skills (C), and Affective Measures (A)

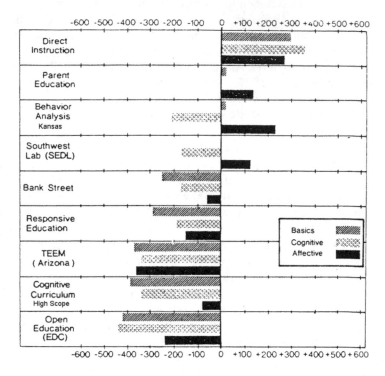

Index of Significant Outcomes

The basic skills consisted of those things that could be taught by rote— spelling, word identification, math facts and computation, punctuation, capitalization, and word usage. DI was first of all sponsors in basic skills. Our average score was +297 (which means that we had a considerably larger number of significantly positive outcomes than the Title I comparison students). Only two other sponsors had a positive average. The remaining models scored deep in the negative numbers, which means they were soundly outperformed by children of the same demographic strata who did not go through Follow Through. The sites that Stallings glorified did poorly in this category. High Scope was –389 and Open Education was –433 (far fewer significantly negative outcomes than the Title I comparisons recorded). According to the Stallings predictions, this outcome might be expected for basic skills.

DI was not expected to outperform the other models on "cognitive" skills, which require higher-order thinking, or on measures of "responsibility." Cognitive skills were assumed to be those that could not be presented as rote, but required some form of process or "scaffolding" of one skill on another to draw a conclusion or figure out the answer. In reading, children were tested on main ideas, word meaning based on context, and inferences. Math problem-solving and math concepts evaluated children's higher-order skills in math.

Not only was the DI model number one on these cognitive skills; it was the only model that had positive scores for all three higher-order categories: reading, math concepts, and math problem-solving. DI had a higher average score on the cognitive skills (+354) than it did for the basic skills (+297). No other model had an average score in the positive numbers for cognitive skills. Cognitive Curriculum (High Scope) and Open Education performed in the negative numbers, at −333 and −450.

On the affective measures, which included a battery of tests that evaluated children's sense of responsibility and self-esteem, our model was first, followed by Kansas. The models that stressed affective development performed even below the Title I average.

One of the affective tests described positive achievement experiences and negative experiences. DI children saw themselves as being more responsible for outcomes than children in any other model. On the test that assessed children's feelings about how they think other people view them and how they feel about school, DI children had the highest scores.

Note that DI was over 250 points above the Title I norm and Open Education was over 200 points below the norm. The Abt Report observed that the high performance of children in our model was unexpected because we did not describe affective outcomes as an objective. The reason was that we assume that children are fundamentally logical. If we do our job of providing them with experiences that show they are smart, they will conclude that they are smart. If they experience success in school that can also be measured in the neighborhood, those experiences serve as fuel for the conclusion that students are competent. At the time of the evaluation, I had heard more than 100 stories of our children helping older siblings learn to read or do homework. The children knew that they could do things the average kid on the street could not do.

The rest of the Abt results were expressed as percentiles. The performance of an average student taking an achievement test is the 50th percentile. The goal for Follow Through had been to achieve the 50th percentile with at-risk children. The average percentile for Title I students was the 20th percentile—less than half that of the average student. The 20th percentile was used as a measure of whether a model produced a positive or negative effect. The farther above the 20th percentile a model is, the better it performs.

The figure below shows the performance of the nine major sponsors in total reading, total math, spelling, and language.

Percentile Comparisons for the 9 Major
Follow Through Sponsors

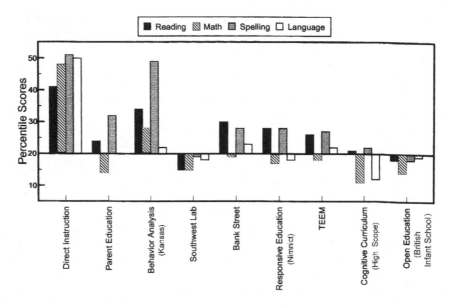

The horizontal line indicates the 20th percentile. As the figure shows, the competition is closest for reading. All but three of the sponsors scored at or above the 20th percentile. For math, only two models were above the 20th percentile, ours and Kansas (Behavioral Analysis). For language, our model was the only one above the 23rd percentile. High Scope (Cognitive Curriculum) had the lowest scores of all sponsors in math and language. Obviously, this data makes a mockery out of Stallings's notion that an untrained observer could make a few observations of classrooms, classify the activities, and draw any kind of valid conclusion about how successful each program was in inducing cognitive skills.

There's more: Not only were we first in adjusted scores and first in percentile scores for basic skills, cognitive skills, and perceptions children had of themselves, we were first in spelling, first with sites that had a Headstart preschool, first in sites that started in K, and first in sites that started in grade 1. Our third-graders who went through only three years (grades 1–3) were, on average, over a year ahead of children in other models who went through four years—grades K–3. We were first with Native Americans, first with non-English speakers, first in rural areas, first in urban areas, first with Whites, first with Blacks, first with the lowest disadvantaged children, and first with high performers.

From a historical perspective the performance of our children set important precedents.

1. For the first time in the history of compensatory education, DI showed that long-range, stable, replicable, and highly positive results were possible with at-risk children of different types and in different settings. Previously, "the exemplary program" was a phantom, something that was observed now but not a year from now. Most were a function of fortuitous happenings, a measurement artifact, or a hoax.

2. DI showed that relatively strong performance outcomes are achievable in all subject areas (not just reading) if the program is designed to effectively address the content issues of these areas. Also, this instruction created lively, smart children who had confidence in their abilities.

3. The performance of all the Follow Through children (but particularly DI children) clearly debunked all the myths about DI. DI did not turn children off or turn them into robots. DI children were smart and they knew it.

4. DI outcomes also debunked the myth that different programs are appropriate for children with different learning styles. The DI results were achieved with the same programs for all children, not one approach for higher performers and another for lower performers, or one for non-English speakers and another for English speakers. The programs were designed for any child who had the skills needed to perform at the beginning of a particular program. If the child is able to master the first lesson, she has the skills needed to master the next lesson and all subsequent lessons. The only variable is the rate at which children proceed through the lessons. That rate is based solely on the performance of the children. If it takes more repetition to achieve mastery, we provide more repetition, without prejudice.

5. The enormous discrepancies in performance between our model and all the others implies that we knew something they didn't know

about instructing the full range of children in the full range of academic skills. We did not buy into the current labels, explanations, or assumptions about learning and performance. The results suggest that our interpretation was right, and that the philosophies of the cognitive and affective models did not translate into effective instruction.

6. The performance of the sponsors clearly debunked the notion that greater funding would produce positive results. All sponsors had the same amount of funding, which was more than a Title I program received. DI performed well in this context; however, the same level of funding did not result in significant improvement for the other models. For all programs there were comprehensive services, which included breakfast, lunch, medical, and dental care, and social services. In this context, the only reasonable cause for the failure of other models was that they used inferior programs and techniques.

7. The Direct Instruction model was the only one that was effective with extremely low performers. We showed that these children could uniformly be taught to read by the end of kindergarten and read pretty well by the end of first grade. Performance of this magnitude and consistency had never been demonstrated in the schools before Follow Through.

8. The relative uniformity of the DI sites implies that DI was better able to make the typical failed teacher successful. Teachers who had not been able to teach children to higher levels of performance were able to do it with our program.

9. Probably most important, the outcome showed that our focus on the moment-to-moment interactions between teachers and children was correct. Most of the other models viewed the problems of instruction in terms of broad interactions between teachers and children, not in terms of specific information delivered in moment-to-moment interactions.

We were not into celebrating, but after work on the day Volume 4 arrived, we had a little party, a couple of beers, and several rounds of congratulations to trainers, managers, and consultants who worked in the trenches to achieve this outcome. Wes reminded us that the game plan was for the winners to be widely disseminated. So we needed to think about tooling up to work with a far greater number of places. We needed to convert some of our trainers to project managers, recruit some of the super-teachers from our Follow Through sites, and get ready to work with lots of Title I programs. Several of our project managers were skeptical about this degree of acceptance, but the rest of us felt that there would be a payoff for the last nine years of work.

RECONSTRUCTING HISTORY AND LOGIC

With the Abt data published, the moratorium on comparative studies was lifted. Wes promptly prepared a long article for the *Harvard Educational Review*, "Teaching Reading and Language to the Disadvantaged—What We Have Learned From Research," which came out in 1977 and gave overviews of our approach and programs, our training, and our results.

Wes anticipated that the article would stimulate great interest. Instead, there was almost no response—no revelations reported by readers who realized that the practices they espoused had led to unnecessary failure or revelations that DI presented a better way to solve problems that had been haunting school districts since the Coleman Report. There were no frantic phone calls from people wanting to learn more about DI, nor calls from reporters asking about the astonishing results. Instead there was a handful of responses, and most were not positive but raised carping issues about the design of the study or the problems associated with accurately measuring cognitive outcomes. Those who carped had earlier accepted the idea that achievement tests documented the performance problems of at-risk students. Yet, when the same kind of achievement-test data showed that their favored programs produced children who failed as miserably as children summarized by the Coleman Report, they rejected the study.

THE GLASS HOUSE

We later discovered that the effort to trivialize Follow Through data had begun before Abt 4 had been released. The effort was initiated by the Ford Foundation, which had been supporting failed educational programs. In January 1977, the Ford Foundation awarded a grant to the Center for Instructional Research and Curriculum Evaluation at the University of Illinois to conduct a third-party evaluation of Follow Through results. Ernest House was project director. He assembled a panel of professionals with national reputations in their fields—Gene V. Glass of the University of Colorado, Leslie D. McLean of the Ontario Institute for Studies in

Education, and Decker F. Walker of Stanford University. This assemblage judged Follow Through data.

The main purpose of the critique was to prevent the Follow Through evaluation results from influencing education policy. The panel's report asserted that it was inappropriate to ask, "Which model works best?" Rather it should consider such other questions as "What makes the models work?" or "How can one make the models work better?"

Glass wrote another report for the National Institute of Education (NIE), which argued that it was not sound policy for NIE to disseminate the results of the FT evaluations, even though the data collection and analysis had cost over 30 million dollars. Here's that part of the abstract of Glass's report to the NIE:

> Two questions are addressed in this document: What is worth knowing about Project FT? And, How should the National Institute of Education (NIE) evaluate the FT program? Discussion of the first question focuses on findings of past FT evaluations, problems associated with the use of experimental design and statistics, and prospects for discovering new knowledge about the program. With respect to the second question, it is suggested that NIE should conduct evaluation emphasizing an ethnographic, principally descriptive, case-study approach to enable informed choice by those involved in the program.

Again, this position is curious for one who apparently believed that data of the same type collected in the FT evaluation earlier documented the problem. Why would the data be adequate to document the problem but not appropriate for documenting outcomes of different approaches that address the problem?

The suggestion that case studies would enable informed choice is not very thoughtful. Qualitative studies work only if they are carefully underpinned with rules about quantities. I'm sure that if the game was for each sponsor to compile descriptions from their high-performing classrooms, DI would have a larger number of success stories than the other sponsors.

Unless there are some number assumptions—like, "How consistently do positive case histories occur?"—The data is useless. Making it even more useless is the depth of description that would be needed to enable an "informed choice." I would guess that each study would require many pages. It would be far more confusing to try to extract information about what works best from these documents than from a few tables that summarize the performance data. In fact, the suggestion for using ethnographic studies was probably intended to make it impossible for readers to find out what worked best. Who would want to wade through possibly thousands of pages of "case histories" to distill a conclusion about which model was more effective?

Glass even argued that all evaluations involving measurable events and data are invalid. "The deficiencies of quantitative, experimental evaluation approaches are so thorough and irreparable as to disqualify their use." What is surprising about this statement is how anybody at NIE could have read it and not concluded that the author was loony. The Follow Through experiment was a teaching experiment involving not a few minutes in the lab, but nine years of cohorts in which students passed through four grades in actual classrooms. This study had huge numbers. Also, the evaluation tools that documented performance of students already included ethnographic descriptions of models (prepared by Nero and Associates).

Another argument that Glass presented involved the "audience."

> The audience for Follow Through evaluations is an audience
> of teachers to whom appeals to the need for accountability for
> public funds or the rationality of science are largely irrelevant.

There are two major problems with this assertion:

1. The Follow Through study was not designed for teachers but for decision makers—school districts, state and federal departments of education—who serve as gatekeepers for what teachers do. The Coleman Report did not result in individual teachers organizing carpools to schlep children from the inner-city to the suburbs. The Follow Through study was not founded on the assumption that teachers enjoyed some kind of democratic world in which every teacher was able to make independent decisions about what and how to teach. Teachers are not decision makers on policy. Policy makers and district officials are. They would be far better informed by the Follow Through results than by any other single data source because only Follow Through provided extensive comparative data of different approaches.

2. Glass could not have seriously believed that even district-level decision makers would read Abt 4. They wouldn't. Glass appealed to NIE because he was concerned about what NIE would say about Follow Through. The final NIE word would make a lot of news and create great interest. In effect, what NIE would say about the program

would become the truth about it. People, press, and historians would be greatly influenced by NIE's stance.

Also, if NIE followed Glass's recommendations, there would be no challenge to the current order of things in education. The Ford Foundation would save face and wouldn't be labeled as a corporate fool for funding foolish programs for years. People in teacher colleges and district administrators would be able to keep their prejudices about children, learning, and teachers. The publishers of elementary-grade instructional material would be happy because no tidal wave would sink sales of instructional material, and school districts would not have to face uncomfortable issues of overhauling both their belief systems and their machinery. College professors could continue to espouse developmental theories and discovery practices as they decry programs that would "divest teachers of their individuality and creativity."

With a statement that downplayed the Follow Through data, Open Education and High Scope, Bank Street College, and Nimnict's program would not be cast as losers, because ethnographic studies might feature one of their "good" sites. All the primitive but well-greased machinery on all levels from state departments of education to classrooms would remain solidly in place, with no challenge. Of course, somewhere in this political milieu were millions of kids whose lives would be greatly influenced by NIE's decision. But as the anti-number philosophy suggests, who was counting?

In 1978, House and Glass published an article in the *Harvard Educational Review*, "No simple answer: A critique of the Follow-Through evaluation." Unlike Wes's earlier article, this one created quite a stir. A shortened version appeared in *Educational Leadership* in 1978.

Although Gene Glass had been president of the American Educational Research Association, the flaws in the arguments the article presented were so conspicuous that they should have been obvious to the man on the street. The article presented two main arguments to discredit the Office of Education evaluation. The main argument was based on a simple value judgment: sponsors should not be compared. Therefore, the Abt focus on the performance of individual sponsors was inappropriate.

House and Glass contended that the evaluation was actually designed to show how *the aggregate of models* performed, not what individual sponsors achieved. The aggregate failed; therefore, the most definitive statement about Follow Through would simply be Project Follow Through failed. In other words, the average of Follow Through students was no higher than those of comparable Title I students. Therefore, Follow Through failed, which means that every sponsor failed. The question of whether individual sponsors actually failed was not considered relevant because it's bad form to compare sponsors.

What seems most curious about this argument is how House and Glass could conclude that Follow Through as a whole failed. That judgment involves a comparison of programs, Follow Through and Title I. Why is it that sponsors can't be compared but larger programs like Follow Through can?

Even more puzzling was how House and Glass could make the obvious distortion that Follow Through was never intended to evaluate the performance of different sponsors. Certainly, this assertion would be contradicted by Follow Through, unless there was collusion between several agencies, including the Office of Education.

The second House-Glass argument was that no approach was successful with all its sites. House and Glass pointed out that there was variability among each sponsor's sites, some performing well and others poorly. Therefore, no single sponsor should be identified as being "successful."

Again, if House and Glass argued that data could not be used to compare sponsors, by what ground rules were they able to compare sponsors with respect to their variability? Logically, Glass and House would have to throw out this argument or reveal themselves as cherry pickers who used comparative data when they needed it and rejected it when it worked against them.

The variability argument was particularly incredible because it was presented by professionals who were supposed to be experts in experimental designs. The most elementary fact about populations is that every observable population of anything has variation. In fact, populations vary across every measurable feature—the size of the lobes on black oak leaves, the shape of snowflakes, the age of computers. So it would be insane to throw out data simply because it shows that there is variability, particularly in this case because only one DI site varied greatly from the seventeen others and only that site performed poorly. Grand Rapids had third graders performing a year lower than third graders in our other sites. The only possible evidence that House and Glass had about the "failure of DI" or the variability was based on one site that openly rejected the model's provisions and had no contact with the sponsor in more than three years. Furthermore, all the higher-echelon bureaucrats in Follow Through and in NIE knew that we hadn't worked with Grand Rapids for years.

SAD SONG OF THE REAL FAT LADY

The official statement that NIE issued was consistent with the recommendations by Glass and House: Project Follow Through did not significantly improve the performance of disadvantaged students over students in extant Title I programs. There was not a word about winners, losers, or about the performance of individual sponsors, just a flat statement that Project Follow Through—an aggregate—failed.

Functionally, this decision showed the priorities of the educational system. It was more palatable for educators to accept that their favored approach failed than it was to admit that an approach in disfavor succeeded. The educators' feelings and prejudices were functionally more important to them than evidence that there was a successful method for teaching at-risk children. Stated differently, these people showed that their beliefs were more important than the millions of failed children who could benefit from effective instruction. Make no mistake, they would not have gone through the various machinations they created if they believed their own rhetoric about how important it is to serve at-risk children.

In the end, sites from all the Follow Through models including High Scope and the Open Classroom were "validated." So the status quo was maintained; the models that had horrible results would remain in good standing; all educational myths were perpetuated. If policy makers wanted to believe in instructional models based on student choice, extensive parent involvement, or discovery learning, they wouldn't have to face the pesky problem of how to support this notion with data. Their collective conscience was clear because all these approaches had been "validated." Someone receiving this information would assume that validated means that the validated approach was replicable and sound.

PAPER TRAIL

The master plan for Follow Through and how information about Follow Through would be disseminated to other schools and agencies was complicated.

The switch of emphasis from sponsors to individual school programs had begun as soon as Abt 4 came out in 1977. The Office of Education established the Joint Dissemination and Review Committee. Its purpose was to screen Follow Through schools that applied for funds to disseminate information about the school's successful program. The review committee scrutinized schools that applied through forms, letters, and interviews. Those schools that made it over these hurdles were "validated." Whether they were High Scope schools, Open Education schools, or DI sites. All received the same size validation.

Not all of our sites that applied for funds made the cut. At least four of them received a rating of B and at least two a rating of C, even though they had excellent performance data. It seemed obvious that there was a conscious effort to keep DI from having more representation than some of the other major models.

Once validated, a school would become a member of the National Diffusion Network (NDN), which consisted of 200 programs, each receiving funds to promote itself to other schools. Of the 200 dissemination schools, only 21 were Follow Through schools, and only 3 were Direct Instruction schools—Flint, Dayton, and East St. Louis. Most of the 200 schools came from a poor list of "effective programs" compiled by the Far West Regional Educational Lab. Very few of these schools actually had data of effectiveness, but neither did at least 14 of the 21 Follow Through sites that were now incorporated into the network.

The National Diffusion Network was possibly well named because it did a good job of diffusing, in the sense of making the effect thin. Instead of being 3 out of the 21 programs to be disseminated, DI was now 3 out of 200, less than 2 percent of the total. And as usual, all "validated sites" had the same status.

Individual schools were eligible to disseminate, but sponsors weren't. The Joint Dissemination and Review Committee ruled that only *schools* could apply for validation, not models.

When we received this news, I thought Wes would go into apoplexy. I had never seen him that angry. I was not a portrait of happiness, but Wes exploded. He quickly recovered and in less than an hour was on the phone, trying to contact senators, representatives, and others who might have some influence.

In October of 1977, Wes and I wrote a letter to Rosemary Wilson protesting Follow Through's position about dissemination. We wrote again in November, after it became apparent that nothing would change. That letter appears in whole, followed by her response. Our letter iterates some of the points I have covered.

UNIVERSITY OF OREGON
College of Education
Department of Special Education

FOLLOW THROUGH PROJECT—"So They Shall Not Fail"

Telephone (code 503) 886-3555
Eugene, Oregon 97403

November 16, 1977

Rosemary Wilson
Office of Education
Department of Health, Education
    and Welfare
7th and D St. SW
Washington, D.C.   20202

Dear Ms. Wilson:

The critical Follow Through issue is a moral one. We have demonstrated
the capacity to teach you and other educators about teaching "poor kids",
turning them on, and assuring that they catch up to their middle-class peers
in academic skills. Our Follow Through achievements, however, don't show
what we are actually capable of doing, because we do not have fully-implemented
sites - only moderately implemented sites. The Follow Through guidelines have
never permitted the kind of total system support needed to provide a full-
fledged demonstration of what poor kids can achieve in grades K-3 if they
receive a fully implemented, uniform, Direct Instruction approach (with
trained teachers, supervisors, and directors).

The moral issue centers on this question: What does Follow Through stand
for? Is it simply an experiment on human beings which has no concern for what
the experiment might reveal for the millions of other "poor kids" who have
serious educational needs? Is your office even remotely justified in treating
all sponsors as equals and shifting (in the past two years) the emphasis from
sponsors to individual sites? Or is this move designed to detract from the
issues of effective approaches and make it seem that "every approach is capable
or producing good results"? We would not have engaged in Follow Through for
the past ten years if we had thought that there would be no attempt to weed
out the inadequate model approaches, to educate both the public and the educational community about how to be effective, and to disseminate information
on how to be an effective model? Furthermore, we would not have perpetuated
our model if it proved to be a hoax; rather, we would have quit Follow Through
with abject apology if the results had shown that our approach did not work
any better than that of the typical Title I program and produced kids who
performed only at the 18th percentile in reading and arithmetic by the end
of the third grade.

According to your letter of October 28, 1977, "No single instructional
approach, including that of Direct Instruction, was found to be consistently
effective in all of the projects where it was tried and evaluated. Therefore,
no overall claim of its effectiveness can be supported."

Rosemary Wilson
November 16, 1977
page 2

   This statement flies in the face of the USOE's own Evaluation Synthesis
(John Evans' office) indicating that there is one model generally effective
in basic skills, cognitive skills, and on affective measures - Direct Instruction.
Your statement also flies in the face of the Abt Report data - not merely in
the face of data showing the relative superiority of Direct Instruction over
comparison groups, but also in the face of absolute grade norm data that shows
Direct Instruction to be the only approach to bring third graders at or near
grade level in reading, arithmetic, spelling, and language.

   Your conclusion that no single instructional approach was found to be
consistently effective is spurious because: (1) Grand Rapids is included as
a Direct Instruction site (for two data points); and (2) the conclusion confounds
program effect variability with control group variability. Variability in
program implementation must take into account absolute grade-level performance.
Grade-level performance is clearly as relevant as statistical significance
because if all kids were performing at grade level (on the average), there
would have been no need for Follow Through. In fact, much of the rhetoric
that led to Follow Through by Robert Kennedy, Commissioner Howe, Bob Egbert
and Jack Hughes, focused on the fact that poor kids perform well below grade
level and are therefore preempted from "higher education" and its concomitants.

   The so-called "variability" among the Direct Instruction sites is accounted
for first by the unwarrented inclusion of Grand Rapids as a Direct Instruction
site for two cohorts. Grand Rapids is not a Direct Instruction site. It is
a Lola Davis site. You know that for most of 1972 and 1973, we did not function
as a sponsor for Grand Rapids, that we did not receive funds for servicing
Grand Rapids after the spring of 1973 when relationships with Grand Rapids
were severed. You also know that Grand Rapids was not functioning as an
implemented Direct Instruction site before the 1972-73 school year. It was
not implemented - not because of our lack of effort - but because the director
had different ideas about what and how to teach. You were involved in this
situation and know quite well our position and the history. Grand Rapids
is the only Direct Instruction K-starting site that performs relatively low
in absolute performance. In fact, Grand Rapids performs an average of 1/2
standard deviation below the mean of other Direct Instruction K-starting
sites. Examine the following summary tables that are based on data from
Abt 3 and Abt 4, which show medium grade norms for Direct Instruction sites.

Total Reading	Total Math	Spelling	Language
3.7	4.2	4.3	4.8
Norm(3.5)→3.5	4.0	4.3	4.8
3.4	4.0	3.9	4.7
3.4	3.9	3.9	4.6
3.3	3.9	3.7	4.5
3.2	3.8	Norm → 3.6	4.2
3.1	3.8	3.4	4.1
3.1	Norm → 3.75	3.4	Norm → 4.0
(2.8)	3.7	3.4	(2.8)
(2.8)	(3.0)	(3.0)	(2.6)
	(2.8)	(3.0)	

   ( ) Grand Rapids   Norm = 50th percentile

Rosemary Wilson
November 16, 1977
page 3

Although there is a variability, note that most of the variability
is _above_ the national norm (with the removal of Grand Rapids). Grand
Rapids is the only site that _consistently_ falls below national norm.
Even the most casual inspection of these data suggests that Grand Rapids
is "different". And you know that it is different because it has not been
implemented as a Direct Instruction site.

In absolute data, Direct Instruction, even with Grand Rapids included,
out-performed the other sponsors by one-fourth to one full standard deviation
on MAT Total Reading, Language, Total Math, and Spelling. Furthermore, we
can document the fact that what can be achieved through the Direct Instruction
approach is only partly reflected in the table above. We can show, for example,
that implementation was not fully achieved in any site and that we can do better.
Our questions to you are: Wouldn't it behoove Follow Through to pursue the
possibility that what we are saying is true? Wouldn't it be of potential value
for educating disadvantaged kids to know what _really_ could be done _with optimal_
implementation? Wouldn't it be valuable to have a bench mark, a standard of
excellence that establishes what can be done and that can therefore serve as
a goal for other projects and schools more generally?

In your letter, you assert: "Since 1968, the program emphasis ... has
been on the cooperative development and evaluation of Follow Through _projects_,
not models ..."

There are two problems with this statement. The first is that it is
historically false. The second is that it places you on the horns of a serious
dilemma.

1. The historical facts are these:

In his history of Follow Through prepared for the Brookings Conference
on Planned Variation, Egbert asserted while referring to the planning going
on in 1967: "With such limited funds, it seemed sensible to change Follow
Through's primary purpose from 'service to children' to 'finding out what
works'. ... Follow Through now focused its attention on developing,
examining, and refining alternative approaches to the education and
development of young disadvantaged children."

Fairley's five-year plan in 1971 was aimed at disseminating successful
models into Title I applications, a project that was terminated because the
data were not yet in. The following quote is taken from the SRI Administrative
History (p. F28, quoted from Haney, 1977, p. 36): "It was clear from Mr.
Fairley's comments that his interest was largely upon overall program effects
and an identification of 'best' individual sponsors to guide decisions about
future Follow Through program scope." [Emphasis added.]

The following statement is found in the first page of the Abt IV Report
on the evaluation of Follow Through which has been accepted by the Office of
Education and due for release to Congress shortly: "As part of this evaluation, the U.S. Office of Education commissioned Abt Associates in 1972 to

Rosemary Wilson
November 16, 1977
page 4

analyze the data generated by the extensive program of testing and
interviewing which was part of Follow Through and to draw from them
appropriate conclusions about the <u>effectiveness of the various models'</u>
<u>approaches to compensatory education.</u>" (Abt IV, 1977, p. xxiii)
[Emphasis added.]

In his history of Follow Through in Rivlin and Timpane's book on
Planned Variation in Education, Elmore states: "The idea of planned
variation experimentation adopted by Follow Through was, of course,
very different. Instead of specifying dimensions of variation and
attempting to limit the experiment to those most susceptible to
definition and replication, Follow Through administrators tried to
select promising, innovative <u>program models</u>, leaving the question
of how these models differed to a later time." (Rivlin & Timpane, p. 36)

Garry McDaniels, former director of Follow Through research,
makes these statements discussing the goals of the Follow Through
evaluation:

"Do the various educational strategies used in Follow Through
have different effects, and do the effects endure?" (Rivlin and
Timpane, p. 47) ... "The planned variation between models of various
sponsors is considered to be a more reliable means of assessment than
natural variation..." (Rivlin and Timpane, p. 48)

You assert that the emphasis of support is and has been on individual
sites, not sponsors. This position, however, does not explain why Follow
Through is organized as it is. If the emphasis is not on sponsor, why
isn't there a "random variation" of approaches used in different sites?
Why were sponsors introduced in the first place? The notion of planned
variation makes very little sense and becomes self-contradictory if in
fact there was no attempt to draw conclusions from a controlled pattern
of implementation across sites. Furthermore, the National Office has
commissioned studies to document the fact that different sponsors
produce different patterns of implementation:

The Nero implementation study (1975) shows that sponsors are
discriminable, that classroom features clearly identify different
sponsors, and that there is a different pattern of performance
across different sponsors. (What was the purpose of this investigation if there was no attempt to find out about sponsors, and
their implementation across sites.)

Similarly, the Stallings and Katkowitz study, funded by USOE,
showed through classroom observations that sponsors were discriminable
in their implementation at different sites and at different grade
levels. The study supported the conclusion that sponsorship is a
viable concept and that sponsor implementation does lead to observable
differences in classroom outcomes and in performance outcomes.

Rosemary Wilson
November 16, 1977
page 5

2. <u>One horn of your dilemma is this</u>:

If you deny (which you apparently have done) the sponsor concept
of Follow Through and deny that what was to be measured was sponsor
capability, not just the capacity of different sites to produce programs,
you make it transparently clear that Follow Through actually conned
individual sponsors into thinking that their efforts would be reinforced
if they produced positive results and that good approaches - those with
uniform potential - would be disseminated. You admit that Follow Through
is a sham and that all sponsors would be equals - those achieving student
performance at the 50th percentile and those at the 15th percentile.

On the other hand, if you accept the sponsorship philosophy of Follow
Through and the idea that the game was, from the beginning, an attempt to
find out about methods, programs, approaches that are effective across
different sites, different types of kids, and different ethnic groups,
you are faced with the conclusion that you are now supporting many sponsors
that have shown precisely no capacity to produce, and in fact are showing
alarmingly consistent negative results.

We do not envy your position. However, we do not have to reinforce
it and continue to be a part of an obvious travesty. We wanted to show
what could be done for the kids. After nearly ten years, we find that
although we succeeded, we have been rejected - not merely by the outside
educational establishment from whom rejection would be a natural response -
but from the agency that has funded us, that required us to hold to a
moratorium on publishing comparative data before 1975, that repeatedly
suggested possible expanded funding of successful models, that posed
as something more elegant than a fancy Title I program. It seems apparent,
however, that Follow Through at the National Level, has become a bureaucracy
with no apparent advocacy for the needs of children.

What other form of significant protest do we have other than quitting
Follow Through, other than by severing association with the kind of non-relevant
educational agencies that we have tried to fight during the past years?

Wesley C. Becker
Professor of Special Education

Siegfried Engelmann
Professor of Special Education

cc: Richard Fairley
    Thomas Minter
    Ernest Boyer
    Robert Egbert
    Mary Berry
    Representative Weaver
    Representative Ullmann
    Senator Packwood
    Senator Hatfield
    Dean R. Gilberts
    Senator Nelson

Rosemary Wilson
November 16, 1977
page 6

References

Abt Associates, Education as Experimentation: A Planned Variation Model,
Vol. 3, 1976, Vol. 4, 1977, Cambridge, Mass. Abt Associates.

Haney, W. The Follow Through Planned Variation Experiment, Vol. 5:
A Technical History of the National Follow Through Evaluation, Cambridge
Mass., Huron Institute, 1977.

Nero and Associates, A Description of Follow Through Implementation
Processes, Portland, OR, Nero and Associates, 1975.

Egbert, R., "Planned Variation in Follow Through," unpublished manuscript,
presented to Brookings Institution's Panel on Social Experimentation.
Washington, D.C.; April 1973.

DEPARTMENT OF HEALTH, EDUCATION, AND WELFARE
OFFICE OF EDUCATION
WASHINGTON, D.C. 20202

DEC 1 9 1977

Dr. Wesley C. Becker
Dr. Siegfried Engelmann
Professors of Special Education
University of Oregon
College of Education
Eugene, Oregon 97403

Dear Sirs:

This is in response to your letter to me of November 16, 1977, in which
you state among voluminous other assertions, that a statement I had made
in an earlier reply to you of October 28, 1977, was "historically false."
Although, as Director of the Follow Through program, I have many constructive
demands upon my time that prevent my entering into what now threatens to
become an endless exchange of unproductive, widely distributed, correspondence
between you and myself; I am compelled to respond to that charge of
falsehood.

Since, on October 28, I was writing a letter to you and not a position
paper as you have now done, I felt it unnecessary to provide annotation
of the sources upon which I based my statements. I do so now, however,
in view of this charge which you have so widely circulated.

The Follow Through Program Manual (draft), dated February 24, 1969, was
prepared and used while this program was under the direction of Dr. Robert
Egbert, whose later unpublished writings your paper quotes extensively.
The program manual contains on page 2, the following statement under
B. Planned Variation in a Context of Comprehensive Services.

> "In February of 1968, the U.S. Office of Education invited a limited
> number of communities (recommended by State officials) to participate
> in a cooperative enterprise to develop and evaluate comprehensive
> Follow Through projects, each of which incorporates one of the
> alternative 'program approaches' as part of its comprehensive
> Follow Through project. Generally, each of the current program
> sponsors concentrates on only a portion of the total Follow Through
> project. The remainder of the program is developed by the local
> community with consultant assistance."

Page 2 - Dr. Wesley C. Becker and Dr. Siegfried Engelmann

Based on the above quotation, I made the following statement in response
to your suggestion that this office recommend your Direct Instruction
Model to the Joint Dissemination Review Panel.

> "This is not reasonable in that it directly conflicts with OE's
> decision that projects, not "models" would be presented to the
> JDRP. This was a carefully considered decision based on the following
> facts.
>
> > a. Since 1968 the program emphasis has been on the cooperative
> >   development and evaluation of comprehensive Follow Through
> >   projects not models.
> >
> > b. No single instructional approach, including that of
> >   Direct Instruction, was found to be consistently effective
> >   in all of the projects where it was tried and evaluated.
> >   Therefore, no overall claim of its effectiveness can be
> >   supported."

In 1968, I was not in the employ of the U.S. Office of Education. The
draft program manual to which I refer, however, contained the guidelines
used by the Follow Through program and its grantees to govern their
operations until June 21, 1974 when, under my direction, the Follow
Through program published in the Federal Register as an interim final
regulation, its first official regulation (39 FR 22342 et. seq.)

I add that "quitting Follow Through" as a form of "significant protest"
was your decision. In my opinion, it is a very destructive one to the
Follow Through program and to the "poor kids" to whom you profess commitment.

Rosemary C. Wilson

Obviously, Rosemary Wilson lied, issuing the same fabrication that House and Glass asserted about Follow Through being designed to assess the aggregate performance of the models, not to compare individual sponsors. Equally obvious, Wilson was told by her superiors what lies she would present about the intent of the Follow Through evaluation. The only real question was how high in the bureaucracy the deception went.

The answer came in 1978, in the form of a letter from U.S. Commissioner of Education, Ernest Boyer, to Senator Bob Packwood from Oregon, one of the politicians Wes had contacted. This letter provides no doubt about Rosemary Wilson lying. It also delivers the twisted justification for rejecting the focus on sponsors. The letter leaves no doubt that the decision came from the top of the food chain, the Commissioner of Education. This letter is frank and honest, but contains desperately confused arguments.

Following is the letter from Packwood to Wes and the accompanying letter from Boyer to Packwood.

United States Senate

COMMITTEE ON FINANCE

WASHINGTON, D.C   20510

April 19, 1978

Wesley C. Becker, Ph.D.
University of Oregon
College of Education
Department of Special Education
Eugene, Oregon   97403

Dear Dr. Becker:

At last I received a response from the Office of
Education regarding my questions on the Follow Through
Program. I have enclosed their response to me with
this letter. It would appear from the letter that the
Office of Education and the President feel that (1) the
Follow Through Program was generally not successful in
producing any definitive results; and (2) that they are
therefore abandoning any continuation of the program.

I would certainly welcome your comments on the
points that they make in their letter.

As you know, the Subcommittee on Employment, Poverty
and Migratory Labor of the Senate Human Resources Committee held hearings on S.2090 which proposed to extend
the Head Start and Follow Through Programs for another
three years. The Subcommittee will be marking up the
bill next week.

I would greatly appreciate receiving any thoughts
you have on this bill, and how I might be of any assistance to you in your program efforts. Thank you for contacting me, and I look forward to reading any comments
you may have.

Cordially,

BOB PACKWOOD

BP/gzp

DEPARTMENT OF HEALTH, EDUCATION, AND WELFARE
OFFICE OF EDUCATION
WASHINGTON, D.C. 20202

MAR 3 1 1972

Honorable Bob Packwood
United States Senate
Washington, D.C.

Dear Senator Packwood:

Thank you for your letter inquiring about the Follow Through Program.
I will speak to your specific questions in order:

1. Since the beginning of Follow Through in 1968, the central emphasis
has been on models. A principal purpose of the program has been to
identify and develop alternative models or approaches to compensatory
education and assess their relative effectiveness through a major
evaluation study which compared the performance of Follow Through
children with comparable children in non-Follow Through projects over
a period of several years. That study had just been completed. A
summary of part of the final result, which was sent to the Congress
last summer, is enclosed; a more comprehensive final report will be
issued in the next few weeks. The evaluation found that only one of
the 22 models which were assessed in the evaluation consistently produced positive outcomes. The central finding of the evaluation was
that there was substantial variation in effectiveness among the sites
in almost all of the models. Accordingly (and this speaks in part to
your second question), we are funding 21 of the successful sites as
demonstration sites this year so that other schools and educators will
learn about, understand, and hopefully adopt the successful activities
and procedures taking place in these effective sites. In summary, while
the initial emphasis of the program was on designing and implementing
models, the evaluation results forced us to shift attention more to successful individual projects. If the evaluation findings had indicated
that the various models tested were either generally effective or generally ineffective, then the subsequent demonstration and dissemination
activities could have proceeded along model rather than individual
project lines. However, with the exception of the Becker-Engelmann
Direct Instruction model, this was not the case.

2. The President's budget recommendation for FY 1979 is to begin a
phase-out of the Follow Through program. The experiment to assess this
particular set of compensatory education models has been completed. It

Page 2 - Honorable Bob Packwood

is felt that future research and development efforts of this nature ought to be carried out by the National Institute of Education. The Administration is proposing an increase of $600 million in Title I of the Elementary and Secondary Education Act which will substantially expand the kind of direct compensatory education assistance which children in the Follow Through sites are receiving.

With respect to your question about funding selected models on an expanded scale, with the exception of the Direct Instruction Model this could not responsibly be done since, as I noted above, positive evaluation evidence for the other models is lacking. The same problem applies to your question about funding sponsors to disseminate information on Follow Through programs on the college and in-service levels. Since only one of the models, and therefore only one of the sponsors, was found to produce positive results more consistently than any of the others, it would be inappropriate and irresponsible to disseminate information on all the models which carried the implication that such models could be expected to produce generally positive outcomes.

I hope this information answers your questions. If I can be of any further assistance, to you, please let me know.

Cordially,

Ernest L. Boyer
U.S. Commissioner
of Education

The first sentence of point 1 in Boyer's letter contradicts the assertion by Wilson, House, and Glass about whether Follow Through was designed to find successful models or to evaluate the aggregate of models. *"Since the beginning of Follow Through in 1968, the central emphasis has been on models."*

Boyer freely admits that policy makers accepted the data as valid. Several references in his letter indicate that he had no doubt that only one model was highly successful, which means that he was aware of facts that had never been shared with states and school districts.

The ultimate conclusion Boyer drew was that if there was only one successful model, it should be treated like all the other models. In response to the question about funding *selected* models, Boyer's logic seems to be that somehow such funding would be irresponsible because there were not selected models, *only one selected model.* So rather than fund that model, the Office of Education assumed it was equitable to treat all models the same and simply promote selected sites. Imagine spending half a billion dollars to draw this conclusion.

The effect Boyer presumed would happen is naïve: *"… we are funding 21 of the successful sites as demonstration sites this year so that other schools and educators will learn about, understand, and hopefully adopt the successful activities and procedures taking place in these effective sites."*

Boyer had data that the effective non-DI schools were aberrations and that they were so elusive that the sponsors could not even train their other schools to do what the successful school did. If there was any validity to the notion that people would visit a dissemination model for High Scope and be able to implement as well as the school visited, the sponsor would have been the first to know about this excellent site and therefore the first to try to disseminate in his other sites. This dissemination failed. The successful school remained an outlier. Therefore, there would be no hope of visiting schools being able to replicate the procedures of this school. In fact, the National Diffusion Network (NDN) did not create more than a handful of success stories for failed schools.

Schools from High Scope and other failed models were disseminated for one reason: to preserve at least a modicum of credibility to all the favored ideas and practices of mainline educational thought. If everybody failed, at least Stallings, Piaget, and the rationale that drove at least 19 of 22 models would not be shown to be grossly inferior to the ideas and practices that innervated DI.

In terms of morality, Boyer's decision not to permit sponsors to disseminate was brutal. Why wouldn't it have been possible to fund us as a model and fund sites from other models? The consistent performance of our model affirmed that our techniques and programs were replicable and that with proper training teachers in failed schools could succeed. Why wouldn't that information be important enough to disseminate? Why did the government feel that it had to initiate some form of affirmative action to keep failed models floating?

Boyer admits that the results didn't come out the way experts predicted. Policy makers didn't have the vision of only one program excelling in basic skills and cognitive skills, or the same program excelling in reading, spelling, and math. They were not prepared for the possibility that this program · would also have children with the strongest self-image.

MANIPULATED DATA?

Earlier, I suggested the possibility that policy makers tried to sour our data by purposely including Grand Rapids as one of our sites. Two sentences in Boyer's letter may confirm this suspicion:

> *The evaluation found that only one of the 22 models which were assessed in the evaluation **consistently produced positive outcomes**. The central finding of the evaluation was that there was substantial variation in effectiveness among the sites **in almost all of the models**.*

If these sentences are considered literally, they imply that in the original report Boyer received, not all of the models had variation. There was substantial variation in *almost all of the models;* however, one *consistently produced positive outcomes.* Possibly the addition of Grand Rapids was an intentional manipulation to create variation and thereby make it possible for conspirators Glass and House to present their argument on variability within models.

Whether or not the data were manipulated, there had been a fairly extensive plot to assure that various bureaucrats told a consistent story about the intent of the Follow Through evaluation and did not contradict one another (at least until Boyer blew it with his letter to Packwood). The parties included House, Glass, the Ford Foundation, Rosemary Wilson, Follow Through, the National Institute of Education, and the Office of Education, all the way to the top.

The extent to which the distorted account of Follow Through prevailed over truth was partly revealed by an online outline of significant educational events that occurred during the 1960s and '70s.

I discovered the outline while doing research for this chapter. The outline was for a college course at Illinois State University, Political Science

233: Politics and Public Policy. The instructor was Gary Klass. The outline went into some detail about the Coleman Report and the Pettigrew interpretation of the Report, which led to bussing. The outline covered the failure of bussing and the failure of Head Start. It did have a note that a preschool produced benefits. That preschool was the Perry Preschool, which is High Scope.

Following the endorsement of High Scope was a heading, *Other Studies*, followed by a one-line reference to Follow Through:

Compensatory education programs show no effect.

Done.

If people like Klass didn't have a clue, the campaign to bury the truth about Follow Through had to be pretty effective.

Another way of measuring the effectiveness of the historical distortions of Follow Through is to tell the truth. On three occasions I talked about our model to non-educational audiences. One was a Chamber of Commerce; the others were business groups that supported different school efforts. The responses were the same. After I gave the facts, at least one member of the audience would say something to the effect, "You're telling us that you achieved all these things in Follow Through but professionals in the field rejected your model. I know some people in education, and they are well informed and committed to do a good job. But you're saying that they would purposely ignore actual facts about student achievement. I've always believed that if someone builds a better mousetrap it will sell. You're telling us that's not true in education. I find that hard to believe. I also question whether the educational system would plot against your program if it was as successful as you claim it is."

After the third talk I resolved never to do it again, and I haven't. But I've had the same experience dealing with administrators—the frown, the headshake, and the confession, "I find that hard to believe."

The saddest part of the Office of Education's conspiracy to propagate lies and intellectual casuistry is that it makes a mockery of the vision that Robert Kennedy had when he argued for evaluation—so that educators would make sensible responses based on the outcome data.

That could have happened only if the Follow Through data were properly disseminated; however, such dissemination was unpalatable to those who had power. Stated differently, on the balance scale of reality, the weight of Jackie, Alan, and all the other poverty kids on one side didn't come close to balancing the weight of influential people, their prejudices, and their financial interests on the other.

However, this failed system could have benefited in the long run if it had an understanding that the process of creating effective programs is greatly different from the approach they used; that there was a theory that explained the details; and that there were people who would have been glad to share whatever they knew about efficient ways of doing it.

During the tumult of 1977–79, I did not participate in the political side of things beyond the letter to Rosemary Wilson. I continued to develop instructional programs and work with our remaining sites, as Wes took on the bulls and the bears. Both left scars on him. After Packwood sent him the Boyer letter, Wes wrote Packwood again. Here's the last part of that letter.

> The basic problem we face is that the most popular models in education today (those based on open classrooms, Piagetian ideas, language experience, and individualized instruction) failed in Follow Through. As a result there are many forces in the educational establishment seeking to hide the fact that Direct Instruction, developed by a guy who doesn't even have a doctorate or a degree in education, actually did the job. To keep those promoting popular approaches from hiding very important outcomes to save their own preconceptions will take formidable help from persons like yourself. We hope it is not too late.

Sorry, Wes. It was too late. The truth about Follow Through was silently drowned like an unwanted kitten, and nobody protested. Outfits like the NAACP and other advocacy or community-action groups should have been outraged, but they were conspicuously mute, apparently lacking the means, knowledge, or commitment needed to be more than paper advocates. The drowning was a complete success.

CHAPTER 6

Follow Through Aftermath

FOLLOW THROUGH SPUTTERS ON

Follow Through didn't die immediately after the formal evaluation in 1977. It grew weak and lost most of its teeth as funding decreased but continued until 1995 in its various effete manifestations.

We didn't quit Follow Through in 1978. Rosemary Wilson was replaced with Gary McDaniels, who had been in charge of Follow Through evaluation. He was right-minded and positive. He talked us into continuing to work with our sites that did not drop out of Follow Through.

We worked hard and tried to keep sites at a high level, but it was more difficult to do because they often did not have sufficient funds to hire aides in K and 1. We didn't receive as much money, so our travel budget was cut substantially; and we had fewer days on site, so we weren't able to address problems as well as we had during the glory days of Follow Through. From a psychological standpoint, it wasn't the same because it was as if the glory days had never occurred. DI retained its grunt-and-spit image, still dubbed an approach that had no regard for children's needs.

We concentrated on serving the students in our sites, but without the expectation that what we did would be recognized. Some of us retained qualified hope that some district somewhere would institutionalize DI practices and set new standards for achievement and service to at-risk children.

I apologized to our trainers and project managers for involving them in the project. I had earlier told them that I was sure we would win the competition, and they would benefit and be recognized for their effort. Instead, we remained irritants in the districts we served and lepers to those outside our sites. People who should have been recognized as valued resources were often targets of scorn.

Although our model continued, Wes didn't. In 1979, Wes left the project and assumed a position of associate dean in the College of Education. He did not drop ties with us or the mission we espoused—at least not at that time. He continued as a shareholder and treasurer of Engelmann-Becker Corporation, so we saw each other once in a while. He continued to teach Ed Psych, and, as usual, he was deeply involved in trying to acquaint his students (many of whom would become school psychologists) with the facts of life in schools. I presented to his class at least once each quarter. But our relationship wasn't the same. We had started to write a book on Follow Through in 1977, when the Abt report came out. We had written drafts of 11 chapters. I tried to schedule times to work on the book with Wes, but he was busy with other projects. His responses were not typical of Wes. He seemed reluctant to work on the book.

The Corp published some instructional material, including the original version of our *Corrective Reading* program. It published a book on reinforcement by Hill Walker, and some beginning-level programs created and field-tested by Alan Hoffmeister at Utah State University. Wes was the principal force in the nuts-and-bolt details of publishing this material.

In 1981, Wes and I founded the Association for Direct Instruction, but he did most of the work. The Association put out a quarterly newspaper. Wes was the editor. He recruited and collected articles, stories about DI implementations, and research studies relevant to teachers and school administrators. The association took over the annual DI conference in Eugene and scheduled four or five smaller conferences in different parts of the U.S.

Doug Carnine replaced Wes as co-director of our project in 1979. The Follow Through Project wasn't the same without Wes, but the size and shape of the battlegrounds didn't change.

In 1981, the U.S. Senate gave us some hope by passing a bill that would increase the funding for effective Follow Through sponsors. In 1982, the Department of Education decided that the most reasonable way to increase funding for effective sponsors was to decrease our funding and increase the funding of failed Follow Through models, those that had never been validated as being any more effective than failed Title I programs.

Doug corresponded with the Assistant Secretary of Education, Jean Benish, and questioned the sagacity of this decision. Here's one of his letters and the response.

Doug

UNIVERSITY OF OREGON
College of Education
Department of Special Education

FOLLOW THROUGH PROJECT—*"So They Shall Not Fail"*

Telephone (code 503) 686-3555
Eugene, Oregon 97403

July 13, 1982

D. Jean Benish
Assistant Secretary
U.S. Dept. of Education
Washington, D.C.   20202

Dear M. Benish:

I'm disappointed that the Department of Education decided
against following the wording of last year's Senate language
which suggested support for effective Follow Through projects
and their sponsors. The Department's decision seems to be to
reward incompetence. If Follow Through projects haven't been
validated after fourteen years, do you think giving their
sponsors more money for the fifteenth year will do any good?
The Senate wording would have the Department disseminate what
works. The Department is giving extra money to what hasn't
shown to work, at least for the last fourteen years.

"Administrations come and go but the logic of the bureaucracy
never came so how can it ever go?"

Best wishes,

Doug Carnine

cc:Sen. M. Hatfield
   Rikki Poster
   Sen. W. Proxmire

UNITED STATES DEPARTMENT OF EDUCATION
WASHINGTON, D.C. 20202

2 7 JUL 1982

ASSISTANT SECRETARY
FOR ELEMENTARY AND SECONDARY EDUCATION

Dr. Doug Carnine
Director, Direct Instruction
  Follow Through Project
University of Oregon
Eugene, Oregon 97403

Dear Dr. Carnine:

This is in response to your letter of July 13 concerning Follow Through
sponsor funding for Fiscal Year (FY) 1982.

The reasons for our funding decisions were outlined in my July 6 response
to your mailgram concerning the same issue. With regard to the language
in the FY 1981 Senate report, we feel that we are acting in the spirit
of that language. By providing somewhat greater support to sponsors with
non-validated projects, we are providing an opportunity for validation
to projects and sponsors that may not have had that opportunity in the
past. In this way, we hope to increase the number of exemplary Follow
Through projects, to the ultimate benefit of the Nation's public schools.

Sincerely,

D. Jean Benish
Acting Assistant Secretary

The logic of the Department of Education again seemed totally political, garnished with a shallow argument that justified affirmative action for failed sponsors, but certainly not failed students. The goal seemed to be to give support to projects that were consistent with prevailing beliefs. If we take Benish's argument seriously, however, we have a glimpse into the Department's belief system—then and now. Nobody on their end completely understands what makes a model effective. They don't believe it is a logical outcome of what is done moment-to-moment in the classroom and how it is done. For them, whatever amorphous ingredient spawns success is either global (like focusing on children's self-image through self-reports) or totally mysterious, but they believe this illusive quality would be vitalized if the failed models simply had more opportunities to be successful. The policy makers did not reason that if the sponsor cannot disseminate effective practices among its participating sites, why would anybody assume that the model would work in sites over which the sponsor had less control?

Also, to believe this "justification" would require erasing all memory of the Coleman Report and the Westinghouse Study. Both studies had extensive data showing that increased money did not improve student performance.

THEORY OF INSTRUCTION

After the Follow Through evaluation, I didn't travel as much. By this time, I despised travel so much that the smell of an airport produced a knot in my gut. For me travel was strongly associated with going places where I had to try to solve problems that often proved to be insoluble or that yielded a bitter compromise that was not worth the amount of effort they required.

Doug Carnine and I decided that it would be productive for us to write a theory of instruction. "Theories of instruction" were not wanting in number, but in substance. There were theories of the brain, theories of cognition, theories of learning. The problem was that none of these theories addressed instruction in a rigorous way. None of them had basic principles and rules that would even suggest some of the more fundamental tenets of teaching, such as creating instruction that is consistent with a single interpretation; or demonstrating how things are the same; or even how much to teach at one time. None of the theories could explain why our approach worked well and the others didn't. The theories didn't address the full range of instruction, from working on simple motor skills to higher-order concepts.

The two "theories" that were closest to a real theory of instruction were

Benjamin Bloom's taxonomy of learning, and Robert Gagne's *Conditions of Learning.*

Bloom's hierarchy suggested the order of difficulty for six different levels of learning: **knowledge, comprehension, application, analysis, synthesis,** and **evaluation.** The problem with the categories is that they tend to evaporate when they are applied to specific applications. How could we possibly judge that a child comprehended something without receiving some evidence that the child was able to apply what had been taught? And how could a learner identify an object never observed before as red unless the learner applied an analysis of what was red and what wasn't?

Gagne was an instructor and his observations were in the ballpark, but his theory is an unholy mixture of things to do when teaching and what the learner is learning. For instance, he specified "nine elements of instruction."

- Gain attention

- Inform learner of objectives

- Stimulate recall of prior learning

- Present stimulus material

- Provide learner guidance

- Elicit performance

- Provide feedback

- Assess performance

- Enhance retention transfer

These suggestions are reasonable, but they are not linked to tenets of a theory. They are just sensible things to do with sophisticated learners. Stated another way, an instructional designer could create a teaching sequence that met all of these criteria but totally failed to teach the learner because the content—the guts of instruction—is not addressed by these steps. Direct Instruction presentations generally meet Gagne's requirements, but so do presentations that fail.

Real theory would have principles that explain every detail of a teaching sequence that is highly effective.

Here's a highly effective sequence for teaching red.

Demonstration of *red*

A white ball appears on the screen.

"Watch this ball. I'll tell you when it's red."

Examples: 1. "My turn: Is it red? No."

2. The ball becomes blue: "My turn: Is it red now? No."

3. The ball turns red: "My turn: Is it red now? Yes."

4. "Your turn: Is it red now?" "Yes."

5. The ball gets bigger: "Is it red now?" "Yes."

6. The ball turns blue: "Is it red now?" ...

7. The ball turns red and moves to the left: "Is it red now?" ...

8. The ball turns green: "Is it red now?" ...

9. The ball gets smaller and turns yellow: "Is it red now?" ...

10. The ball gets smaller and turns red: "Is it red now?" ...

The learner responds to possibly four more examples. Then the projected images change. The screen shows a dozen flowers of different sizes and shapes. Five are red.

"Some of these flowers are red and some are not red."

The teacher points to a red flower. "Is this flower red?" ...

The teacher points to a white flower. "Is this flower red?" ...

And so forth, with possibly six more examples.

The presentation is effective because it clearly shows what red is and what it isn't. This is not an amorphous judgment, but one based on many details of the presentation. For instance, the changes are dynamic; only one thing changed for the first three examples—the color; the narrator labeled the examples as red and not-red. These statements paralleled changes in only one feature of the ball, the color. Therefore, that "color" is the *only* feature that the teacher could be describing as "red" versus "not-red."

The dynamic presentation does not require the learner to compare two static objects, just one, as it changes. So, from the standpoint of communication, it is as streamlined as possible. This is a logical analysis, not an analysis based on empirical evidence, or one based on the learner, but one based on the nature of the concept the learner is expected to learn.

After Doug and I agreed that the field needed a real theory of instruction (one that addressed the logic of all the details of effective instruction), we embarked on writing one—*Theory of Instruction: Principles and Applications* (1982; 1991). We designated it "a job," which means that we set a daily time slot—usually an hour and a half—when we would work on it.

We followed the same development format that we use for writing programs. We proceeded at a relatively fast rate, but not superficially. We didn't want great personal investment in what we wrote because we'd have to look at it later, and we wanted to be able to rip it apart with the same vigor we would critique someone else's work. If it stood up to scrutiny, that was good. But we really didn't mind changing it if it had problems because the changes hopefully would make it better.

We didn't start with an outline, do a chapter, and then redo it. When we started out, we didn't know what the chapters would be. Rather, we tried to start with the guts of what we were trying to develop and go as far as we could before we saw that there were important gaps in what we'd written, which would mean that our explanation didn't generate what we knew to be true about children's learning behavior.

At the time we wrote the book, we had taught just about everything to every type of kid or adult, including people with just about any handicapping condition. So we had a good understanding of the range of behaviors to expect, the kind of mistakes and problems learners had with different types of material, and the fe atures of programs that are successful in teaching various skills and information. That's what the theory had to predict or explain.

As we constructed the theory, the logical analysis would sometimes predict behavioral outcomes that had not been studied empirically. For each of those cases, Doug conducted an empirical study, with kids, and with a design that would demonstrate whether our logical analysis predicted the learning outcome. Doug was very good at designing and conducting experiments. Most of them had two matched groups of children. One group received the treatment. The other didn't. The tests of outcomes showed how the experimental group changed as a function of instruction, compared to the "control group."

At the time we wrote the book, Doug had already conducted more controlled studies than most investigators do in a lifetime. Before the Follow Through evaluation came out, he had conducted 19 of them. Nearly all involved procedures we used in Follow Through. The studies compared outcomes of our procedures to those of traditional approaches. For instance, he did studies on the extent to which young, at-risk beginning readers benefit from engaging in independent, silent reading. The answer was none. If anything, the practice tended to galvanize the mistakes they made because they received no feedback when they worked independently, so they simply practiced the same mistakes or inappropriate strategies they made when they read aloud to a teacher.

Doug worked with about ten Ph.D. students during this period. Doug would specify the details of the experiment. He would create or assemble whatever material was needed. His cohorts would recruit subjects, set up the experiment, run it, and analyze the data.

Doug followed this procedure when we worked on the theory book. If we drew a unique logical conclusion about behavior, Doug would indicate that he knew of no experimental data on this issue and would ask if I knew of any empirical data. The answer was usually "no," so Doug would conduct a study. For example, in the theory, we specified "templates" for teaching any basic non-comparative concepts, like *rake, laugh, red,* etc. The demonstration of *red* follows this basic template. The first two examples are negatives (not-red balls); the third example is a minimally different positive (red ball). From a logical standpoint, the negative-first sequence would convey more precise information about red the first time an example is identified as red. If the examples were reordered so the sequence of examples began with the first two positive examples of red (examples 3 and 4 in the sequence), learners would theoretically have less information about what the label red referred to than they would if the negative examples came first.

If the first example in the sequence is labeled "red," the label could convey all kinds of possible meanings to a naïve learner. The reason is that the projected image labeled as "red" is an example of an indefinitely large number of concepts—thousands of them. This is an amazing assertion, but you can identify the concepts by simply asking the question, "Could this be an example of _____? Could this be an example of a round shape; of something in this room; of something larger than a penny; of something smaller than a garage; of something that is not square; or of something projected on the wall? The answer is yes, which means that *this same image could be used to teach or demonstrate any of those other concepts.* For instance, if you were teaching the concept, round versus not-round, you could use image 3 or 4 as a positive example of *round*. If you were teaching the concept of something larger than a penny, you could use the same images as positive examples of larger than a penny, and so forth for all the concepts listed above, and for thousands of others (theoretically an infinite number).

Understand that this image is not a positive example of everything. It's not an example of something square, something on the floor, something you eat, or a grandmother. The game of teaching the concept efficiently involves first recognizing this basic fact about any concrete example and then reducing the possible interpretations to one as efficiently as possible.

This may seem like a very picky orientation, but that's what a theory of instruction is designed to do—provide all the information that is relevant to creating effective instruction.

So, when we were designing model templates like the one for red, Doug conducted at least one experiment for every detail of the template. Doug did a total of ten studies on the template for *red*. One addressed whether the dynamic sequence is superior to one that presents a series of static examples. For this study, 40 preschoolers were taught the concept of "diagonal." The teacher used a straight stick and moved it to create a series of examples that were either diagonal or not diagonal. Those in the "dynamic change" group passed the test of generalizing the concept to unique examples in 20.6 trials. Children in the "non-dynamic change" group required 56.4 trials. So the empirical evidence confirmed the logical analysis.

Doug did three large studies that addressed the number of differences between positive and negative examples. One study involved five groups of preschoolers. All children received the same positive examples. (A positive example of red is red; a negative, not-red.) Each group, however, received unique negative examples. For one group, positives differed in only one way from the negative (like those in the sequence for *red*). For the next group, the negative examples differed in two ways (which, for the example of *red*, would be a difference in color *and* possibly in the size of the circle). The next group had negatives that differed in three ways from the positives (possibly not red, larger, and oval, not round) and so forth to the fifth and final condition, which had only positives, no negatives.

As the logical analysis predicted, the children who received negatives that differed in only one way from positives outperformed all the other groups, and the poorest group was the one that was shown no negatives. Note that the vast majority of traditional teaching demonstrations do not have any negatives, or, if they do, they are greatly different from the positives in an attempt to make the learning "easier."

Doug conducted two studies involving the juxtaposition of the examples (which example follows which example). The experiment configured the same set of examples different ways. The format suggested by the analysis produced the best learning outcome.

Doug also did studies on the presence of irrelevant features, and studies on wording variations and wording consistency. The results of all the experiments upheld what the logical analysis predicted.

These again are picky details, but that's what makes the difference—saving ten trials here, thirty there, avoiding inducing a misconception that will later require re-teaching. The result is acceleration and greatly increased confidence of children that they will learn what the teacher tries to teach.

Consider the unfortunate teacher who goes out of her way to make the directions and "tasks" more interesting by varying wording. Her presentation may sound better to the naïve observer, but she has greatly compromised the clarity of what she is trying to teach. In the same way, the teacher who doesn't know the details of the positive and negative examples will do what intuitively makes sense, which guarantees that her presentation will be more difficult for the naïve learner. Intuition might dictate that a concept would be easier to teach if the presentation did not involve positive examples that are minimally different from negatives. The outcomes of intuition are not supported by either logic or experimental outcomes. A long list of popular practices (such as first teaching students fractions that have 1 as the numerator) make no sense logically or empirically.

Because the theory we developed addressed all the issues of creating effective instruction, the theory is not simple. I taught Theory of Instruction as a graduate-level course for eight years. Both the course and I received relatively low ratings. The main problem was that most students had not taught hard-to-teach children and did not appreciate the level of detail that the successful teacher presentations had to meet. Also, students often had trouble with assignments, most of which required them to design tasks and series of examples for teaching something; or to critique and fix up series of examples that had problems. (Some students were comfortable working from college textbooks, but unpracticed in creating presentations.) Because some students were quite knowledgeable about teaching low performers, I felt as if I was in a bind. If I taught to them, I would totally lose the others.

So, I agreed with the student evaluations of me. Paradoxically, I didn't do a stellar job of doing what the theory was all about; however, I don't think the theory can be simplified. As we point out on the first page of the text, the analysis of cognitive learning involves three different analyses—the analysis of behavior, the analysis of knowledge systems, and the analysis of how information is communicated to the learner. Each analysis has unique principles.

The analysis of behavior involves data, observations of how students perform under different conditions. The analysis of knowledge systems reveals what the core concepts are and how they are chained to create more complicated knowledge concepts. The analysis of communication addresses what the teacher says and does. This analysis has principles for such things as showing sameness across the range of positive examples.

Doug and I worked on this project for over three years. When it was completed (probably the fifth draft of some parts), the manuscript had 900 pages with more than 200 figures and tables.

Then came the hard part—finding a publisher. We knew it might be difficult because the theory book was like our instructional programs in that the theory didn't follow a traditional outline for books on "instructional design," and the book could not be comfortably positioned as a textbook or simply an academic work. Furthermore, it was very doubtful that more than about five percent of the instructors who would teach such courses or review the book for a publishing house would be "comfortable" with it and what it does. Prentice Hall had published the book that Carl and I wrote; but neither Prentice Hall, McGraw-Hill nor any other top publisher was interested in the book. Irvington Publishers published it in 1982. There were very few sales of the book, no publicity, and no recognition that this text might be important because it revealed all the secrets of those who conducted the most effective preschool and primary-grade programs on record.

Irvington Publishers folded a few years later, and again, no major publisher was interested in *Theory of Instruction*. The Association for Direct Instruction finally published it, so it would be available to the few who were interested in it. Bob Dixon wrote the preface to the ADI edition. Bob is a very talented person who came to me with an idea for teaching spelling. His idea was based on what he called morphographs, the smallest units of meaning that are spelled the same way. Bob and I wrote a series of successful spelling programs based on morphographs.

In Bob's preface to the theory book, he observed:

> *Theory of Instruction* is the articulation of a theory—not in the atheoretical sense "theory" is used in educational jargon, but in the more precise sense well established among scientists and philosophers of science ... 1) it is exhaustive in that it covers everything from the most basic motor skill instruction to the highest order thinking skills, and 2) ... it is parsimonious.

(The ellipses before "it is parsimonious" indicate that Bob was not parsimonious.)

The overall impact the book has had on technical understanding of instructional design is minimal, even though it has enormous implications for designing effective instruction.

SELF-SPONSORED SITES

During the first eight years of Follow Through, Follow Through funded over 50 self-sponsored schools. These schools are based on the assumption that local schools know more about their children and the problems they are experiencing than remote writers of instructional programs or sponsors who are not knowledgeable about local children. Because local teachers know more about the children, they are better prepared to orchestrate effective instruction for them. There were 15 self-sponsored districts, and many implemented in more than one school. If Follow Through had been limited to the 15 self-sponsored communities, it still would have been the largest educational experiment ever conducted. In California, for instance, three districts were self-sponsored: Los Angeles, Stewart's Point (Native Americans) and San Diego. We later worked with San Diego and almost worked with Los Angeles, but L.A. did not submit its proposal on time and didn't get funded. When questioned about this faux pas, a district official indicated that it wasn't a very large grant, under $5 million, so the proposal somehow got lost.

The other self-sponsored communities were: Honolulu; Van Buren, Maine; Prince George County, Maryland; Great Falls, Montana; Dade County, Florida; Portland, Oregon; Detroit; Chattanooga; Puerto Rico; Corpus Christi; Morgantown, West Virginia; and Riverton, Wyoming. The children spanned the full range of demographic variation rural and urban, non-English speakers, Blacks, and Native Americans.

The performance of these sites would be important to those in the educational community who believed that teacher autonomy and collaboration would transform failed schools into effective ones. Nearly all of the self-sponsored sites promoted teacher autonomy and school autonomy. They permitted enormous latitude in how teachers developed material and practices to meet the needs of children, and nearly all sites had provisions for teachers working collaboratively to meet the children's need. If judged on the appeal of goals and practices, these sites should have been 10s. In fact, all failed. Incredibly, the self-sponsored sites performed below the average of the Follow Through sponsored sites, which was considerably below the level of children in Title I schools.

In 1977, we began working as a sponsor in San Diego. The San Diego self-sponsored program had been implemented in the seven lowest schools in the district. The school populations were mostly Hispanic, some Black, and a few Southeast Asian. In the seven schools, third graders performed at the 11th percentile. In 1977, Gary McDaniels indicated that San Diego could no longer continue as a self-sponsored site, but had a choice of being sponsored by Kansas or by us. The district selected DI because a high-ranking administrator in the district supported DI. We thought this was a good omen because it hadn't happened in any of the other larger cities we'd worked with.

At the time our model was selected, San Diego had just lost a desegregation suit. Judge Loren Welsh ruled that it was not practical to "desegregate" the district through bussing. Instead, he ordered the district to implement effective programs for all minority students. He also indicated that he would monitor the district's progress.

The illusion that San Diego would be cooperative with us quickly evaporated. In fact, San Diego's administration proved to be the most deceitful and non-cooperative one we had worked with. That judgment may partially result from the fact that we had more interaction with the administration than we had in other districts. In the book, *War Against the Schools' Academic Child Abuse*, I list a series of deceptions we encountered. One had to do with teaching English. The administration insisted that we had to install the district's "bilingual program," which was poorly conceived and provided extensive instruction in Spanish before introducing English. We indicated that we would not use the district program, but would use our beginning language program and teach everything in English, starting in K. The following excerpt from the book describes the district's response:

> One day, we received a letter from Lisa Sanches, an assistant superintendent, informing us that according to State bilingual regulations and district regulations, kids had to be taught in their native language first.

> There it was in writing and very official looking. Of course, it was a lie. We called the state director and the legal counsel for bilingual programs, in Sacramento. Both indicated that no such regulation existed, that the methods for instructing the kids were not specified, except that the instruction should be designed so the kids were able to participate. The district continued to give us static on the issue of bilingual kids. We were required to get "waivers" from parents, but the waivers did not seem to make it from the central office in a timely manner, so we made up our own waivers.

In a progress report on the District's implementation of effective programs for the minority children who were not in Follow Through, Judge Welsh observed that the district did not excel in veracity.

> The credibility of the district with this Court has deteriorated because of lack of candor. Statistical analyses in district evalua-

tions are changed from report to report in order to exaggerate claimed successes and minimize failures.

A paradox of the district's program was that it left the Southeast Asian children with no language program. The district policy prevented teachers from teaching English; these children could not speak Spanish; no teachers could speak Hmong or Vietnamese, so the children were left somewhere in limbo.

The district hoped to comply with the court order by creating its own program, which the district thought would be as good as ours. (Again, the logic seems to be that if we did it, why couldn't the district do it without going through the steps we do in developing a program or even understanding the steps.) The district program was named Achievement Goals Program (AGP). It used coaches and had classroom observations, just as we did. It even had scripted presentations, just as we did. The difference was in the scripts. Theirs were sophomoric in both structure and content.

The district commissioned teachers and miscellaneous others to create these scripted lessons. The project proved to be more costly than district administrators had anticipated. Not only were the teachers who created the material virtually absent from their schools; the district went over the estimated cost of the entire project on what it paid for paper and reproducing lessons, and the paper cost alone was more than a million dollars above the estimated cost for the whole project. When we received this news, one of my colleagues joked that they may have purchased their paper from the University of Illinois.

After the second year of AGP, San Diego did an evaluation that compared the results of the San Diego Follow Through first graders with minority children in the AGP program. Both groups of first graders had similar numbers—64 percent were at or above grade level at the beginning of first grade; 60 percent were at or above grade level at the end of the first grade. The conclusion was that the AGP was successful, as good as the Follow Through program.

The problem with this interpretation was that our schools had 64 percent of the kids at or above grade level at the beginning of first grade. Even the district should have known that the lowest seven schools in the district obviously don't have children who start at this performance level. Fewer than seven percent of our entering kindergarteners performed at or above grade level. The reason for the high performance at the end of kindergarten was our kindergarten program. There was good teaching in many kindergartens. Our children left K above the

50th percentile. Non-English-speaking children who had been in school all year performed so well in English that you couldn't tell that nine months earlier they hadn't been able to understand any English.

In contrast, the AGP students entered first grade with over 60 percent of the students at or above grade level. That performance was not caused by an effective K program. These were minority children, but not minority children who were at-risk. They entered school as high performers.

AGP failed emphatically. It was replaced by the Rainbow Project, which also failed emphatically.

Our Follow Through Project went well in San Diego, but the director was not a help, mainly because he also did not excel in veracity. He pretended to support the project, but he did many things to undercut it. The project went well because it had a tenacious project manager, Phyllis Haddox; good trainers (including Adrienne Allen, Gary Johnson, and Mariam True); and three outstanding on-site supervisors who were employed by the district and were on a career ladder. The supervisors were very intelligent and dedicated young women—Bonnie Nelson, Rita Colton, and Kimiko Fukuda. I could not believe that such a sour district could have such talented people. All three quickly caught on to teaching DI and supervising. During the first year, they visited classrooms with Phyllis, observed and rehearsed what she did, and carried out the assignments she gave them. Phyllis reported that they were the smartest supervisors she had ever trained.

By the second year, they were performing very well on their own. Phyllis and the consultants helped them out when they got stuck, but they didn't get stuck very often. There was a lot of work for everybody because much of the teaching was substandard and the district created problems.

I didn't help matters in San Diego. One morning a reporter from the *San Diego Union* interviewed me with regard to the court order and how the project was going. I answered his questions until he asked about the AGP processes. I told him I would rather not answer the question. He said, "Well, off the record, what would you say?"

I said, "It's a zoo." And elaborated.

The next morning, while a trainer, Phyllis and I were having breakfast in the hotel, a district administrator marched over to our table, slammed a newspaper on the table, and directed me to the prominent article in which I was quoted as labeling the operation a zoo. I didn't deny saying it but tried to explain that the reporter said it was off the record. I later called the reporter, who apologized but told me that there is no such thing as remarks that are "off the record." I wished that I had known that earlier.

One of the more memorable out-of-school events I experienced in San Diego was the time it rained. Some of the schools we worked with were on the southeast side of the city, on top of a plateau-like area. To get back to the hotel, we would go down streets that crossed very large culverts (probably eight feet high) and capacious channels, which were dry—except one time.

We were finishing up at Logan School when it started to rain—pour like a Midwest cloudburst. Our hotel was down at Mission Bay. To get there, we tried to take the normal route, but when we came to the first culvert, I understood why they had been constructed. The water cascading down the hill not only filled the culvert but left the bridge more than a foot under rushing water. We went back and found another route that wasn't flooded, but we saw a lot of overflowing culverts and near waterfalls. Part of the hotel's parking lot was flooded, with a couple of rows of cars half under water. The exceptions were the VW bugs. Four were floating around like water bugs.

It was fun working with the supervisors, teachers, and children in San Diego but a real pain working with the director or the central administration. After the third year we worked there, the support from the district was so unhelpful that we seriously considered dropping the site. The Federal Liaison was Susan Green. She set up an evening meeting with the Follow Through director and supervisors. The meeting was held at Disney World in Orlando, where Follow Through was having a business meeting on funding.

As others were outside laughing and squealing, we sat in a nondescript, large room where I experienced the most draining, frustrating, but uplifting meeting I have ever attended. The meeting began in the early evening. During the first two hours, Phyllis and I presented a litany of problems, such as the director giving the parent group false information and the essential changes in San Diego's slippery operating plan not occurring. For each problem, the director would give a canned response. Some of the discussions became heated—at least for everybody but the director. He calmly denied most of the problems and indicated that plans were in place for others to be solved.

The meeting went on late into the night. In the middle of a discussion about the way the site supervisors were to spend their time, Bonnie Nelson changed the topic. She was an attractive African American who had great passion for helping at-risk children. She looked at the director and said, "I know I'm probably going to be fired for saying this, but I'm going to say it anyhow. Ralph, you're a liar and you lie a lot." She counted on her fingers as she recited events and issues he had lied about. Her voice became louder as she spoke. At one point Susan Green tried to interrupt her. Bonnie hollered, "No!" and continued listing items. When she finished, the room was very silent, except for the sounds of happy tourists outside. Nobody talked for possibly ten seconds. The director showed no more emotion than you would expect if he had just been told, "Today is Thursday."

Susan started to steer the conversation back to her outline of issues when Rita Colton interrupted. Rita was a petite, young woman who appeared to be about as "American" as someone could be. She had reddish hair and a very quiet manner. She was enormously talented. Although she spoke with no accent, she had been raised speaking Spanish.

She announced, in tones not as loud as Bonnie's but with great conviction, "I have to agree with Bonnie. You do lie, Ralph." She recited a list of his lies and reiterated some of the points that Bonnie had made.

I almost knew what was going to happen next. Kimiko Fukuda was a young Asian woman, very efficient and hardworking. After Rita finished, Kimiko said, "I have to go on record agreeing with Bonnie and Rita. You are a liar, Ralph." She added an instance the others hadn't covered and confirmed some of the observations the others made.

The director remained unmoved by what these women did, but I was moved, not because I thought what they said would result in changes in the management of the site, but because they were on a career ladder to high-paying positions in the central administration or in another district. Troublemakers do not go far up the career ladder. They are tagged as people with an attitude problem, which is intolerable in a large school district. These women knew that, but they showed the conviction to put kids first, above political concerns and possibly their future. I don't remember how the meeting ended, but I'll never forget part of it.

We worked with San Diego the following years. Bonnie and Rita later left San Diego. Bonnie became principal of an at-risk school, and implemented DI, at great personal cost. She not only trained her teachers and monitored them; she conducted before-school and after-school classes for older non-readers. Her school achieved very good performance, and positive press, but good data is generally not welcome in a school district unless the data is the result of the district's programs or is consistent with what the district believes.

An almost universal formula for insulting the district is to achieve better performance with at-risk students than the district is achieving with middle-class children who use the district-adopted material. That's what Bonnie did. The result was that the district made it so tough for her, she left the school. Bonnie's last DI school was in Chula Vista. The school was very successful. In 2006, the superintendent showed his respect for what she had achieved by reassigning her to a completely failed school where she would not be able to use DI.

Rita went back to being a classroom teacher in a small community near San Diego, where she worked with low performers. DI programs were not on the adopted State list. At the time, the State policed districts and schools that were not using whole language, and particularly those that were using DI. Rita could not purchase programs or use them in the open. Phyllis sent her programs, which she used on the sly, before retiring.

Kimiko remained on the career ladder, became a district administrator in San Diego, and effectively denounced what she had seen and learned in Follow Through.

THE DISSEMINATION PERIOD

The dissemination phase of Follow Through occurred from 1988 to 1995. In 1988, there was still no data that the failed approaches worked, and the Office of Education was still funding these approaches.

During this period, I remained one of the directors of our project. Doug quit as director in 1983. He was followed by Phyllis. Directorship did not seem like a very popular job.

As part of the dissemination phase, we worked with four new sites that were new only in name and location. They had good potential but generated the same implementation problems we had encountered in the earlier manifestations of Follow Through. The new sites were Bridgeport, Connecticut; Camden, New Jersey; Moss Point, Mississippi; and Seattle, Washington.

Bridgeport did well. It even installed *Corrective Reading* for older non-readers, and it had some very good teachers. During a visit I made to Bridgeport, a trainer mentioned the problems they were having with the low performers in another school. She indicated that these children were crack cocaine victims. I told her I had never worked with such children and wanted to see them. We drove to the other school. After I worked with some of them, I told the trainer that if these children showed the effects of their mothers' crack cocaine habits, there must have been a lot of crack cocaine mothers back in the sixties in Champaign-Urbana, because these children performed just like the lower ones we had worked with in the preschool. They entered school very low, but could learn with careful instruction.

The schools in Camden, New Jersey also did well. The director was strong and the schools had better discipline than I'd seen in most schools in this part of the country. The site even tried to take steps to institutionalize DI practices, but the proposal became bogged down in politics and never got past the planning stage.

At the end of one trip to Camden, I got very nervous because my ride to the airport was over a half hour late. We had driven to Camden from Bridgeport, but I was to leave from Philadelphia, and we were in New Jersey. When my ride finally arrived, I indicated that I was sure I would miss my flight.

The driver smiled and said, "Don't get upset. We'll be there in five minutes." I didn't know how close Camden was to the Philadelphia airport, but I found out and felt stupid for not looking at a map.

Moss Point, Mississippi was a site that had interesting outcomes. Paul McKinney served as the site's project manager. He was a second-generation manager, trained by Glenda Hewlett. Before working with Follow Through,

Paul was the instructional director for a three-county program in northern New York (BOSE). The project served special needs and at risk-students in all grades and achieved very good data. It was the first to use some of the new instructional programs we developed.

We worked with two schools in Moss Point and with two principals who had greatly different orientations. The principal in Creole School implemented the program passionately, and the children became passionate about learning. Third graders earned stars for each book they read outside of class. The chart with the stars was in the hallway. It went up one wall and half way across the ceiling. Working with this school was a rewarding experience. As Paul put it, "It's like heaven."

The principal in the other school made only a superficial effort to implement. We nagged and tried, but in this version of Follow Through, we really didn't have sufficient funds to do more than nag and try.

The achievement of the Moss Point schools showed the differences in results that occur when the program is well implemented or poorly implemented. The lackadaisical school had lackadaisical data. The third graders scored only slightly above the average for Title I schools. That was unfortunate because this school was largely White and Creole was predominately Black. It was politically incorrect for Blacks to outperform Whites, but Creole had unprecedented data. Its third-graders were second highest in the state in reading and third highest in language. It outperformed private academies and some elite White schools.

A regional director in the State Department of Education called Paul and commended him on the outstanding data. He then asked how it was achieved. After Paul gave a brief explanation of the program, the director said, "If you think I'm going to go around the state and promote that Direct Instruction crap, you're crazy."

The district did nothing to support Follow Through and Creole School. In fact, district administrators concluded that the model didn't work well. The evidence was that one of the schools did not perform well, so the model obviously was not reliable. Paul and I tried to point out that no other poverty school in the state had ever performed as well as Creole and that the other school was not well-implemented. Paul tried to appeal to others in the State Department of Education but was unable to contact anybody who was "in charge" of disseminating information on successful approaches.

Over the next couple of years, the district clipped the wings of the Creole implementation so it never had another chance to fly.

Our fourth new site, Seattle, did well in K and 1, but not comparably well in grades 2 and 3. The teachers in K and 1 were fairly strong, but they were not responsible for the high performance in K and 1. Most of the children in the Follow Through program had gone through CAMPI preschool. They entered K reading pretty well.

Phyllis was the site's project manager. She did a good job, and the site didn't seem to be highly resistant; but it never made the progress it should have. Margo Fitzgerald still lived in Seattle but was no longer working for CAMPI. I wanted her to be the project's on-site coordinator. She declined my invitation, saying, "I've taken enough shit for one lifetime." She had. She had been teacher trainer and coordinator for the CAMPI preschool for over ten years. The project had been evaluated by the district twice and by an outside evaluator once. All showed the same thing: inner-city children in CAMPI outperformed comparable children, and even outperformed the district average in one study. The CAMPI graduates had significantly higher performance at third grade, significantly fewer referrals to special ed, and a significantly higher percentage of graduates going into programs for the gifted and talented.

In fact, years before Seattle became a dissemination site, I had received a call from a district administrator, asking me if I could talk at a conference the district was having in two days. The late invitation occurred because the administrator had just received one of the evaluations. I did the presentation to a policy group, and there was expansion of CAMPI to other schools and "temporary units." But Margo received no recognition for her role in CAMPI's success.

In the end, she fought political battles to maintain the integrity of the instructional programs, but the performance level slipped, so Margo did what Rita Colton and a lot of our other trainers did—quit and went back to the classroom. She worked with upper elementary students who had been referred because they had learning difficulties. She loved working with them. She knew that she was changing their lives, and they knew it, too.

After Margo declined my request for her to be the Seattle on-site coordinator, I called one of the people we had worked with much earlier. She had been a good teacher and trainer. Even though she had never managed a site, we didn't train her in the details because I assumed she knew what to do. It wasn't until the third year of the project that I discovered that I was wrong and at least some of the site's problems were magnified by the on-site coordinator. We solved some of the problems, but I felt bad because we hadn't identified the training problem a lot earlier.

I saw Margo once during this period. I was to deliver a keynote address for a CEC (Council for Exceptional Children) conference in Seattle. Margo met me at the airport. We joked a bit, and then she asked what I was going to say in my talk. I told her that I didn't have any idea, which was true. I wasn't particularly worried because I figured that something would come to me.

I asked her if she liked working with older kids. She said, "Oh, yeah," and gave an account of the kids she was currently teaching. She indicated that this group started out particularly sour because they didn't really believe that they could learn to read. She said, "But now, they are into it." She told me, with great animation, about some of the things she was doing with them and how turned on they were.

She had introduced spelling earlier in the year. "So I play games with them by spelling words. Like the other day, I told them, 'I am looking forward to what's going to happen because I love V-A, C-A, T-I-O-N.' " She spelled the word very rhythmically.

The kids asked, "What's that?"

"You'll have to figure it out. Listen again: I love V-A, C-A, T-I-O-N. What is it that I love?"

Hands went up. One kid said, "Valentines."

"No, no. That would start out V-A-**L**. The thing I love is spelled V-A, **C**-A, T-I-O-N. Hey, think of what you know. You know the sounds V and A and C, so you should be able to get the first part of V-A, C-A, T-I-O-N."

They got it and figured out the word. The next day she asked who could spell the word *vacation*. Most of them could.

After she gave me a few more examples of what she was doing to get them to work harder, I told her, "You just gave me my speech, if you don't mind me using your examples."

She didn't mind, and I used them in my speech, which I presented to a large audience. The message I delivered was that turning kids on to instruction is something any good teacher does because when kids are turned on, they work harder and learn faster. Turning on older students who have a history of failure involves some form of letting them know where they've been, where they are now, and where they're going; and what evidence suggests that they will be able to get there.

When kids are down and are having trouble, you build them up by comparing what they couldn't do when they started the year and what they are able to do now. This comparison provides them with evidence that they have learned a lot, which means they're capable learners.

Comparing where they are now with where they will go gives them incentives to learn, particularly if they have evidence that they are making good progress. I presented the *vacation* example and pointed out how it stretched Margo's students and challenged them to take the next steps in learning how to spell.

I concluded the talk by saying something like, "No, Virginia, good teaching is not mechanical. It involves artistry, but all the artistic skills can be taught. Thank you, Margo."

TRADITIONAL INSTRUCTION

Bob Mattson (the associate dean who brought our project to Oregon) described a school district's chain of command as having loose coupling. The top of the chain specifies things in non-technical detail. A directive or standard may be something like, "Teach fraction skills to kindergarten children." The directive may specify the fractions to be taught, but that's as detailed as it gets on this level. A teacher's manual or instructional program translates these general statements into more specific "suggestions" like, "Show the relationship between whole numbers and fractions ... Point out the unity of fractions in describing the amount of milk that remains in a bottle ... or ... the length of the second part of the trip compared to the whole trip ... "

This level of detail is still very loosely coupled to what the teacher will say about fractions and what the children will see. The assumption is that teachers are proficient at bridging this gap, but there's no evidence that they are. The Follow Through data showed that teachers who fashioned their own instruction were not successful.

In 1981, Don Steely and I did a study that directly addressed the issue of how much teachers rely on instructional material, and how effectively they interpret, expand, and ask questions to teach skills and concepts that are presented in the students' textbook. The teachers in this study worked with average students, not at risk students.

We first analyzed the more popular reading programs in grades 4 to 6. All had the same format. They presented a series of topics over the course of the year—main idea, fact versus opinion, context clues for word meaning, cause and effect, key words, and a few others. Each lesson would take a few days. The lessons were in cycles so that a lesson on main idea would occur now and would be followed by lessons on all the other topics. After this round of lessons, the cycle would then be repeated to further develop the topic. On the average, the lessons for any given topic occurred about every 50–60 school days.

We interviewed 17 teachers on questions about critical beliefs and facts. "What percent of the children should master any skill that is taught?" The answer from our sample was that 86 percent of the students should answer the item.

"What percent of the students master *main idea*?" The answer from our sample was 58 percent of the students.

After the interview, the teachers were taped teaching two topics from the program they used. All teachers were taped teaching *main idea*. Teachers selected the other topic. They were instructed to teach the way they normally would.

We analyzed the teaching and compared it to the directions and specifications provided by the program. We designed tests that evaluated how much of what was taught was learned by students. The testing occurred immediately after the teaching of each topic. Each test was custom designed, so that it used the same language specified in the book and presented items very similar to those the teacher had presented.

The analysis of the programs (which occurred before the teaching) implied that the teaching would be unsuccessful. An example I gave earlier was the teacher who urged the children to identify the "whole main idea." The problem was created by the programs and by the examples it presented. For the first example, the main idea was the first sentence. For the next two examples, the main idea was either the first sentence or the last sentence. The final example contained no sentence that expressed the main idea. This sequence is analytically crazy. You don't give naïve students three examples of a sentence expressing the main idea followed by an example that breaks this rule, without warning or preparation.

The tapes of each teacher teaching showed that the teachers followed the specifications of the program very closely. Their verbal reports indicated that they deviated from the directions more than they actually did. They asked a fair number of additional questions and added some explanations, but they presented all the examples the material indicated and followed what wording the teacher's material suggested.

The comparison of their teaching with the directions and specifications of the programs they used showed that no teacher taught better than the program. In other words, they tried to improve on what the program presented, but they didn't know how. The fact that no teacher taught better than the program specifications casts doubt on the assertions that teachers are able to adapt and respond to the students in a way that is superior to a canned program.

The program may be viewed as a limiter. Except for an occasional exception, a careful analysis of the program reveals how the best teachers will perform. Where the program has logical problems, the observed teaching has predictable performance problems.

The most frightening thing the tapes revealed was that the programs for grades 4, 5, and 6 taught the same thing for each topic each year, with no great increase in sophistication. Unfortunately, the performance of students did not improve from grade to grade. The same percentage of students made the same kinds of mistakes and the teachers had the same frustrations (except the sixth-grade teachers, who tended to be more resigned to the futility of their efforts).

The data showed that only ten percent of the students mastered *main idea* and only a little more than half of them got a score above 50 percent correct. The topic that had the lowest scores was *context clues.* Only 15 percent of the students got half or more of the items correct. No student achieved mastery. Overall performance across all topics showed that 12 percent of the students achieved mastery at the level of 90 percent correct. Interestingly, the topics that educators suggested were most important— higher-order skills like identifying main idea and using context clues—were the areas of poorest student performance.

The questionnaire we designed revealed that the teachers were aware of the mastery problems. Teachers indicated that over half of their students needed one more week of instruction on just *main idea.* We sent the same questionnaire we used with the teachers we taped to 3,000 other teachers in grades 4 through 6. About 500 responded. Their responses were quite consistent with those of our teachers.

I wrote an article on this research for the *Association for Direct Instruction News* (Spring 1982). I ended with this observation:

> This study made me feel very sad, not so much because the results surprised me, but because the tapes of the teachers revealed both concern and a lot of raw talent. Most of the teachers who volunteered for this study were clearly intelligent people who were trying very hard to do an important job. Their verbal responses and the questionnaire responses suggest that these teachers are quite aware of the ... learning problems that their students experience. They know, for example, that students tend to confuse the title or the first sentence with the main idea. Teachers simply don't know how to avoid this problem, how to teach in a way that will help solve it, and how to provide explanations and examples that correct the problem. As it is, their talent, their potential to be super-teachers, is unfulfilled, in the same way the potential of their students is.

WESLEY ELEMENTARY

Wesley Elementary School is located in one of the lowest socio-economic areas in Houston—Acres Homes. Almost all children are African-American. In 1975, Thaddeus Lott became Wesley's new principal. He grew up in this neighborhood and was willing to take on battles to install and maintain whatever worked. He installed DI.

The school was large, about 850 students. This large number made it possible for Wesley to have homogeneous groups for the fastest-moving children and the slowest. By 1977, Wesley had star teachers. The most outstanding was Loraine Killion. She had a unique experience that allowed her to teach the same students in grades 3, 4, and 5.

She frequently called me about technical difficulties. Her questions were good, and from her descriptions of problems, I could tell that she was tuned into the performance of her students. Over the years, the categories of her questions changed. At first, they addressed problems. When the students were in the fifth grade, the questions were more along the lines of what they should do now that they have completed all the programs we had. Her children were very smart and good at learning. They read a lot. By the time they completed grade 5, they had read more than the average ninth grader.

Killion loved her kids, and they reciprocated, calling themselves "Killion's Kids." She sent me a picture of them wearing their Killion's Kids t-shirts and smiling broadly.

I have stacks of correspondence from her kids. Three things are striking about them. One is that she did not format what they were to write in their letters, the way many teachers do. Instead of putting up a model on the board that has one paragraph that tells about this and another that tells about that, she told them the broad purpose of their letter, and they wrote. No two letters are the same. Some children wrote extensively about their personal experiences.

A second characteristic of their performance was their handwriting. Loraine wrote in a classical cursive hand, with letters perfectly formed, all slanting the same way, and slight flourishes on the descenders for final g and y. When I started writing this part, I laid out ten of her students' papers and one that she wrote on lined paper. I asked several colleagues if they could tell which one was written by the teacher. Three of the people I asked looked at the papers and said something like, "What do you mean? They're all written by the same person." Nearly every student in the class wrote like Killion—the same slant, the same letter formations, and the same flourishes.

The third characteristic of her students' writing was that they obviously used the new vocabulary words they were learning. Some examples were cute. When they were sixth graders, one student wrote, "Why haven't you answered my last letter? Are you indolent?"

Their scores in fifth- and sixth-grade reading and spelling were unprecedentedly high, far above grade level. When they graduated, Killion missed them so much that she had trouble working with other groups. She spent a lot of time keeping track of Killion's Kids and trying to get her mind into teaching third grade, but her separation grief wouldn't permit her to let go. She left Wesley at the end of the next school year.

I thought Wesley would suffer without Killion, but the school had generated new stars. Lott hooked up with an exceptional DI trainer, Carolyn Schneider, who would produce a lot of stars in Texas over the next thirty years. She trained Wesley's teachers and coordinators, and Lott saw to it that details were executed in his school. He didn't spend nearly all of his time in his office, the way most principals do. He visited classrooms regularly and checked on specific problems to assure that they were being addressed. He held his teachers and coordinators to high standards and he was intolerant of teachers who did not work hard. The result was that his teachers were technically proficient in teaching reading and spelling, particularly in K and 1.

Years later, I saw a tape of several educators and teachers from Wesley discussing instruction. The discussion started with a global topic about teaching and interacting with children. The moderator asked a young blonde teacher from Wesley several questions, and her answers were neither learned nor precise. Then the discussion turned to issues of instruction, and although I had never seen her teach, I knew she was a star. One of the other participants said that there was a problem in completing a lesson during the allotted time. She said, "No. You can just about always finish the teacher-directed part of the lesson in 24 minutes." She then went on to assign the number of minutes for letter reading, word reading, and story reading. The fact that she could achieve these times indicated that her children were placed properly. Also, they were firm on all the skills and information she had taught earlier. (I knew that in Wesley, she would not be able to just skim through the lesson. Her children were at mastery.) Later in the discussion, a question of correcting mistakes came up. The Wesley teachers gave very precise and technically knowledgeable responses.

Lott had many battles with the district, largely because the performance of his students made the administration look bad. His students were thoroughly outperforming the White middle-class children. The district tried many times to figure out ways of making him drop DI, but Lott was very strong. He also got lucky. A politically influential group became interested in the performance of kids at Wesley, contacted the producer of *Prime Time,* and reported on the current situation in Houston. The district was currently asserting that Wesley had high scores because the school cheated on achievement tests.

Prime Time documented some of the assertions by administrators and recorded the witch hunters from the central office going into classrooms, trying to find evidence of teachers teaching test items. The witch hunters tested the lower performing students, trying to prove that they really couldn't read. Wrong.

The segment aired in 1991 and created quite a stir in Texas. The segment showed the superintendent telling flat lies about Wesley. It showed the goon squad rummaging through classrooms and hassling teachers, but finding nothing. The students could read as advertised and there was no evidence of cheating.

The theme of the story was strong—a dedicated man fought the bureaucracy and won. What struck me about the *Prime Time* segment was that there was not a word about the instructional material or approach the school used. The presentation gave the impression that if anybody fought for kids the way Lott did, they would succeed. That, unfortunately, is a distortion. The children did well because the programs did not limit the teachers' ability to teach.

The ploy that Houston Independent School District used after the *Prime Time* scandal was to try to disarm Lott and get him out of the school. The district offered him $20,000 more in salary to become district director of *maintenance*. He laughed when the district made the offer. I laughed when he told me about it.

Lott was definitely not the kind of person who could be bribed. He stayed on as principal of Wesley for eight more years. I knew the commitment he had to make. Because of the *Prime Time* coverage, Houston got a new superintendent. With great verbal show of support, the new superintendent set up a Mickey Mouse DI program in seven schools. The program was scarcely better implemented than the classrooms in Grand Rapids and showed no great gains.

RITE RESULTS

A few years after the Wesley feature on *Prime Time,* the Houston Livestock and Rodeo Foundation set up the RITE foundation and hired Lott to install a reading program in eight high poverty schools in Houston. Lott hired some of Wesley's star teachers to train teachers in RITE schools, and Lott saw to it that the teachers performed well. The schools used DI in grades K–2. The project expanded over the years and is currently serving about 25 schools.

The Foundation kept data on the performance of its students. In 2001, the Texas Institute for Measurement, Evaluation, and Statistics published data on 5,000 RITE students and an equal number of comparison students in Title I programs. The study was pristine from an experimental standpoint. Comparison children were carefully matched in performance and demography with the students in the RITE project.

The study presented data on second graders who had been in the RITE program one year, those who had been in two years, and those who had been in the program the entire three years. The students came from 20 RITE schools and 20 comparison schools. Students took the Stanford Achievement Test. Here's a bar graph that shows the outcomes at the end of grade 2.

Stanford Achievement Test Word Reading Percentile
All Second Graders

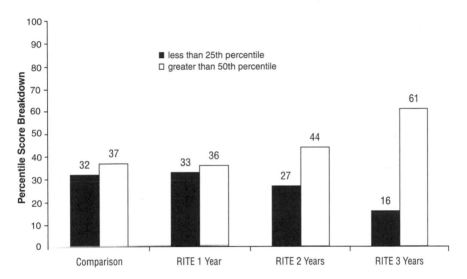

The first pair of bars shows the performance of non-DI second-grade students. The black bar shows that 32% of the children scored below the 25th percentile. The white bar shows that only 37% of the students scored above the 50th percentile. The next pair of bars shows that students who were in RITE only one year performed about the same as the comparison students.

The difference between the bars is greater for two years and strikingly greater for three-year students. After being in the program three years, only 16% of the students were below the 25th percentile, but 61% were above average. That is very impressive data that would be difficult to discredit because it involved such a large number of students.

One criticism of DI is that it is only effective in the beginning levels. Not so. The RITE children who finished second grade on average completed the third level of the program. The gap between the percentage of high performers and low performers is much greater for three-year students than it is for two-year students. Therefore, students must have learned a great deal during their third year.

To the best of my knowledge, and that of colleagues, no other foundation picked up on this obviously impressive formula to improve performance of at-risk children, and no school district, including Houston, seems to have used the RITE data as the basis for replicating what RITE did. Instead, foundations fund limp practices like trying to associate role models with reading (professional athletes reading to kids), or by staging events that celebrate reading. These attempts are based on the notion that if kids are motivated, they will read. In fact, they punish low performers who know they can't read by showing how important it is to read and showing the happy faces of children who do what low performers have unsuccessfully tried to do for years.

After Lott retired, Wesley school continued to do well because procedures were institutionalized. Over the years, the operation became a little fuzzier, but the school still does a pretty good job.

Lott called me while I was writing this book. He said he had no particular reason, just wanted to exchange pleasantries. I don't throw bouquets around much, but I told him how much I respected him and appreciated what he did by continuing to battle a very strong enemy. In other words, he is a true hero.

HIGH-SCOPE, LOW BUDGET

The story of Wesley and the RITE Foundation stand in sharp contrast with what happens in educational circles if there is a hint, any kind of hint, that DI is bad or that children in a fuzzy program outperform DI students. The most outrageous example was a follow-up study conducted by High Scope. Back in the '60s, the Perry Preschool (which is High Scope) did a study of three-year-olds and four-year-olds who were in three different programs—in traditional nursery school, in DI, and in High Scope. All attended half-day preschool programs. Our language program was used with the DI three-year-olds. The language program and a small part of our reading program were used with DI four-year-olds. The teaching of each subject took about 30 minutes a day.

One follow-up study occurred nine years after the children graduated from the preschool and started kindergarten. This follow-up asserted that children in DI had more social problems and behavioral problems than students in the High Scope preschool or the traditional nursery school. The report concluded that these differences were caused by differences in the preschool.

Here's a response I wrote to a newspaper that endorsed the report.

> To accept the High Scope study as having any relevance, one would have to assume the following fatalistic stance: 15 extremely low-performing ghetto preschoolers (IQs below 85, which are **extremely** difficult to find among four-year-olds) who received one or two years of preschool instruction, **followed by 9 years of regular-school instruction**, and who (like the subjects in their comparison groups) had an average of 2.5 encounters with the law, were so influenced by their preschool experience that whatever differences were observed in their **verbal responses** to questions presented at age 16 were caused by differences in the respondents' preschool experiences, not by any intervening influences (even though these response differences were not statistically significant in showing valid differences in the rate of reported "antisocial" or "illegal" activities across the groups). We are to believe that by being engaged in group work and performing on oral-language activities (which the children generally liked to do, but which occupied only about 30 minutes of their daily routine) children would be so anesthetized to their environment that intervening experiences in the family, on the streets, and in school—no matter how powerful they were—would have only a tertiary influence on their subsequent development. All this without a shred of sound evidence.
>
> If we subscribe to this fatalistic position, we should probably shut down the schools because they can't possibly compensate for what happens to the children when they are four-year-olds.

My response did nothing to convince traditionalists or the newspaper, which published snippets of what I wrote.

This High Scope study was widely quoted; however, the follow-up report that came out nine years later, when the students were 23, received many times the amount of press coverage. The study was published in a monograph, and as an article that appeared in *Early Childhood Research Quarterly*. The conclusion the study drew was that DI caused a significantly higher percentage of felony arrests than the comparison approaches. The alleged cause of this outcome was the DI reading program and its scripted lessons.

This study was cited over 3,000 times in newspapers and educational publications. It was used to try to throw out successful DI programs in various cities, and it created a lot of problems for us. In every place we went, we were greeted with questions about the bad social effects DI has on children or with assertions that DI creates antisocial behavior.

I wrote a response about the alleged rigor of the study. I pointed out that the investigators claimed that they interviewed 52 of the original 68 subjects, but they only interviewed 49. This kind of discrepancy does not occur in a respectable study. Not all the former students were found. Of those found, there wasn't a good male-female balance. Only 36 percent of the High Scope group were male, compared to 47 percent for the DI group. This difference was important because males are more likely to have encounters with police than females. Also, the subjects were not well matched in the number of years they were in the preschool. All members of the High Scope group went through two years of preschool. Eight of the 15 DI children attended only one year, as four-year-olds. A significantly higher percentage of DI subjects remained in Ypsilanti at age 23— 84% for DI, 64% for High Scope, and 44% for the nursery school graduates.

Michigan was the only state in which records were searched. This convention provided a great advantage to High Scope and nursery school because fewer subjects lived in Michigan. The study reported that 8 of the 19 subjects that could not be found had arrest records, but only 5 of the 19 had arrest records. With this correction, there were no significant differences in arrest rates for DI and the other treatments.

Here's the final argument I presented:

> But even if we permit the inclusion of all subjects and accept the figures presented for felony arrests, we still face the problem of conviction data. **The study shows that ... there are no statistically significant differences in convictions, only in arrests.** So, unless arrest data is a more reliable indicator of guilt than conviction data, the study does not establish the suggested outcome that DI causes crime.

The High Scope study shows how desperate the system is to maintain its belief in magic. Educators showed no interest in the performance of the 5,000 DI children in the RITE study, but exhibited great concern with 15 DI children in the High Scope study.

Years later, several studies showed the opposite outcomes. One was conducted in the Seattle area, with a much larger number of students. This study received very little press.

"20/20" TV COVERAGE

Educators generally espouse liberal beliefs. The liberal political camp perceives Direct Instruction is an insult to sense and sensitivity. It insults by contending that one size fits all, that teachers should be divested of their individuality and their ability to respond intelligently to the individual needs of children. Teachers are forced to read scripts and treat children as robots, not living, developing beings.

This clash of belief systems with facts played out in a "20/20" segment on Direct Instruction, which aired in October 1995. John Stossel interviewed me at Coleman Prep School in San Diego, which achieved very good results using DI with middle-class children. The crew filmed me presenting tasks to children in kindergarten who performed well and went on to receive many academic awards in high school.

John Stossel seemed to appreciate what he saw. Many questions he asked, however, suggested that we addressed only basics.

The "20/20" segment also showed a cut of me from 1966, working with the first group of children who had completed the Bereiter Engelmann preschool. These children had been out of school for a month and received no warm-up before the filming. They showed off by working math operations that very few children completing second grade could have performed. These children had not yet entered first grade.

I don't watch all the "20/20" programs, but I've only seen one in which Stossel and Barbara Walters disagreed. At the end of the segment on DI, Stossel said that the approach works.

Barbara Walters pointed out that it was simply rote learning and that *whole language,* the current enlightened approach, eschewed teaching by rote.

I found her response disappointing. Clearly, she was not influenced by what the segment presented, but by what liberals believe should be effective. Nothing positive came from the "20/20" segment.

SKY'S THE LIMIT

During the period that Follow Through limped along, we worked with out-of-control students from our local school district. We also did a summer program for these kids, managed by my son Kurt, who trained the staff in the procedures and operated the program. We worked on academics, established rules of how students were to behave, told them the rules before sessions, reinforced good behavior, and punished inappropriate behavior. The kids learned far more than they did in their regular school program. We tried to talk the district into following up on the gains that we had achieved and to continue with the programs and training practices that we used. The district never did anything along these lines.

One out-of-control student the district sent us was Sky, a high-IQ kid of 14 who seemed well mannered and socially sensitive until somebody pushed one of the many buttons that sent him into an undiluted rage. He threw things and issued colorful threats laced with foul language. He hurled insults, yelled and spit, and became dangerously aggressive. The district sent Sky to us after an incident in which Sky became so enraged over the behavior of one of the kids in his special class, he pushed the kid's wheelchair into a busy street. This act was particularly disturbing because the kid was in the wheelchair.

The director of special ed for the district brought Sky over and told me confidentially that he was quite sure we would not be able to do much with him. He said, "I know I'll continue to have problems with him until he leaves the school system."

The hardest kinds of behavior to change are those that occur infrequently. If it requires more than 20 or 30 trials to change a well-established behavior, and if the behavior occurs possibly once every five days, it would take 20 or 30 weeks to change the behavior. Sky's misbehavior occurred infrequently, partly because the teachers went out of their way not to provoke him. The program that we used with Sky was designed to change his low-frequency responses into high-frequency responses so we could change his behavior more quickly. The program was pretty simple. We would do things to provoke him. He would respond by switching into his Mr. Hyde mode. We would then force him physically to follow the commands—"stand up," and "sit down"—until he complied on at least 20 consecutive repetitions without hurling insults, spitting, cussing, or resisting.

His behavior was fascinating. He would yell and resist violently for the first ten trials or so. Then he would follow the commands, but with a running commentary. "You're assholes. You can't do this to me. It's illegal. I'm calling the cops."

During all this, we would remind him that after he stopped all his non-compliant behavior, he would still have to do 20 more stand-ups.

At around 50 trials, it was as if a wave of reason washed over him and Dr. Jekyll emerged. The first signs would be an observation like, "Boy, this really makes your legs tired, doesn't it?"

From then on (through stand-up 70 or so), there would be no negative behavior, and often statements of contrition. "I know I shouldn't behave that way." Following the completion of the series, we would return to the situation that caused the problem. We would try to provoke him again. He would not respond with aggression or resistance. We would then require him to give a verbal commitment about how he would behave in the future.

Initially, there was very little correspondence between his verbal commitments and his future behavior. When he went into a rage, and we reminded him of his verbal commitments, he would say something like, "Fuck commitments. Fuck you."

During the time Sky was not acting up, we engaged him in academic work. After two months, he had very few outbreaks, and he didn't require as many stand-ups for his good side to return, so I decided it was time to transition him from stand-ups. I told him that the next time he acted up, I was just going to put him in a time out room, where he would stay until he was quiet for at least five minutes.

He went into a rage about ten minutes after he arrived next morning, and I put in him in the office next to mine (which was vacant at the time). He yelled and threw things. From time to time, I reminded him that the longer he was out of hand, the longer he would have to stay in the room. Over the morning, I reminded him possibly five times, but by noon, his rage had not modulated at all. He was still cussing and throwing things around. A little after one, he was still out of control, and I decided to use stand-up. I put him through a hundred stand-ups, and he went through the familiar metamorphosis. After finishing the stand-ups, he was contrite. I told him he had to straighten out the room before he could leave. He said he would and apologized for making a mess. As I was walking from the room, he said, "You could have saved yourself a lot of trouble by doing that four hours ago."

My first reaction was, what a weird comment. Then I recognized what he was trying to tell me. Forced stand-ups were the only vehicle that had ever caused him to gain control of himself. He was as addicted to stand-ups as some smokers are to nicotine gum when they try to stop smoking.

His statement showed me that the transition program (time out) would not be effective and had to be replaced by something that would use stand-ups but that would turn control of the stand-ups over to Sky. Designing the program was a challenge because when he was out of control, he did not respond to directions to stand up.

What we came up with was a lecture that we repeated. "You can't take charge of yourself unless you get mad at yourself. Stop getting mad at everything else. Get mad at yourself for being such an asshole. Get mad and do something about it. Make yourself stand up and sit down until you're back in control. Get so mad at yourself that you'll be able to control yourself."

For the next few weeks he didn't blow up frequently, and there were no reports of bad behavior at school; however, he did blow up a couple of times, and each time I told him in a very angry voice, "Get mad at yourself and make yourself stand up. Then come into my office. I expect to see you there soon." I would leave the room (never observing what he did), but soon, he would come into my office to apologize and make promises about how he would behave in the future.

We returned him to full-time school and received information from his teacher that he was not disruptive. I never heard of further problems, so I assume he was okay. The director of special ed never acknowledged that his bleak prediction that Sky couldn't be changed was wrong.

ASAP

In 1993, we set up an organization to install full-school DI implementations in all grades—K through 5 or 6. One goal was to avoid some of the problems we'd had working with Follow Through schools. One problem was that the K–3 implementation divided the school into two camps, DI and anti-DI. Also, we observed many instances of children doing very well through third grade and then not progressing much in grades 4–6. We felt that we could show far greater acceleration in schools that implement all the DI programs well in grades K through 5 or 6. We had learned a lot about training teachers; we had programs that could accommodate six or more years; and we had done a lot of work with failed students in the upper elementary grades.

The name of our new organization was Accelerated Student Achievement Program (ASAP). It would not have the person power or the clout of our Follow Through model. So we had to devise some provisions that made schools easier to work with and that permitted us to get reliable information on teachers and students in ways that required fewer on-site hours. We solved the cooperative-school problem by requiring ASAP schools to have a buy-in of at least 80 percent of the teachers and requiring the school to secure a commitment from *all* teachers to implement the program. The two major tricks we devised to identify problems without the kind of person power we'd had in Follow Through were show-off lessons and weekly conference calls.

The show-off lessons were rehearsed before the teacher presented them in front of the trainer or on-site coordinator. We specified lessons that had critical skills. Performance on these skills predicated success or failure on new skills that were scheduled soon in the instructional sequence. For example, when teachers direct children to read words from their readers, the teacher says, "First sound ... next sound ..." as the children touch under each sound and say it. Several lessons before these tasks appear is a task that simply tells children to touch under sounds. "Touch under the first sound ... Touch under the next sound ... touch under the next sound ... back to the first sound ..."

If children are sloppy on this task, the first reading task will be a disaster. The teacher will say, "Touch under the first sound," and possibly none of the children in the group will perform correctly. The teacher will physically move the fingers under the sound and then try to present the next task, but the timing will be so bad that it is impossible for the children to sound out the word.

Teachers are told in advance that they may practice the show-off lesson two times with their students before presenting the lesson in front of a trainer or coordinator. The goal is for the lesson to be perfect, with neither teacher nor children making any serious mistakes. If children follow the directions to touch under the first word, the next word, and the next word, they are well prepared for the next step—touching under each sound as they say it.

The trainer observes the entire show-off lesson. Through this single observation, the trainer is able to identify children who are too low for the group, determine whether the children are at the proper lesson, and diagnose virtually all the current problems that the teacher and the students have. The idea is that if the teacher has problems so severe that she is not able to teach to mastery following two rehearsals, the problem is serious. The teacher's performance shows the trainer precisely what needs to be done. It also shows both teachers and students the level of performance they are expected to achieve. Later in the program, teachers rehearse show-off lesson fewer times before presenting them to an audience. Show-off lessons proved to be a very efficient way to communicate with teachers and to identify teaching problems they had.

Another technique we used to get information in a timely way was weekly conference calls between key people on the site and on our end.

Ideally, the call involved the principal, coordinator, and grade level coaches on one end, and the trainer and possibly the project manager on the other end. The purpose of the weekly call was to review all the problems the school was working on, to identify new problems, and to establish remedies for these problems and indicate who would execute the remedies. (The remedies involve either some form of training or modifying the set up, including changing who teaches specific groups.)

These calls are important because the more the principal knows about specific implementation problems, what the assignments are for solving them, and what progress is achieved, the more the principal's role becomes that of instructional leader of the school.

Utah was the first state that had ASAP schools. The relationship occurred as a result of a talk that I gave in Salt Lake City on serving at-risk students. The participants were "mentor" teachers from around the state. Following my talk, another presenter showed tapes of teachers teaching. Although these teachers were presented as models of what to do, their performance was terrible. They didn't know much about correcting or presenting.

After the talk, the co-organizer of the conference, Ken Revis, had lunch with me and then drove me to the airport. Revis asked me what I thought of the mentoring system. I told him I thought the mentors lacked technical skill. Instead of taking my observation as an insult, he said, "Well, what should we do to correct it?" I presented some ideas. One was to set up model schools that could serve as demonstration centers and that could accelerate the performance of at-risk students. He liked that idea.

I was amazed by the rate at which the plan was formulated and executed. The project would be a partnership between Utah State University, Utah State Department of Education, and people from the University of Oregon. The first meeting that led to the formation of ASAP occurred in January, 1994. By August, the funds had been appropriated; the schools had been selected; the on-site supervisors had been identified and trained; the schedules, materials, and operating procedures had been specified; grade-level coaches had been identified and trained; a one-week training had been completed; and the schools were operational.

The schools had been identified by the selection committee, which was composed of members from Utah State University and the Department of Education. Steve Kuckic was the person in the Utah State Department of Education who engineered the preparation.

The ASAP schools were designed to avoid some of the problems encountered in Follow Through. At least 90 percent of each selected school's faculty agreed to participate in the project. The participating districts agreed to provide support to the implementation for five years, to transfer any teachers from the school if they did not wish to participate in the project, to waive district requirements for texts and content, and to involve the entire schools—all grades, all subjects, and all details (from daily schedules to specific curricular requirements, teaching procedures, and systems of monitoring and training teachers). Also, the principal of each school was judged to be a leader capable of executing the requirements.

The remarkable performance of Steve Kuckic's team did not reflect the State's philosophy. There was an ongoing war between the hard-minded and those who promoted *whole language*. Salt Lake City, the surrounding counties, and the State Department of Education were overwhelmingly in support of *whole language* and opposed to highly structured approaches. Interestingly, by this time, California (the first to adopt *whole language*) had finally discovered that it didn't work and was in the process of "questioning" it. The new twist that supported *whole language* in Utah came from the National Association for the Education of Young Children. It was called "developmentally appropriate practices," which basically reiterated the early-childhood educators' circular argument of using failure of some children to read as evidence that the children were not ready, not that the instruction failed. Promoting the notion of "developmentally appropriate practices" was clever because who would suggest engaging children in instruction that was not developmentally appropriate?

Although the NAEYC's philosophy gives a superficial impression of being thoughtful, it is basically a license for schools to fail. It clearly stated and continues to predict that a percentage of children will not learn to read by the fourth grade. Some of us suggested changing the acronym for "developmentally appropriate practices" from DAP to DIP (developmentally inappropriate practices).

ASAP predicted that there would be no reading failures in grades K and 1 by the end of the first school year—no learning disabilities; no dyslexic children; no failures caused by single parents, attention deficits, fetal alcoholic syndrome, or crack. The objective was to leave no doubt that the procedures we use are developmentally appropriate for the children. The project further predicted that both boys and girls would be represented as high-math performers (as opposed to the current trends that show high-math performers to be overwhelmingly boys). Although the ASAP position was that current budgets were adequate to support full-school implementations, Utah was an exception. It appropriated less than $2,000 per student each year; the average district in the U.S. at that time allocated more than $6,000 per student.

Our obvious disrespect for the NAEYC and the state's educational stance did not set well with the Utah State Department of Education. There were heated debates within the bureaucracy. One was between department people and some faculty from Utah State, which ran a very good Direct Instruction training program. Steve Kuckic was a moderator for this debate. He told the two sides to bring in the research evidence that supported their position. The stack of papers the child developmentalists brought in was about eight inches high; that of the empiricists was about two inches high. Every one of the empiricists' studies presented empirical data. None of the child developmentalists' exhibits had any relevant empirical data. All were either case studies or philosophical arguments based on questionable premises (like how "natural learning" occurs). The debate resulted in no resolution. Everybody came away with confirmation that their stance was right.

The three ASAP schools were selected from a pool of 14 candidates. Valley View was in the Ogden School District, north of Salt Lake. The school did not look like a failed school. It was almost new, set in a fairly well-manicured neighborhood, and built according to the philosophy that students are greatly influenced by their surroundings. The belief was that open space would provide them with a sense of freedom and various other emotional benefits. Because of noise and traffic problems, open areas in the school were partly walled up when we started working there and more walls were to come. Although Valley View did not look like a failed school, it performed either 23rd or 24th in a district of 24 schools.

The other two ASAP schools were Gunnison (in the town of Gunnison, which is about 120 miles south of Salt Lake City), and Monroe (near the town of Richfield, about 40 miles south of Gunnison, in the heart of the coal mining part of the state). Both Valley View and Gunnison were new to DI, but Monroe had been using DI before becoming an ASAP school. Monroe's principal was a strong leader. The teachers were mechanical but did reasonably well.

Our prediction of all children reading by the end of the first year proved to be a challenge. Most of the first-grade teachers were capable and smart. Some of the kindergarten teachers were difficult to train. Valley View had the most serious problems in kindergarten. We had an aide teach reading because the classroom teacher was a nice, well-meaning lady, but not yet prepared to teach.

We met the prediction. All children in all schools read by the end of the first year, some of them not as well as comparable children would read in the following years, but passably well.

During the following four years, the performance of all schools improved, particularly in the early grades. Tim Slocum from Utah State conducted a study that compared the kindergarten performance of the three schools with comparison schools that were supposed to have the same demographic characteristics, but which were quite a bit higher.

The results showed that 91 percent of the ASAP children scored above average and that 50 percent of the students scored above the 90th percentile, compared to 21 percent above the 90th percentile for the comparison schools.

During these years, my son Owen was the primary trainer for Valley View, and the school did well. It received an award for being an exemplary school. District administrators visited the school and were obviously impressed by the performance of the students; however, they responded indifferently to our proposal of replicating what occurred in Valley View. In fact, they removed the principal, Maureen Newton, and replaced her with a person who was not well organized and did not do a very good job.

With open spaces converted to classrooms of often-irregular shapes, Valley View became something of a maze, with angled corridors and dead ends. It took me quite a few trials to learn how to go from the K classrooms to the office, but I was close to mastery by the time we stopped working with the school. I was also almost reliable at navigating from K to the upper elementary classrooms (which were on the other side of the office). I often didn't know whether I was going north, south, east or west, but I learned some helpful landmarks. One of our consultants quipped that the children would have to be pretty smart to find their classroom.

The school that impressed me most was Gunnison Elementary. To get there, you drive south from the Salt Lake airport through what our consultants referred to as the moonscape, areas with little vegetation and striking rock formations. The major industry in Gunnison was (and is) a prison, which is inside the city limits. The teachers of the school were as smart and reliable as any I've ever seen. They were also eager to learn.

During the first part of the first year, however, I was appalled at the performance of some students. We used the *Corrective Reading* programs with the majority of students in grades 4–6. There was one group in the upper elementary grades that was as screwed up as any group I'd ever seen. The students showed signs of having been mistaught in every way possible. We directed various teachers in grades 4–6 to teach that group for a period or two. Afterwards, I assembled the teachers and told them, "Put that group in your memory, because that's what it is going be—a memory. During the time that we work in this school, you will NEVER, NEVER see another group like that!"

They never saw one. (And that group got fairly well straightened out by the end of the school year.)

One of the reasons Gunnison had potential to become a spectacular school was that it had a very low student-turnover rate, compared to the other schools we had worked with. We figured that possibly more than 75 percent of the students who began in K or 1 would go through the sixth grade.

After the first couple of years, the fifth and sixth grades inherited children who were far above grade level, and these teachers were models of technical proficiency. Students completing the elementary-school sequence were very impressive.

I believed then and believe now that the achievement test results for Gunnison were doctored by the State so the reported scores were substantially lower than what they really were. I say this because the Gunnison sixth graders "scored" around the 58th percentile, slightly above the average of the comparison groups, but Gunnison students performed far above the reported level.

I understand that I'm making an ugly suggestion, particularly since I have no hard evidence. But there is data that may support my suspicion. For example, when the first cohort of children to go from first grade through sixth grade reached the eighth grade, it had the highest scores on the SAT ever recorded in the school. 17 of the 86 children in this class—20 percent—scored at or above the 90th percentile overall. It would be spectacular for five students from the school to achieve such outstanding results. Seventeen is amazing.

This cohort graduated from high school in 2006 with the highest GPA and the highest number of college scholarships in school history.

Earlier we had engaged in some battles over the way the junior high was to interface with the elementary school. Here's part of the letter I wrote in 1999 to Rodney Anderson, principal of the elementary school and a really good guy.

> I have to meet with ... the superintendent. I want the superintendent to know that he has to adjust the Junior High so that it accommodates our students. We didn't go through all the work of accelerating the students so the school district can decelerate them in Junior High. We are giving them gifted kids and precious few low performers. The ground rules are that the district is to respond accordingly.

A specific controversy had to do with math. The elementary school petitioned the junior high to put our graduates directly into algebra, which was traditionally an eighth-grade subject. Our sixth graders had completed the sixth level of our math program, had awesome fifth-grade and sixth-grade math teachers (Loraine Sorenson and Crystal Childs) and performed extremely well.

Both the superintendent and the junior high math teacher argued that seventh graders could not go into algebra. We told them to make up a test of what they needed to know and see if the students could pass it. They made up the test and the students passed it, with no difficulty.

The response from the junior high school was an accusation that Crystal cheated, by giving the students the answers. After a couple of go-rounds, the junior high math teacher made up another test with different items. He sent a teacher to monitor the students as they took the test, and Crystal had to leave the classroom during the testing so she would not be able to cheat.

The students passed the test. They not only went into algebra along with the eighth graders; at the end of the term, our seventh graders placed first, second, fourth, and fifth in the class.

For these reasons, and others, I don't really believe that the achievement test data the State reported was accurate.

UTAH AND ALASKA

Alan Hoffmeister, an Aussie who believes in data, was a professor of special ed at Utah State University. He played a key role in ASAP. He had worked with Ken Revis (who studied under Hoffmeister) on establishing the committee that identified the ASAP schools. Alan was knowledgeable about instruction. He had designed and field-tested programs; he had taught kids and had installed a very good teacher-training program for special ed.

I went to Logan, Utah quite a few times to work with their program. One time I did a demonstration with low performers to a large group of teachers. I worked with different students and explained to the teachers what I did and why. Alan told me later that those who set up my talk scoured the northern part of the state to find the toughest cases they could find. One was a five-year-old who did a lot of crying and was totally noncompliant to any directions his teacher gave. One of the many things he would not do (and his teacher didn't believe he could do) was ride a tricycle. She brought a trike to the demonstration and showed the kind of tantrums he threw when she tried to seduce him into riding the trike. She wanted to see how I would go about training him to use it.

I suspected that the child knew how to do it, but didn't want to. I would never be able to find out whether this guess was right or wrong unless I induced some degree of compliance. So what I did was work on compliance, not on trike riding. I used a technique that we call the hard-task paradigm. The logic of it is simply that if the child is compliant on a series of tasks that require quick responses, and this series is followed immediately by the task you're interested in, the child will comply. If the child does not perform well, the reason is that the child doesn't know how to do it, not that he is being noncompliant.

I was interested in "ride the tricycle." The tasks I presented were simple tasks that I could prompt physically, like "stand up," "sit down," "touch your head," and others he probably understood.

I told the audience that I would present tasks until he was compliant and didn't cry for ten seconds. The child was quite noncompliant, and I worked with him for more than 15 minutes. Finally, he complied to a couple of tasks without crying.

The trike was behind him. As soon as the child met the compliance criteria, I said, "Good job. Now get on that tricycle and ride away." He sprang from his chair and did it. A lot of people in the audience gasped. All the demonstration proved, however, was that he knew how to ride the trike, and he understood my directive. There was absolutely no question about whether he would try to comply. If he hadn't ridden the trike I would have known that he didn't know how to do it and would start the training there.

One of the more interesting adventures I had with the folks at Utah State occurred before ASAP, and it occurred in Alaska. Alan called me and explained that his number-one trainer, Tina Rosen, was going to be working with the school in Barrow. Could I come up for a couple of days in October and help orient the teachers? Yeah, sure.

It turned out that I was very busy before the trip and didn't look on the map to see where Barrow was. I took one bag with my typewriter in it and donned a corduroy sport coat. It wasn't until the plane from Portland arrived in Anchorage that I found out that Barrow was the farthest north community in Alaska, 340 miles north of the Arctic Circle.

From Anchorage, I transferred to Wien Airline. It had one stop, in Fairbanks. Everybody had to get off the plane. When we returned, the front half of the plane had become an area for mailbags and other cargo. My bag was in a heap of stuff piled outside the plane. I retrieved it and sat next to a construction worker. I asked him what he was going to do in Barrow. He told me that he was there to build a chimney, which would be part of Barrow's new sewage system. He explained that the current system had problems. Sewage was dumped into a large, very deep pond south of Barrow. The problem was that water remained so cold that solid waste wasn't decomposing, just building up. He told me, "They sent divers down to the bottom and they found turds that were almost a hundred years old in perfect condition." So the plan was to incinerate solid waste with a furnace that had a tall chimney.

He told me that he had a contract for over $200 a day, which was very high for that time. I commented that the chimney would be pretty expensive. He said, "My cost is nothing. It costs over $20,000 just to ship the fire bricks from California to Barrow."

I felt a bit stupid getting off the plane without a coat in this featureless, grassy tundra. The sun was very low in the south and the wind vigorous.

Barrow had a population of less than a thousand people and one elementary school. Everything except rifles and shotguns was outrageously expensive. Even though you could buy a rifle for a reasonable amount, the cost of ammunition was probably four times what it was in the contiguous states.

A hamburger in the cafe near the school cost $3. (In Oregon at that time, a burger of the same quality cost 50 cents.) The Naval Arctic Research Laboratory fronted the ocean a couple miles from Barrow. The lab presented an incredible contrast with the community. Its dining room had an opulent dinner buffet—steaks, chicken, salmon, fresh fruit and vegetables, and a lot more. Two chefs were available to fix anything you wanted, from eggs Benedict to corned beef hash. Tina and I stayed at the research lab. For us, everything was free.

One project the research station was currently conducting was a study of the behavior of arctic wolves. At least 30 of them lived in cages behind the lab. They were beautiful animals, very tall, with expressionless faces and blue eyes. The ensign who showed me around pointed to an attractive bitch and said, "Don't let their calm looks fool you. Just last week a visitor put his finger inside this fence. She calmly walked over and bit it off."

You could set your watch by their morning howling. It occurred at 6:55, first with one, and within moments, all wolves (even the pups) joined in an eerie chorus.

A Navy car drove Tina and me to the school, which was connected to housing units by wooden tunnels. We first observed teachers working with the children. The teachers were ineffective. They did a combination of mother-henning the children around and spoon-feeding them by responding with them. "Say the days of the week. Sunday, Monday, Tuesday ... " Only a few children responded, and they responded after the teacher cued each response. It seemed that most children were extremely deficient in language.

I told the teachers that language was the first thing they needed to teach. They said that the children wouldn't respond. When I indicated that I wanted to work with a group of children, the teachers insisted that the children wouldn't respond to a stranger. I started a group of eight primary-grade children at the beginning of the language program. Only one or two of them responded at first, but within a few minutes all were responding. I pointed to different pictures and asked, "What is this?" If they couldn't say "a dog" or "a cat" or "a boy" or "a girl," I told them the name, then gave them repeated practice in saying it and practice in identifying the referent. I gave them lots of praise and little treats for responding well.

I was surprised when I presented the first *yes-no* question. I pointed to a picture of a dog and asked, "Is this a dog?" They didn't say anything, just looked at me with strange expressions. Some of them raised their eyebrows. I said, "My turn: Is this a dog? Yes. Your turn: Is this a dog?" Again, nobody said anything, just looked at me with raised eyebrows. Their teacher caught my attention, raised her eyebrows and said, "This means *yes*."

I first told the children, "Say *yes*." I repeated the task a couple of times. Then I did "my turn" again. "Is this a dog?" I raised my eyebrows and said, "Yes." They smiled. "Your turn: Is this a dog?" They raised their eyebrows and said, "Yes."

The children picked things up very fast. We worked with different groups during the morning. In the afternoon, we started training the teachers. This part did not go well. Two teachers seemed disinterested. The others seemed hostile. They had many picky questions about the appropriateness of our approach and about "language acquisition."

We worked with the teachers the entire next day. We had them practice presenting tasks, reinforcing appropriately, and correcting mistakes. Then we had them work with groups of children. The teachers did not seem to try very hard and remained negative. At the end of the day I was pissed. I told them that they could make a big difference in the children's lives, but it would require work. I said, "You can do it, but it's not going to happen unless you go at the job with the understanding that if you don't do it, nobody else will. For these kids, you're their salvation." The teachers responded with sour looks.

My plane was scheduled to leave the next morning. Tina was supposed to be on the same flight, but at breakfast, she told me that she wanted to stay and work with the teachers for the rest of the week. I told her I thought they were hopeless. She disagreed and said, "I think I can bring them around."

I said, "Good luck," and shook my head knowingly.

I had worked with Tina before. I knew that she had a laser focus on helping kids and teachers. I knew she was capable of working with tough cases, but I didn't believe it was possible for anybody to work with those teachers.

I underestimated her tact and tenacity. She called me early the next week and reported a complete turnaround. When she left, the teachers were working with the children in reading and language. The teachers were both pleased by their performance and positive when they presented. I asked her what she did to achieve the turnaround. She said, "Nothing special, just kept working with them. They were scared, but they got over it." Tina was scheduled to go back to Barrow in a couple of weeks. She said, "I'm really looking forward to it."

The rate of teacher turnover in Alaska was incredibly high. In some districts the average teacher stayed for less than one school year. Barrow had a high teacher-turnover rate, but the project went well for several years. Tina trained new teachers and kept the student performance high, far higher than that in comparable Indian schools in Alaska.

Tina was not only a very dedicated trainer; she was also an incredibly good person. She lived alone as if she had taken a vow of poverty. She rented very modest apartments in poor neighborhoods and used boxes as chairs. She gave probably 75 percent of her earnings to charity and lived on the rest. She worked daily, tutoring neighborhood children before and after work. The only payment she received for this work was the pleasure she experienced when she taught children. She received no recompense for many of the days she worked with Barrow. I would guess that the same pattern held for at least half of the teaching and training she did. Although she was a Ph.D., she never mentioned it or suggested that she needed more recognition for what she did. She had a single agendum in her life, to help kids and teachers. Everybody who knew her or worked with her knew this about her, including the teachers in Barrow.

Unfortunately, those in the State Department of Education didn't show much respect for what she did. During the third year she worked in Barrow, Alan Hoffmeister received a call from a top bureaucrat in the State

Department of Education at Juneau, who said that he had found out that Alan might know something about why the Barrow children had such high scores on achievement tests.

Alan explained the consulting and training the teachers received and how the high scores reflected the improved performance of the children.

The bureaucrat said, "You misunderstand. The scores are—What should I say?—*unrealistically* high. I thought you might know how the school is doing this."

Alan got angry and told him that he should get on a plane, go take a look, and he would see that the scores were "unrealistically high" because the children were performing at unprecedentedly high levels, not because there was any cheating on the test. The bureaucrat did not follow Alan's suggestion.

LOCAL STUFF

The rule we've always followed with respect to instruction on the local scene is that if somebody comes to us with a problem and seems committed to trying to solve it, we'll work with them.

As a result of this policy, I spent a lot of time one year working as a volunteer with trainers in our local Educational Service District (ESD). The district had a program for special-needs kids in one of the local high schools. I worked with the teachers at this center and with field people who were supposed to solve problems in the various schools served by the ESD. I did a lot of demonstrating, both with individual students and with groups. At least one of the trainers I worked with did well and used procedures and techniques I demonstrated. The ESD administration, however, neither institutionalized any of the practices nor showed great interest in them.

Possibly the most frustrating interactions we had with our local district, Eugene 4J, occurred in the 1990s. Hill Walker, a friend and colleague at the University of Oregon, took the first step in setting up what was supposed to be a cooperative program between selected U of Oregon staff and the school district. The plan was to identify the lowest schools in the district and train the principals and staff in these schools in effective practices.

The strategy we wanted to set up was based on two facts: nearly all at-risk schools have a high annual turnover of students, possibly 20 percent or more; and this transient population has something of an underground railroad. The pattern is pretty much the same in all districts. Locally, when these students are in the district, they are in one of three or four schools about 90 percent of the time. So, if all the schools in this circuit were implemented with the same programs and procedures, the receiving school would be able to place students in the same program they had been in, at nearly the same lesson, and continue with nearly seamless instruction that used the same procedures as those in the other school.

This plan seems sensible, but we have never been able to interest any school district in using it. (Chicago's District 10 had procedures that were effective, but the entire district used DI, so within-district movement was not as great an issue as it is where most of the schools did not use DI.) Earlier, we had submitted a proposal to Title I to fund a study that investigated the effects of the program on the lower one-fourth of the student population, but the application was rejected.

About half a dozen of us volunteered to work with the district. I had some reason to believe that the plan would be adopted because the district superintendent had been in special ed, and I had worked with her. She knew what could be done with DI. Before the superintendent arrived at the designated meeting place, our group went over our roles and what our minimum requirements would be for the district—basically that we would do all the training and all the set up, and the district would back us and install procedures for collecting data and assuring performance of teachers and aides. I indicated that Doug Carnine and I would take responsibility for the academic end; Hill would be in charge of the behavioral end.

When the superintendent arrived at the meeting, we went over the proposed organization. After we finished, she said that there were parts of the plan that were unrealistic. Then she declared, "I cannot tell a principal what to do."

We said in unison, "What?"

She explained that her role does not imply such invasive interactions. If the participating principals wanted to do the program, she would give them permission. If they didn't, however, she could not and would not intercede. She stressed that she could not specify how they were to do their job.

I asked, "You mean, even if the kids are failing and what the principal is currently doing is failing, you can't give him a direct order about what to do?"

"That is correct."

We tried a couple of other tacks—appealing to her concern for the kids, pointing out the great savings a successful program of this type would provide the district with respect to special ed placement and the like. We suggested that if she installed something like this, she would be a pioneer who provided a model of how to be effective with at-risk kids.

Her response: "No, I'm sorry, but I cannot tell a principal what to do."

After about the fifth time she said that, I stood up and said, "I'm out of here," and I was.

I was appalled by the apparent moral inconsistency of putting the interests of the principals above those of the kids. The school is not designed for the benefit of principals. This sort of schoolmen-know-best orientation belongs in the 13th century. Imagine a doctor who used unsanitary practices but had a supervisor who could not tell him what to do.

The laissez-faire stance of the district, however, was a sham that was in sharp contrast with the dictatorial stance the district takes on some issues. Coburg School was repeatedly reminded that it had to comply and use district-mandated programs. To obtain permission not to use adopted programs, the school had to jump through many hoops and make frequent trips to the district office and to Salem, where the principal was basically on trial, even though his school performed quite a bit above the average school in the district.

No cooperative venture between the University and the school district materialized. The district continued to use its superficial democratic principles.

ABSOLUTE PITCH

One of the more interesting studies we did involved trying to teach first graders absolute pitch. A person with absolute pitch is able to listen to a musical note and identify it as B or D or whatever. Paul Williams, a Ph.D. student, did most of the work for this study. I knew that absolute pitch could be taught, because I taught it to my oldest son, Eric, when he was four and five. It's just another one of those skills that involves learning highly unfamiliar discriminations.

When I taught Eric, he had very good relative pitch, which meant that he could sing on key. (People who have poor relative pitch sing off key.) The way I taught him absolute pitch required him to hum the note I specified. I'd say "middle C," and he would hum a note. I'd then play middle C on the piano and see if it matched the note he hummed. During earlier lessons, we'd first do a warm-up series of tasks. I would tell him which note I would play. I would play the note. He would hum the note, then I would ask about a series of other notes. For instance, I would tell him I would play A. After I played it, he would hum it. Next I would play another note, possibly in a different octave. He would hum it and identify it.

Because most of the first graders Paul worked with did not have good relative pitch, we couldn't use the kind of program I'd used with Eric. To use that program, we'd first have to teach them to carry tunes, then teach absolute pitch. We didn't have time for that kind of intervention. But the fact that most of them couldn't accurately hum tones played on the piano raised serious questions about how much they would be able to learn from the instruction.

We wanted to conduct an experimental study, so we needed a comparison group. We didn't want to use subjects that performed at the same level as our students did because the study wouldn't show much if our students performed better than the comparison group after the training. So we used comparison students who *had* very good relative pitch and who had opportunities to learn absolute pitch. These were musicians who played band instruments. Trombone players, for instance, have frequent situations in which they must produce specific notes through combinations of slide movement and lip configuration.

A large group of gifted high school band students who had played instruments for over six years was scheduled to attend a summer course at the University of Oregon. We made plans to use them as our comparison subjects.

At the beginning of the spring semester, we set up daily "music" periods with the first graders. The instruction ran for an entire semester. For part of each period, we sang songs. The songs had some instructional value and they were fun. They also served as breaks between the time students worked on identifying notes.

We would work on absolute pitch for about ten minutes of each period. The work started with pretty simple tasks. Paul would play a note on the piano and identify it. For example, "Listen: ... That's A. What is it?"

He would then play a series of other notes, some of which were A and some of which were not. He'd ask, "Is that A?"

For the early identification tasks, the notes children were to identify were fairly far apart (A, D, and G, for instance). When children became pretty firm on discriminating these notes, more difficult discriminations were introduced (A, C, F, for instance). As students improved, the tasks got more challenging. Children had to perform "cold" with no warm-up or practice that gave them comparative information about the notes. The children became pretty good at identifying notes by the end of the semester. Some of them were over 90 percent accurate.

During the first week the band students were in Eugene, we tested 40 of them individually on the same test we used with the first graders. Each student identified a series of 15 notes that were accurately recorded on tape. The notes were played in different orders.

We scored performance on a scale that gave 3 points for a correct response (identifying D was worth 3 points), and 1 point for identifying a note that was off by one letter. (Identifying D as C or E was worth one point.)

The results were interesting. The average score for the first graders was higher than that of the gifted band players. However, no first grader got a perfect score, but two band players did.

The study showed a couple of important things about absolute pitch.

It is not an all-or-none thing. It can be taught. And the number of people who have absolute pitch is probably more than the estimates suggest. Some estimates are that absolute pitch occurs in one out of 10,000 people. If our sample of band players is representative, the number may be closer to one out of 25 for people who are proficient with musical instruments.

CHICAGO AGAIN

In the late 1980s, Jerry Reinsdorf, owner of the Chicago Bulls and White Sox, wanted to build the United Center on the west side of Chicago. Years earlier, attempts to replace Soldier Field with a stadium on the west side resulted in enormous hassles, partly because the people who lived in this neighborhood fought it. Reinsdorf took preventative measures against a recurrence of resistance by negotiating with community groups before starting construction on the United Center and promising, among other concessions, support for education.

At that time there were local "boards." The first educational attempts Reinsdorf introduced were designed to educate and upgrade parent groups by teaching them about school budgets, priorities, and curricula. The Interfaith Organizing Project (IOP) did not believe that this effort made significant impact. One of the organizers saw the *Prime Time* segment on Wesley School and arranged for a visit to the school. The visitors were very impressed by what they saw and decided that they would promote using the Direct Instruction model in neighborhood schools.

Lott, who was working with Phyllis Haddox at the time, called her and told her about the apparent plans. After several delays, five or six at-risk schools were implemented in Chicago. The implementation was ragged, without sufficient time scheduled for core subjects and without provisions for ongoing training. So the performance of most schools was spotty. A couple of exceptions were the schools that had Adrienne Allen as their trainer.

Adrienne is one of the five best trainers I've ever observed. She was my assistant for a while. She is sensitive, has a great sense of priorities, and teaches mastery techniques very well. Over the years, I have been able to identify superstar teachers Adrienne trained by their impeccable timing.

The two Chicago schools she worked with, Hearst and Goldblatt, made tremendous improvement. The fact that Adrienne worked with these schools meant that the principals listened to what she said needed to be done and did it or tried. If they hadn't, she would have quit the same day, not because she was a quitter but because she had no tolerance for principals who put the teachers' desires above the needs of the children. She has done a lot of good over the years. Unfortunately, she's also done a lot of quitting. (Eventually, she left both Chicago schools.)

In 1995, the mayor of Chicago took over the school district and installed George Vallas as "CEO." The idea was to run the district as a business. The problem was that the district had an organization that preempted accountability, which meant it could not be run as a business. There was no data tracking to identify problems in the classroom, no single person in the central office responsible for the performance of a given school, and no clear expectations about what the teachers were to accomplish except to have children pass state and local tests of achievement.

Unlike the scenario portrayed by our local superintendent, who could not give a principal a direct order, principals in a place like Chicago were bombarded by directives from a host of superintendents and officials whose roles were not coordinated.

A principal in a failed Chicago school could receive conflicting information on specific issues from the superintendent in charge of elementary education, the director of reading or math, the Title I director, the director of bilingual education, the school's probation officer, the regional educational officer, and the local board. The district also had an accountability department that had the power to place principals, but rarely became involved in specific issues of instruction. The director of the Accountability Department, like other underling administrators in Chicago, went out of his way to provide Vallas with good news. (Vallas was not highly tolerant of either bad news or those who delivered it.)

The Chicago DI program changed when Vallas took over. It now became a part of the district. Ten schools, some of which had been doing DI, were to receive financial support as well as training. The money went through Malcolm X College.

The main problem with the plan was that the commitment of funds from the district was verbal. Jerry Silbert, who was now involved in the project and was responsible for providing training, committed $60,000 to trainers who were scheduled to work with the schools. It took a very long time for the district to release the funds that Jerry had promised. As a result of the payment format, Jerry couldn't offer trainers a contract. Several did not want to work in Chicago without a contract.

The implementation was spotty, but the children in the DI program performed higher than comparable students before the Vallas era. Even though the Accountability Department was feeble, teachers knew that they were in the school to teach and manage the children.

In 1996, ASAP became a vendor in Chicago (under the name Center to Accelerate Student Achievement). All vendors were equal, and the district did not monitor the results obtained by different vendors, or try to assure that the model was implemented or even closely observed. The irony was that although the school district brought in vendors to provide evidence of what could be achieved with outside support, the vendors were supposed to adhere to district procedures that would guarantee failure.

When we applied for vendorship, we insisted that the district waive requirements that were in opposition to provisions of the model. The district hired us but never provided a waiver on anything.

We worked with five failed schools. Three had the potential to become models. They had good teachers and adequate direction from the principal. About the only way to succeed in these or any Chicago schools was to convince principals to do what we told them to do, not what the multi-voiced district told them.

The schools were supposed to follow a variety of unenlightened mandates. For instance, three of our schools had an after-school reading program. The reading material used to instruct children in this program was not our program, which was used during the school's regular reading periods. It was a whole-word reading program mandated by whatever superintendent or officer was in charge of after-school activities. I protested to the director of the Accountability Department, a guy who formerly had been a principal in an affluent suburb and rarely went to the inner-city schools to discover what was going on. After I described the problem with the after-school program, he said, "I don't really understand why you're concerned about it. That's not anything you're responsible for. You're only contracted to work with the children in the regular-school day, not after school."

I tried to explain that there aren't two groups of children, the ones we work with and the ones who go to the after-school program. They are the same kids with the same problems, the same confusions, and the same need for a consistent program.

I told him that we would conduct the after-school program for free. It never happened and I don't believe he ever got the point.

We had a similar problem with one of the other schools. It had a Title I pull-out program that did not use the same material students used during their regular reading period. This was a very common model for Title I. We fought the principal and advised the teachers that they should simply provide more practice in DI during the pull-out periods.

The school that I felt had the most potential was Carver Primary, a school of 1,200 children in grades K through 3. The two main reasons it had such potential were that it had a large number of pretty good teachers and a fair number of stars; also, it was large, which meant that it was easier to address problems and to maintain homogeneous groups for all subjects.

One serious problem with small schools is that unless there are possibly one or more teaching aides in *every* classroom, the school won't work. If the school does a good job, its students in grades 3 and beyond will be far above the performance of incoming students. Virtually all incoming students will perform far lower than continuing students. Where do you place these students appropriately if you have just one classroom per grade level and one teacher in each classroom for grades 2 through 8?

If the school has only an occasional student entering the school mid-term, it will not be a serious problem, but most failed schools have high annual turnover rates. Ultimately, small schools face the dilemma of holding higher groups back so that the incoming students put in the groups will be taught. In other words, the small school that has a high rate of student turnover guarantees that it will not have students performing well in the higher grades.

In a school like Carver Primary, it would be possible to dedicate two classrooms per grade level that accommodated new students entering the school. At the same time, it would have the capacity to maintain the top groups at flank speed. In other words, the large school has far greater capacity to serve all students because it has a far greater potential to accommodate a wider range of incoming students. Wesley Elementary did a good job of exploiting the potential of a large school.

Carver never reached its potential. The two major problems were: (1) the inputs by district literacy consultants and the regional superintendent were in direct conflict with what we were trying to tell teachers to do; and (2) some district procedures were not only unenlightened but inhumane. Among the more unenlightened was the practice of placing the school's best teachers in grades 3 and 5. The reason was that students were tested on the State test in these grades. The good teacher was supposed to cram loads of information into the children so they would pass the test.

Our priority was to put the best teachers in K and 1, where they would guarantee that children learned the basics and would be able to perform well in subsequent grades. We did not engage in "test prep cramming" to artificially inflate the children's performance; instead, we assumed that if we provide children with a solid foundation, in the end they will catch and pass the others. Along the way, their test performance will document their proficiency.

The most inhumane requirement the district installed was that all instruction on a particular grade would use only "grade-level" programs. If children were in the third grade, they were to be taught exclusively with grade level material and only with this material. The paradox was that third-grade incoming students were never tested to determine which grade level was appropriate or whether they could perform on grade level material. Rather, the procedure was simply to dump them in the third grade and then to systematically punish them. The chances of these students being able to perform in a "grade level textbook" approximated zero.

The Chicago board, which installed grade-level instruction, apparently didn't know that if children are performing far below grade level, immersing them in third-grade material won't increase their skills. It will simply present them with an uninterrupted series of tasks they can't handle. This practice provides children with evidence that they are failures, induces low self-images, and greatly increases the likelihood that they will reject the institution that issues this punishment.

Even the District house organ, *The Catalyst*, suggested as strongly as it dared in this political arena, that the grade-level mandate might not make the good-idea list. For us, the plan presented another area in which we had to convince our principals not to do what the district mandated but to do what made sense.

Vendors (also called external partners) were supposed to work with all grades. In a couple of our Chicago schools (Herzl and Abbott) the lower grades did well, but the upper division was shabby, largely because the principals did not require teachers to follow the requirements of our program.

Because of the multiple inputs from different departments within the bureaucracy, all our schools treated our input as suggestions, not as something they should follow. There were no sanctions for a school not implementing the model.

The worst school we had in Chicago, Smyth, was a study in how to reduce a school to a travesty. They put non-English-speaking children in a district program that did not teach English. Among the parade of principals in this school were those that made sweet promises that were never fulfilled, and those that did a lot of excuse-making. The probation officer of the school recommended programs that were at odds with the content and practices of our programs. The literacy consultant also directed the school to use programs and practices that were inconsistent with our approach.

We resigned from Chicago because there was no hope we could implement beyond what several trainers referred to as the "half-assed" level. Before resigning, we wrote a letter to the head of the Accountability Department indicating what conditions would have to be met before we would consider continuing with the schools. We required three changes:

1. There would be no conflicting input from the bilingual office, Title I, regional education officers, literacy consultants, directors of transition and summer programs.

2. There would be adequate training time—at least four full days for summer training and at least an hour a week early in the school year for ongoing in-service training.

3. A person of authority in the central administration would be designated supervisor of the principal and all personnel, would be entirely in charge of each school, and would have the power to make whatever adjustments were necessary for the schools to become completely implemented in all subjects in all grades.

The head of the Accountability Department never responded to the letter. We gave our notice of resignation from Chicago in April of 1999, with considerable regret. Like Follow Through, none of the schools we served was completely implemented, but nearly all (with the exception of Smyth) performed quite a bit better than schools of comparable demographics. I would have loved to show what could have been accomplished in Carver, Daily, Abbott, and Herzl, but we never had the chance.

DEVELOPMENTALLY DELAYED CHILDREN

Possibly the best implementation we ever had before the new millennium was a program for developmentally delayed young children. This label is another way of saying seriously retarded. Most of the children had some language, but were seriously behind.

The program was great because everybody involved was a star teacher. Gary Davis was the director of the operation, a hands-on director who could demonstrate with the children and had a clear idea of what could be achieved and how to do it. In addition to being smart and efficient, the teachers were tireless.

We installed many procedures we had used on the Down syndrome project in the '70s. We revised the written material and labeled the new work *The Low Performers' Manual* (available free online: Zigsite.com). After children completed the program the manual describes, they had the skill needed to go into the language program we use with at-risk children in preschool and kindergarten.

I loved visiting the project because it was a treat to see such talented teachers in action. One time, I brought a visitor over when a new child was scheduled to begin the class. This visitor was a prominent psychologist from Portland who worked with developmentally delayed children. His role was more along the lines of testing children and then turning them over to what sounded like a weak training program.

Our new child didn't arrive at the scheduled time. So the visitor and I observed teachers working with children. The visitor commented on the teachers' "uncanny intuitive sense" and their ability to structure tasks so the children responded at a high rate.

He observed that our teachers had enormous natural ability, and he seemed particularly impressed by the way the children responded to the reinforcement teachers provided. I told the visitor that they were very smart people, but all of their teaching behavior had been trained. He shook his head as if to say he wasn't convinced.

The assessment that we used with incoming children provided us with precise information about the children's skill level and their compliance, but it was administered in less than ten minutes. Our visitor indicated that the placement procedures they used in Portland required several hours and involved formal meetings attended by many participants. He expressed doubt that a ten-minute assessment could possibly yield sufficient information.

The teacher who tested the new child had given this test many times and ran through the testing routine without referring to any material. She first directed the child to touch an object. The child picked it up. She quickly demonstrated touching as she said, "Touch ... touch." On the child's next turn, he again picked up the object.

She gave him a series of other commands—stand up, touch your nose, touch your head. I gave our visitor a running commentary on what she would do next. I told him that she would now change her demeanor so that she was doting. She did, "Oh, you're such a hard worker. Would you like some candy? Well, would you stand up for me?"

I told the visitor that she was testing the child's degree of compliance and identifying the ways the child had learned to control adults. Then I told him that she would next become very fast-paced and upbeat. She did.

When the test was completed, I pointed out that we had all the information we needed to place the child. I summarized that he had some language, lacked a lot of basic vocabulary, did not understand *yes-no*, was a little noncompliant, but not bad. I said, "So we will run through the low-performing program and use the action track from the beginning language program. We'll skip any tasks that involve *yes-no* until he completes about lesson 30 in the language program."

He said, "Yes, but you don't know about his emotional stability, IQ, and other important developmental factors."

I said, "We know all we need to know to place him and start teaching."

He said, "But the person who will teach him has not observed the test. So what kind of records do you provide?"

I said, "The person who did the testing is the teacher. And she has all the information I just told you."

He said, "Do you mind if I ask her about the placement?"

"Go ahead." He did.

She started out, "He's a little noncompliant, but he shouldn't be a problem." She then went on to reiterate the same placement schedule I had indicated.

The psychologist shook his head and said, "I had no idea that instruction and placement could be so efficient. You've given me a lot to think about." I told him that if diagnosis is to work, it must clearly imply where the child is to start and what he will be taught first. I don't know how much he thought about it, but I never heard from him again.

GOODBYE TO A GOOD GUY

Wes devoted some of his "free time" to writing the book *Applied Psychology for Teachers*, a very ambitious work that covered everything related to effective practices and background information—from behavioral principles to the theoretical underpinnings of effective instruction and how to interpret data on student performance. I believe that Wes considered this book his ultimate achievement, an opus that positioned effective teaching and the analysis of learning in a framework that could be comprehended by undergraduates and that would establish DI as at least a contender in the field of education. The work, positioned as a textbook for undergraduates, was published by SRA in 1986. It was a colossal work—472 pages, in 8½" x 11" format, with 275 references (over 11 pages).

It was another false hope. The book did not sell, was not adopted by more than a handful of the faithful, and after only a few years, was discontinued by SRA. No other publisher was interested in it. I recently bought a copy of it online. It was in very good condition and cost $4.50.

Wes and Julie were divorced in 1980. Wes continued in his role as associate dean until 1992, when he became involved in political wars with the College of Education and quit the University. After retiring, he refused to talk about education. On three or four occasions, I tried to discuss the Follow Through book we had started. I got the same response each time. He said that he would talk about golf or other sports and the stock market, but that was all. He declined to talk about the Association for Direct Instruction, or about anything else related to education. He told me, "That is something from a past life. It's dead and I have no interest in it."

In 1993, Wes sold his shares in Engelmann-Becker Corp and moved from Eugene to Sedona, Arizona. There was no going-away party or celebration because he didn't want one. Just before he left, I asked if there was anything I could do for him. He asked if I would give him a painting I had done of a lion. Yes.

I called him several times in Arizona to see how things were going. Not well. I called him once around noon and he sounded as if he'd been drinking. His leg had gone bad so he couldn't play golf, and the stock market had not been kind to him. His son David lived with him for a while but left. Wes never remarried and lived alone. A couple of times I asked him when he was coming back to visit us in Eugene. He seemed to entertain the idea, but it apparently didn't make the serious-planning list. I never saw Wes again after he moved to Arizona.

CHAPTER 7

The New Millennium

PAINTING A NEW LANDSCAPE

The first months of the new millennium were relatively seamless with the preceding one except for the changes in records that were keyed to the first two digits of the 20th century: 19_ _. By now, my life had changed a lot. My children were adults, and Louella (Lou) Bradley was my partner. Also, I no longer wrote in the evenings. Instead, I painted. The main reason for the change in activities was that I had written a book, *War Against the Schools' Academic Child Abuse*. The title indicates what it was about. Like the book you're reading, it was painful to write, so after I completed it, I vowed to change my evening routine. At first my after-dinner behavior was fairly aimless—watching TV, reading occasional articles that were far removed from education, and tinkering around.

Bernie Kelly was the catalyst for my change to painting. She is one of my co-authors, who had grown up across the river from Liverpool, England, and become almost religious about helping at-risk students. She first used DI when working with a class of rowdy 7- to 13-year-olds near Barnstable, the final dumping ground for students who could not be accommodated by the education system. She taught five different DI programs and followed the programs to the letter, even though she questioned some of the language the stories presented. For example, in the *Corrective Reading* program, one story tells about a bum who answers the door wearing pants and suspenders. Her students got a great charge out of that description because in England, it translates into something like, "A rear end wearing underwear and a garter belt answered the door." That would present a quaint image.

Bernie later came to the University of Oregon to study with us. She thought she was enrolling in the master's program, but she had actually signed up for the Ph.D. program. She got her Ph.D. quite quickly, with virtually no bumps in the road.

Bernie co-authored some of the math programs with Owen, Doug, and me. After we finished working one day, I mentioned to her that I was considering painting. She indicated that she had done some watercolor painting and listed the virtues of watercolors. She cautioned that it was difficult because "one cannot indiscriminately paint one color over another." She also pointed out that one doesn't paint white but, rather, leaves white areas unpainted.

I indicated that I might go in that direction. I liked the idea that one doesn't have to clean one's brushes after a session. I'm not highly organized, and I knew that if I painted with oils, within days, my brushes would have ossified stumps where they formerly had bristles.

Bernie checked on my progress regularly. "Have you started painting yet?"

I told her regularly, "No, but I'm getting ready." Actually I hadn't done anything. One day she brought in a bag full of material—paints, paper, brushes. She said, "Here. Now you have no excuse for not getting started."

She asked about my progress almost daily, but I had no progress. After the painting material sat on my kitchen table for over a week, I started to feel guilty about not painting. So I tried it, and for some reason, my first attempts were pretty good. I showed Bernie my fourth picture, an ocean wave spattering against a rock and sending a fountain of water into the sky. It was good. She liked it. I thanked her for introducing me to watercolors.

I've painted ever since. The thing I like most about it is that after a few hours, a painting is done, in contrast with my other pursuits, which seem to take forever to complete. In 2000, I sent my friends and coworkers the 2000 calendar of my pictures, the fifth one I'd done. (I still do them. My website, Zigsite.com [Pic o' the Month], shows those for the current month and preceding years.)

PUBLIC INFORMATION ABOUT PROGRAMS THAT WORK

In 2001, the Bush administration presented a paradox. It had taken a sensible stance with respect to education. On other issues, however, the administration seemed to be close to 180 degrees off target. This combination of virtue and vices made it difficult for us. I don't think that more than ten percent of the people I worked with were Republicans; however, I believe all of them endorsed Bush's educational strategies.

At least part of the reason for the administration's sensible educational stance was Doug Carnine. In the 1990s, he had set up NCITE (National Center to Improve the Tools for Educators.) He did a remarkable job of reaching the part of the establishment that had awareness of its weaknesses as well as scientists who recognized the need for basing educational practices on data. Starting in 2001, Doug was extremely busy providing input into federal programs and policies. The central message that he tried to get across was that policy makers needed to set up programs based on what works. Doug spent much of his time in D.C. and the rest working with people who influenced what went on in D.C. He was on the road at least half of the calendar days. He went to D.C. at least three times a month. Although only about one out of every seven promising leads actually showed any promise, Doug had at least ten projects in the works at any time. He observed, "Getting one out of seven is enough to keep me busy."

Doug had some influence in special ed legislation. One of the things he campaigned for was changing the legislation for "learning disabilities," a field that followed one of the more insane practices ever used in education. According to this legislation, the "learning disabled reader" was a child in the normal IQ range who had not learned to read. The odds are a hundred to one that this child became "disabled" when reading instruction began, in K or first grade. The legislation, however, provided no remedies in K, or in 1, or in 2, or in 3. In grade 3, however, the child—who was now far behind his peers and who had three years of evidence that he was a failure—was *identified* as "Learning Disabled." Doug campaigned for the early identification of "learning disabled children" and for early intervention. It is much easier to provide remedies for these children if their problem is identified early. So the formula Doug advocated for seemed almost simple-minded: Identify the problem as soon as it occurs, and use data-based programs to provide an early remedy. This concept was very hard for traditionalists to understand or accept.

Doug couldn't promote DI and couldn't push for the total abandonment of the "learning disabilities" label, even though he knew that these children—who numbered in the millions—could be turned around with DI in less than a year if the problem is identified early.

In fact, the change in machinery necessary to implement this "revolutionary" approach was substantial. There had to be new ground rules for identifying children who were not meeting reasonable progress goals for beginning readers, and procedures for providing remedies with "scientifically based" programs. Influential groups fought it, partly because they wanted to believe that there are special children who learn differently from the normal child. This premise becomes a self-fulfilling prophecy, if the approach used to teach children creates a relatively high rate of failure and if there are no means for assessing children until the third grade.

Doug also had some influence on Reading First legislation, which provided early intervention programs for at-risk children. Again, his message was simple, but very controversial: Use what has been demonstrated to work. Install procedures that permit early identification of program failure and provide for early remedies.

On a practical level, this plan would fail if there were no reliable tool for evaluating the progress of children learning to read. This tool would need norms or "benchmarks," and procedures for testing children early, and in a way that would provide evidence of the extent to which every individual child was meeting those benchmarks or was failing.

The tool many educators used was DIBELS (Dynamic Indicators of Basic Early Literacy Skills). DIBELS samples actual oral reading behavior of individual children (not a pencil-and-paper test). Children are tested at least three times a year—at the beginning of the school year, during the middle, and at the end. The test provides norms or benchmarks that indicate whether each child is progressing well.

The part about districts providing timely remedies is still a problem because this is a new game for the states and the districts. The traditional game is to install a program and keep it in place until a designated time for adopting new programs. Reading First calls for a more flexible procedure that is based on student performance. If the average at-risk child is failing, the district is to conclude that something must change and respond intelligently. Although there are sources of information about such programs (which means it should not be an insurmountable task for the district to find one), most states still seem to be pretty weak in recognizing that retaining poor programs won't work.

CONSUMER INFORMATION ON WHAT WORKS

Interestingly, information about what works comes from the American Federation of Teachers. In 1998, the AFT published a report, "Seven Promising Reading and English Language Arts Programs." DI was one of them. The first part of an AFT article that summarizes the list provides a refreshing, frank description of the problem.

> If you compared the amount of time most people spend deciding what car to buy with the amount of time most schools spend selecting a program for teaching students to read, you'd probably find that the car-buying decision was the more thorough and time-consuming. One reason is that car buyers have a

huge array of guides, ratings, checklists and other resources available to help them evaluate their options and make an educated choice. Teachers and administrators, by contrast, have little objective material on which to base what is undeniably a vital decision for the future success of our students.

Although most of the approaches listed are not very effective with lower performers, the goal was noble.

A year later, an even more remarkable document came out, *An Educator's Guide to Schoolwide Reform*. It was fairly thorough and showed that only two approaches in the elementary grades, Direct Instruction and Success for All, had substantial evidence of effectiveness. What was particularly remarkable about this document were that the organizations contracted to have the study conducted:

- American Association of School Administrators

- American Federation of Teachers

- National Association of Elementary School Principals

- National Association of Secondary School Principals

- National Education Association

Both major unions (AFT and NEA) were involved in funding this report. One might assume that because of the involvement of these organizations, the findings would be widely distributed and would have substantial impact on consumer trends. The report was widely distributed and may have increased interest for some programs, but it did not lessen the hostilities against DI or significantly increase adoptions of DI. In several cites served by the NEA, there was great antagonism toward DI and no attempts to support it. We contacted the national office of the NEA and pointed out the problem. The response we received was that the national office did not have control over local chapters in these matters.

Although the guide provides fairly valid information about programs that have demonstrated effectiveness, the guide was not used much.

The outfit that has reliably provided information about what works has been AIR, the American Institutes for Research. As I indicated earlier, AIR has listed DI several different times as an effective approach. AIR, however, is not without fault, particularly in its latest evaluation of the effectiveness of full-school implementations (2005). It again identified only two programs that had substantial evidence of effectiveness in the elementary grades, DI and Success for All. This report addressed something that had not been considered in earlier evaluations, the "effect size" of different models. The report concluded that the effect produced by both DI and Success For All was "moderate," not large.

The authors of this report adopted two questionable procedures to make this conclusion possible. The first was to treat all studies as equals. Whether the study involved 15 students or 5,000, the study earned one point. In its evaluation of DI, AIR included the RITE Institute study, which involved 5,000 children and a study of a poorly implemented school that involved fewer than 50 students. The RITE study showed huge effect sizes for DI. The other study showed virtually none. Because these two studies received the same weighting, the effect size for the RITE institute children was greatly neutralized by a handful of children.

The person in charge of the AIR evaluation was one of the investigators in the poor study. We called him and pointed out that the study had a section in which the authors admitted DI wasn't implemented properly. He observed that there had been serious discussions in the evaluation business about the "intent to implement." He pointed out that his group believed that the study should be included in the evaluation because the people who were involved were sincere and attempted to implement.

Can you imagine this kind of logic applied to other domains, such as evaluating medications? If one of the studies showed no effect but clearly did not use the medication as prescribed, the study would be included if the investigators thought they were doing what they were supposed to do. If schools evaluating DI do not carefully follow the technical details that are required by the DI model, studies involving these schools are not evaluating DI or its potential, regardless of how unassailable the investigators' intentions are.

There's more. Although the DI Follow Through model showed very large effect sizes and evaluated possibly four times the number of students in the RITE study, no Follow Through studies were included in the AIR evaluation. The reason was that AIR decided not to include any studies conducted before 1985. When we talked to the director on the phone, I asked him what justification there was for this decision. His response was that the AIR decision was based on "current industry standards." I pointed out that the Follow Through study was far superior in design to anything since, particularly because it had provisions to help sponsors implement with fidelity. Such provisions were unheard of in subsequent studies.

His response was basically that industry standards are industry standards. It seems that AIR has the same orientation that we battled in Follow Through—attempts to make it look as if there are more highly effective programs than there are, and to position DI so it is not the undisputed winner. Also, I'm sure that AIR has some input into what are considered "industry standards." And if it wanted to, it could set new "industry standards." In any case, even with its machinations, AIR still had to rate DI in the highest category of available programs.

MORE MIXED MESSAGES AND BAD LOGIC

The same problems that characterize Follow Through logic influenced the direction of Reading First. The initial goal of the drawing-board version of Reading First was to require the use of *evidence-based* instructional programs with students who were at-risk of failing. That means evidence of effectiveness.

There were "compromises," which changed the "definition" of programs to be used, to "research-based." The difference is that an evidence-based program has substantial evidence that it is effective; a research-based program simply possesses some of *the features of programs that are effective.* For instance, effective beginning reading programs use some variation of phonics instruction to show that the letters signal specific sounds of the word. A research-based program would be one that had the feature of presenting "phonics" even if the program had no evidence of effectiveness. The result was that most programs that met the criterion of being "research-based" were poorly designed and were not effective with at-risk populations.

Regional educational labs published long lists of programs that met the "research-based" criteria. DI was one of the least popular programs on these lists. As closely as we could calculate, only about five percent of Reading First funds were used to purchase DI material.

I wrote an article that dealt with the illogical nature of this research-based logic, "The Dalmatian and Its Spots." The article points out that it is illogical to conclude that any program having the same features as an effective program will be effective. The faulty argument is: All effective programs have certain features; therefore, all programs that have these features are effective.

An exact parallel would be to say: all Dalmatians have spots; therefore, any dog with spots is a Dalmatian. There are zillions of dogs that have spots but are not Dalmatians. In the same way, there are many programs that have the broad features of programs with data of effectiveness, but that are not effective. The article I wrote appeared in *Education Week.* I didn't receive one rebuttal because there isn't one.

The primary advisor involved in the creation of Reading First, Reid Lyon, was interviewed in 2006 about his beliefs and what he had learned from

Reading First. He was asked: "What particular instructional programs do you endorse in order for teachers to implement what you've learned through your research?" He replied, "I have never nor will I endorse a program." This response is particularly curious because in his testimony to Congress he indicated that only DI and Success For All have strong data. Just as the Office of Education had voluminous data that DI worked, yet refused to disseminate this information, Lyon had even more information that DI works; yet he wouldn't endorse DI.

The parallel between Reading First and Follow Through logic does not end here. Lyon indicated that the reason for changing the selection criterion from programs that are successful to programs that share features of successful programs was, "There weren't enough programs that went through that level of rigor; so many programs would be screened out and only a limited number of programs would be available." Lyon's rationale is almost identical to that of Secretary of Education Boyer, who indicated that no Follow Through models could be disseminated because only one succeeded.

Again, the reasoning seems to be based on the idea that it is morally important to have a large number of programs available, whether or not they have been demonstrated to work. Of course, there is a middle ground that could keep the scheme from being totally irrational and provide for the possibility that some of the candidates for endorsement were capable of achieving positive results. Reading First could have *identified* programs that have significant data and *acknowledged* other programs that have some of the features of the programs with significant data. In this way, Lyons would be able to provide a desperate teacher who wants to know what works with an answer that still preserves his strange belief that he would never endorse a program. He could say, "Well, I can't endorse a program, but I can tell you that the two programs with the asterisk after their names have significant data of effectiveness. The other programs don't, but they have basic features in common with the programs that are known to be effective. Your choice."

Lyon also uses a variation of Follow Through's affirmative action for failed programs. He states,

> It is important to note that we designed Reading First so that it would also stimulate publishers and program developers to develop and test programs scientifically to ensure their effectiveness. This is a very slow culture change, but there is some indication that the major publishers are beginning to move in this direction.

In other words, "Screw Alan and Jackie. We're involved in a slow process here, so we'll just have to face the fact that current students aren't very important compared to current publishers that publish effete products. Affirmative action for these failed publishers comes first."

I suppose that if one considers the publishers to be more important than the kids, this position makes sense. If this is the case, a straight message to the teacher would be something like, "Understand that we are playing this game of 'Mum's the Word About What Really Works,' so you'll just have to recognize that your concern for kids is not our primary concern."

Indeed, the process of "culture change" is slowed even more than it has to be by reinforcing failed publishers.

FALLEN COMRADES

Although the first months of 2000 were relatively seamless with the preceding century, things changed in the fall. Wes Becker and Bob Mattson died within three days of each other. Wes died on October 29, Bob on November 1 (his wife Sandra's birthday). These men died for greatly different reasons.

Bob died at 74 from the ravages of cancer, but he died with dignity. He and Sandra lived in the country. In the months before his death, Lou and I tried to visit him on the weekends, either on our way out to the land at Veneta, or on the way back. Until Bob became incapacitated, he kept horses. Even during the time he made frequent visits to the hospital for his heart and his cancer, he built awesome furniture in his shop. About two months before he died, he started to lose weight. Lou predicted that he would die soon. She had befriended a lot of elderly people and knew the symptoms that presage death.

I said, "Well, we probably shouldn't go out there so frequently. He probably doesn't want company." She told me that I had stated a common misconception—"This is the time they want company and need it." She explained that their life is hell and they're frightened. Visitors provide some diversion from their pain and anguish. So we continued to visit Bob and Sandra.

I spoke at Bob's funeral. Near the podium was a large picture of Bob as a young man in his Navy uniform. I had given a great deal of thought to what I would say about Bob and what he stood for. I pointed out that one of the more obvious things he did was to assemble possibly the most talented group of people ever assembled in a department of special education. He was comfortable with mavericks because, for Bob, the issues were not of form but function. If people produced results, he supported them.

I told of the two events that seemed to crystallize his character. One occurred in his shop. He built a flat for me—a shallow wooden box without a top that I later used to grow Coulter pine seedlings from seeds. The flat he built was technically perfect in every dimension and feature. Yet, he made it in less than five minutes as we talked, and he didn't use a ruler, just his eyes. To me, this was one of Bob's characteristics—his belief that even if a job is simple, it is to be done with technical precision.

The second event was a discussion that Bob and I had about conservation. After I made some observations, Bob said, "The basic principle behind conservation is simple: Leave the world in better condition than it was before you were there," which is what I believe Bob tried to do. I concluded my talk by saying that I would miss Bob a lot.

Wes's death came as a great shock. I hadn't been in touch with him for months. I knew he was getting frequent tests, but I had no idea that he would die at 73. We felt we should do something to honor him and decided to hold a memorial service for him in Eugene. We put a notice in the paper, made many calls, and arranged to hold the service in the church that Wes had attended (the Unitarian Church).

A lot of people showed up for the service, including Don Bushell, Wes's daughter Jill (who is a professor of biopsychology at the University of Michigan), his son David, and his ex-wife, Julie (who lived in Florida). We took turns telling Wes stories and feeling sad.

I said, "Those who worked with him were routinely amazed, not only by his skill, but the speed with which he could do things. Perhaps his most impressive quality, however, was the strength of his will. In the face of terrible setbacks and impossible deadlines, Wes prevailed. If he promised to get something done by a particular time, it was not only done on schedule, but done very well."

Several others echoed this observation. One researcher who studied under Wes said something that I had observed many times, the amazing speed at which Wes could identify glitches in raw data or elaborate calculations. About the time I was looking at the first few numbers on a spreadsheet of data, Wes would point to a set of scores in the middle of the display and say something like, "It's impossible for them to have a correlation of point 9 with these data. These scores account for no more than 5 percent of the variance." Possibly a minute later, I would see what he meant, but if I'd figured it out on my own, it would probably have taken closer to an hour.

I pointed out that even with the incredible number of things he had to do, Wes was a good dad (a lot better than I was during the Follow Through years). Wes's daughter Jill expanded on this theme. She told about some of the nice things he had done and indicated that the only time he lied to her was a couple of months before he died. She had visited him in a hospital in California. The last thing she said before leaving was, "Now, you take care of yourself. I'll be back in three months."

He said, "I'll be fine."

The clinical causes of Wes's death had to do with his liver, kidneys, and blood pressure. One of the contributing causes was that he probably drank too much. These may have been the measurable causes, but the psychological cause was that he killed himself. When the establishment rejected Wes and his beliefs in data, he rejected education. To do that, he had to reject a huge part of himself. The image of himself that he had to maintain afterwards was one with many amputated parts, the hollow core that could survive on what had been peripheral interests. When his physical health failed, he had nothing.

The sad part of this equation was that Wes had to reject himself not because he did anything reprehensible but because the establishment made a mockery of his beliefs and accomplishments. Jill believes that someday he will be recognized for his singular contribution to Follow Through. I hope she's right, but I can sympathize with Wes. It is not very comforting to know that you can help thousands of kids and teachers, but you lack credibility and have no access to these victims. It hurts to see your professional beliefs trampled by educators who cling desperately to myth and folklore.

A colleague recently showed me a picture from the '70s, taken at a "Zignic" (a picnic at the Veneta property for all our trainers and friends). Six people, including Wes, Bob, and I, were wearing t-shirts with the motto, "Show me the data." For Wes, it was a way of life.

How is Wes remembered? In 2003, the College of Education at the University of Oregon launched a fund-raising campaign to support construction of a mega-building to house the College. Part of what the planners did was to make up a price list for "dedications." If you want an office named after somebody, donate $25,000, and the plaque goes up. For a decent-sized classroom, the ticket is about $100,000.

Shortly after the list came out, Doug called me about raising enough money to have a classroom named after Wes. I told him that we shouldn't have to pay anything. My feeling was that the College should have dedicated an entire wing to Wes, with no donation required. The College didn't see it that way. Doug is currently trying to negotiate the price of a plaque for both Wes and Bob at the entrance to the Clinical Services Building, which was one of Bob's projects.

Three other people we worked with died far too soon.

Valerie Anderson died of cancer in 1996. She was 57 years old.

Susan Green died of cancer in 2002. She was 59 years old.

Tina Rosen died shortly after she finished consulting in Barrow.

GET YOUR GOAT

Returning to 2001, we heard rumors that there were plans for President Bush to visit successful sites and publicize their success as part of the administration's campaign to increase awareness of programs that worked with at-risk children.

The visit happened in one school, but it did not generate the intended message about the children's performance and the administration's educational posture. In September, President Bush visited a second-grade classroom in Booker Elementary School in Sarasota, Florida. The teacher was Sandra Daniels. The President observed as she taught a group of 18 children lesson 60 of the second level of our reading program (*Reading Mastery*, Level 2).

The story they read was a simple one in respect to plot, but very important with regard to instruction. Some long-vowel words that had been in the "funny" font appeared for the first time in regular print.

The story presents word pairs that children confuse unless they are skilled readers: *at* and *ate, cans* and *canes, mad* and *made, pans* and *panes, caps* and *capes.*

Words like *capes* are tricky because the "final e" is not the last letter in the word. So from the standpoint of decoding, this story is very challenging for the emerging reader.

The teacher had good presentation skills. The children were at mastery and seemed pretty proud of themselves. They were on schedule to read very well by the end of the school year.

President Bush sat in front of the group and followed along in his copy of the reader, as the children completed the first part of lesson 60. Just before the children read the story for that lesson, "The Pet Goat," an aide whispered to the President that there had been an airborne attack on one of the New York World Trade Towers. The date was 9/11/01.

The documentary, *Fahrenheit 9/11,* showed the President's behavior in the classroom. He seemed unmoved by the message of the attack and sat impassively as the teacher directed the reading of the first page of the story.

the pet gōat

a girl got a pet gōat. she liked to go runniñg with her pet gōat. she plāyed with her gōat in her house. she plāyed with the gōat in her yard.

but the gōat did some thiñgs that made the girl's dad mad. the gōat ate thiñgs. he ate cans and he ate canes. he ate pans and he ate panes. he ēven ate capes and caps.

one dāy her dad said, "that gōat must go. he ēats too many thiñgs."

the girl said, "dad, if you let the gōat stāy with us, I will see that he stops ēatiñg all those thiñgs."

her dad said, "we will trȳ it."

so the gōat stāyed and the girl made him stop ēatiñg cans and canes and caps and capes.

The attack understandably eclipsed whatever educational plans the administration had with horror, concern about victims, and questions of retribution and justice.

Through *Fahrenheit 9/11*, "The Pet Goat" became something of a symbol of the President's indecisiveness. For some, the book that contained the story became a collector's item; for others the story became a departure point for political satire. In 2005, articles about the story and the authors appeared in publications that range from *The New Yorker* to the Italian version of *Vanity Fair*.

I was saddened to be associated in any way with the 9/11 tragedies and found it ironic that the publicity the episode received put our program in such a horrible context. As a CNN reporter told me, "Whether you like it or not, that story is part of history." A reporter from *The New Yorker* put it this way, "Well, everybody, gets to be in the national spotlight for 20 minutes." I didn't like the color of that 20-minute light.

Dennis Baron, Professor of Linguistics at the University of Illinois, wrote a piece for *Education Week* in which he tried to draw parallels between the President's action and the instructional program, "The President's Reading Lesson."

Here's part of the response I wrote.

> Mr. Baron didn't think much of the teacher's presentation and seemed particularly bummed out by the fact that the presentation was "scripted." In a way, that's ironic. I believe Mr. Baron would have no trouble recognizing a good performance in a legitimate theatre. The performers are following a script. In a very real sense, the teacher is an actor. The criteria for an outstanding performance are different from those for the stage, but they mark the difference between a successful communication and a failure. If these criteria are best achieved with the support of a script, why would it be any more of a problem here than in the theatre? ...

> The most odious and contrived shot that Mr. Baron took at Direct Instruction is a suggested parallel between the behavior of those children and that of President Bush. If Mr. Baron had an inkling of the amount and quality of work that goes into teaching kids to read as well as those kids read, the small number of people who are able to do it well, or the fact that if children don't learn to read well by the 3rd grade, they're educationally dead, he might appreciate how grotesque it is to suggest that they will behave as Mr. Bush did when they try to "wrest

meaning from an unfamiliar passage." All passages they read are unfamiliar until they have read them. And if Mr. Baron wants to discover the extent to which these kids would behave pusillanimously, he could write them an "unfamiliar" passage that starts with his major premise, "Your 2nd grade teacher shortchanged you," then explain the reasons—the low expectations ... the "script" ... her boring table-thumping ... My bet is that they would not only wrest meaning from the text but would provide Mr. Baron with a very spirited response to every point he believes he's made—either verbally or through "the written word."

NIFDI

In 2000, my son Kurt came back to Eugene to work with us. Kurt had been associate director of the Russian, East European, and Central Asian Studies Center in the Henry M. Jackson School of International Studies at the University of Washington (an organization with a less-than-catchy title that required four full lines on Kurt's business card). In Eugene, Kurt became director of the National Institute for Direct Instruction, NIFDI, which had replaced ASAP. The reason for NIFDI was that ASAP was not a non-profit organization. To work with some districts and to apply for federal grants, organizations had to have non-profit status.

Kurt worked primarily with Vicky Vachon and Gary Davis, the two senior project managers of NIFDI, and with Mary Gleason, who was in charge of training. Vicky is an exceptional trainer who lives in Vancouver, BC and maintains a travel schedule that is close to impossible. Some of her most impressive implementations are in Kansas and Nebraska. She works well with administrators, partly because she is very knowledgeable about how our programs fit in with administrative rhetoric and state standards. (This is not a trait that all of us share.)

Mary Gleason was definitely the most organized and efficient person in NIFDI. She had worked with me at the University for years, setting up classrooms so that teachers could present a good model for student teachers placed in the classroom.

In 2000, NIFDI was starting its fourth year of working with 13 Baltimore schools. The arrangement with Baltimore came about through a sequence of unlikely events. Perhaps the most unlikely event was Muriel Berkeley, who formed the Baltimore Curriculum Project and set up a venture involving Baltimore Public Schools and Core Knowledge Foundation, established by E. D. Hirsch. The Baltimore Curriculum Project

agreed to write lessons for the "Core Knowledge sequence" (but not necessarily to use them). The project initially tried to use these lessons in 13 of
the lowest-performing schools in Baltimore.

The Core Knowledge sequence is outlined in a book that has the same
name. A blurb for the book explains that the outline covers specific knowledge to be taught in grades K–8: language arts; American and world history;
geography; visual arts; music; math; and science. The content specified in
the sequence "compliments the general skills and objectives typically found
in state and local curriculum guides."

The problems with the sequence are legion and result from the way in
which curricular guides were formulated. They were committee efforts and,
like many committee efforts, there was nobody who knew when to say,
"No." Consider the various objectives for second-grade music and how they
probably came about. A committee member says, "Well I think second
graders should learn something about reading music." That sounds reasonable. Another says, "They should learn the broad classes of musical instruments—percussion, stringed, wind, keyboard, and electronic." That sounds
doable. "What about learning to sing major scales and learning to relate the
do-re-mi to the keyboard octave of middle C?" Okay. "They could learn the
song about Doe, a deer, a female deer; Ray, a drop of golden sun; Me, a
name ... " Why not? "They should certainly sing songs, not just scales, and
they should sing different genres of songs—patriotic music, religious music,
and popular music." Hell of an idea. Put all these suggestions together, add
a few more "reasonable ideas" and you have an unmanageable mess. None
of the suggestions is bad in itself, and no committee member wants to say,
"No, that's not a good thing to do," so the unholy aggregate is born.

Multiply the unmanageability of the music sequence by about ten, and
you have a rough idea of how unmanageable the sequence would be in an
at-risk school (which probably doesn't have a piano or keyboard for the
second-grade classroom). The Core Knowledge second-grade sequence was
not tried out with children to determine either the possibility of being able
to schedule the teaching or, more immediately, exactly what the teacher is
supposed to do to cover this material outlined for the second grade.

So the Abell Foundation found itself in a bind. Part of its job was to try
to create lesson plans for all the curricular areas that were to be taught. Part
of the job was to train the teachers. The biggest part, however, was to coordinate things so the effort was effective with low performers.

Early attempts failed, and it was apparent that the children needed something else. Fortunately, the Baltimore Curriculum Project had Dr. Muriel
Berkeley. She reminds me a lot of Tina Rosen. She is dedicated but humble
and unassuming. She is well-off (her husband was president of the
NASDAQ stock exchange at the time), but she works long hours at her job

and is completely dedicated to providing at-risk children with a good education. Also like Tina, she has a Ph.D. but never uses it to posture herself as being superior. Muriel had been a teacher and had high standards for her students. She'd suffered the inevitable frustration of trying to teach lower performers without proper instructional tools. Her heart remained in teaching, and her experiences provided her with a reality check that is rare in people who work with foundations.

Muriel was determined to find something that worked. After running through several false hopes, she came across Direct Instruction, phoned me, and indicated that she wanted to meet with me to discuss the Baltimore situation. At the time, we were working with the Utah schools. I told her that before we got together, she should visit those schools so she had a clear idea of our procedures and the DI curricula.

She did and thought DI was what she had been looking for. We had a good meeting. She told me about the Baltimore Curriculum's involvement with Core Knowledge, and I made it very clear that NIFDI would not work in a school that used Core Knowledge, and would not compromise so that the program consisted of some DI and some Core Knowledge. I pointed out that if a school has a "mixed program," the role of NIFDI in achieving high performers would probably be credited to either Core Knowledge or to some kind of magic that involved Core Knowledge and DI. I told her that if there was specific information that she wanted taught, she should tell me about it and we would write a sequence that teaches it.

She wrestled with minor machinations so the project still retained the label of "Core Knowledge," but was undiluted, full-school DI. She came up with the plan that DI would be used with all students who entered school below grade level. That included just about all the students. So the problem was solved and we agreed to work with the schools. We pointed out that she needed consensus from the faculties in these schools and that a good plan would be to reassign teachers who didn't want to participate.

With one exception, the schools we worked with ranged from low to the lowest. Possibly the most notorious school in the district at the time was City Springs. It was in a high-crime Black neighborhood and had the lowest achievement scores of the 119 elementary schools in the district. The average performance of the students in City Springs when we started was below the 10th percentile in all grades and all subjects. 98 percent of the students were on free-and-reduced lunch schedule, which is used as an indicator of the poverty level of schools.

Two of our trainers visited City Springs in the spring before the implementation began. Their summary statement was, "It's a zoo; totally out of control." Children were running through the halls when they were supposed to be in classrooms. In many classrooms, kids were fighting and throwing things. Most teachers had no control over the children. During recess, the behavior of children on the playground could be conservatively described as rowdy and dangerous for the younger children.

The school had a new principal, Bernice Welchel, who had grown up in the neighborhood and was committed to providing children with the kind of education that would permit them to leave the neighborhood and have a better life. At the time she became principal, however, the job seemed impossible to most observers. The *Baltimore Sun* carried an article that expressed this view.

City Springs proved to be as challenging as any school we've ever implemented. I gave an illustration in chapter 3 of the kindergarten teachers trying to control their children, and the trainer telling them that things will get worse before they get better. That was a theme for the whole school. The students had been reinforced for their behavior. They knew they could get away with it, so when we robbed them of their "freedom," they would try harder to reinstate it.

We knew that we had to turn K and 1 around before the school would start to show real progress, so we put a lot of trainers in these grades and scheduled extra days when trainers were on site. The teachers were bad. One of the first-grade teachers had her children under control, but she didn't follow Wes's plan of catching them in the act of being good. Instead, she made it clear that if she caught somebody in the act of being bad, there would be negative consequences. Unfortunately, she was the best model of maintaining an orderly classroom that we had in these grades.

Some of the other Baltimore schools we worked with were almost as low as City Springs. Arundel was one of them, but the behavioral management was better there than in City Springs, which meant that when the principal ordered a substitute for an absent teacher, one would show up around 50 percent of the time. In contrast, substitutes always refused to go to City Springs, which made the job of turning the school around even more difficult during the winter, when several teachers were absent, and the logistics made it problematic to put two classrooms of children in a single room or disperse children to several other rooms.

During our first year in Baltimore, City Springs had a locked-door policy. The outside doors were locked when the morning bell rang to assure that no children would leave and no crazies would come into the school (such as the irate parent who came into the school with a knife and chased Bernice around).

This part of the locked-door policy was not unique to City Springs. Most inner-city schools had locked doors. In City Springs, however, not only were the outside doors locked. In the morning, Bernice locked the doors to all the classrooms so that children would not turn the hallways into a combination war zone, fun house, and social center.

Progress in turning the school around was slow, and if the school had weak leadership, it never would have happened. When I visited City Springs during the second year of the implementation, Bernice first took me to three classrooms that looked okay, but certainly not outstanding. Then she said, "Those are my best teachers. They give us something to build on, but I don't know what to do about some of the others." She took me on a tour of possibly six teachers she judged to be her worst. I had suggestions for half of them. After we observed the rest, Bernice asked, "What do I do about those teachers?"

I told her that I didn't know, short of getting rid of them. She responded, "That won't happen soon. What do I do in the meantime?" I didn't have any answers except for us to do the best we could by using aides or other school personnel to work in those classrooms.

Replacing teachers is not a routine assignment for a school as notorious as City Springs. The only teacher the district sends to replace a failed teacher is either a first-year rookie, a misfit, or a reject from other schools. Teachers not in these groups typically have other options, and they won't go to schools like City Springs. After the first year, 19 new teachers were installed. The new population of teachers was not much better than the teachers they replaced. So the second year was like starting over—rolling a rock up a hill one more time.

The misfits often had good potential and became high performers. Some of the rejects were as bad as the teachers they replaced. For first-year teachers, the City Springs experience went beyond culture shock—more like undiluted horror. Nothing in their college work had prepared these rookies for City Springs. Most of them came in with expectations of teaching and interacting with students that were shattered within the first hour in the classroom. Even those who had studied "behavioral principles" were quickly traumatized by the rude realities of City Springs.

The county presented another barrier to improving City Springs and our other Baltimore schools. Salaries for teachers in Baltimore were significantly lower than in the three counties that surround the city of Baltimore. These counties wanted good teachers because the population of the counties was growing while that of Baltimore had been shrinking. So there was a market for our better teachers. As their skills increased, the probability that they would defect to one of the counties increased. A rough guess is that we lost 15 percent of our teachers every year to the counties. A pattern for the younger teachers was to work two years in a DI school and then defect to a county school. I couldn't blame these teachers. Some actually lived a lot closer to their new county school than they did to their former city school.

Another reason for the slow process of change in City Springs was that the options for dealing with poor teachers in a failed school are far fewer than they are in a well-implemented school. In well-implemented schools, it is possible to arrange the schedule of a good teacher or aide so she teaches some of the academic skills in a weak classroom. Another option is to combine a couple of classrooms, put the better teacher in charge of the classroom, and assign the poor teacher to monitor how children are performing. As the poor teacher improves, she assumes more responsibility for teaching. This arrangement presents a positive model for the poor teacher, shows her what is expected in student performance, and familiarizes her with the material that is to be taught.

These options were generally not available for many City Springs classrooms. Of the second-year teachers, at least one couldn't even read the script and another seemed to be insane; however, some of the teachers and aides got a lot better. The coordinator worked patiently with one first-grade teacher who could scarcely read and who could not produce the sounds for the letters and combinations that she was trying to teach to the children. She wanted to learn; she worked hard; and she became much better. After one practice session with the coordinator, she gently put her hand on the co-ordinator's forearm and said tearfully, "Thank you so much. Nobody has ever worked with me before." She was a certified teacher, however.

A serious problem in the upper grades was that some teachers did not know the content of what they were trying to teach. They needed to go through the program as students before trying to teach it.

As City Springs progressed slowly, Arundel Elementary improved quickly, especially during the first year. The principal was strong, and the average kindergartener read fairly fluently by the end of the year. Students in the early grades were on schedule to do very well. Performance in the upper grades, however, was poor.

My son Owen was the trainer for this school, and he did a good job. But it required a lot of work. When he wasn't on site, he kept in touch with the principal about specific problems that threatened the Arundel implementation. During the second year of the implementation, I was very impressed with the talent of most of the teachers in K–3.

We had some very good coordinators in Baltimore, but City Springs may have had the best—Anayezuka Ahidana. I had known her since May of 1969. Baltimore had schools using DI in the early grades at that time. I spent a few days observing in classrooms. I gave several talks, and I demonstrated with four-year-olds. The day before I was to demonstrate, the teacher who was to supply the children asked what kind of students I wanted to work with. I told her, "The lowest you have." She asked whether it wouldn't go better with the highest, and I told her no. She told her friend, another frustrated young teacher, Anayezuka (whose name was then Margaret

Brown), about the upcoming demonstration. Anayezuka attended it.

I taught the four-year-olds to count, and to say some sentences they couldn't say like, "This is a pencil." (At first they said, "Di pencil.") I also taught them a couple of prepositions. After the demonstration, Anayezuka asked if she could go with me on a tour of some DI classrooms the next day. Yes.

She brought along a third teacher, Karen Seitz, who would become Karen Davis; go to Champaign in the fall with her husband, Gary, and enroll in our graduate program; work in Follow Through as an on-site trainer in Providence; and finally move to Eugene and become a co-author of several reading and language programs.

Anayezuka wanted to join Karen and Gary but couldn't. When we started working with Baltimore 30 years later, she was a teacher there. I was pleased when she agreed to work as coordinator at City Springs. She had everything a trainer needs to achieve stardom—full understanding of the programs and how to solve the full range of instructional problems. She had the ability to show a teacher who is having trouble teaching something exactly how to do it; and she had dogged persistence and dedication to the job. When we later asked her if she wanted to become a project manager, she declined, pointing out that she saw her role as working directly with teachers and kids.

City Springs would not have turned around the way it did without her. It certainly would have become better—even a lot better. But the turnaround for City Springs was spectacular. Understand, however, it had three strong forces keeping it on a true course—Muriel Berkeley, Principal Bernice Welchel, and technician Anayezuka. It would be rare to find three people of their strength who dedicated themselves to improving a hopeless school. Muriel's daughter, Helen, shared Muriel's convictions. She taught first grade at City Springs for two years and did an excellent job.

By the spring of 2000, City Springs' neighborhood hadn't changed. Nor had the middle school across the street, which was still loud, disorderly, and had regular visits from the police. City Springs, however, had changed. It was far from the lowest school in the district. First-grade performance had improved from below the 10th percentile to the 75th percentile in reading. The school had order. Children had bought into the role of being good students. There was a lot of positive reinforcement and greatly improved teaching.

With K and 1 in place and getting better, the scene was set for the subsequent grades to inherit higher performers and achieve better results. If the performance of children remained at around the 75th percentile, the improvement would be spectacular. Over the next three years, however, the teachers in K and 1 continued to improve and the performance of their students reflected this improvement.

In 2001, first graders achieved at the 80th percentile in reading.

In 2002, first graders achieved at the 91st percentile in reading.

In 2003, first graders achieved at the 99th percentile.

City Springs first graders had gone from the lowest in the district to the highest. The fifth graders did not achieve as high as the first graders, largely because of more than 20 percent annual turnover of students; however, by 2003, the fifth-grade performance was one of the highest in the district, well above average: the 87th percentile in reading and the 79th percentile in math. One classroom had finished the sixth level of the DI programs and completed a middle-school textbook on U.S. history. As I pointed out earlier, when these students visited Monticello, the tour guide indicated that their group was the most intelligent the guide had conducted.

The other schools we worked with also improved a lot, but not as much as City Springs. Here's the first-grade reading performance of 11 schools we had worked with during the entire period.

Reading Scores in NIFDI Baltimore Schools
GRADE 1

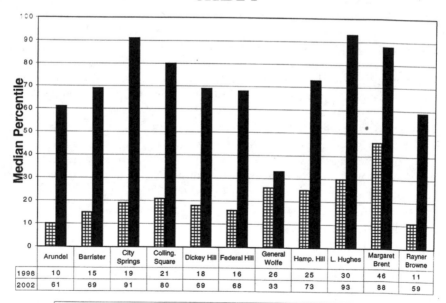

	Arundel	Barrister	City Springs	Colling. Square	Dickey Hill	Federal Hill	General Wolfe	Hamp. Hill	L. Hughes	Margaret Brent	Rayner Browne
1998	10	15	19	21	18	16	26	25	30	46	11
2002	61	69	91	80	69	68	33	73	93	88	59

⊞ 1998   ■ 2002

Note that in 1998, City Springs, Arundel, Federal Hill, General Wolfe, and Hampstead Hill were in their second year with NIFDI. That's why City Springs was no longer below the 10th percentile. In 2002, all schools but one were above the 50th percentile; 9 schools were above the 60th percentile; and 4 schools—more than a third of the schools we worked with—achieved at or above the 80th percentile. In 2003, all schools performed at or above the 50th percentile.

Some of the schools did not show great improvement. The worst was General Wolfe, which had an almost annual succession of principals who ranged from poor to very poor. Ironically, although this school was only a few blocks from City Springs, it served a population of children considerably higher than that at City Springs.

Arundel did not reach its potential. It acquired a new principal who did not implement the program as wholeheartedly as the former principal had. Although Arundel slipped, several schools were performing in the same range as City Springs—far above average.

All the other Baltimore schools (non-DI schools) improved during the school years 1998 to 2003. The reason was that the district scrapped the whole-language reading program it had used and adopted a better phonics program. So the district first graders (outside the DI schools) went from the 37th percentile in reading to the 54th percentile. During this time, the DI schools went from the 32nd percentile to the 66th. So even though the district ended the period above average, the DI schools started lower, ended higher, and out-gained the district average by 18 percentiles. Bernice received a citation from President Bush in 2003, as part of the first-anniversary celebration of the federal program, "No Child Left Behind."

How did the district respond to this data? It didn't exactly deny the outcomes, just tended to trivialize them. The district had what some of us called a bad case of premature elucidation and assumed it didn't need to master the details of how to manage and maintain a successful implementation before doing it. The superintendent took over one of our schools and ran it herself, but with higher funding than our schools. The performance in this school slipped. The district took over most of our other schools and managed them through a department whose head knew far less about instruction than he would have to know to improve poorly implemented schools or maintain the higher schools at the level they had achieved. The district implemented its model of managing and supervising these schools. Student performance slipped.

The Abell Foundation managed to keep three schools, Collington Square, Hampstead Hill, and City Springs. They continued to perform well; however, in 2004, NIFDI had a falling-out with City Springs. The school wanted to go in a different direction than the one that brought it to where it was. The school believed that it should place more emphasis on test preparation. We indicated that we would not work with the school if it chose that direction. It chose that direction, and NIFDI dropped it in the spring of 2004. That hurt. Anayezuka left the school to work in Hampstead Hill. Muriel kept City Springs but required it to follow the NIFDI guidelines.

The good news about Baltimore was that we had finally been able to show what could happen in very low-performing schools if they implemented the model more faithfully and in more grades than schools did in Follow Through. There was almost a perfect parallel between how well schools followed the details of the model and how well students performed. Also, it was inspiring to work with people as dedicated as Muriel, Bernice, and Anayezuka.

Baltimore and the press did not respond with awe to what had to be the most remarkable turnaround in the history of education (and one that required no less than a supreme effort). One article in the *Baltimore Sun* quoted a district bureaucrat who suggested that the reason City Springs was able to do so well was that it was a small school. General Wolfe is a small school and it was the lowest performer of our Baltimore schools.

NIFDI continues to work with Collington Square and Hampstead Hill.

THEORY OF LEARNING

Don Steely is an adventurous person. One of the more adventurous things he did was to sail a 28-foot-long boat from California to Hawaii with only one other person on board. The trip took 18 days.

I enjoy working with Don. He has co-authored several instructional programs with me. He is extremely bright and creative, and he is good at playing devil's advocate. He has extensive knowledge of instructional design and learning phenomena, and he has worked with the full range of learners, from non-English speakers to naïve learners. He has worked with deaf students in California, Missouri, Idaho, and Texas. In California, he worked with deaf high school students. They performed above the eighth-grade level by their senior year. That performance is over twice what deaf seniors had historically achieved.

At the opening of the new millennium, Don and I were two years into a project that would take nearly three more years to complete—writing a theory of learning. We worked on the project just about every working day from 7:00 to 8:30 a.m. There were a couple of interruptions in our schedule, but before we were finished, we had gone down four or more blind alleys and had written many pages that we had to throw away.

Our goal was to write a rigorous theory of learning, one that could serve as a basis for designing machines that could perform the basic kind of learning that humans and other animals do—learning from concrete examples (not from verbal presentations). The idea was that we would establish the fundamental rules required to learn from examples then scaffold verbal learning, responses to reinforcement, and other phenomena onto that foundation.

So we wrote and scrapped over 2,000 pages on learning from examples. From a strict theoretical standpoint, these attempts didn't make it. We knew they didn't make it because when the foundation is laid properly, all the phenomena that we know are true would follow more or less automatically, with the simple addition of a detail here or there related to (and only to) the new structure that was to be added. If we had to expand or change the foundation at this point, we knew immediately that we had not framed the foundation properly. So we would scrap what we had written, go back to the beginning and reconfigure the foundation so it supported the various phenomena we would later address.

After a year's worth of trying to set the foundation, we finally recognized why our attempts failed. Learning does not occur in the abstract. Every time we discovered that the foundation was not stable, it was because we had to address the *performance* that occurred when something was learned. For instance, we teach a cat to run from sudden illumination. We put the cat in a dark setting it has never been in. We illuminate the setting suddenly. The cat runs to darkness. Was this an instance of learning? The cat had never performed in this situation and had never produced the exact response it produced on this occasion. But was this learning or simply performance—an application of what had been learned to a new setting? After the false starts, we finally figured out that it is not possible to describe learning rigorously without starting with performance.

The best starting point was with organisms that perform without learning—like bees, ants, and others that inherit the content and rules that are needed to perform without learning them. The worker bee, which lives only about a month, has an extensive hard-wired system that permits the bee to do remarkable things, like communicate not only the distance and direction of sugar, but also indicate how high it is above the ground. In a great demonstration, experimenters put sugar high in a tree and brought some bees to the location. Experimenters then put a second cache of sugar on the ground directly below the tree. Bees that had been to the site were removed from the hive and not permitted to "guide" others. The others went to the sugar high in the tree but did not discover the sugar at the base of the tree.

There was no learning involved in this illustration, simply the application of hard-wired knowledge to a specific concrete situation. The first response to this situation may be, "Of course, there was learning. The bees discovered where the sugar was." If you follow this notion to its logical conclusion, you would have to conclude that every time an organism does something as elementary as climbing an unfamiliar hill, "The organism learned to climb that hill," or contend that the last instance of the cat running from sudden illumination was learning because it performed in a unique situation.

A fact of performance is that if we showed that an unknown mammal ran from sudden illumination, we could not tell from its behavior whether that behavior was learned or hard-wired. If we had taught the behavior, it would be exactly the same as the hard-wired behavior would be.

We know what is required to teach the behavior. This fact is very important because all the discriminations that would be required to induce the performance through learning must be possessed by the organism that performs the same way sans learning. We have to present instances that are consistent with the rule, "Run from sudden illumination." To do that, we have to make the sudden illumination far less reinforcing than running to a dark place. We could achieve the goal most easily by following the onset of illumination with a loud noise or a shock that would continue until the organism ran.

If we wanted to be sure that the learner learned behavior consistent with the rule, "Run from sudden illumination to darkness," we would have to make sure that we varied details of the setting so the learner did not learn to run to a predetermined spot, or did not learn to run to darkness only in the place we had provided the initial training, in which case, the organism could learn the rule, "Run from illumination in this room."

Once we had provided the organism with practice in other places and at different times of day, we would be able to predict that the organism would perform in a new setting exactly the same way the organism with the inherited behavior performs in that setting.

What does all this mean? That both organisms now have a rule that is functionally the same. The rule the hard-wired organism has must have the same information and the same urgency as the rule we induced. Therefore, whether we like it or not, a cockroach that runs from sudden illumination has that rule and that sense of urgency.

Furthermore, the application of that rule to a particular setting is the same for both organisms. When sudden illumination occurs, the organism must be able to distinguish dark areas to direct the behavior of running there. No, these behaviors cannot be "reflexes" because the particular responses the organism produces are not only different from one setting to another; they are also referenced to different physical locations. As the dark places change, the behavior changes.

From these facts, Don and I inferred the logically necessary features of a hard-wired system that performed intelligent behaviors. The basic premise that drove our inferences was that if the behavior is the same across organisms or situations, the mental functions that create that behavior must be functionally the same (but not necessarily the same with respect to neurological structures). The behavior of the two animals that ran from illumination is the same; therefore, the fundamental functions of the mental systems needed to support these behaviors must be the same.

We further inferred that the behavior observed must have two independent components. One component accounts for those aspects of the response pattern that are the same from one situation to the next; the other component explains those aspects of the response pattern that are different from one situation to the next.

What is the same across all applications implies the details of a "general rule" that the organism's mental system possesses and applies under specific conditions. Illumination occurs and the animal runs to darkness. Or a particular pheromone is presented, and the animal does a ritualistic dance. The other component accounts for why performance is different from one setting to the next. No two instances of running to darkness have exactly the same set of responses. No two instances of the ritualistic dance are exactly the same.

All occurrences of the behavior that are governed by the same rule are clearly influenced by unique details of the current setting. If the dance occurs on a steep rocky area, the specific details of the dance are clearly adaptations to the unique terrain.

Because details of the setting influence performance, the system must have not only the means to receive information about the setting, but also the capacity to create a plan consistent with the observed variations of behavior.

The inferences become more complicated at this point because they focus on specific details of the mental system that are logically necessary to account for what is the same and what is different about inherited behaviors. At this point most of the people who have tried reading the final version of the theory get lost or reject it. One reason is that the theory asserts that animals functionally must have emotions. These are needed to "motivate" the learner to respond. If it is no more reinforcing to do something than it is not to do it, the organism wouldn't do anything, predictably.

Also, producing the responses requires some form of "consciousness" to plan and direct variations in responses. Some readers have indicated that our reasoning is anthropomorphic. Not really. The beetle that runs from sudden light is not drawn to the darkness by a magical magnet. Rather, it is logically essential for the beetle to recognize the dark place and make decisions about how to reach it.

Once the theory establishes the two systems (one for motivation and one for planning and directing responses) we have reached the point at which we can explain learning as simple scaffolds to this system. In the end, the theory passed our test of showing the full range of motor and cognitive learning as progressive extensions of this foundation. The theory is logical, and I believe it is logically unassailable, but I suppose it seems as far out as our notions about instruction. For instance, I tried to set up a relationship with a man-and-wife team in New York that has written on brain phenomena and MRI's. I told them I would like to work with them on particular issues about learning that might be elucidated though MRI technology. I suggested that it would make communication easier if they read the first couple of segments of the book *Inferred Functions of Performance and Learning*. I didn't hear from them for several months, so I called. I couldn't reach them. So I wrote a letter, but they did not respond. So I wrote two more letters to which they did not respond. Apparently, they thought that Don and I were so loony we didn't deserve any communication, not even a simple response, such as, "Not interested, thank you."

Because the theory is built on logical inferences, it is probably strange to some, including those who build intelligent machines, especially because the readers aren't familiar with learning phenomena, such as the learning of unfamiliar content or learning from examples. But when they seriously approach the process of learning from examples—which is what basic learning is all about—they'll appreciate our theory (or somebody else will "invent" it).

Earlier, I observed that there were a couple of interruptions in our schedule for working on the book. The most serious one occurred on August 1, 2001. Don had built a remarkable house in the country about 20 miles from Eugene. It was like something out of Alice in Wonderland. It had 12 different levels, which were orchestrated into the equivalent of 3 stories. Don was cleaning gutters on the roof, which is steep. He secured himself with a hemp rope and went to work. As he cleaned the east-side gutters, the rope was tight around a corner of the chimney, rubbing against a metal flashing that had a razor corner. As Don moved around, his movement caused the flashing to saw through the rope. Don fell four stories, landing right next to a large stump, which probably would have killed him if he had landed on it. The fall pulverized his right heel bone and badly disfigured his left foot and ankle. After six operations, Don's doctors exercised their last option and amputated his left leg just below the knee.

Don wears a titanium prosthesis, but he gets around far better than I do. Shortly after we finished the book, I had spinal surgery, which left my right leg without much in the way of motor nerves to the quadriceps muscles. For a while, Don and I were a pair of gimps. We joked about the possibility that we were being punished for writing the theory book.

LOU AND DEVIN

I've been accused of suggesting that any children, regardless of how low they are, can learn if the instruction is careful. Not so. When I first met Lou Bradley's son, Devin, he was three and she was frantic. When Devin had been less than a month old, he almost died from pyloric stenosis. He survived the surgery, but he suffered serious brain damage. Lou desperately wanted him to be normal, but by age three he didn't talk, except to say "mama," and he was a serious behavior problem.

When she brought him to me, she asked, "Will he be able to catch up?" I told her that I didn't know. We would start where he was and teach him as fast as he could learn. I couldn't predict how fast or how much he would learn.

His initial learning rate was very slow and did not improve. He's now in his thirties. He's good-natured most of the time, and he works part-time at Goodwill Industries. His favorite activity when we go to the land at Veneta is to use a machete to trim dead branches from the trunks of Douglas firs. He's good at it. His speech, language, and cognitive performance are low. I can't always understand what he's trying to say, but Lou is good at it. And Devin keeps learning things and making verbal observations that are more complicated than the ones he made ten years ago. But he is still sometimes unreliable on *yes-no,* and his accounts of things are not always accurate. The more emotionally charged a situation is for him, the more accurate his reports are. However, if you asked him an hour after breakfast what he had for breakfast, he would probably say, "I don't know."

Devin laughs raucously at TV shows that have even the slightest hint of being funny (so raucously that he often drowns out the character's next sentence or two). He adores his father who takes him on outings every other weekend and to Belize for a couple of weeks every winter. If Devin discovers that he's going to Belize in the next few days, he becomes totally and frantically preoccupied with the prospect, asking "Belize soon?" about a thousand times. Lou doesn't typically let him know that he's going until the day of departure, but Devin is quite perceptive and if there is any hint of anything associated with the trip, such as a suitcase that is not in its usual place, he'll start asking about Belize.

Devin has relatives in Belize, and he is accepted down there. He goes lobster fishing with the others and has a great time.

Devin requires a great deal of maintenance and supervision. Lou provides it. Her mother, unfortunately, is in poor health and also requires maintenance; and unfortunately, I require maintenance, too. Since my spinal surgery, it is difficult for me to do things like shop for groceries. Lou does that for me.

I am deeply indebted to Lou. She's a wonderful partner, a good friend, and a very strong person.

THE PROGRAM FROM HELL

Starting around 2000, school districts finally began to harvest the fruit of *whole language* in the high schools and middle schools—students who couldn't read well (or scarcely read at all), and students who knew very little about math. This revelation raised a furor in some states and resulted in resolutions like "graduation standards" and "high school exit exams" for math and reading. The state that sparked this movement was California, which issued reasonable guidelines for identifying students who needed help and the kind of intervention needed.

The reason it took so long to identify that students were frightfully behind was largely that middle schools and high schools were not set up to teach basic reading or math. They had syllabuses in place. So teachers presented the textbooks and math assignments that were called for on particular grade levels. The students who attended class and seemed to be working received passing grades, even though they often could not do any of the work or understand much of the textbook.

One of the people who spearheaded the change in teaching failed high school students was Bonnie Grossen, one of my co-authors. She had been a middle school special ed teacher and had taught *Corrective Reading*. She later went back to graduate school and received her Ph.D. in special education.

Then Bonnie and Bernie Kelly worked for two years in Africa, teaching children in the Village of Mkhuhlu, in the Eastern Transvaal region. They also taught under-qualified teachers in Hoxani College. The women left Africa in 1990, when the revolt against Whites made it quite dangerous for them to remain.

After Bonnie returned to the U.S., she and I co-authored levels 5 and 6 (for fifth- and sixth-graders) of a program called *Reasoning and Writing*, which teaches students how to identify faulty arguments and how to write critiques that point out flaws in these arguments.

Bonnie became involved with high schools and middle schools in California. The first one was Goethe (locally pronounced "Gatie"), a middle school in Sacramento. The students scored somewhat below the 20th percentile on grade-level standardized achievement tests. That performance level greatly exaggerated the students' skills, however. When Bonnie tested them individually, using a test that had norms for many grades, a frighteningly high percentage of Goethe's students scored at the 0th percentile in reading.

Bonnie, who often tries to work on too many things at the same time, designed an elaborate system for teaching these students reading decoding, reading comprehension, language, math, and writing. She adapted different combinations of the *Corrective Reading* programs and upper-level DI programs for students with different performance profiles. Then she worked with the school to establish schedules and mobilize all staff and train them to teach students. In Goethe, all teachers, plus some ancillary staff, taught reading, writing, and language to all students who performed well below grade level.

Bonnie labeled her program REACH and developed manuals for placing students, arranging schedules, and using the various programs in the REACH arsenal. This effort was the first organized program that made it possible for teachers to teach older students at a level appropriate for their skill.

The program produced great gains in student academic achievement and in student attitudes about school. In Goethe's 7th and 8th grades, students learned as much in one year as they had formerly learned in two. The percentage of students at grade level increased from 23 percent to 47 percent. Students liked the instruction because they realized that they were able to succeed and learn things they had grown to believe they couldn't learn. Most passed newly adopted graduation requirements. The REACH system was later picked up by other California schools and by some schools in Florida.

One of the areas not covered well in the REACH system, however, was math. The need for effective high school math programs was magnified when states began adopting math requirements for graduation. In some states, like California, a graduation requirement stipulated that all students needed to pass a test of "algebra." Those who did not pass the test did not graduate.

The definition of "algebra" that California used is far different from the algebra I studied in high school. The new conception is greatly watered down but still quite ambitious for the lower performers, who constitute a high percentage of the California school population. The requirements were further watered down by the scores that students had earned. Performance slightly better than 50 percent correct was considered "passing."

On Valentines Day, 2003, Bernie, Owen, Doug, and I had our first meeting on designing the exit math program. Bernie wrote a journal entry that portended the nickname of the program. She observed that the meeting was congenial and then added, "We'll see how we do in the year ahead, which is what the project will probably take." In fact, it is now 2006, and if we keep on-task, we may be done by January 2007. After about two years of working on this program, I began referring to it as "the program from hell." It had to be the most difficult program I have ever co-authored. Part of the problem was the incredible discrepancy between what lower-performing students actually knew about math and what they would have to know to pass the test.

The typical student is weak in basic math facts (like $13 - 7$ and 6×8). The student has a very poor understanding of fractions and what they are. For these students, fractions are "less than 1." The students have no scheme of how fractions relate to division and to whole numbers. Students are weak on multiplying fractions, weaker on adding or subtracting fractions that have the same denominator, and incapable of adding or subtracting fractions with

unlike denominators $\left(\dfrac{4}{9} + \dfrac{1}{6} \right)$.

These students do not understand how to find the perimeter or the area of figures. They can't figure out the circumference or area of circles. They are often able to work division problems that divide by a single-digit number, but can't work problems that divide by a two-digit number. The students know virtually nothing about the coordinate system, and nothing about analyzing lines on the coordinate system (their slope; where they intersect the y axis), or constructing lines from equations.

The skill level needed to pass the test is roughly .8 of a light-year from where students begin. Many items on the test require students to solve sophisticated word problems.

The tests have problems that require knowledge of algebraic principles ($3r + 7 = r - 2$), problems that assume knowledge of scientific notation (What is the scientific notation for .002591?), and problems that assume knowledge about geometry (What's the volume of concrete needed to form the illustrated stairway?).

On the surface, there is no possible program that could teach these skills in one year or even two years. The program would require jamming four or more years of knowledge into the program and doing so in a way that *lower performers* would be able to master at least most of it.

We initially thought we should design a program that spans two years. After asking around, we discovered that in most situations, two years were not available for students who desperately needed the program, so we figured we'd do the best we could to fit everything into a one-year program that could also be used in situations that had more than one year available.

So another reason for "the program from hell" label had to do with the amount of material to be taught and stuffing it into a one-year package that would be relatively effective. The next reason had to do with the logistics for the co-authors working on the program. Typically, when we work on programs, I type the material; co-authors sit next to me, provide input about what to write next, and what's wrong with what we have just written.

The logistical problem was that Owen and I were in Eugene, Oregon, and Bernie was now in Pacific City on the Oregon coast, over two hours away.

We solved this problem by using a computer hookup called Timbuktu, which permitted Bernie to see my computer screen. With speakerphones, it seemed possible for us to have the same kind of interactions we would be able to have if Bernie were sitting with us.

The problem with this setup had to do with the phone system that connects Pacific City to the rest of the world. While someone talks, that person cannot hear somebody on the other end who is trying to interrupt. So, if Bernie launched into a 150-word observation, presented at Bernie's typical speaking rate (close to 175 words per minute), Owen and I had to wait for nearly a minute to issue our comment, which often was something like, "That's not what we meant."

We had initially assumed that after revising the first draft, we'd be able to try it out, do some fix-ups, field-test those modifications that were significant, make final changes, and be done with the program. The process actually required three fairly complete field-tryouts, which means three elaborate revisions of the program. Even with all the revisions, nobody is satisfied with all the details of the program.

The incredible amount of work the program required is another reason it got its informal label. (At this time, we're still arguing with the publisher, SRA, about what its official title will be, however, none of us really thinks that "The Program from Hell" would work, even as a subtitle.)

Our main objective in designing the program was to make the content manageable and realistically teachable. To do this, we had to change basic ways that a lot of things are taught. We had to create "inventions" that permitted us to teach all the content typically taught through more than one separate "topics" as one topic, which involved only one procedure, not many.

Possibly the biggest challenge was to take the intuitiveness out of solving word-problems and to provide rigorous procedures for translating the information presented in these problems into equations. With respect to how well we did this, I think the program is certainly among the best we've ever developed. Our inventions were great. Some resulted in procedures that were so simple that after we figured them out, we shook our collective head and wondered why we couldn't have seen something so obvious within a minute or two (rather than many hours).

For example, students have a lot of trouble working probability problems that refer to trials. Even simpler problems are difficult for them. "A spinner has 10 segments. Three are red. If the person takes 120 trials, about how many times would you expect the spinner to land on red?"

Our plan was for students to set up the problem so that the first fraction tells about the spinner and the other tells about trials, $\frac{3}{10} = \frac{?}{120}$.

The difficulty students have is in discriminating which fraction tells about what, and where the numbers belong in the fraction (top or bottom).

In our first version of the program we created various exercises that addressed where to write the numbers. Although the plan seemed simple, students had serious problems. They tended not to get it because we were not teaching it well. We kept trying to create some kind of template that made sense to them and somehow simplified or unified the details that they couldn't get.

The invention we came up with was embarrassingly simple. It was the most elementary example that showed the relationship of the spinner and the trials.

We labeled the two fractions and presented values that showed exactly where the numbers should go.

Object	Trials
$\frac{3}{10}$	$\frac{3}{10}$

The top numbers are "winners"; the bottom numbers show "all" (all the parts or all the trials).

Now, all the explanations were greatly simplified:

For the object fraction: *How many parts in all are on the spinner?* 10. *How many of those parts are red?* 3.

So the fraction is $\frac{3}{10}$.

A rule relates the fractions: The fraction for the object tells about the fraction for trials.

For the trials fraction: *What's the number for all the trials?* 10. *What's the number of winners you would expect?* 3.

"If the object has 10 parts and 3 parts are red, you take 10 trials and expect to get 3 reds."

After working with various examples that had the same fraction on both sides, we told students that the fraction for the trials could be any fraction that is equivalent to the fraction for the object. For the example above, any fraction equivalent to $\frac{3}{10}$ tells about the trials: $\frac{6}{20}, \frac{9}{30}, \frac{12}{40}$. Now, students have a scheme for understanding the basis for probability equations and where the numbers go.

Again, this solution to structuring the teaching is so obvious, after the fact, that it's hard to imagine how coming up with it could cause serious brain sores.

Perhaps the most extensive invention we created addressed one of the more frustrating problems I had experienced when I taught Upward Bound high school students—how to configure problems that tell about rate or proportion. We wanted to teach as little as possible that would enable students to handle the full range of word problems. As I pointed out in chapter 1, students had difficulty with rate problems. "If a car travels 45 miles per hour until it goes 180 miles, how long does the trip take?" The typical manner for teaching this problem type is to present an equation that

names the units: $H \times \dfrac{M}{H} = M$ (hours times miles per hour equals miles).

Even if students learn this equation, they have difficulty in determining where the numbers go and even what kind of unit is to be named in the answer.

Our invention did not require students to memorize any equations, but simply write the equation a problem described. This invention came about after Bernie, Owen, and I had a lengthy debate about whether these problems should be taught as ratio problems or multiplication problems. Bernie voted for ratios; I voted for multiplication; Owen was leaning toward multiplication because it would probably be tidier for problems that required more than one equation.

The discussion became "vigorous." I finally said to Bernie, "The multi-

plication form, $A \times \dfrac{B}{A} = B$, applies to all possible extensions involving

multiplication. Bernie pointed out that so does $\dfrac{B}{A} = \dfrac{B}{A}$. I argued that the

multiplication equation provided a better parallel to the wording of rate problems. The fraction refers to the two units for "rate"; the other values refer to single units.

The conversation ended with Bernie saying, "I emphatically disagree." This, of course, was one of the myriad times one or more of us had emphatically disagreed. I hadn't figured out how the scheme would relate to all word problems, but I *emphatically* believed that this was the most efficient way to go. When we hooked up on Timbuktu the following morning, Bernie announced, "I've changed my mind." She then gave a detailed analysis of how multiplication could be applied to the full range of problems.

It was awesome. We fiddled with bits and pieces of it, but basically followed the scheme she outlined.

Students first determine if the word problem involved multiplication (which means it had a part that told about the related units—feet per day, sheep in pens, hours per mile, houses built each year, and so forth).

Next, students identify the unit named in *the question the problem asks.* That's the unit that will be named in the answer.

Next, students write the letter multiplication equation that ends with the unit the question asks. If the question asks, "How many <u>feet</u> will the reservoir rise in six years?", it asks about feet; so students write: $Y\left(\dfrac{F}{Y}\right) = F$.

If the question asks, "How many <u>years</u> will it take the reservoir to rise 36 feet?" students write the equation that ends in Y: $F\left(\dfrac{Y}{F}\right) = Y$.

With this scheme, students are not required to learn different "formulas" or equations. They simply analyze the word problem to see if it involves multiplication. If so, they write the equation based on the units and the question the problem presents, solve the problem, and answer the question the problem asks. The answer consists of a number and a unit name—the same unit name that appears at the end of the equation with letters.

I would love to be able to go back in time to the days of Upward Bound with knowledge of this scheme. I know I could have taught all the students I was not able to teach to mastery.

Although Bernie and Owen and I had many "spirited" discussions and frequent disagreements, we knew from the first tryout results that the program was a winner. A large majority of students who completed only the first 2/3 of the program passed the math exit exam for California.

The program from hell may not be popular, because it is so different from traditional text material that middle schools and high schools use. The program has a workbook, a textbook, and a scripted teacher presentation book. We included the workbook because we have to teach things very quickly. For some problem types, the workbook greatly reduces the amount of copying and writing that would be required to work some problems; permits students to apply newly-taught discriminations at a high rate; and permits students to quickly work problems that are cumbersome without a workbook (like drawing lines on the coordinate system).

GUAM

In 2002, the administration of Guam Public Schools sent out a request to possible providers of DI to implement reading in all 26 of the Guam elementary schools. Years earlier, Gary Davis had done a lot of training in Guam, and he reported that some of the teachers did very well.

NIFDI was selected as the provider. For the first time, we were in a potential position to show what could be achieved on a district level. To work effectively in Guam, we had to figure out an efficient system. Airfare to Guam was not cheap and required about 24 hours travel time. Because of the expense of the trip, both in time and money, trainers could not go to Guam for only a couple of days. Trips had to be scheduled so the trainer was working in Guam for at least 10 days. Also, conference calls with Guam would be awkward because their time was 18 hours ahead of ours. Our 3 p.m. is Guam's 9 a.m. of the next day.

We got a break that didn't seem too positive at the time. The school we worked with in Chester, Pennsylvania (probably the most dysfunctional district we had worked with) had disintegrated and had turned over the schools to the Edison Project, an organization with no serious evidence of effectiveness. We tried to argue that because our school, Columbus Elementary, had achieved great gains and was substantially outperforming comparable schools in the area, the district should retain us in this school. Unfortunately, there was really nobody of authority to listen to this appeal. The board was not really a board, and the district was no longer an independent district, but was nominally under state control.

The person who suffered the most was the assistant principal, Donna Dwiggins. She was an experienced DI trainer who had been hired by the district (when there had been a district). Donna served as coordinator and on-site trainer. She was devastated by what happened to her school. She appealed to the Edison Project to manage the school financially but permit NIFDI to continue doing the instructional side. Edison would have no part of this proposal. (After a year, the Edison Project pulled the plug on the implementation, which cost the Edison project nearly $250,000.)

Enter Guam. For us to work efficiently in Guam, we needed a full-time, on-site trainer-coordinator who could also work with administrators. Donna, who was now working in a private school, definitely filled the bill; however, would she consider moving to Guam and living there? Without hesitation, she said "Yes." And we had the keystone in the educational arch.

Initially, I wasn't satisfied with our agreement with Guam. I didn't think we had enough on-site days to create great first-year gains. Also, NIFDI generally works with full-school implementations only, but in Guam our agreement was limited to teaching reading (except for kindergarten and first grade, which would have reading and language).

Another concern was the performance of Guam students on achievement tests. They scored at a much higher level than I would have expected. There was also a serious discrepancy between the students' performance on the National Assessment of Educational Progress (which was very, very low) and their performance on achievement tests. (One would expect the scores to be quite similar.) One concern was that if the achievement-test results were "inflated" it would be difficult to show improved scores. Also, the lack of a language program in all grades would compound the problem.

I wasn't completely optimistic about the Guam project because NIFDI had recently lost several good schools in Hawaii to the State Department of Instruction, which was bent on installing balanced literacy and showed no interest in the superior performance of our schools. I hoped that we wouldn't encounter the same kind of problems in Guam.

Surprisingly, the administration in Guam was the opposite of what I had feared. The superintendent, Juan Flores, was everything an implementer could hope for. He wanted to see the program succeed. He studied the program, observed it in the classroom, went to schools with Donna, sat in on initial training sessions, asked a lot of good questions, and seriously tried to address problems of implementing the program.

Also, the person in charge of Federal Programs, Ernestina Cruz, and the administrator, Rose Rios, were effective and fully supportive of the program.

The first year was a little ragged because some of the teachers were low, and not all the schools had a full level of commitment; however, the implementation looked good for being its first year, and all the signs were positive.

The second year went very well. We began work with seven middle schools. The language programs were added. Although there had been a mass retirement of principals, this problem was not as severe as it would be in some places. The set-up in Guam made it clear to the replacement principals what reading programs, language programs, and schedules would be in place. Teachers were improving and some of the schools were starting to look like models that we could use to show other schools how to do it better.

The third year presented some problems. The most serious problems during the third year were created by the school board from hell. In all the years we had worked with schools, we had never worked where the administration supported us and the board opposed us. Initially, three members of the Guam board were opposed to the project. One board member, Jose Cruz, was the ex-president of the University of Guam. One of his problems may have been that our project was not happy with the teachers who had graduated from the University of Guam. It was sometimes hard to determine exactly what bothered Cruz. Several people I work with read documents that expressed his reasoning and confessed that they had no idea what he was trying to say.

A second member apparently thought our project was unfair because his kid was placed in the middle instructional group, not the top group. A third board member had a wife who was a teacher. She didn't believe in the DI philosophy because it was too narrow and restrictive.

The Pacific Daily News observed,

> Few residents were interested in running for the Guam Education Policy Board two years ago resulting in last-minute campaigning and a nine-member board with four members who were elected as write-ins. [Two board members] were elected with less than 1 percent of the votes in their district.

One reason the board earned its informal appellation as the board from hell was that it had no rules of order—not Robert's Rules or those of anyone else. Board meetings were characterized by members yelling, interrupting speakers, and engaging in liberal doses of name-calling. Another reason for the board's label was the hellish decisions it made. One had to do with Superintendent Juan Flores.

The board became highly critical of Flores. During an evening board meeting that continued past midnight, board members interrogated Flores. He indicated that he felt sick and left the meeting. Following some further discussion, the board fired Flores and sent a messenger to his house at 4 a.m. to give him formal notice of his status.

On the following day, the *Pacific Daily News* wrote, "Gov. Felix Camacho yesterday chastised the board and several of the decisions it has made since being sworn in, saying he personally believes its members should be recalled."

One of the chastisements had to do with the board's decision that schools were to adopt a schedule for teaching DI that provided significantly less time for DI activities. This modification of the schedule was in violation of Guam's District Action Plan.

The board member in charge of curriculum (Rosa Polomo) later argued before the Guam Senate that the contract with No Child Left Behind did not call for second reading periods and the board was justified in eliminating these periods.

The committee read her the part of the contract that contradicted her assertion about the schedule. She countered by saying that she had been working from a draft copy of the contract, not the final version, and that her copy had no mention of second periods. She later brought in her copy and presented it to the committee. She displayed some of the marked-up pages to show that it was indeed a draft. However, a 30-second investigation of her document disclosed that it too contained the part that specified the second reading periods.

The Feds impounded the funds that were to be sent to Guam for the '06–'07 school year. The impounding meant that the DI implementation would have a considerable setback because the district was unable to purchase instructional material. We petitioned SRA to allow teachers to reproduce whatever pages were needed to teach until the district could order new material. (SRA holds the copyrights and without their permission, copying the material could create problems.) SRA granted permission, which I thought showed that SRA was interested in the success of the project.

Although the trials with Guam may slow the rate of implementation, I thought that the events in Guam were more positive than events in any larger district we had worked in. The district attempted to institutionalize the program so that it could not suddenly disappear without record, on the basis of a whim or change in philosophy. There has been serious talk about reconstituting the board and changing the scope of issues the board addresses. The Guam community shows a healthy understanding that more highly skilled students will benefit both the community and the students. One of the most incisive descriptions of DI was written by a member of the Chamber of Commerce, Carl Peterson. He and other members of the Chamber of Commerce's Education Committee visited Carbullido Elementary School. Here are parts of the account he wrote for the *Pacific Daily News*.

> The first thing the principal and school DI coordinator did was present the report for the previous week—a stack of paper 1½ inches thick covering every single class for the week, every subject and every student's progress for each day. They knew exactly what the progress of every student was, their mastery of the content ... kinders were way ahead of the scheduled benchmarks; they were already working on Reading Mastery 2! ... We watched first-grade students reading at a third-grade level. The story unit they were reading integrated a number of science and social studies facts into the lesson. The children didn't see it as a science class; they were learning science in interesting story forms ... fourth and fifth graders were in reading level 5 [reading] the story "Buck" by Jack London. They were learning geography and history—the Yukon and the gold rush—through the story ... We were actually dumbfounded. We realized that all one would have to do is go to the classroom and see the amazing progress ... When asked, the staff said none of the policy board had been in any DI classrooms at Carbullido.

The fact that the Chamber of Commerce would have enough interest in the program to visit schools places Guam in a very exclusive group of communities. The newspapers carry frequent articles on the project, so that the part of the community that is normally naïve about what occurs in schools that serve lower performers is aware of what the Guam schools do.

Guam still has a basic problem, which is that the school day is short.

The daily reading, language, and math schedule consumes about 4½ hours in the primary grades, which is about the full day after lunch and recess are added. The board complains about this, and I agree. As the students become more proficient, we will modify the schedule so the core subjects require less class time in grades 2 and above.

The Guam Senate is considering new legislation for the hiring and firing of superintendents. Several people in the Chamber of Commerce have expressed interest in running for the board so that students will be represented more by people whose central concern is with the health and prosperity of Guam.

SCRAP URBAN SCHOOL DISTRICTS

In 1982, I wrote an angry article, "Advocacy for Children," that expressed the premise that the system (not simply the district) will not respond to data or reason. Here's part of the conclusion:

> Optimists suggest that changes will occur within the system and that the strategy for affecting change is through an evolutionary process ... I have seen too many good projects disappear to believe that such a benign approach will work. The system is too self-supporting, too intertwined, too powerful to roll over because of mild internal irritations. It will respond only to loud voices and demands from a strong power base outside the system. The crisis is already at a critical level. What is needed to create a productive response is a mobilized effort that points the finger at the law, the colleges, the districts, the educational publishers, the state and federal funding agencies, and the unions—in other words, at the entire system.

I believe the experiences we've had in working with many school districts since I wrote this angry appraisal provide ample evidence that the system is functionally as sick now as it was then. I think that the most productive way to effect fast change in the system is to reform school districts. If they are reformed, a strong domino effect would put pressure on colleges of education to provide districts with technically proficient teachers and pressure on publishers to design material that is technically sound and has evidence of effectiveness.

Reforming urban school districts, however, will require strong pressure from outside the system because districts cannot be reformed from within, partly because the magnitude of the changes makes the task daunting. The central problem is that districts are not constructed so that children and their performance are the central focus of the administration. Decision makers are not really concerned with learning about more effective ways, but are concerned with institutionalizing what they would like to believe in, and using rhetoric, guile, and force to assure that they squelch any attempts to stray from the mandated blueprints. In the simplest terms, if an outsider who has potential to greatly reduce failure tries to work with the district, the district requires the intruder to follow district policies that guarantee various degrees of failure. The resulting paradox is that the only way to gain access to children and teachers who need help is to agree to use ineffective practices.

The book, *The Great School Legend,* written by Colin Greer in 1972, points out that public schools have never been designed to teach all children and have always resulted in at least half of the children failing. The reason is that despite the schools' rhetoric, they are structurally sorting machines constructed to weed out the common and select the few who meet the challenges the schools present. To change schools so they are consistent with their rhetoric about caring and serving all children requires a new machine, not another disguise for the sorting machine. Virtually none of the current instructional practices would survive. To appreciate why significant reform initiated by districts is highly unlikely, consider the nine primary ways districts would have to change and how far these changes would take districts from their current operating plans and functions.

1. Child Advocacy: Students' interests would be formally represented in all district decision-making, including union negotiations.

2. Evidence-based adoptions: Procedures for adopting instructional programs would be based on evidence of effectiveness for both the programs and the training needed to maintain them.

3. Accountability: The district's organizational design would have "nested accountability" for each at-risk school, which makes one person in the central administration responsible for everything that goes on in that school.

4. Decision makers' technical knowledge: The superintendent and all central-office personnel who make significant decisions on curricula or training teachers would have working knowledge about the technical details of instruction and of the effectiveness of programs that are installed.

5. Well-designed learning environment: Classrooms would be organized to maximize student achievement, with students grouped homogeneously for academics and placed appropriately, with adequate and coordinated schedules, with performance projections maintained, and with students' performance data used to make decisions.

6. Current data: The primary function of the district's research department would be to process current data on children's performance and note where remedies are not provided in a timely way.

7. Functional memory: The district would maintain records of various programs and training packages used in the past and provide ongoing comparisons of the past results with the current performance of students.

8. Ongoing training: Skilled trainers would provide in-class coaching and in-service training for all teachers who need it.

9. Teacher placement: New teachers would be tested in actual teaching settings before they were hired, and trained (if necessary) before they were assigned.

With the exception of the Reading First requirement that the district is to respond to poor data, possibly by adopting another approach, urban districts have none of these provisions; however, each provision is sensible. If the school's central function is to instruct, why wouldn't the district have an advocacy function that represents children's interests? In the same way, there seems to be no compelling justification for the district adopting material that has not been demonstrated to be effective. Also, teachers need training in using any effective program.

I could write extensively on each of the nine provisions and why each is necessary if the school is to serve lower performers, but I'll just hit some of the highlights,

Child advocacy: The district provides some advocacy in the non-instructional aspects of the school—in the free-lunch program and the medical-dental program. It may even have a productive counseling program. In most at-risk schools there is not even a pretense of trying to place children appropriately in instructional sequences or use instructional sequences that are on the students' skill level.

If the district had advocacy for children, it would have both something like a department of internal affairs to police the system and a staff of experts, people who are technically knowledgeable about instruction of teachers and children. In concert with the research department, they would identify areas in which a school is not operating effectively and fix the problem.

Another area in which the children's interests should be represented is the negotiations with teachers' unions. The negotiating parties are the union and district representatives. A parent representative may be present, but not anybody who has detailed technical knowledge of teaching and of the teaching outcomes that are being achieved in the various classrooms; therefore, there is no voice for what the children read, simply what the adults in the union and district deem acceptable.

Program adoptions: Any form of serious advocacy for at-risk populations would overhaul the procedures the district uses for adopting instructional programs. Selections of programs need to be based on evidence of effectiveness. Furthermore, the district needs to consider not only the likelihood of the program being effective but also the potential of training even lower-performing teachers to be effective in teaching the program. If the district thought a program had potential but did not have compelling evidence of effectiveness, the district would conduct a small field-test in which the program would be fully implemented and seriously evaluated. The results would determine whether the program is effective enough to install on a larger scale. The district would not rely on committees or personal opinions from anybody who has not been associated with highly successful projects (as measured by student performance).

School districts are not organized so they first try out possible instructional programs or reform models on a small scale before implementing them in all their schools. Districts are performing experiments on human subjects; ironically, however, a graduate student in special ed who proposes testing a new, untried program for a dissertation has to present evidence that the experiment will produce results no worse than current programs and practices. Furthermore, the student has to indicate a plan B, specify the criteria for knowing when the experiment is failing, and specify the procedures for executing plan B. Finally, the student has to obtain consent from parents if there is a possibility of harming subjects.

The American Psychological Association has professional standards based on the central notion of doing no harm. In the case of program adoptions there would probably be no harm if the district first ran a small-scale study to show that a proposed program did no harm, not just by doing a tad better than the preceding adoption, but by meeting achievable standards of student performance. Even if DI were installed, the district would fulfill the no-harm requirement only if it installed adequate training and organization.

Urban districts have no provisions for doing any of the above.

Nested accountability: The purpose of the nested accountability is to assure that all the schools' efforts are aligned. All input for the schools would be funneled through the single person responsible for the instructional performance of that school (and with any school-related conditions that affect student performance). One such director might have charge of four or five schools. There would be no language-arts consultants who provide input that is opposed to the language programs the school uses. There would be no contradictory directives from the central office and trainers. The administrator responsible for the school would assure alignment among the school's summer programs, after school programs, federal programs, and special education programs.

Technical knowledge of decision makers: A necessary requirement is that all district-level personnel who are involved in decisions about instruction must have knowledge about the technical side of teaching and how to use small-scale studies to evaluate the potential of programs. Unless this requirement is met, the administration will make poor decisions about programs, teacher training, and poor responses to observed learning problems. There would be no district directors of elementary education who view instruction as broad issues that are framed in a way that insulates them from being questioned about results with lower performers. Directors must be technicians, whose passion is not to play house using living children or be a powerful boss, but to help the teachers and students do a better job.

It would also be important for superintendents or CEOs to have an understanding of the technical side of instruction, particularly of the steps that are to be followed to validate instructional programs. Superintendents should have the knowledge needed to resist modish ideas that have "appeal" but no data. They should also have a good sense of the classroom realities and what is realistically required to engineer significant improvement. (They should not believe that simply by creating "partners" and having counselors, active parent groups, and provisions for teachers to "collaborate" significant reform will result.)

Formal memory: A memory is important for a district that does not want to make the same mistakes 5 years or 20 years later. With a memory of both effective approaches and ineffective ones, the district would be able to compare current outputs with past outputs, something virtually no urban district is able to do. The reason that districts do not have memories is so they can pretend they are improving. Every seven years or so, when the district "adopts" new material and "standards," it is easy for the district to sell the idea of a change because what had been used hasn't worked. Occasionally, however, there has been something that worked a lot better than what is being currently proposed. Successful approaches should be recorded, remembered, and used as a yardstick for evaluating current approaches.

Skilled trainers: Consistent with the reformed district's central focus on identifying problems and providing timely solutions, the district would need skilled trainers. Without them, the district would be like a magnificent machine with no provisions for lubricating gears and bearings. These trainers are not lecturers or inspirational performers for district-mandated "in-service training," but people who can go into the classrooms where teachers are experiencing problems, show how to correct the problems, and train teachers in executing techniques that correct or avoid the problems.

Teacher placement: No unqualified teacher or aide would have an instructional role. Before instructional personnel are placed in a classroom, they would be tested on both the content they were to teach and their ability to teach programs they will be assigned.

Districts would certainly argue that all these changes would be far too expensive. That's not true. Once set up, the system would be no more expensive than what is in place now. Districts would argue that teacher unions would not endorse this plan. I don't know of any compelling reasons unions could cite for not accepting the plan. Just as the coal mining union had to accept change brought about by technology, teachers' unions would have to accept it.

LESS THAN SUPER SUPERINTENDENTS

In some ways, the superintendent or CEO is the key figure in a successful district effort. It seems paradoxical that school boards go through elaborate screening processes before hiring a superintendent, even though the chances are probably ten to one that the person they select is completely naïve about the central function of the district—instruction. Earlier, I presented examples of naïve superintendents. Four more recent examples involving DI illustrate that superintendents tend to remain naïve and arrogant.

One example occurred in California. The *Ventura County Star* carried an article in 2003, titled "Effective Reading Program Must Go," which indicated that the only school in Ventura County, and one of 109 in the state to receive a citation for achieving exemplary progress, was forced to drop their program. NIFDI had earlier worked with that school, and it was a pretty good performer, far better than other schools with comparable demography. The district replaced DI with a program that has limited evidence of effectiveness, but that had been adopted by California because it met State "standards."

The county superintendent justified scrapping DI this way: "We want to make sure all schools are using the same curriculum. Why not something based on the standards that are going to be taught?" So in the end, the fact that the program achieved impressive performance and met standards more relevant than the California Standards was far less important to the superintendent than it was to maintain alignment with cavalier state standards.

The second illustration involves San Diego. A recent superintendent, Alan Bersin, wrote an article that appeared in the *San Diego Union-Tribune* in which he endorsed a paradigm shift "centered on productivity that evaluates everything we do and every change we consider from evidence of its impact on improving the quality of instruction, and hence student achievement." The central notion that his article presents is that "growth in student achievement must be education's key metric."

In developing his case for "maximizing productivity," he refers to the scientific revolution, Ptolemy, Copernicus, and changes created by labor leaders. He addresses the issue of "why there has been so little change in public education over the past 40 years, in spite of endless and recurring reform." He points out that educators contend that change takes a long time (7 to 10 years), but positive change is rare. His solution is that we should welcome charter schools and others that compete with public schools. Bersin's assumption is that through competition, better ways will emerge.

He concludes with rousing rhetoric. "We educators should remind one another of this fact: it's the teaching and learning that matters. If our students and teachers don't succeed at greater rates and in greater numbers, the franchise is doomed."

So in very broad strokes, he presents a sensible message consistent with the one outlined above. And he may now actually believe what he writes; however, his record reveals that he could have been the poster example of a naïve and arrogant superintendent.

How would a concerned, knowledgeable superintendent like Bersin actually do things to maximize the output in San Diego schools? He would consult sources of information about what works, like the report, *An*

Educators' Guide to Schoolwide Reform. He would check history to see what had worked earlier in San Diego. He would assemble people who were involved in successful interventions, like those of DI in the lowest performing schools in the district. And he would seek advice and consult with those who have demonstrated expertise about how best to implement, expand, and maintain successful programs.

How many of these steps did Bersin take? None. He installed one of his cohorts, Anthony Alvarado, as "Chancellor in Charge of Instruction." Alvarado promptly installed two failed approaches, whole language and very fuzzy math. Was there any tryout, any serious data that they would work? No. Both programs failed and continued to fail in San Diego, but there was no response from the central administration. Finally, Alvarado was strongly encouraged to leave town (not by the administration, but by the public).

Under Bersin's leadership there were no safeguards, no current data, no systematic observations of failing classrooms, no plan B. There was simply the standard arrogance of the urban school district.

An interesting footnote to the Bersin story is that his next job was not a step down based on the poor showing in San Diego, but a sizable step up. In April 2005, Governor Arnold Schwarzenegger rewarded Bersin by making him Education Secretary for the State of California. Schwarzenegger also appointed him to the State Board of Education, so he would have the capacity to put his stamp on educational policy for everything in the whole state.

Arnold should have known better. Before becoming Governor, he ran an after-school athletic program in D. W. Griffith, an L.A. middle school. The school used DI. Arnold was so impressed with the math instruction that he made participation in the athletic program contingent on students completing their math assignments. He indicated to a trainer that he couldn't understand why DI wasn't used more extensively. Perhaps in a couple of years, with Bersin at the educational helm, he will have a better understanding. Bersin recently endorsed legislation that provided separate standards for non-English speakers. This legislation would have institutionalized more educational discrimination by not teaching Hispanics English. The bill passed the California House and Senate. To Arnold's credit, he vetoed it.

A third example of questionable superintendents is Chicago. While Vallas was CEO in Chicago and we were implementing in five schools, I tried to contact him at least four times. I wrote letters and made calls that didn't reach him. In the letters, I outlined a simple proposal. Do a little study in which you waive the district requirements and try out DI in the schools we're already working with.

I promised that we would show much greater gains than we were already showing. I received no response to these letters.

Currently, a new superintendent in Chicago is making the same mistakes that Bersin made. The new superintendent, Arne Duncan, installed Barbara Eason-Watkins as Chief Education Officer. She had been a principal who used a kind of do-all, good-will approach that involved everything from mobilizing parents to immersion in literacy. She had good results in her school, but the gains were suspicious, particularly the way they disappeared in the upper grades after she left. If these gains were based on real skills, the students would have performed well for several years after the termination of the program.

Even if the approach worked in her school, would it work in others? Duncan apparently did not consider the possibility that it wouldn't. Chicago is currently advertising that last year produced the largest performance gains ever recorded on the Illinois Test of Basic Skills. That's interesting, but not impressive. The gain was a little more than one percent. The high school I attended in Chicago, Fenger High, reported that 7.4 percent of its students were at or above grade level on a standardized achievement test. That's 1 out of every 13½ students.

Duncan also endorsed a new nostrum, the small school (called Renaissance Schools in Chicago). Like the open classroom, they are supposed to create magical outcomes, but like the open classroom, the small schools will inevitably fail if there is significant student turnover and the schools use programs that have little evidence of effectiveness.

Duncan apparently didn't direct any search of the past; didn't find the records of Joe Rosen and his success in District 10; didn't contact teachers or trainers like Adrienne Allen, who had considerable success in Chicago; and didn't contact us about what happened in our Chicago schools.

Instead, Chicago threw out DI. According to a *Sun Times* article, Eason-Watkins performed an evaluation of DI. "A committee of 50 teachers, principals, and literacy experts evaluated several reading programs, and DI received the lowest scores…" That rating is a familiar echo from California—the program with best performance record receives the lowest ranking by adoption committees.

When the committee rated DI the lowest program evaluated, however, that judgment didn't provide information about DI, simply about the committee and why using such committees can't work.

The last example of poor superintendents involves Lewis Lemon Elementary School in Rockford, Illinois. Its experience paralleled events that occurred in Wesley Elementary, in Gunnison Elementary, in Ventura County, in Chicago, in San Diego, and in Follow Through. The story pretty much follows the familiar plot lines. The principal, Tiffany Parker, installed DI and provided the training and support needed to make the program very successful. In 2003, Lewis Lemon's third-grade students ranked second out of 35 schools in Rockford, in spite of the fact that 80 percent of Lewis Lemon's students were Black, and 85 percent were poor. The only school that outperformed it was a school for the gifted. In Rockford, White students traditionally outperformed Blacks by a wide margin. In 2003, Lewis Lemon achieved much greater equity: 97 percent of Black students and 92 percent White students met standards on the Illinois test.

The success story became compromised by a new superintendent in Rockford, retired Colonel Dennis Thompson, who followed the Bersin model of school management. He brought his deputy superintendent with him and established her as curriculum director. Her mission was to install "balanced literacy," which is the new name for *whole language*.

In 2004, the district accused Tiffany Parker of cheating. A witchhunt (just like the one in Houston) followed but did not disclose evidence of cheating. The superintendent was determined to show that foul play was afoot and arranged to retest the students on another test, just the way Gunnison's district did. Also, Tiffany Parker was banned from the classrooms during the testing so she could not cheat. The outcome echoed the one in Gunnison: the students achieved the same high performance on the second test.

The next ploy was for the district to direct all schools, regardless of their performance, to use "balanced literacy." Here's part of the memo sent out by the deputy super to make sure that Tiffany's Christmas was less than merry.

Sent: Fri 12/17/2004

To: Elem School Principals; Reading Coaches; Reading 1st Literacy Coaches; Curriculum Coordinators

Subject: Reading Programs

I have tried to be sensitive this year to reading initiatives that schools already had in place. However, as time goes on, I realize that it is imperative that we all be on the same page ...

In the fall of 2005 all elementary schools must be on board with balanced literacy. Please let your coaches and district reading coordinators work with teachers second semester to initiate this transition.

This was an audacious memo because the district was receiving Reading First funds to support the program in Lewis Lemon. The district mandate for all schools to adopt balanced literacy was in violation of the district's Reading First contract. The response from Reading First was to inform the district that it would lose its Reading First funding. But like the city of Denver, which lost its funding for not complying with its Reading First contract, Rockford remained firm in its decision.

Tiffany Parker protested. Members of the school board protested. The parents of children in Lewis Lemon protested and demonstrated. The scandal was reported in many newspapers, including *The New York Times*. Carrie Watters, educational reporter for *The Rockford Register Star*, wrote a series of articles that were critical of the district's stance. In one she pointed out that Tiffany's college training was in the approach the district was now mandating. She quoted Tiffany: "I was trained in balanced literacy. I got so frustrated over not meeting the needs of my kids ... I had training, reading coaches, high levels of support," but it didn't work and the children failed.

In January of 2005, Tiffany Parker was removed as principal from her school because she refused to comply with the orders from the super and his deputy. Tiffany had scheduled a meeting with parents. When she arrived she discovered the super and his deputy had taken over the meeting and were passing out big lies to the parents.

So this part of the story is reminiscent of Follow Through logic: DI works; therefore, the administration will assure that it does not spread. Imagine the incredible commitment required by the super and his deputy to proceed in the face of national, highly negative publicity and a loss of $681,000 in Reading First funding. Imagine how important this issue must have been for the super and his deputy to take over the parent meeting and stamp out DI. Clearly, Tiffany Parker posed an enormous threat to them and, equally clearly, they did not want to find a better way or receive data that poor Black kids could succeed. Their behavior suggests they were clearly on a kamikaze mission.

This story ends something like all the others. The orders for removing Tiffany stood, but she sued the district and the district negotiated a settlement. So she inflicted some harm on the district and had some hollow recompense for the insult she received, but like Bonnie Nelson, she was removed from her school for serving her children and providing them with life skills.

The saddest part of the equation is that there is no punishment, aside from possible social scorn, for the super and his deputy. When performance of the children in Lewis Lemon falls—and it absolutely will fall—there are no provisions for retribution, several pounds of flesh from those who would abuse their power the way these two zealots did.

Superintendents who lack means or commitment to find out and install what works are not in a minority. In fact, possibly all urban school districts are headed by superintendents or CEOs who have almost no instructional literacy. Part of the problem lies in their responsibilities. These leaders spend most of the time fulfilling PR functions, working on grants and budgets, and performing a variety of administrative functions. They couldn't have time to serve as directors of the instruction unless most of these functions were handed off to a business administrator. Under the traditional organization, the superintendent simply finds a hatchet person who is "on the same page" as the super, and ands off the main job of the district to this chancellor or deputy (who ironically was never interviewed by the board or considered when selecting the super); yet, this person makes the critical decisions about interactions between teachers and children.

The resulting district operates like a hospital that has nobody with technical skill, only administrators.

One of the more remarkable responses of district officials and policy makers occurs when they receive information that not only did the DI Follow Through model outperform all the other models in everything, but that our schools were not fully implemented and that we could achieve substantially higher levels of performance in sites that were fully implemented. A district that has maximizing student performance as its primary objective would want to implement the model as soon as possible, because that outcome has important implications for maximizing the performance of at-risk children in the district.

Over the past 35 years, we have presented the information about the lack of DI implementation and the request to show what could be achieved to more than 30 districts. Not one expressed any interest in finding out what could be achieved, even though the cost of the demonstration would be negligible compared to the cost of installing programs that fail or programs that provide only a hint of what could be achieved with fully implemented, effective programs and support components.

Given that it would be highly unlikely for any district concerned with the performance of children to turn down this request, the only compelling conclusion is that none of the districts we approached—not one—had children's performance as a high priority. When told that the full-blown implementation could not occur unless the district waived those policies that were in opposition to the model's provisions, district personnel gave the universal response, "Oh we couldn't do that. Your program would have to comply with all our district regulations and standards."

The district's sense of order demands that there are no exceptions to whatever the district establishes as standards. Ironically, the district professes to promote flexibility and expresses revulsion over programs that are "lockstep"; however, the district repeatedly requires everybody to "be on the same page" even if the district's procedures are failing. This seems to be a lockstep way of thinking.

The district won't be repaired with minor changes. Its fabric, philosophy, and logic must be replaced. Its systems and functions must be overhauled so they address technical details of the performance of teachers and children— with the unwavering understanding that teachers and kids can be taught far more effectively than they are now.

Perhaps the most constructive way to commence an overhaul of the district would be to require it to implement DI fully in one or two at-risk schools. The extent to which the district fails to achieve student-perform- ance outcomes achieved by comparable, well-implemented DI schools reveals specific weaknesses in the district that must change before the district has an operating format that can maximize the acceleration of at- risk students.

I make this suggestion for using DI not because I believe that our programs are the only conceivable ones that could do the job or because I will make money from this arrangement, but because our approach is a known commodity that will produce very predictable outcomes if it is fully implemented. In fact, I would promise to refund whatever royalties I receive from district sales for a period of five years to any urban district that accepts this proposal.

THE STATUS QUO

I've made several references to building a better mousetrap. The original saying came from the famous American essayist, Ralph Waldo Emerson. He wrote, "Build a better mousetrap and the world will beat a path to your door." If Emerson's quote addressed the actual strategies of U.S. education, it would go something like this: "Build a better mousetrap and the educa- tional community will lie about either your mousetrap, where your door is, or what constitutes beating a path to a door."

What makes the system dangerous is that it has the power to maintain the status quo and do pretty much what it decides to do. Those who benefit from the status quo will dig deep to find some twist, angle, or peripherally- related nugget that they can use to keep the machinery functioning as is. If there is a lesson to be learned from Follow Through, it is that the system will fight any threat to its structure and beliefs, and will probably win, because it has the power to get second opinions from what it purports to be experts, like Glass, House, Rosemary Wilson and Commissioner of Education, Ernest Boyer. Together, they changed Project Follow Through from an attempt to find out what works to an attempt to assess the aggre- gate performance of the Follow Through models even though such an attempt makes little sense. No district or school could adopt the aggregate but, rather, specific models from the aggregate; therefore, information about the aggregate is useless without information about specific models.

The conspirators scoured the estimated 25,000 pages of information on Follow Through to come up with something they could fashion into a crude justification for not disseminating models. The best they could come up with was to argue that all models had great variation in effectiveness, and the stipulation that models should not be compared. Even this scenario wasn't possible without including Grand Rapids as a DI site and then lying about the intent of Follow Through.

When it came to a showdown, the educational establishment showed through its behavior that despite its elaborate rhetoric about concern over the welfare of at-risk kids, it wouldn't endorse DI simply because it was not consistent with prevailing educational prejudices.

In none of the districts we had worked with was there any systematic adoption, expansion or institutionalization of what we had shown. Some continued to have a project as part of the National Diffusion Network. Not one, however, attempted to redesign its machinery so the district's operating format was more like what we did in Follow Through.

Over the years, not one superintendent or high-ranking bureaucrat of any urban school district has contacted us to find out what we did to be so successful with at-risk students. They uniformly beat a path far from our door.

THE INSPECTOR GENERAL'S REPORT

As I indicated earlier, Reading First was not designed to be of great benefit for DI. One reason was that no program names were mentioned during the negotiations between the Reading First Department and the states. Those training people from a state department of education could not even say something like, "*Reading Mastery* has a strong history of success."

Another reason Reading First did not do much for DI was that the criterion the department used for accepting instructional programs in a state plan was simply that the program's design was consistent with "scientifically-based reading research." A large number of instructional programs meet this criterion, although most of them are quite ineffective with at-risk students.

Early in 2005, the Inspector General's office initiated an "audit" of Reading First. One of the petitioners for the audit was Robert Slavin, the founder of Success for All. He pointed out that two "programs" that have the strongest track record (SFA and DI) are not receiving any play from Reading First. Slavin pointed out that these "programs" incorporate training, and other components the legislation specifies, but the Department has focused only on the level of "instructional material," not broader programs.

As part of this investigation, Jerry Silbert, Doug Carnine, and Jean Osborn were interviewed. The *Final Inspection Report* came out in September 2006, and listed five violations the Reading First Department committed. The first three were relatively trivial—changing the composition of a review panel, releasing an assessment review without permission, developing a package that "obscured the requirement of a statute." The other two infractions seemed serious: intervening to influence a state's selection of reading programs; and intervening to influence the reading programs being used by local educational agencies after the application process was completed.

These issues are particularly sensitive because there are several laws that prohibit the Federal Government from exerting any influence over the curricula used by states. For example, section 9527 of the Federal Legislation on Policy states:

PROHIBITION OF ENDORSEMENT OF CURRICULUM

Notwithstanding any other prohibition of Federal law, no funds provided to the department under this Act may be used by the department to endorse, approve, or sanction any curriculum designed to be used in an elementary school or secondary school.

The inspection report named Doug Carnine and Jerry Silbert as being involved in the last two infractions listed in the report. The charge was that they were parties to an effort to influence Maryland to include *Reading Mastery* on its list of core programs.

If we back up a few steps and consider both the law and the situation in Maryland, the infraction takes on a different complexion. The goal of Reading First was to require schools to select reading and training packages that work. The legislation opens with four purposes of Reading First.

One is "to provide assistance to state and local educational agencies in selecting or developing effective materials ... programs, learning systems, and strategies to implement methods that have been proven to prevent or reme-diate reading failure within the state."

Another purpose is to provide assistance "in establishing reading programs for students in kindergarten through grade 3 that are based on scientifically based reading research, to ensure that every student can read at grade level or above no later than the end of grade 3."

These statements of purpose are strong and pointed. The states are not to install poor programs but those with track records of success.

Obviously, Reading First legislation does not match up well with the prohibition against endorsing programs. By its selection and rejection of applications, the department is endorsing specific programs. The central question is: Exactly what constitutes an endorsement of a product? Is it an endorsement if a department representative says, "*Reading Mastery* meets the department's requirements and the stated purposes of the law"? The Inspector General's report assumes this is an endorsement.

Logically, it would seem that achieving the purposes of Reading First would create some situations in which there would have to be discussions of specific programs. These discussions would not be endorsements but conditional statements of effects or facts.

For instance, if the state of Maryland did not include *Reading Mastery* on its list of core reading programs, the material could not be purchased with Reading First funds. Therefore, any successful schools that were using it would have to discontinue using the programs. This situation would create a dilemma because it is a program that has "been proven to prevent or remediate reading failure within the state." It is "based on scientifically-based reading research," and it has come closer than any other program in demonstrating that "every student can read at grade level or above not later than the end of grade 3." To deny schools access to this program would clearly not be consistent with the intent of the law.

This scenario describes exactly what happened in Maryland. The interaction between the Reading First department and Maryland was not to require any district to **select** *Reading Mastery,* simply to inform the state that if *Reading Mastery* is not available to schools, the DI schools in Baltimore would not be able to use Reading First funds to purchase the material.

Including the program on the list did not compel any local district or school to select DI. In fact, the inclusion of *Reading Mastery* on the list did not result in any new adoptions of the program in the entire state of Maryland. The program was purchased only by those Baltimore schools that had been using DI since before 2000.

The Baltimore incident provided almost the entire basis for the critical two items listed in the Inspector General's report. Many newspapers picked up an AP article about this report. The article indicates that the director of Reading First

> ... repeatedly used his influence to steer money toward states that used a reading approach he favored, called Direct Instruction, or DI, a phonics-centric program that was developed by a researcher associated with the University of Oregon. In one case, he was told a review panel was stacked with people who backed that program.

With all this illicit support of DI, the program should have shown great sales increases. Of the 50 states, only 15 had lists of program choices. Only

10 of these lists included DI as an option. In these states, Reading First schools overwhelmingly selected the top-selling commercial programs, not *Reading Mastery*. DI had virtually no additional sales in some of these states.

For example, in Oregon, 50 Reading First schools were funded. Four of them used DI as a core program. Three, however, were using DI before Reading First. So the increase was $1/50$ (2%). As noted above, the number of new schools adopting DI as a core program in Maryland was zero. As close as I can tell, the increases in DI sales from new implementations funded by Reading First was not more than 2%.

The Complete K–12 Newsletter provides an even broader view of the relative influence of Reading First on sales of *Reading Mastery*. Its 2004–05 listing of the percent of market penetration achieved by the top selling 22 reading programs shows Harcourt's *Trophies* ranked first with penetration of 12.8% of the market; followed by Scott Foresman's *Celebrate Reading* with 11.9%; followed by *McGraw-Hill Reading* at 9.6%. *Reading Mastery* is not in the top 10 programs, the top 15, or the top 20. It stands as the 21st program on the list of 22, capturing 1.2% of the market—which means its sales were less than one tenth of Harcourt's *Trophies,* and that 98.8% of the market does not use DI.

Congressman George Miller from California, a member of the House Committee on Education and the Workplace, came out with the most vitriolic attack against Reading First, calling for "wholesale housecleaning at the Education Department." With appropriate rhetoric of concern for the welfare of children, he summed up the problem this way:

> Corrupt cronies at the Department of Education wasted taxpayer dollars on an inferior reading curriculum for kids that was developed by a company headed by a Bush friend and campaign contributor. Instead of putting children first, they chose to put their cronies first. Enough is enough.

Miller even sent a long letter to the Attorney General petitioning him to bring criminal action against these perpetrators. Although it's reassuring to know that there are watchdogs out there making sure that evildoers are punished, it would serve Miller's cause better if he had even an inkling of what he's talking about. The same company that publishes the DI program publishes not only *McGraw-Hill Reading* but also the Wright programs, so the supposed crony link with a publisher seems pretty weak. Not one detail of the DI program was "developed" by the publisher. And no, Congressman, the DI reading program is not exactly an "inferior reading curriculum."

The result of the Inspector General's scourge was that the University of Oregon received a lot of bad publicity. So did Doug. Shortly after the scandal, Doug was "disinvited" to speak at two places that had invited him. A reputation that he built over 35 years is sullied. But the real issue—the impossible or undefined relationship between the ban on endorsing curricula and both the goals and the requirement for the department to "assist" states—is not even considered an issue.

Chris Doherty, the department head for Reading First, is a straight arrow. His wife, Laura, was one of the people Jerry trained to work in the Chicago DI schools, an extremely challenging place to learn the game. The training conditions were not ideal, which meant that he would observe her teaching and provide her with a long list of things she did wrong. She prevailed and became an excellent teacher and supervisor.

In 1996, she and Chris worked in Kenya with inner-city, middle-school boys from Baltimore. The goal of the project was to remove students from their environment and provide them with intensive instruction for two years in a new school, built for this project—Baraka. (The film *Boys of Baraka* documents the project.) Laura was in charge of curriculum and training. Chris was the director and administrator. Both Laura and Chris, however, maintained a schedule that required them to teach DI programs all day long.

Chris and Laura later moved to Baltimore, where she worked with NIFDI's schools and Chris later became Abell's executive director of the Baltimore Curriculum Project. Laura continues to work with NIFDI. She is tireless and completely dedicated to seeing to it that poverty children receive good instruction.

Chris has a great deal of firsthand knowledge of DI and the realities of teaching, supervising, and attempting to institute change. He also knows what it means to dedicate himself completely to the welfare of at-risk children. It strikes me as being unfair that he is punished for being knowledgeable about DI and what it can do to change the lives of children. I don't have firsthand knowledge of what went on in Reading First, but I seriously doubt that Chris did anything to steer funds to the U of O or to violate the intent of Reading First. He is not that kind of person.

THE REPUBLIC REVISITED

Possibly the writer who best anticipated the mindless rejection of the DI Follow Through data was Plato. In *The Republic,* Plato presents an allegory of a cave. People who inhabit the cave are prisoners, in chains, with their head in a fixed position. They see only shadows of things, not the actual things. Understandably, they come to believe that the shadow figures are the real things. Plato argues that if these prisoners were removed from the cave, they would not be able to look at real figures. Furthermore, they would not experience revelation because the shock would be too much for them, and they would deny that what they see is real. Plato points out that the person who is unenlightened about the truths of jurisprudence is like those people in the cave who think that shadows are real figures. And like the people in the cave, they must proceed slowly, in stages, toward enlightenment.

I think that allegory pretty well sums up why the Follow Through data was so soundly rejected. For educators, accepting the Follow Through outcomes would be like rejecting their reality—what their college mentors told them, what their colleagues tell them, and what they personally believe.

To accept the data and take action commensurate with the truth would require erasing and replacing everything the at-risk school does from how children's performance is monitored to how to teach foundation skills and "higher-order thinking."

An example of the shock created by exposure to Follow Through data occurred in a 1974 meeting in D.C. The various Follow Through sponsors were to provide brief descriptions of their project and tell something about results to about 500 educators who were associated with the Office of Education. Wes couldn't go to the meeting, and neither could Doug or I. So Linda Carnine was recruited to present. She indicated that she was scared because she had never presented before an important group, but she put her calm face on and spent about 15 minutes describing our project. During most of that time, she presented data. She later reported, "I'll never forget their expressions during my talk. They were in pain. Some of them were angry and made angry faces. Others wiggled around in their chairs waiting for me to finish."

After receiving information about student data far more impressive than anything they had heard of before—such as the reading performance of third graders in East St. Louis—the audience had no questions, not one.

Linda observed, "If the setting had been in a place where you throw rotten tomatoes at bad acts, I would have been covered with rotten tomato juice by the time I finished." She added that the general consensus seemed to be, "Well, I'm glad this is finally finished so we can go on with our lives."

In Plato's terms, Linda made them look directly into the sun, and they were not prepared for it. They had no questions because they either had already rejected the information she presented or they were trying to figure out whether their mental system was to file it under the category "Things to forget," "People and things we hate a lot," or "Trivia that has nothing to do with me." Each member of the audience received a measure of solace from the reassuring response of everybody else in the audience. These were people who were viewed as knowledgeable. Obviously, they didn't like what Linda said. So there would be no reason for any rational person to like what she said.

In 2006 the *Utah Special Educator* did an extensive feature section on

me. I had an interesting phone conversation with the editor, Michael
Herbert. I found out that we had a lot of things in common—interest in
motorcycles, tree planting, photography, and painting. In the introduction
to the feature, he wrote,

> Use the phrase "Direct Instruction" or "DI" in the midst of
> veteran teachers and you are sure to get strong and immediate
> reactions. Those who know it best and use it, love it; many who
> do not use it, hate it; but few are ambivalent and without an
> opinion.

Michael told me that he came away from his training at the University of
Utah with a bad opinion of Direct Instruction, and it wasn't until later that
he learned that what he had assumed to be the truth was not true, simply
conclusions based on trying to establish shadow figures as the real things. In
an email to me, he wrote,

> It's a sad commentary on education when great things are
> allowed to go away and a crime when lies and lack of knowledge
> move us away from best practices … We are doomed to repeat the
> same mistakes if not mindful of history.

What are the reactions of teachers who use DI and therefore have an
opportunity to leave the cave? During Follow Through we gathered data
on teachers' feelings. Most indicated that they hated the program at first
and began to like it only when they saw that they were able to teach things
they had never been able to teach before and teach children they had not
been able to reach. Note: This enlightenment did not result from philosophical predispositions about world beliefs or from politically tainted
beliefs about the liberal line versus the conservative one. The changes in
their beliefs did not result from "theories" of learning, or accounts of DI.
Enlightenment sprang from "learning by doing," taking the steps toward
the mouth of the cave.

Teachers have an opportunity to move toward the sunlight. Generally,
administrators are insulated from this kind of enlightenment, because what
they know about children and teaching comes in the form of sterilized
second- or third-hand accounts, not from hands-on activities. This is not to
say that administrators and college professors could not learn the truth
about DI from written descriptions, just that it is highly improbable. We
have had contact with several administrators who hated DI, but who
changed their minds when they had to teach in a classroom. A vocal denun-
ciator of DI was a professor at the University of Oregon. As part of a

project she was doing with children in the primary grades, she taught in the classroom. She later wrote me a long letter apologizing, and decrying her earlier descriptions of DI. She wrote, "It actually does work and it's a pleasure to use."

THE GOOD GUYS

I've written about a few of the outstanding people I've worked with, but I haven't mentioned some that have produced outstanding results and that have been amply punished by the educational system for their efforts.

Specifically I haven't mentioned trainers—Janie Feinberg, Ed Schaefer, Molly Blakely, or Maria Collins. These are excellent trainers. Janie was responsible for training the teachers and principal in Lewis Lemon in Rockford. I had met Janie over 35 years ago when I did a training session for young DI trainers SRA planned to use. She was one of them. During Follow Through, Janie managed our site in Bridgeport and did a commendable job. Her company is J.P. Associates.

Ed Schaefer is another superior trainer. For years, he was a school principal and put on lively summer training sessions in Rahoba Beach, Delaware. Ed works with Paul McKinney and Molly Blakely. Their company is Educational Resources Incorporated (ERI).

Molly had been a student at the U of O, a gifted teacher who became one of our principal trainers in Utah. Maria Collins has worked with a number of successful DI implementations in Chicago, Milwaukee, and other cities in the Midwest and Southwest. She does training for SRA, and is one of the best large-group trainers of teachers I have seen. I had to follow her session once in Madison, Wisconsin, a humbling experience.

Also, we have worked with splendid advocates. Sarah Tarver is a professor of education at the University of Wisconsin. She is a rare, classically educated scholar who has a technical understanding of instruction and arranges for college undergraduates and graduate students to learn about effective teaching practices. She has run several good formal studies in Wisconsin. One showed the superiority of DI math over discovery approaches. We have worked with some excellent people who have completed Sarah's Ph.D. program (like Carrie Beck).

Bryan Wickman started working for the Corp in 1978. He was 17 years old, and his duties consisted mostly of gofering. Starting in 1981, when the Association for Direct Instruction was formed, Bryan became Wes's assistant. Bryan still works for ADI, but his duties have changed over the years. He is now the organization's president.

Geoff Colvin is an Aussie who specializes in managing students who are out of control. He has been both colleague and buddy since he moved to Eugene in the '70s. He and I wrote a book on generalized compliance training and a rubric for identifying authentic Direction Instruction programs. We've felled trees, worked in schools, and played pool together. I have three photos of Geoff and me that were taken decades apart. In all of them, we're in the country, wearing work clothes, smiling, and each holding a can of beer.

Finally, Cathy Watkins and John Lloyd have been our pals and colleagues for many years. Cathy is a professor at the U of California in Stanislaus. She trains teachers and provides them with educational literacy. She wrote an extensive academic critique of the Follow Through evaluation, *Project Follow Through: A Case Study of Contingencies Influencing Instructional Practices of the Educational Establishment*. John is a professor at the University of Virginia. He has an incisive understanding of learning theories, including inferred functions. His wife, Pat, is an excellent teacher and trainer. Both Cathy and John are witty, totally outraged by the system, and committed to reform.

WHAT NEXT?

Writing this book took about ten months, but it was an epoch of emotion. Digging in the past is not something I like to do. I figure that the past is dead and it shouldn't become inert baggage carried into the future. My orientation has been to accept the past, learn from it, and move on.

Reconstructing the events of Follow Through was like revisiting an ancient coliseum that has an underground network of dark places and passages littered with ancient correspondence and other documents that must be illuminated. The light reveals much of what had been forgotten and immediately discloses why it had been forgotten.

My investigation did not answer all the questions of what happened, so it required contacting people who might remember some of the details I'd forgotten. These interactions were bittersweet because in most cases, I have great respect for the people I contacted, and it was good to talk with them, possibly for the first time in several years, but the topic and the details I asked about saddened or angered them as much as these topics affected me. So in the name of investigation, I spread sadness and anger.

My hope was that reconstructing this painful account would not simply document the irrefutable hypocrisy and incompetence of the educational establishment or the damage it has done, but would show that my colleagues and I succeeded in doing something noble—something that required an enormous amount of work and personal commitment. I'm tired of seeing the system rain scorn and rejection on people who have rare skills that could help the system do a far better job than it has ever done.

People who devote even three years trying to implement positive change in schools need thick skin because the system attacks their beliefs, sullies their motives, and insults their competence. Some of the people I work with have been at it for over 35 years. The primary reason they persist is that they believe they can help teachers and children who will categorically fail unless they receive help now.

Nearly all the ancient papers I reviewed were even more sour than they smelled, but a few revealed facts that I hadn't attended to at the time they occurred. For example, I knew there had been a letter from Boyer but I had never put it under the magnifying glass. At the time, it was just another crazy letter that seemed as irrational as those by Wilson and the folks who managed the Joint Dissemination and Review Committee. So some good derived from the investigation—finding evidence that there had been an elaborate plot to reject (and possibly distort) the Follow Through results.

Another bitter justification that emerged from my investigation was that none of the failed models that were funded, disseminated, and refunded achieved positive student performance. No miracles occurred, so the hopes of Boyer and others who thought that somehow these approaches could succeed were not fulfilled. It's not possible to make bulldozers out of egg crates or effective instruction out of wish lists.

Also, a few of the documents I reviewed were positive and restored the hope that there are at least some people who actually have a passion for the truth and who accept it as well as its implications.

One letter was written in the 1990s, near the end of the dark ages of whole language. It came to me from Bob Egbert, who had firsthand evidence of the political machinations that affected the ultimate interpretation of the Follow Through evaluations. Here's part of that letter.

> No one who was not there during the early years of Head Start and FT can know how much your initiative, intellect and commitment contributed to the development of [your] programs. You simply shook off criticism and attempts at censorship and moved ahead, because you knew you were right and that what you were doing was important for kids ... Ziggy, despite what some critics have said, your program's educational achievement success through the third grade is thoroughly documented in the ABT reports. Your follow-up studies have validated the program's longer term success. I am completely convinced that more extensive studies of multiple outcomes, which the Department of Education has been unwilling to fund, would provide a great deal more evidence for your program's success.

A long time ago, I resolved to do what I could to improve instruction, particularly for lower performers, and that's what I'm going to continue doing. It's time for me to leave the icons of the past. Certainly, I'll continue to be outraged at the failure occurring in schools. I'll lament the millions of children who are victims of a sick system, but I'll continue trying to show what can be done with careful instruction.

I hope that this book will create some interest in non-superficial reforms of the system, but if it doesn't, it doesn't. I've written what I think needs to be said, and I hope it provides enough scandalous facts to justify a realistic response to the procedures and rhetoric of the schools.

Who will engineer needed changes in the schools? I don't know, possibly nobody. I know only that positive reform measures won't occur unless they are presented in a loud voice, backed by machinery with enough clout to fight and win the battles that must be fought and won if districts are to be transformed from their top-down arrogant structure into one that is scientific, that has the performance of teachers and students as its central reference point, and that fashions all details of the new system so they comply with Wes's demand: Show me the data.

My uncle Fred used to recite a poem to those who whined, "If this had happened" or "If that had happened":

> If wishes were fishes and fishes could fly,
> If horseshit were biscuits, we'd eat till we die.

With all due respect to the wisdom of this verse, I can't tear my mind from several *ifs* about the reception to the things we've done.

If the system had responded to our attempts to show what could be done in preschools, a lot of children could have learned basic academic skills and entered first grade with an honest head start.

If the Feds had permitted us to present data on the Upward Bound program at the University of Illinois, there would have been information about specific instruction that could have helped a lot of high school students.

If Follow Through had disseminated information on our model's performance, a lot of students who failed because they received poor instruction would have been successful.

These *ifs* refer to helping "a lot" of students. How many is a lot? A colleague of mine made what he indicated was a conservative estimate: 5 million since 1978.

The final *if*: If a mind is a terrible thing to waste, the educational establishment is guilty of incomprehensible waste.

END

About the Author

Siegfried Engelmann is Professor of Education at the University of Oregon and Director of the National Institute for Direct Instruction. He has authored over 100 instructional programs, ranging from beginning reading to elementary chemistry and earth sciences. His principal efforts have focused on at-risk, deaf, Down syndrome, and autistic children. He has authored 50 chapters, 95 articles, and 20 books on educational psychology and instruction, including *Theory of Instruction* (with Carnine). He received the 2002 Award for Education Research from the Council of Scientific Society Presidents.